sama!

Hiro Fujiwara

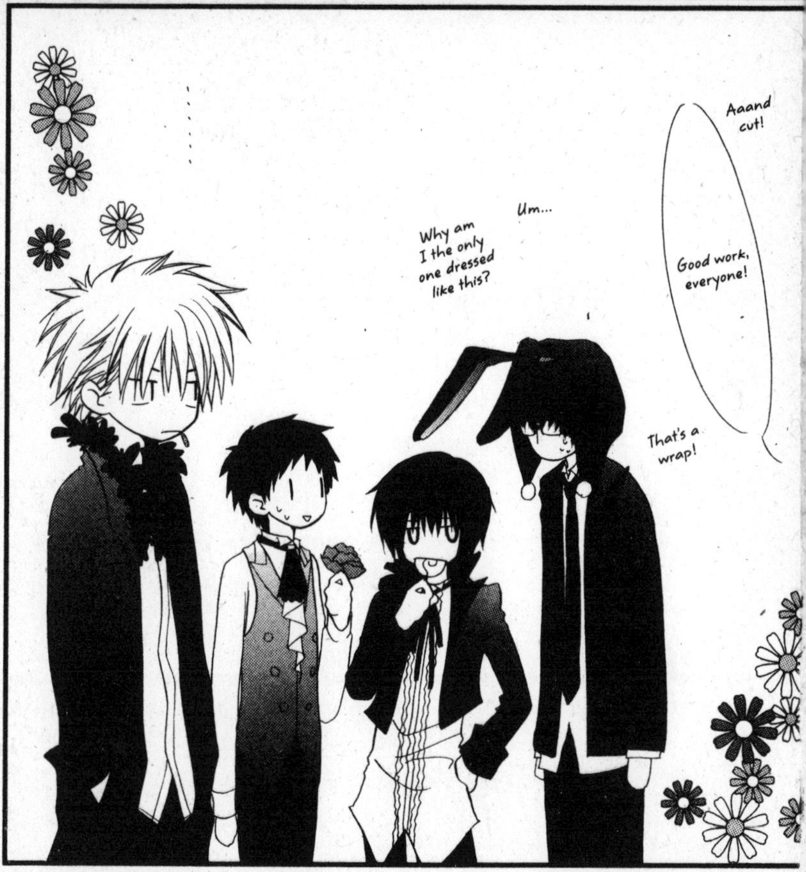
Aaand cut!
Good work, everyone!
That's a wrap!
Um...
Why am I the only one dressed like this?

Maid Sama! Volume 6
Created by Hiro Fujiwara

Translation - Alethea & Athena Nibley
English Adaptation - Karen S. Ahlstrom
Copy Editor - Joseph Heller
Retouch and Lettering - Star Print Brokers
Production Artist - Michael Paolilli
Graphic Designer - Roderick Pio Roda

Editor - Lillian Diaz-Przybyl
Print Production Manager - Lucas Rivera
Managing Editor - Vy Nguyen
Senior Designer - Louis Csontos
Art Director - Al-Insan Lashley
Director of Sales and Manufacturing - Allyson De Simone
Associate Publisher - Marco F. Pavia
President and C.O.O. - John Parker
C.E.O. and Chief Creative Officer - Stu Levy

A  Manga

TOKYOPOP and 🐱 are trademarks or registered trademarks of TOKYOPOP Inc.

TOKYOPOP Inc.
5900 Wilshire Blvd. Suite 2000
Los Angeles, CA 90036

E-mail: info@TOKYOPOP.com
Come visit us online at www.TOKYOPOP.com

KAICHO WA MEIDO SAMA by Hiro Fujiwara
© 2008 Hiro Fujiwara All rights reserved.
First published in Japan in 2008 by HAKUSENSHA, INC., Tokyo
English language translation rights in the United States of
America and Canada arranged with HAKUSENSHA, INC., Tokyo
through Tuttle-Mori Agency Inc., Tokyo
English text copyright © 2010 TOKYOPOP Inc.

ISBN: 978-1-4278-1690-0

First TOKYOPOP printing: October 2010
10 9 8 7 6 5 4 3 2 1
Printed in the USA

Maid Sama!

Hiro Fujiwara

Vol. 6

by
Hiro Fujiwara

HAMBURG // LONDON // LOS ANGELES // TOKYO

♥ WELCOME HOME, MASTER! ♥

Please allow me to introduce all the ladies and gentlemen who appeared in earlier volumes.♥

Maid

President

MISAKI AYUZAWA (HIGH SCHOOL JUNIOR)

AN INDOMITABLE STUDENT COUNCIL PRESIDENT BY DAY, BUT A WAITRESS AT A MAID CAFE BY NIGHT!! BRILLIANT BOTH IN ACADEMICS AND ATHLETICS, HER SPECIALTY IS AIKIDO (ALL ACHIEVED THROUGH MASSIVE HARD WORK AND DEDICATION). AT WORK, THEY CALL HER MISA-CHAN-- A SMART, COOL-HEADED MAID!

TAKUMI USUI (HIGH SCHOOL JUNIOR)

THE SCHOOL HEARTTHROB. HE ACCIDENTALLY DISCOVERED MISAKI'S SECRET AND, INTRIGUED, HAS TAKEN TO FOLLOWING HER AROUND. HE'S SUPER SMART, GREAT AT SPORTS, AS GORGEOUS AS THEY COME AND UNBEATABLE IN A FIGHT--THE PERFECT MAN. BUT AS FAR AS MISAKI'S CONCERNED, HE'S ALSO THE DEMON KING OF SEXUAL HARASSMENT. LATELY, HE'S BECOME MAID LATTE'S #1 CUSTOMER.

SEIKA HIGH SCHOOL

 Yukimura
THE VICE PRESIDENT OF THE STUDENT COUNCIL, HE ALWAYS TRIES HIS HARDEST. HIS SPECIAL SKILL(?) IS CROSS-DRESSING.

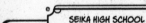

 Sakura
ONE OF MISAKI'S PRECIOUS FEW FEMALE CLASSMATES. "MISAKI, WE LOVE YOU!"♥

 Shizuko
A FRIEND OF MISAKI AND SAKURA. SHE'S ALWAYS COOL AND LEVELHEADED.

 Kanou
A FIRST-YEAR STUDENT PROFICIENT IN HYPNOTISM. HE'S UNCOMFORTABLE WITH WOMEN.

Shirokawa

The Idiot Trio

Sarashina

Kurosaki

FORMERLY OPPOSED TO THE PRESIDENT, THESE THREE DISCOVERED MISAKI'S SECRET AND ENDED UP BECOMING HUGE "MISA-CHAN" FANS.

Cafe Maid Latte

MISAKI'S PART-TIME JOB-- THE STAFF ALL EAGERLY AWAIT YOUR RETURN, MASTER.♥

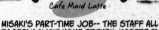

Satsuki

THE MANAGER. SATSUKI UNDERSTANDS MISAKI'S SITUATION AND HAS BEEN AS ACCOMMODATING AS POSSIBLE. SHE IS 30 YEARS OLD AND QUITE GIVEN TO FLIGHTS OF FANCY.

Honoka

Nephew

 Aoi Hyoudou (AOI)

The Maids

Subaru

Erika

Other

STUDENT COUNCIL PRESIDENT OF THE OBSCENELY RICH MIYABI GAOKA ACADEMY.

Tora Igarashi

♡ NOW, PLEASE ALLOW ME TO SUMMARIZE THE EVENTS OF THE PREVIOUS VOLUMES. ♡

MISAKI, THE STUDENT COUNCIL PRESIDENT OF THE PREVIOUSLY ALL-MALE SEIKA HIGH SCHOOL, SPENDS HER DAYS VALIANTLY BATTLING TO PROTECT THE GIRLS AND KEEP THE BOYS FROM RUNNING AMOK. HOWEVER, BRAVE MISAKI HAS A LITTLE SECRET--SHE WORKS AT A MAID CAFE! NOW FOLLOWED AROUND BY USUI--WHO DISCOVERED HER SECRET BY ACCIDENT--MISAKI MUST FIND A WAY TO CONTINUE HER CRAZY DOUBLE LIFE AS A MAID AND A PRESIDENT!♥

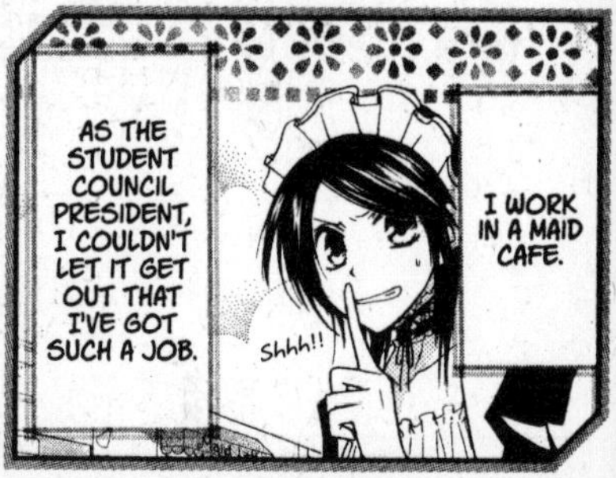
I WORK IN A MAID CAFE.
Shhh!!
AS THE STUDENT COUNCIL PRESIDENT, I COULDN'T LET IT GET OUT THAT I'VE GOT SUCH A JOB.

WILL MAID LATTE BE BOUGHT OUT?! KANADE MAKI, THE HEIR OF THE MAKI DINING GROUP, WANTS TO PURCHASE THE BUILDING THAT HOUSES MAID LATTE IN ORDER TO START A BUTLER CAFE. HE ALSO HAPPENS TO BE A STUDENT AT MIYABI GAOKA. IS TORA IGARASHI REALLY BEHIND THIS?!

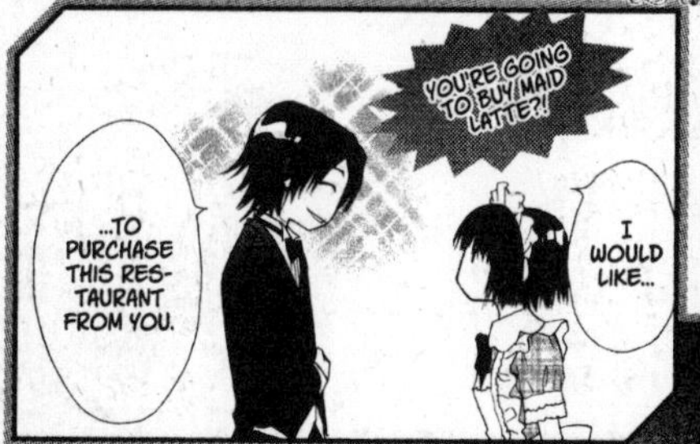
YOU'RE GOING TO BUY MAID LATTE?!
I WOULD LIKE...
...TO PURCHASE THIS RES-TAURANT FROM YOU.

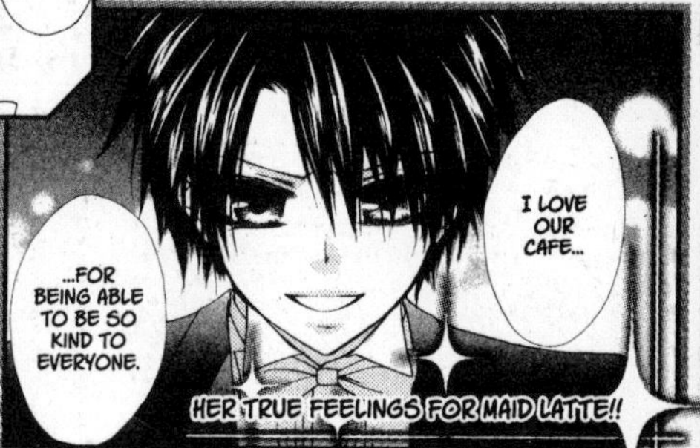
I LOVE OUR CAFE...
...FOR BEING ABLE TO BE SO KIND TO EVERYONE.
HER TRUE FEELINGS FOR MAID LATTE!!

"I HEREBY VOW TO PROTECT MAID LATTE!!" MISAKI AND COMPANY INFILTRATE THE MAKI-SPONSORED FOOTMAN AUDITIONS. WITH SOME HELP FROM USUI, MISAKI SUCCESSFULLY DEMONSTRATES THE SKILLS SHE LEARNED AT MAID LATTE AND REVEALS HER INTENSE LOVE FOR HER CAFE! MISAKI'S SINCERITY CAUSES MAKI TO GIVE UP ON HIS PLAN, AND MAID LATTE IS SAVED.

MEANWHILE, DURING THE FOOTMAN AUDITIONS, USUI INJURED BOTH OF HIS ARMS PROTECTING MISAKI. WHEN MISAKI GOES TO VISIT HIM, SHE IS DESPERATE TO NURSE HIM TO HEALTH--MAKING HIM RICE GRUEL AND GIVING HIM A SPONGE BATH, ETC. ♥NEW AND UNFAMILIAR FEELINGS FOR USUI BEGIN TO BUD INSIDE MISAKI...OR DO THEY?!

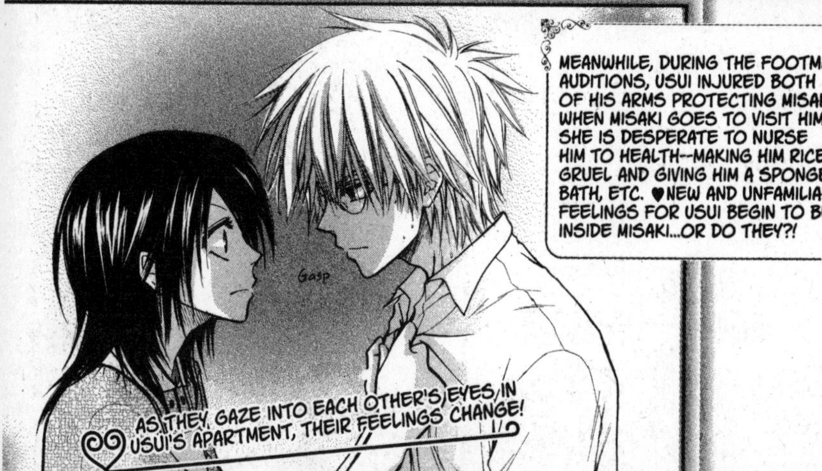
Gasp
AS THEY GAZE INTO EACH OTHER'S EYES IN USUI'S APARTMENT, THEIR FEELINGS CHANGE!

WELL THEN, PLEASE ENJOY, MASTER!♥

Cafe **Maid** **Latte**

6

CONTENTS

Cafe **Maid** **Latte**

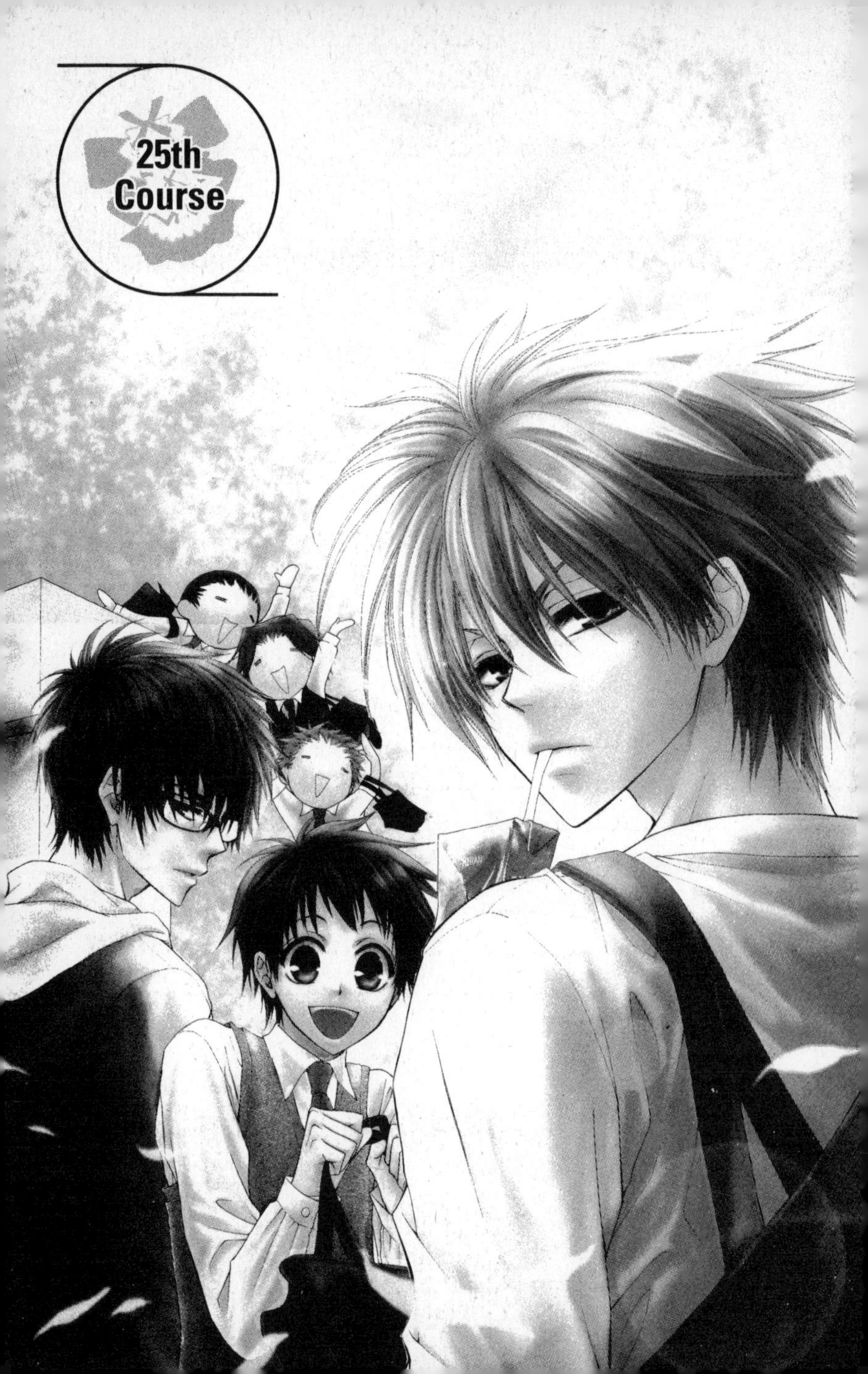
25th
Course

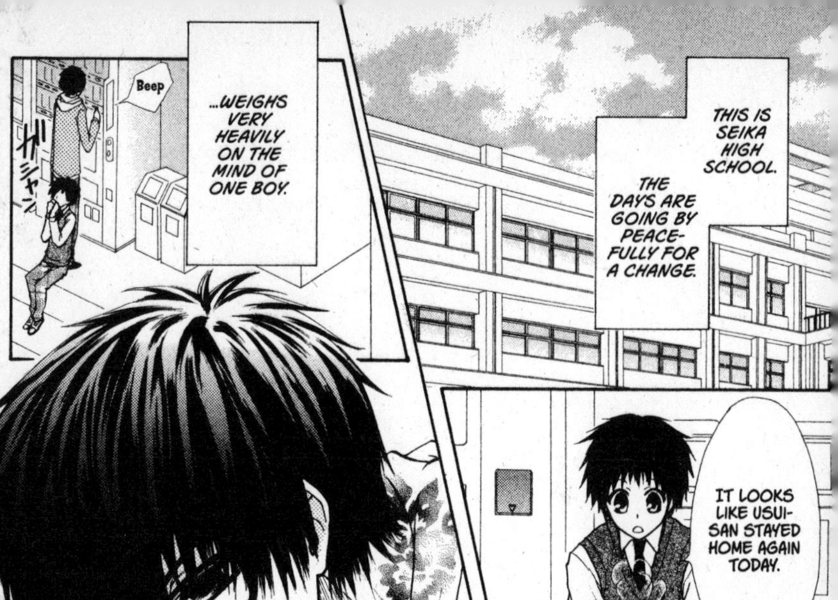
THIS IS SEIKA HIGH SCHOOL.
THE DAYS ARE GOING BY PEACE-FULLY FOR A CHANGE.
IT LOOKS LIKE USUI-SAN STAYED HOME AGAIN TODAY.
I wonder what happened to him.
IN THIS PEACE, THE FATE OF TAKUMI USUI, MAN OF MYSTERY...
...WEIGHS VERY HEAVILY ON THE MIND OF ONE BOY.
Beep
ガシャン
OH...
Kachak...
Class 1-7
Soutarou Kanou
Special skills: Hypnotic suggestion, people-watching

Question Corner

Question 1

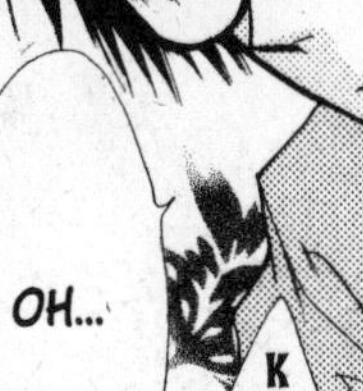

Here I am again. I'm the author.

Q. What are you into right now?

A. That's such a broad question, I don't know how to answer. If you mean music, recently, I listen to a lot of Akeboshi-san and Rie Fu-san. Calm singing voices are the most fitting for background music when I'm working. And of course, I never get tired of Utada Hikaru songs, no matter how many times I listen to them.

When I want more energy, band-style music is a must.

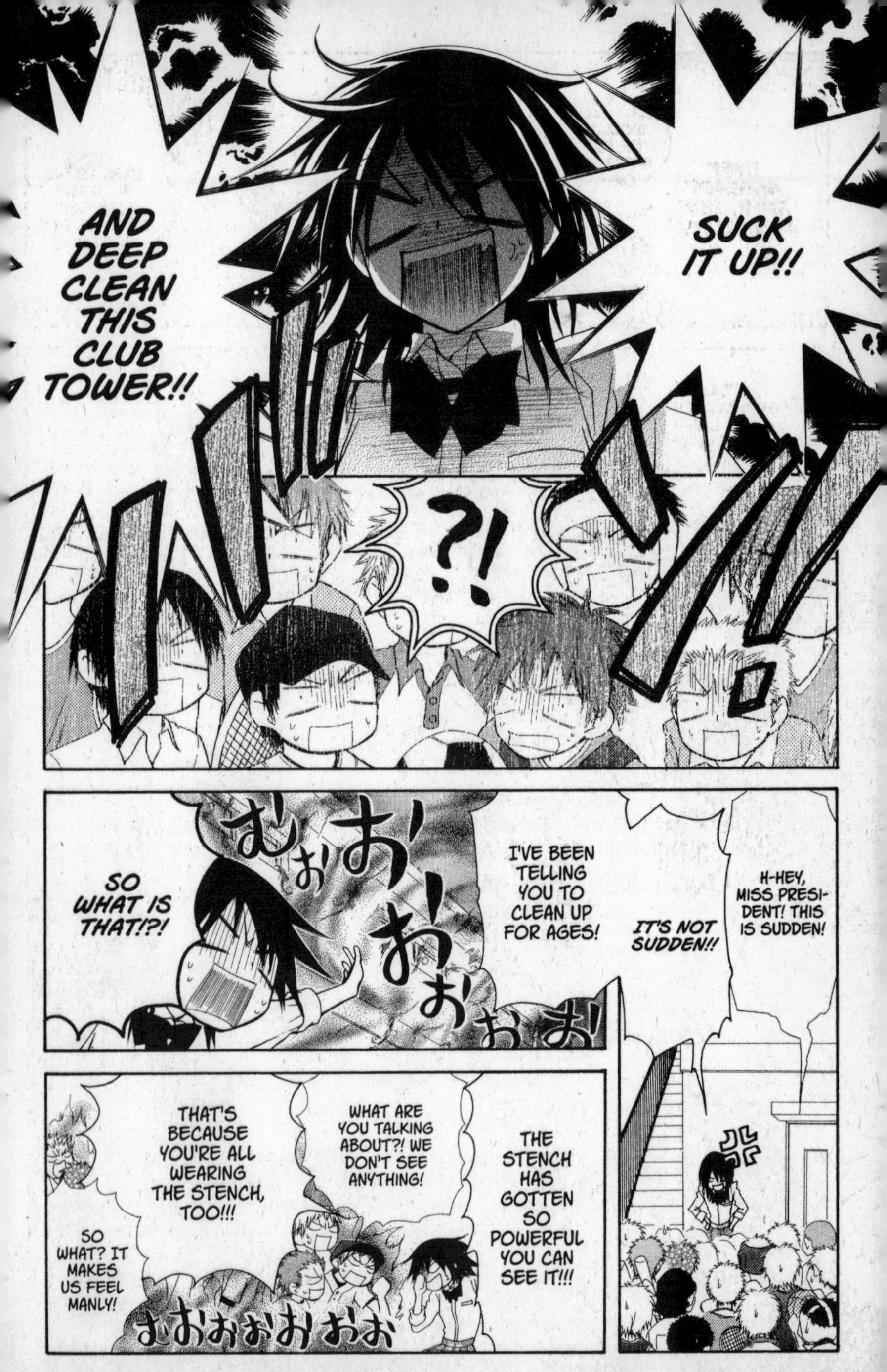
SUCK IT UP!!
AND DEEP CLEAN THIS CLUB TOWER!!
?!
H-HEY, MISS PRESIDENT! THIS IS SUDDEN!
IT'S NOT SUDDEN!!
I'VE BEEN TELLING YOU TO CLEAN UP FOR AGES!
むぉお!お!お!ぉお!
SO WHAT IS THAT!?!
THE STENCH HAS GOTTEN SO POWERFUL YOU CAN SEE IT!!!
WHAT ARE YOU TALKING ABOUT?! WE DON'T SEE ANYTHING!
THAT'S BECAUSE YOU'RE ALL WEARING THE STENCH, TOO!!!
SO WHAT? IT MAKES US FEEL MANLY!
ぉおおぉおおぉ

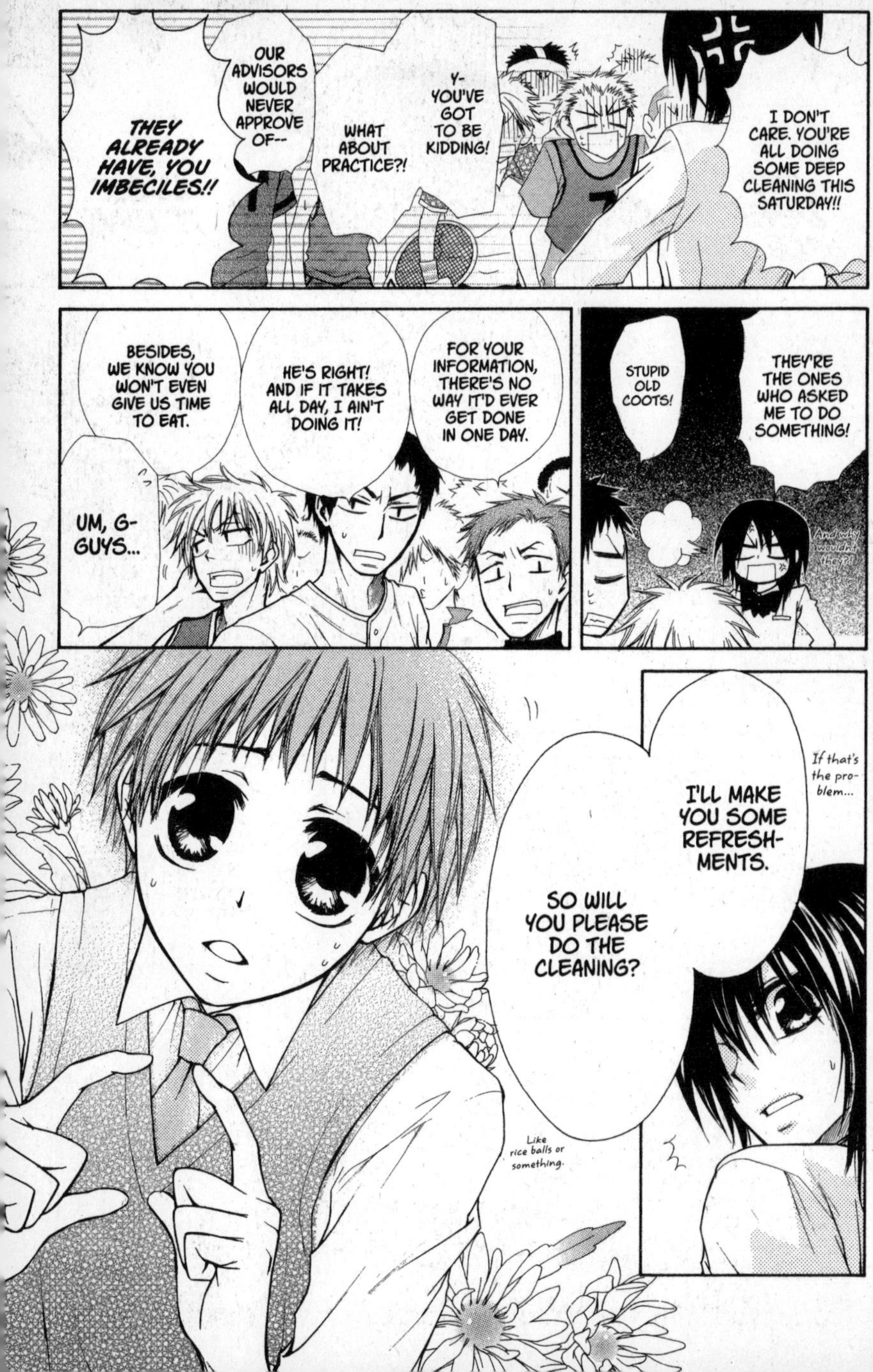
I DON'T CARE. YOU'RE ALL DOING SOME DEEP CLEANING THIS SATURDAY!!
Y-YOU'VE GOT TO BE KIDDING!
WHAT ABOUT PRACTICE?!
OUR ADVISORS WOULD NEVER APPROVE OF--
THEY ALREADY HAVE, YOU IMBECILES!!
THEY'RE THE ONES WHO ASKED ME TO DO SOMETHING!
STUPID OLD COOTS!
And why wouldn't they?
FOR YOUR INFORMATION, THERE'S NO WAY IT'D EVER GET DONE IN ONE DAY.
HE'S RIGHT! AND IF IT TAKES ALL DAY, I AIN'T DOING IT!
BESIDES, WE KNOW YOU WON'T EVEN GIVE US TIME TO EAT.
UM, G-GUYS...
If that's the pro-blem...
I'LL MAKE YOU SOME REFRESH-MENTS.
SO WILL YOU PLEASE DO THE CLEANING?
Like rice balls or something.

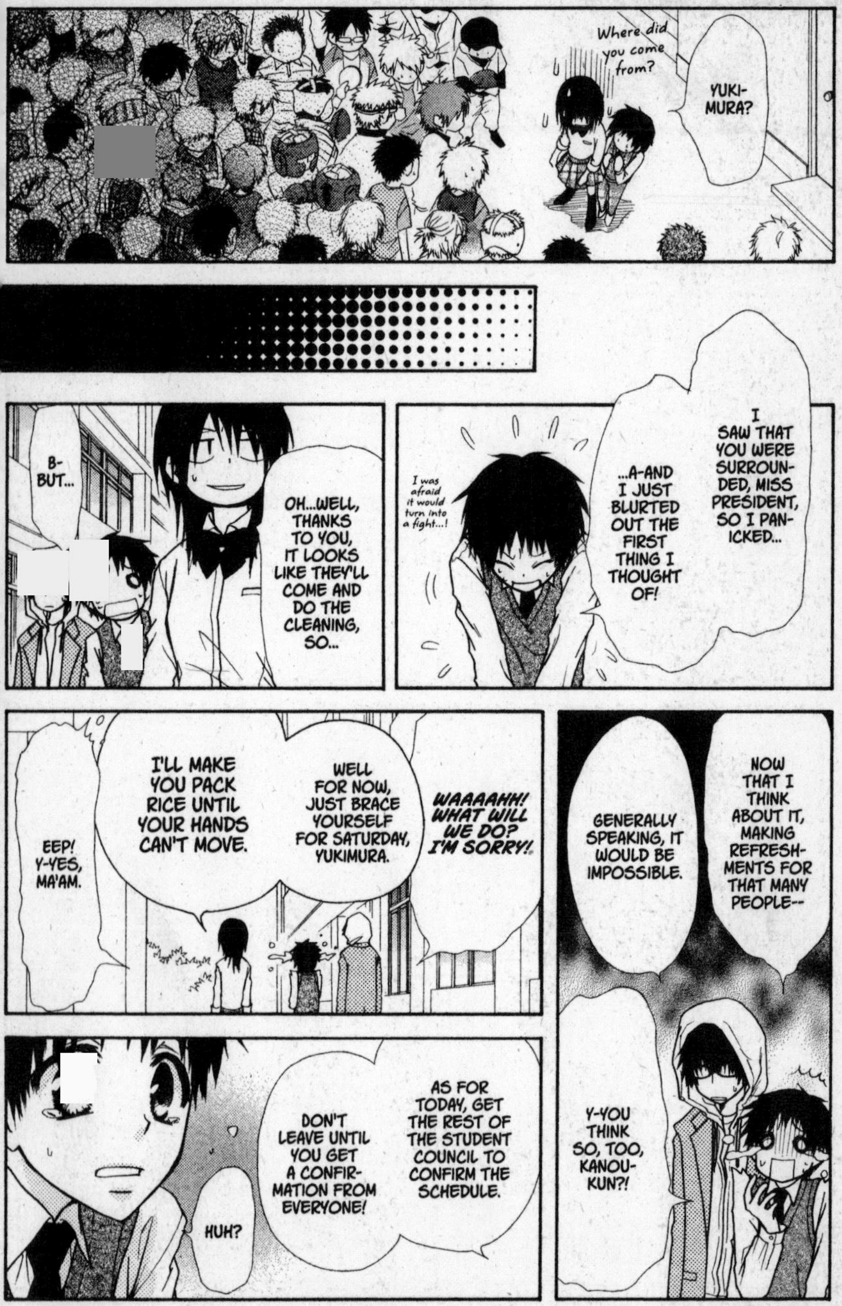
YUKI-MURA?
Where did you come from?
I SAW THAT YOU WERE SURROUN-DED, MISS PRESIDENT, SO I PAN-ICKED...
...A-AND I JUST BLURTED OUT THE FIRST THING I THOUGHT OF!
I was afraid it would turn into a fight...!
OH...WELL, THANKS TO YOU, IT LOOKS LIKE THEY'LL COME AND DO THE CLEANING, SO...
B-BUT...
NOW THAT I THINK ABOUT IT, MAKING REFRESH-MENTS FOR THAT MANY PEOPLE--
GENERALLY SPEAKING, IT WOULD BE IMPOSSIBLE.
Y-YOU THINK SO, TOO, KANOU-KUN?!
WAAAAHH! WHAT WILL WE DO? I'M SORRY!
WELL FOR NOW, JUST BRACE YOURSELF FOR SATURDAY, YUKIMURA.
I'LL MAKE YOU PACK RICE UNTIL YOUR HANDS CAN'T MOVE.
EEP! Y-YES, MA'AM.
AS FOR TODAY, GET THE REST OF THE STUDENT COUNCIL TO CONFIRM THE SCHEDULE.
DON'T LEAVE UNTIL YOU GET A CONFIR-MATION FROM EVERYONE!
HUH?

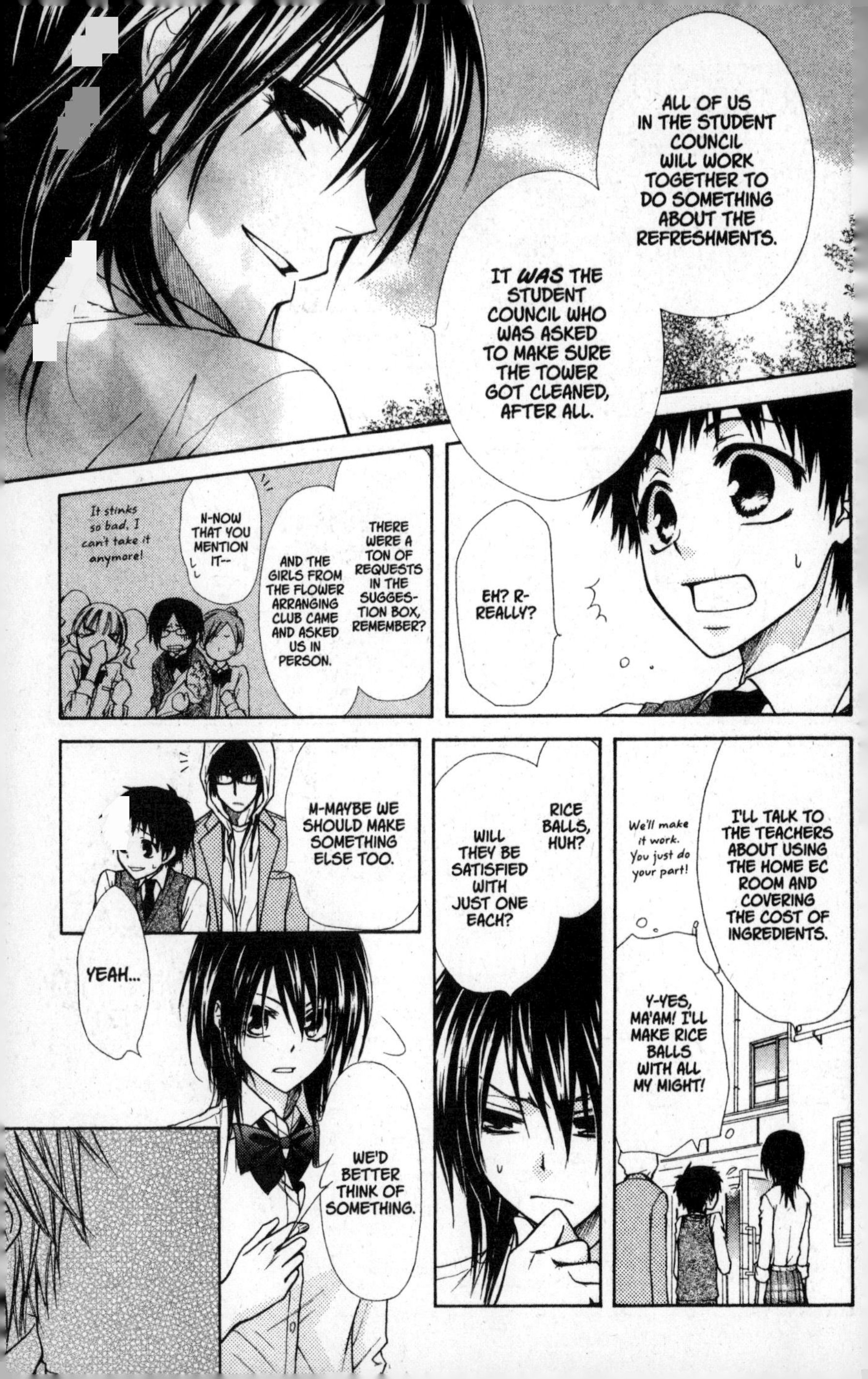
ALL OF US IN THE STUDENT COUNCIL WILL WORK TOGETHER TO DO SOMETHING ABOUT THE REFRESHMENTS.
IT *WAS* THE STUDENT COUNCIL WHO WAS ASKED TO MAKE SURE THE TOWER GOT CLEANED, AFTER ALL.
EH? R-REALLY?
THERE WERE A TON OF REQUESTS IN THE SUGGES-TION BOX, REMEMBER?
AND THE GIRLS FROM THE FLOWER ARRANGING CLUB CAME AND ASKED US IN PERSON.
N-NOW THAT YOU MENTION IT--
It stinks so bad. I can't take it anymore!
I'LL TALK TO THE TEACHERS ABOUT USING THE HOME EC ROOM AND COVERING THE COST OF INGREDIENTS.
We'll make it work. You just do your part!
Y-YES, MA'AM! I'LL MAKE RICE BALLS WITH ALL MY MIGHT!
RICE BALLS, HUH?
WILL THEY BE SATISFIED WITH JUST ONE EACH?
M-MAYBE WE SHOULD MAKE SOMETHING ELSE TOO.
YEAH...
WE'D BETTER THINK OF SOMETHING.

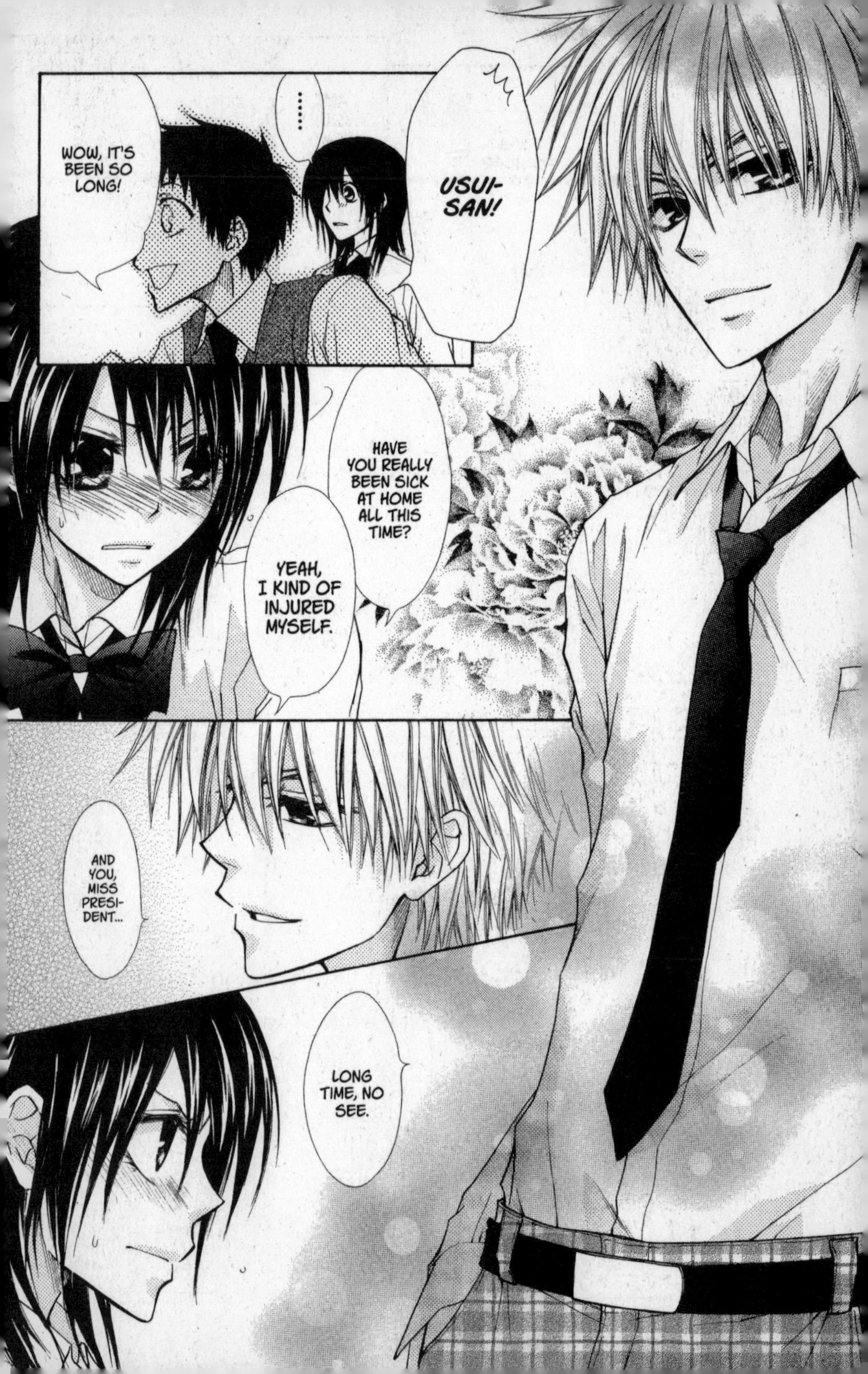
USUI-SAN!
......
WOW, IT'S BEEN SO LONG!
HAVE YOU REALLY BEEN SICK AT HOME ALL THIS TIME?
YEAH, I KIND OF INJURED MYSELF.
AND YOU, MISS PRESIDENT...
LONG TIME, NO SEE.

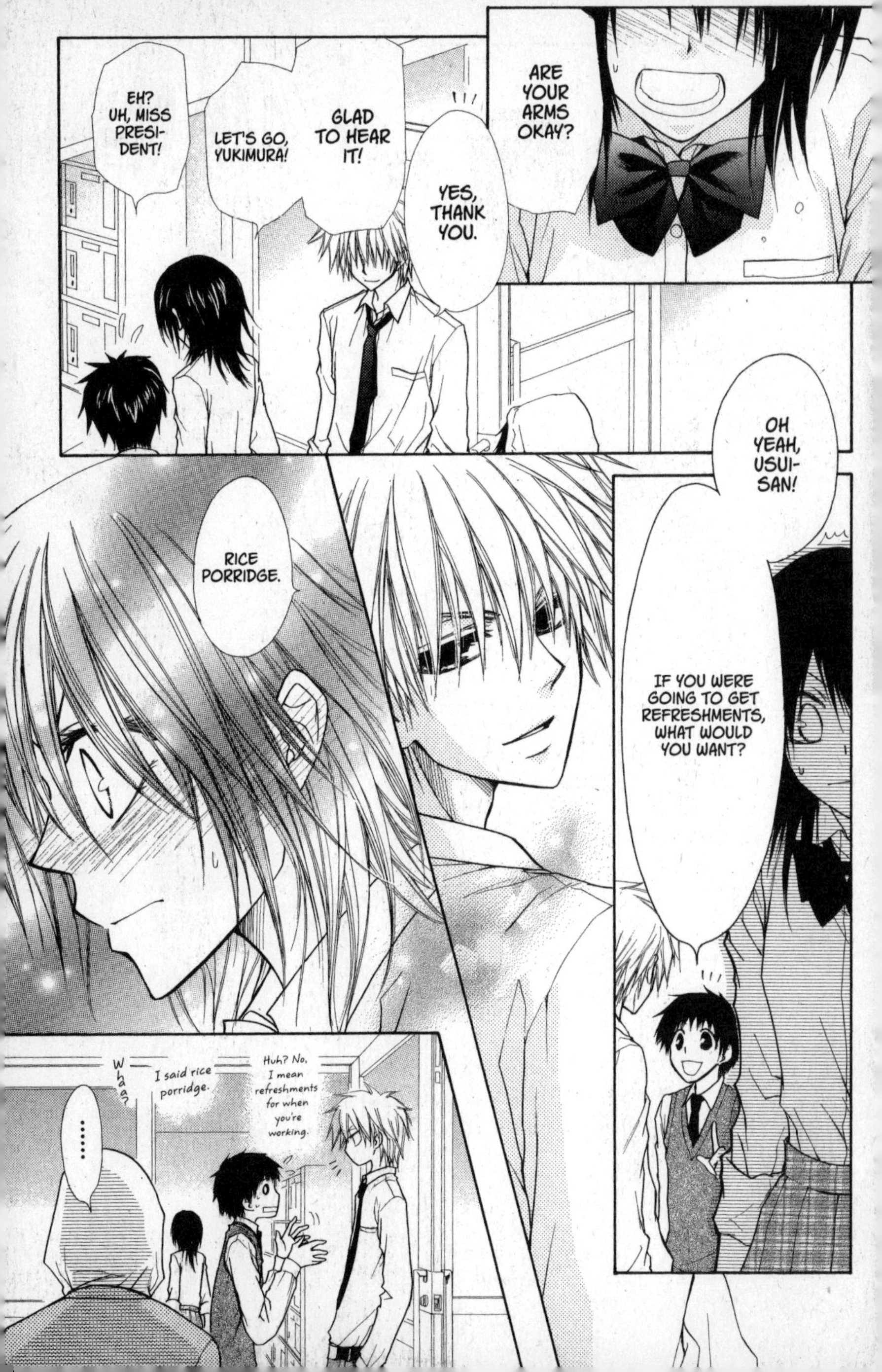
ARE YOUR ARMS OKAY?
YES, THANK YOU.
GLAD TO HEAR IT!
LET'S GO, YUKIMURA!
EH? UH, MISS PRESIDENT!
OH YEAH, USUI-SAN!
IF YOU WERE GOING TO GET REFRESHMENTS, WHAT WOULD YOU WANT?
RICE PORRIDGE.
Huh? No, I mean refreshments for when you're working.
I said rice porridge.
Whaa?
......

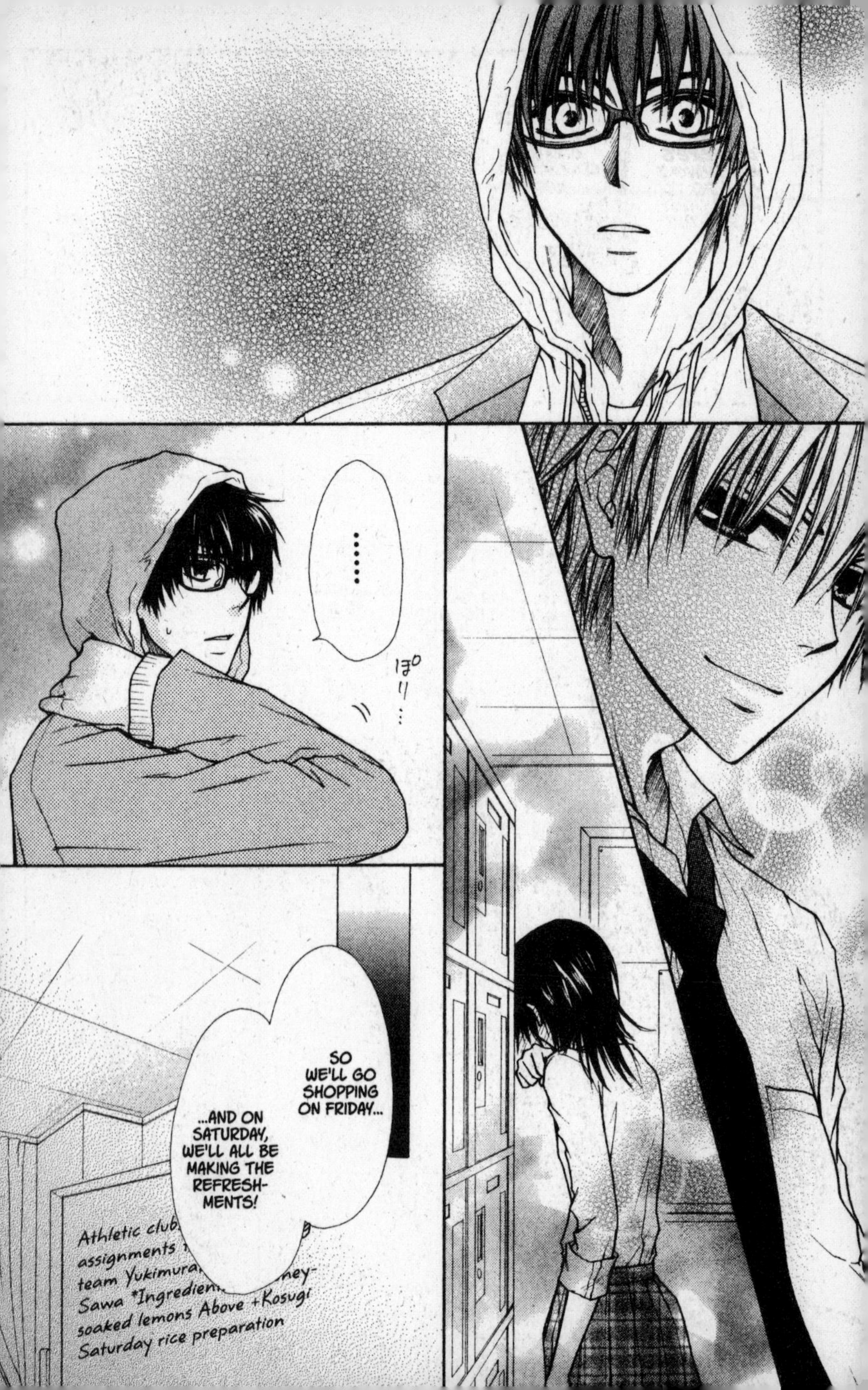
……
ぽり…
SO WE'LL GO SHOPPING ON FRIDAY...
...AND ON SATURDAY, WE'LL ALL BE MAKING THE REFRESH-MENTS!
Athletic club
assignments
team Yukimura
Sawa *Ingredien ney-
soaked lemons Above +Kosugi
Saturday rice preparation

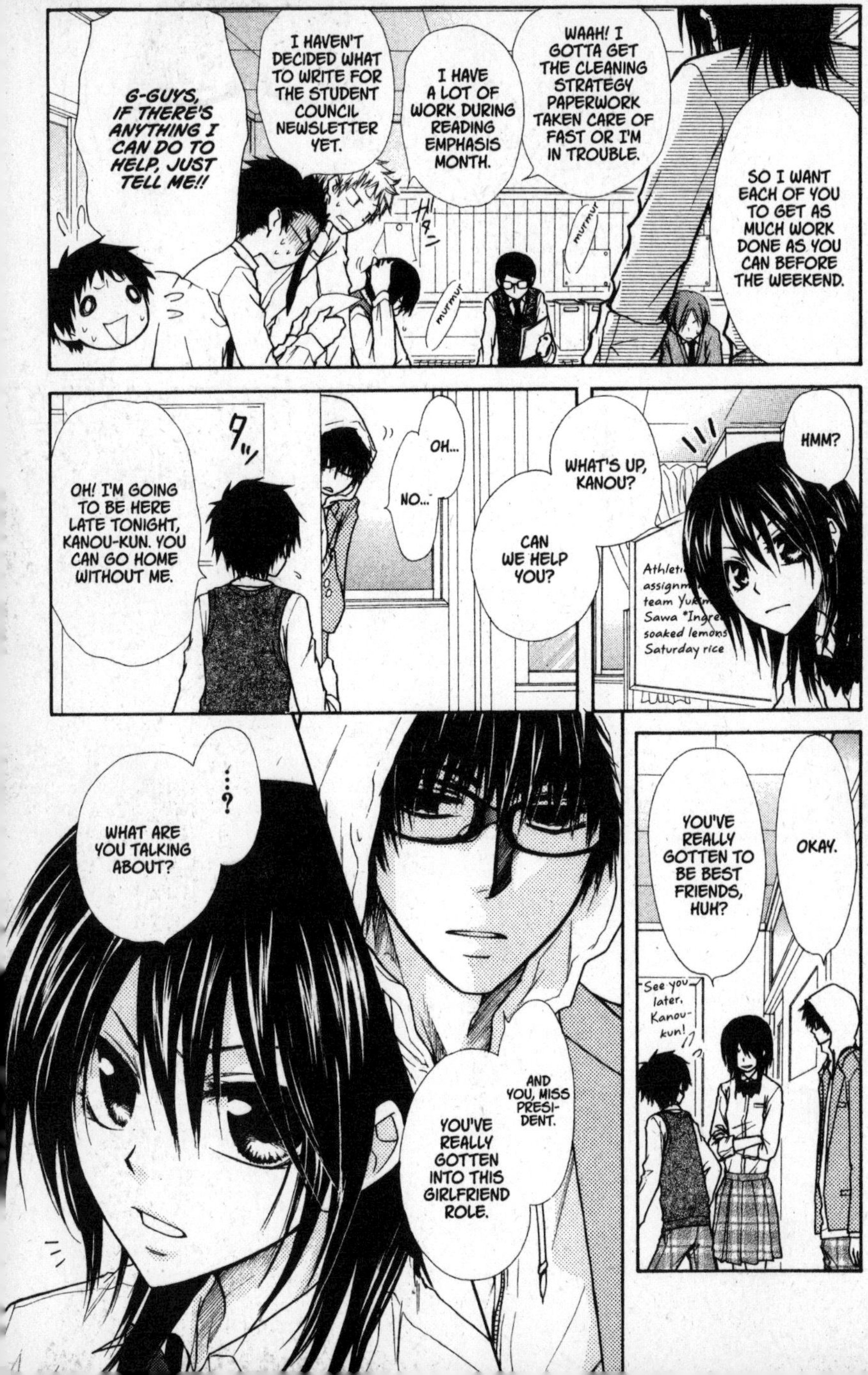
SO I WANT EACH OF YOU TO GET AS MUCH WORK DONE AS YOU CAN BEFORE THE WEEKEND.
WAAH! I GOTTA GET THE CLEANING STRATEGY PAPERWORK TAKEN CARE OF FAST OR I'M IN TROUBLE.
I HAVE A LOT OF WORK DURING READING EMPHASIS MONTH.
I HAVEN'T DECIDED WHAT TO WRITE FOR THE STUDENT COUNCIL NEWSLETTER YET.
G-GUYS, IF THERE'S ANYTHING I CAN DO TO HELP, JUST TELL ME!!
murmur
murmur
HMM?
WHAT'S UP, KANOU?
CAN WE HELP YOU?
Athleti
assignm
team Yuk
Sawa *Ingre
soaked lemons
Saturday rice
OH...
NO...
OH! I'M GOING TO BE HERE LATE TONIGHT, KANOU-KUN. YOU CAN GO HOME WITHOUT ME.
OKAY.
YOU'VE REALLY GOTTEN TO BE BEST FRIENDS, HUH?
See you later, Kanou-kun!
AND YOU, MISS PRESIDENT.
YOU'VE REALLY GOTTEN INTO THIS GIRLFRIEND ROLE.
...?
WHAT ARE YOU TALKING ABOUT?

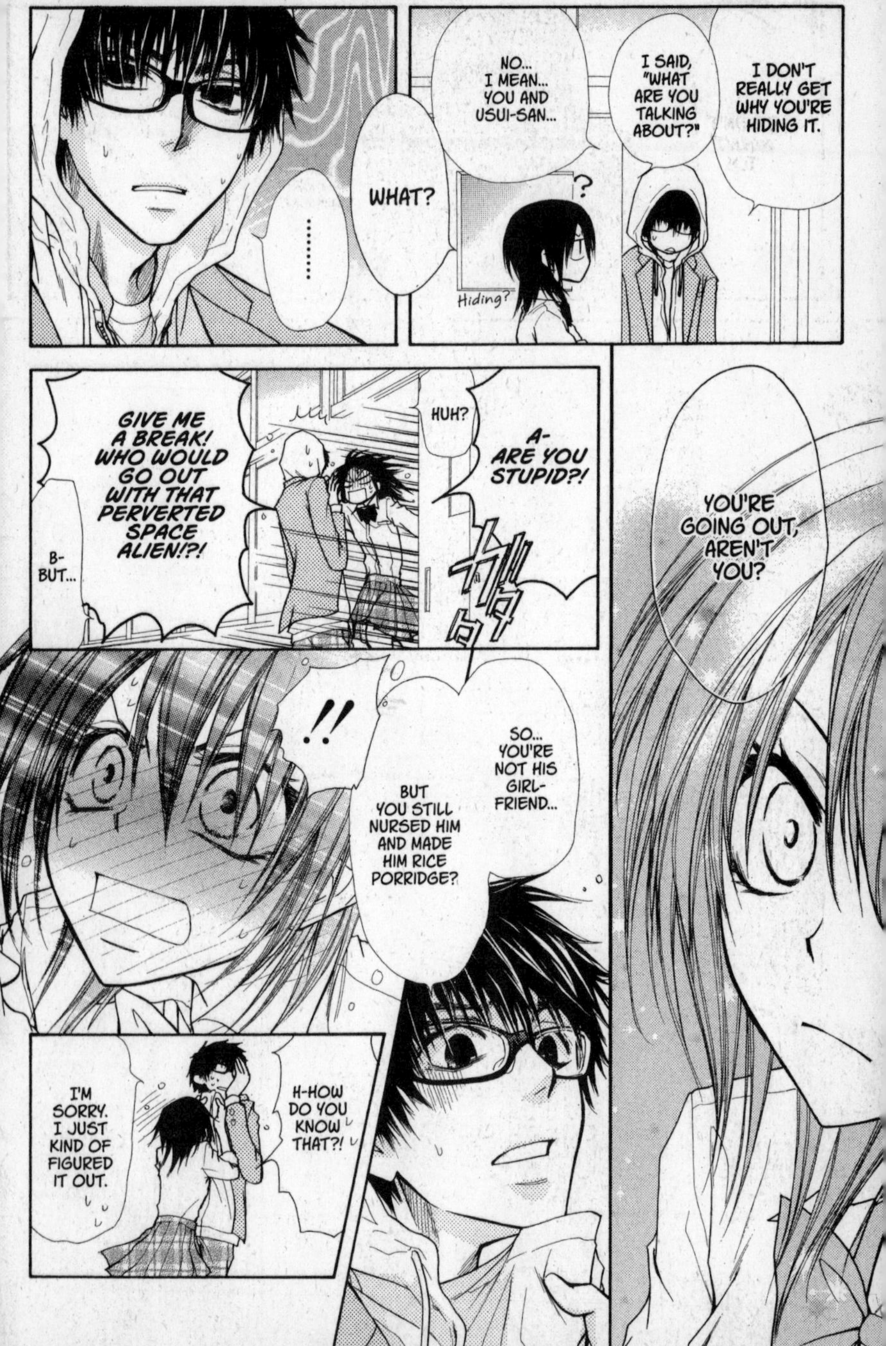
I DON'T REALLY GET WHY YOU'RE HIDING IT.
I SAID, "WHAT ARE YOU TALKING ABOUT?"
NO... I MEAN... YOU AND USUI-SAN...
?
Hiding?
WHAT?
......
YOU'RE GOING OUT, AREN'T YOU?
A- ARE YOU STUPID?!
HUH?
GIVE ME A BREAK! WHO WOULD GO OUT WITH THAT PERVERTED SPACE ALIEN!?!
B- BUT...
!!
SO... YOU'RE NOT HIS GIRL-FRIEND...
BUT YOU STILL NURSED HIM AND MADE HIM RICE PORRIDGE?
H-HOW DO YOU KNOW THAT?!
I'M SORRY. I JUST KIND OF FIGURED IT OUT.

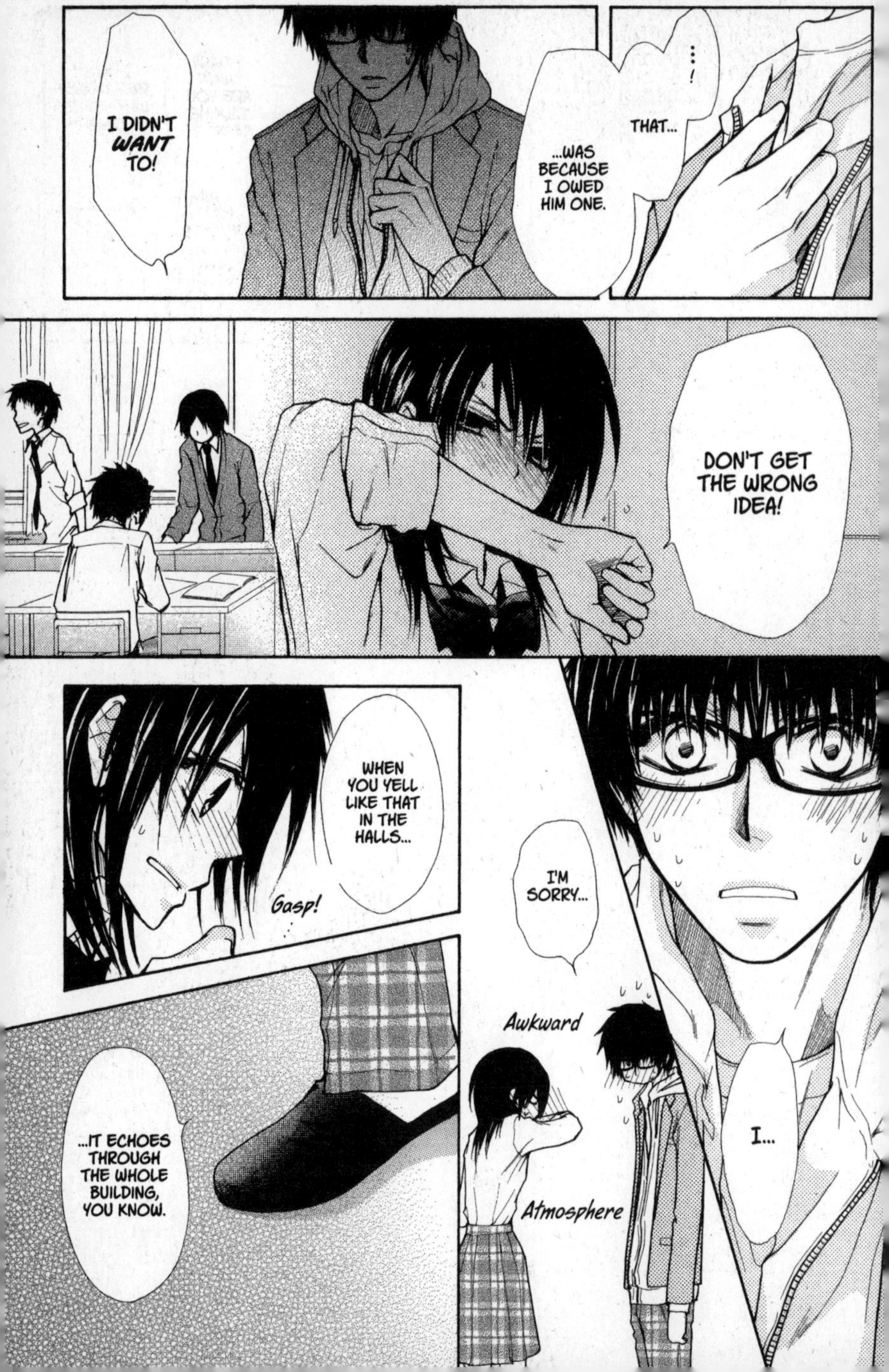

...!
THAT...
...WAS BECAUSE I OWED HIM ONE.
I DIDN'T *WANT* TO!
DON'T GET THE WRONG IDEA!
I'M SORRY...
I...
Awkward
Atmosphere
WHEN YOU YELL LIKE THAT IN THE HALLS...
Gasp!
...IT ECHOES THROUGH THE WHOLE BUILDING, YOU KNOW.

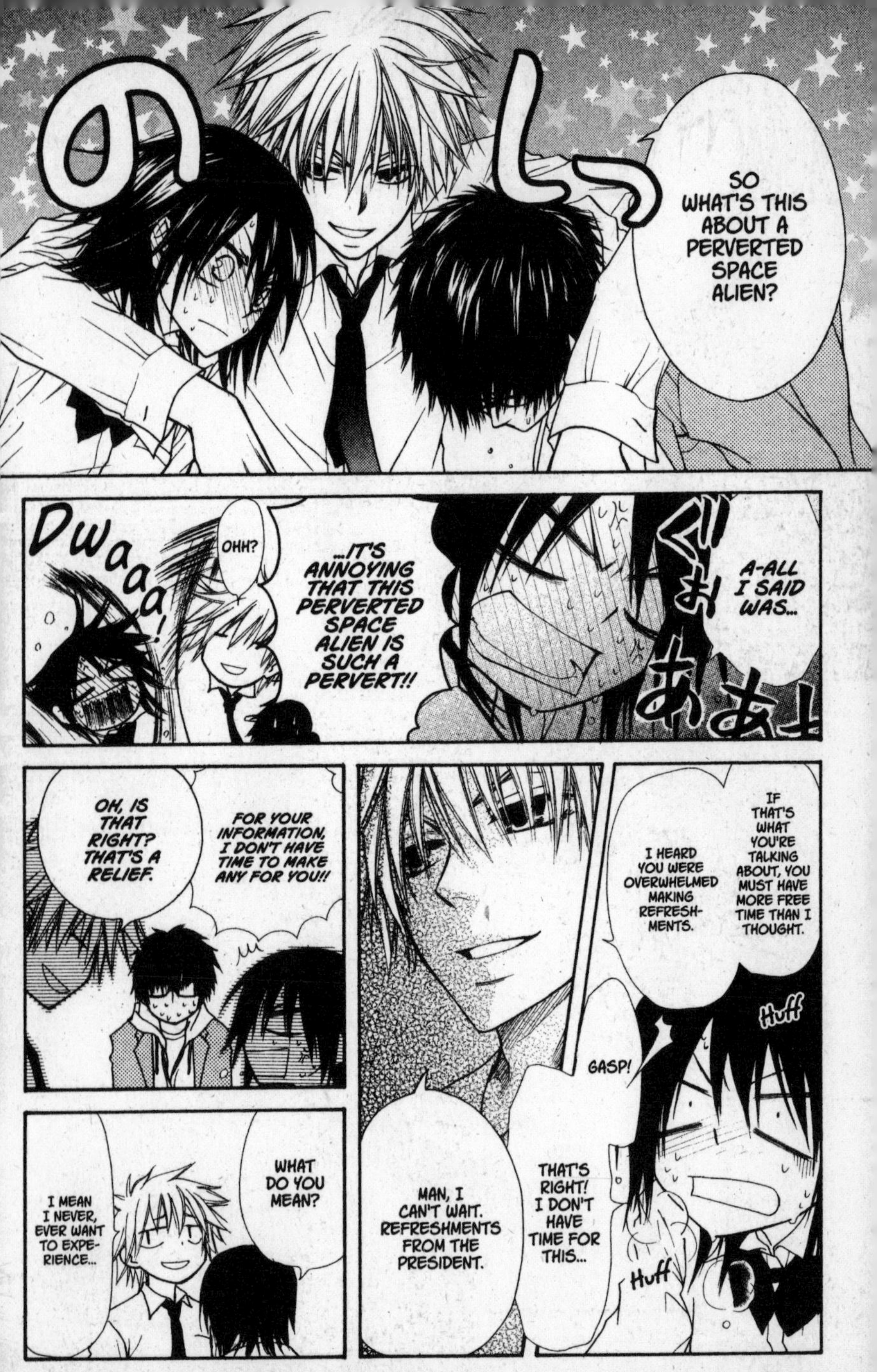

のしっ
SO WHAT'S THIS ABOUT A PERVERTED SPACE ALIEN?
A-ALL I SAID WAS...
...IT'S ANNOYING THAT THIS PERVERTED SPACE ALIEN IS SUCH A PERVERT!!
OHH?
Dwaaaa!
IF THAT'S WHAT YOU'RE TALKING ABOUT, YOU MUST HAVE MORE FREE TIME THAN I THOUGHT.
I HEARD YOU WERE OVERWHELMED MAKING REFRESH-MENTS.
Huff
GASP!
THAT'S RIGHT! I DON'T HAVE TIME FOR THIS...
Huff
MAN, I CAN'T WAIT. REFRESHMENTS FROM THE PRESIDENT.
FOR YOUR INFORMATION, I DON'T HAVE TIME TO MAKE ANY FOR YOU!!
OH, IS THAT RIGHT? THAT'S A RELIEF.
WHAT DO YOU MEAN?
I MEAN I NEVER, EVER WANT TO EXPE-RIENCE...

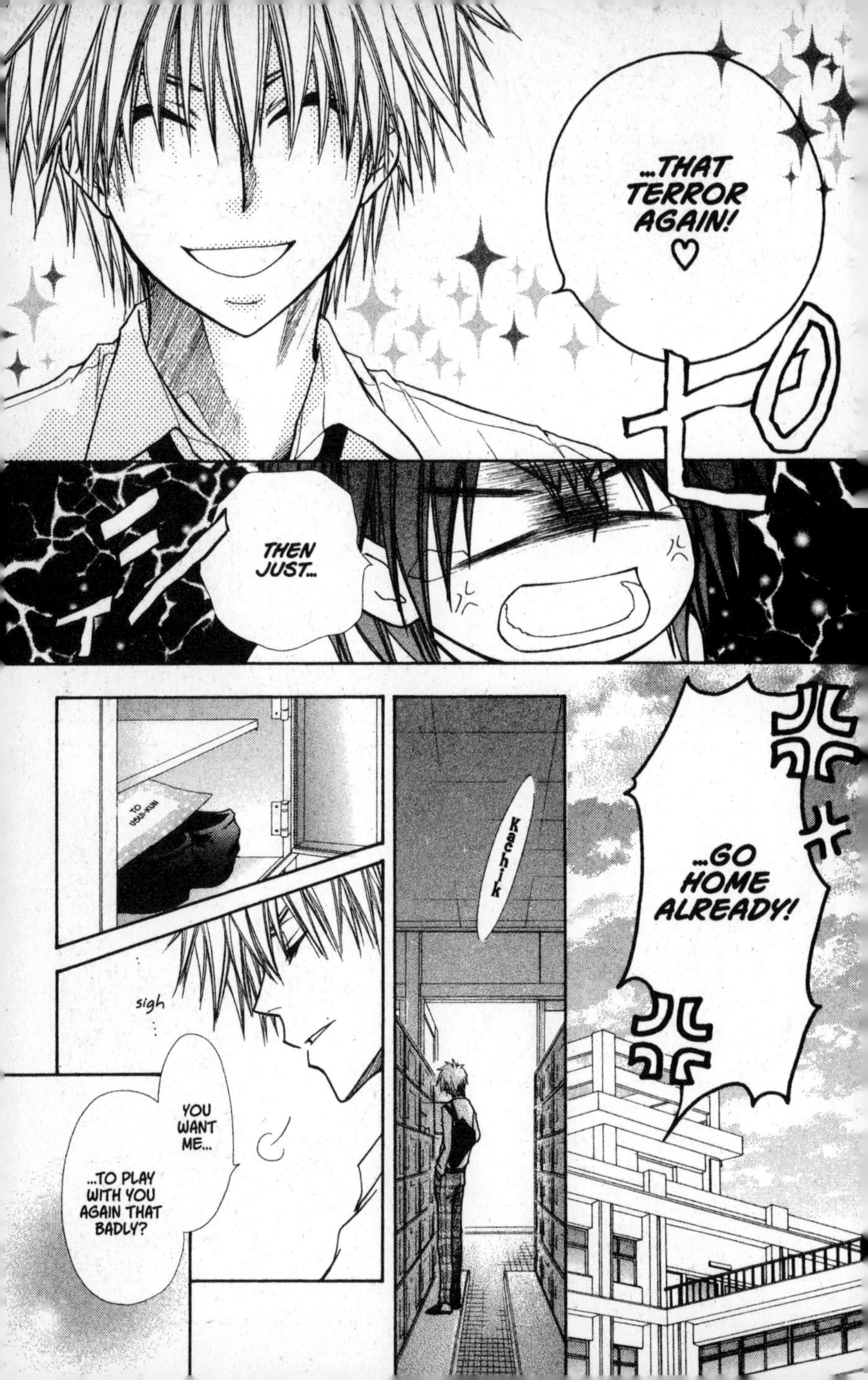
...THAT TERROR AGAIN! ♡
THEN JUST...
...GO HOME ALREADY!
Kachik
TO USUI-KUN
sigh
YOU WANT ME...
...TO PLAY WITH YOU AGAIN THAT BADLY?

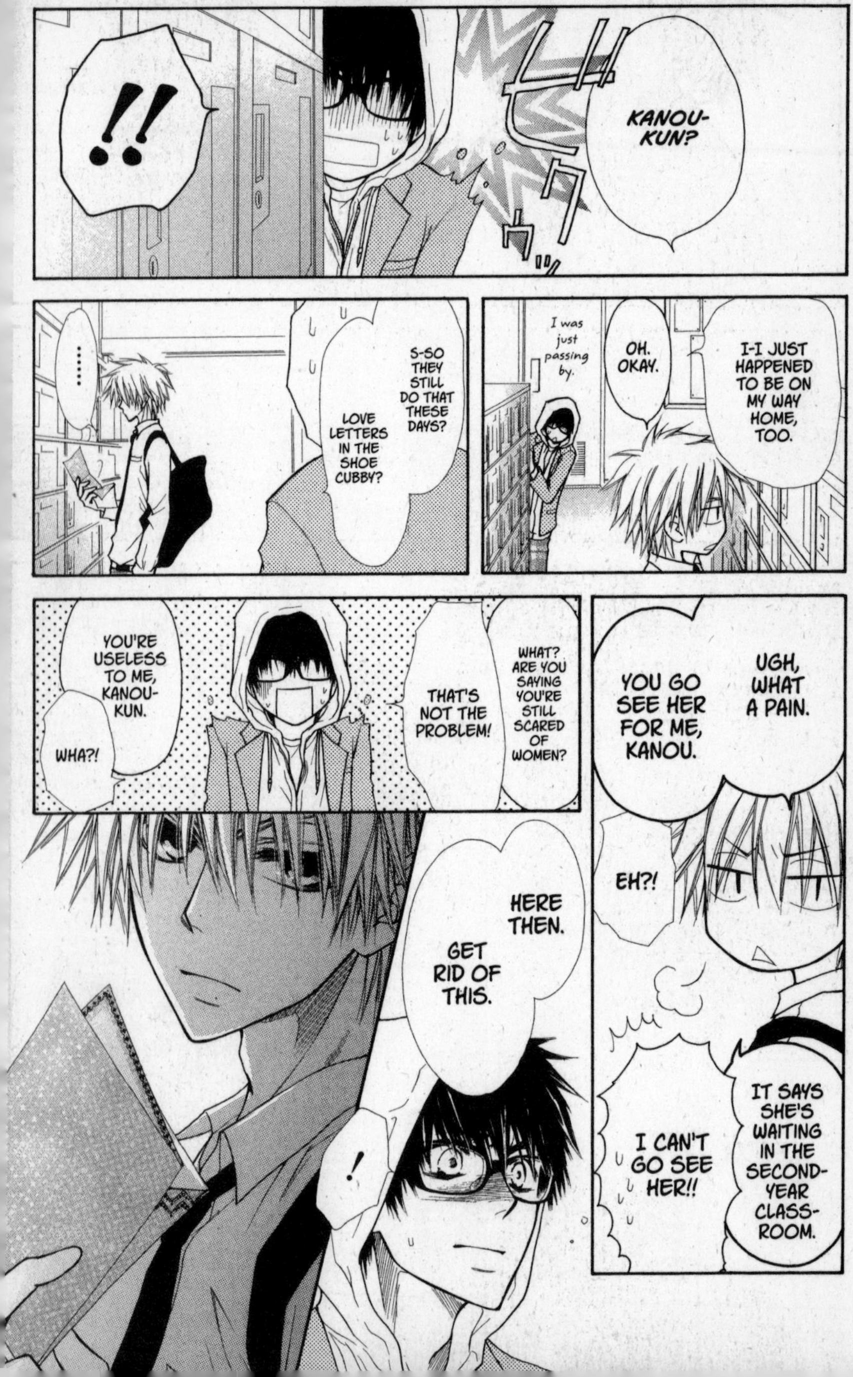
KANOU-KUN?
!!
I-I JUST HAPPENED TO BE ON MY WAY HOME, TOO.
OH. OKAY.
I was just passing by.
S-SO THEY STILL DO THAT THESE DAYS?
LOVE LETTERS IN THE SHOE CUBBY?
......
UGH, WHAT A PAIN.
YOU GO SEE HER FOR ME, KANOU.
EH?!
IT SAYS SHE'S WAITING IN THE SECOND-YEAR CLASSROOM.
I CAN'T GO SEE HER!!
WHAT? ARE YOU SAYING YOU'RE STILL SCARED OF WOMEN?
THAT'S NOT THE PROBLEM!
YOU'RE USELESS TO ME, KANOU-KUN.
WHA?!
HERE THEN.
GET RID OF THIS.
!

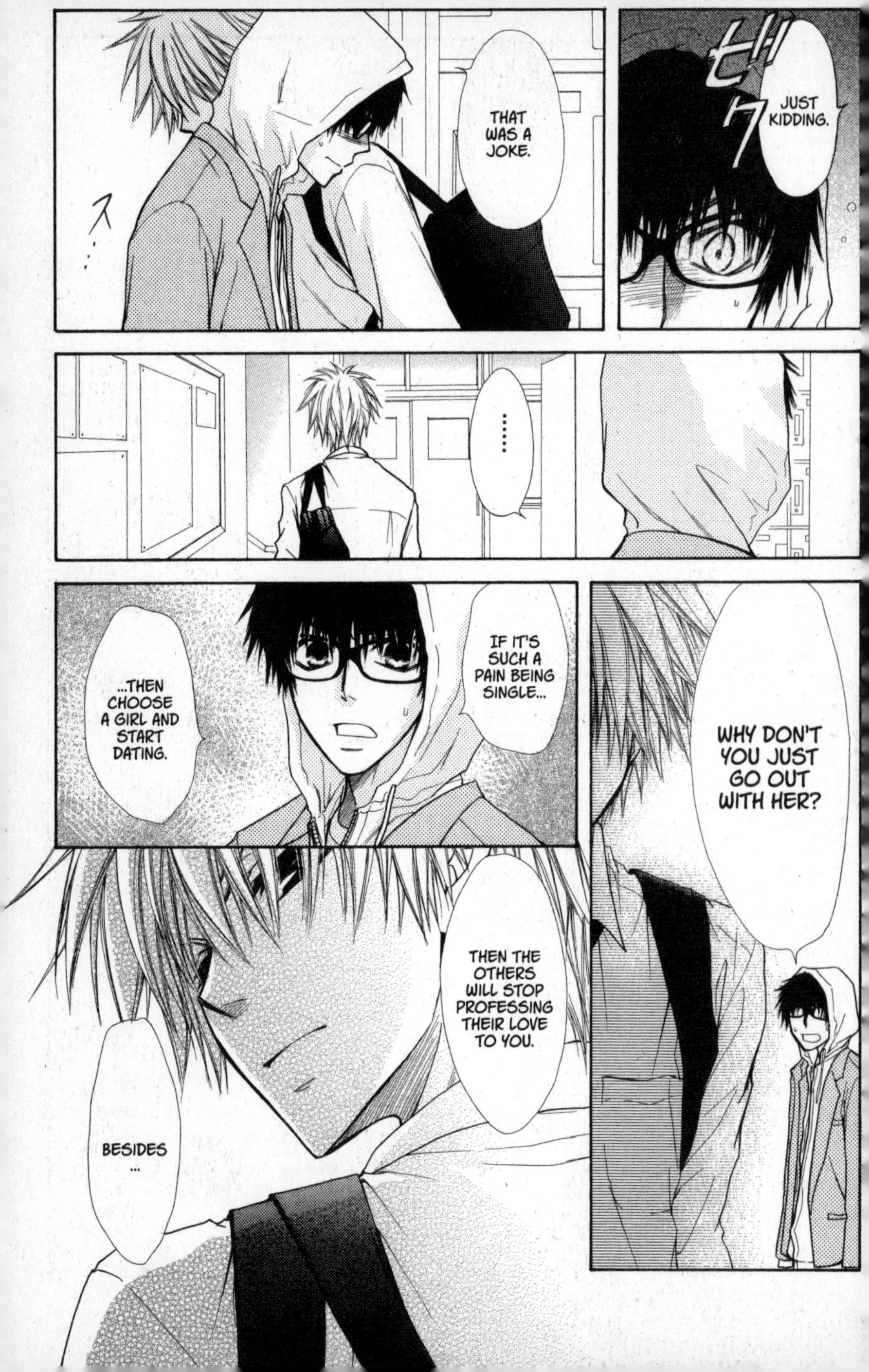
JUST KIDDING.
THAT WAS A JOKE.
......
WHY DON'T YOU JUST GO OUT WITH HER?
IF IT'S SUCH A PAIN BEING SINGLE...
...THEN CHOOSE A GIRL AND START DATING.
THEN THE OTHERS WILL STOP PROFESSING THEIR LOVE TO YOU.
BESIDES ...

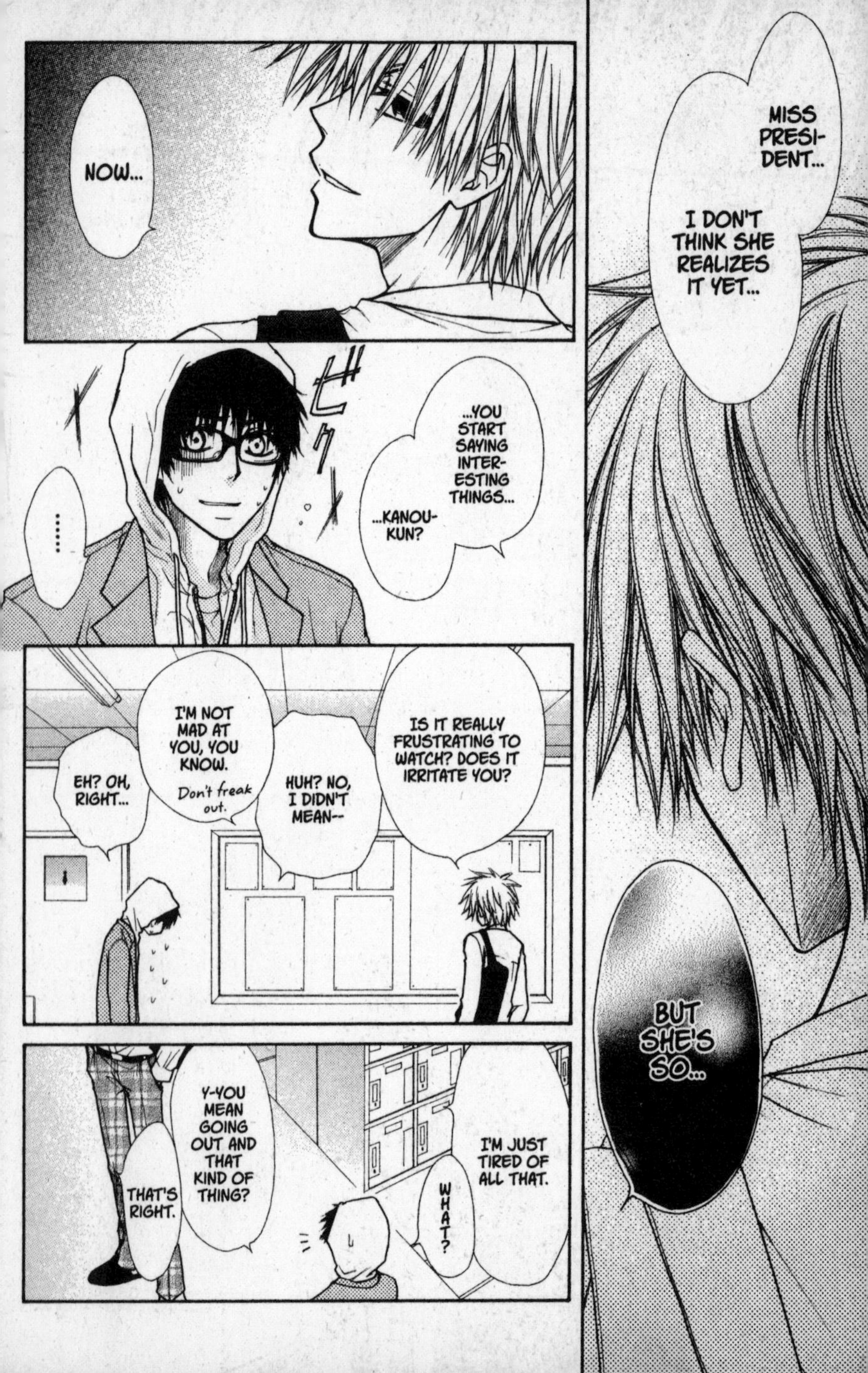
MISS PRESIDENT...
I DON'T THINK SHE REALIZES IT YET...
BUT SHE'S SO...
NOW...
...YOU START SAYING INTERESTING THINGS...
...KANOU-KUN?
......
IS IT REALLY FRUSTRATING TO WATCH? DOES IT IRRITATE YOU?
HUH? NO, I DIDN'T MEAN--
I'M NOT MAD AT YOU, YOU KNOW.
Don't freak out.
EH? OH, RIGHT...
I'M JUST TIRED OF ALL THAT.
WHAT?
Y-YOU MEAN GOING OUT AND THAT KIND OF THING?
THAT'S RIGHT.

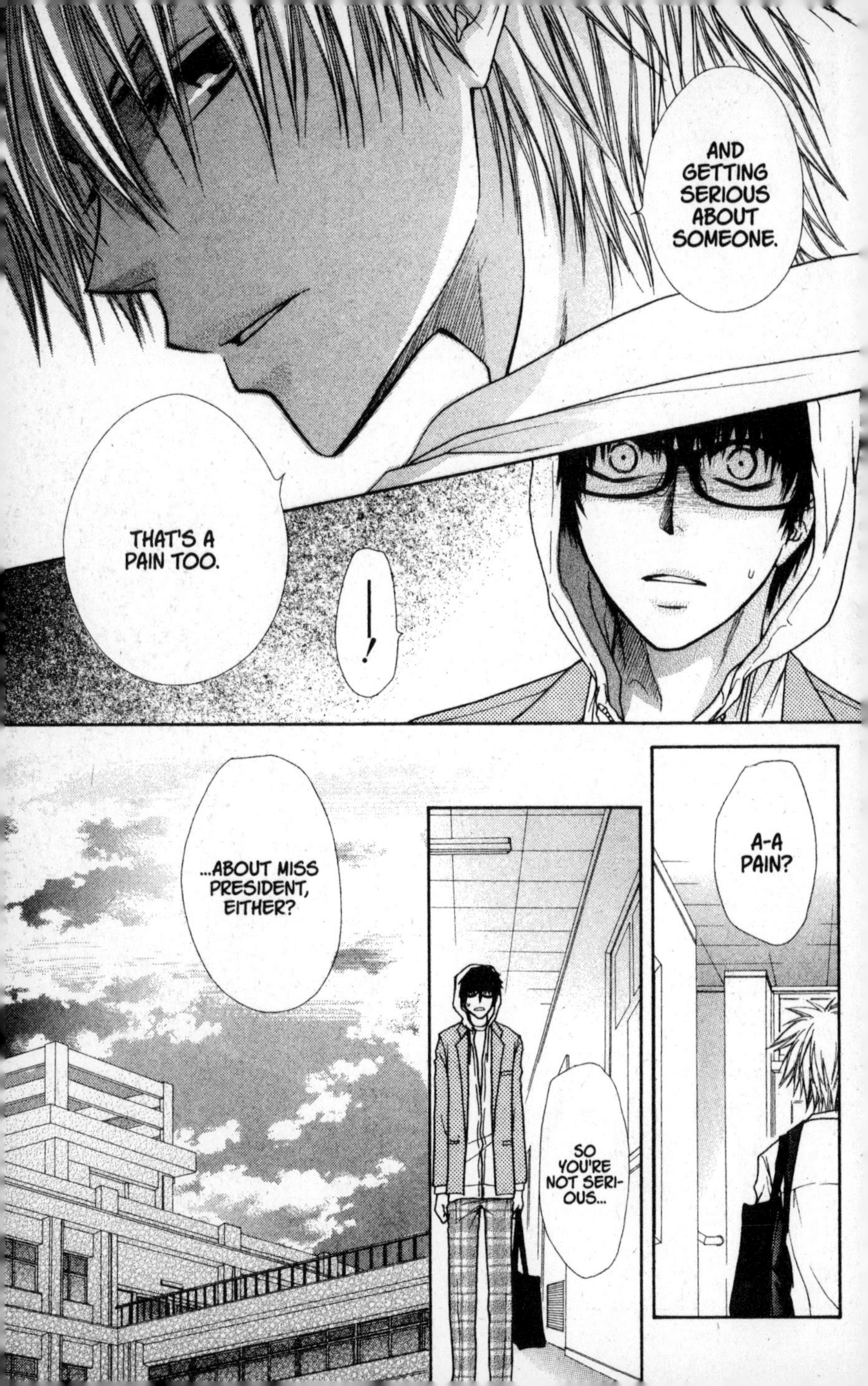
AND GETTING SERIOUS ABOUT SOMEONE.
THAT'S A PAIN TOO.
!
A-A PAIN?
SO YOU'RE NOT SERI-OUS...
...ABOUT MISS PRESIDENT, EITHER?

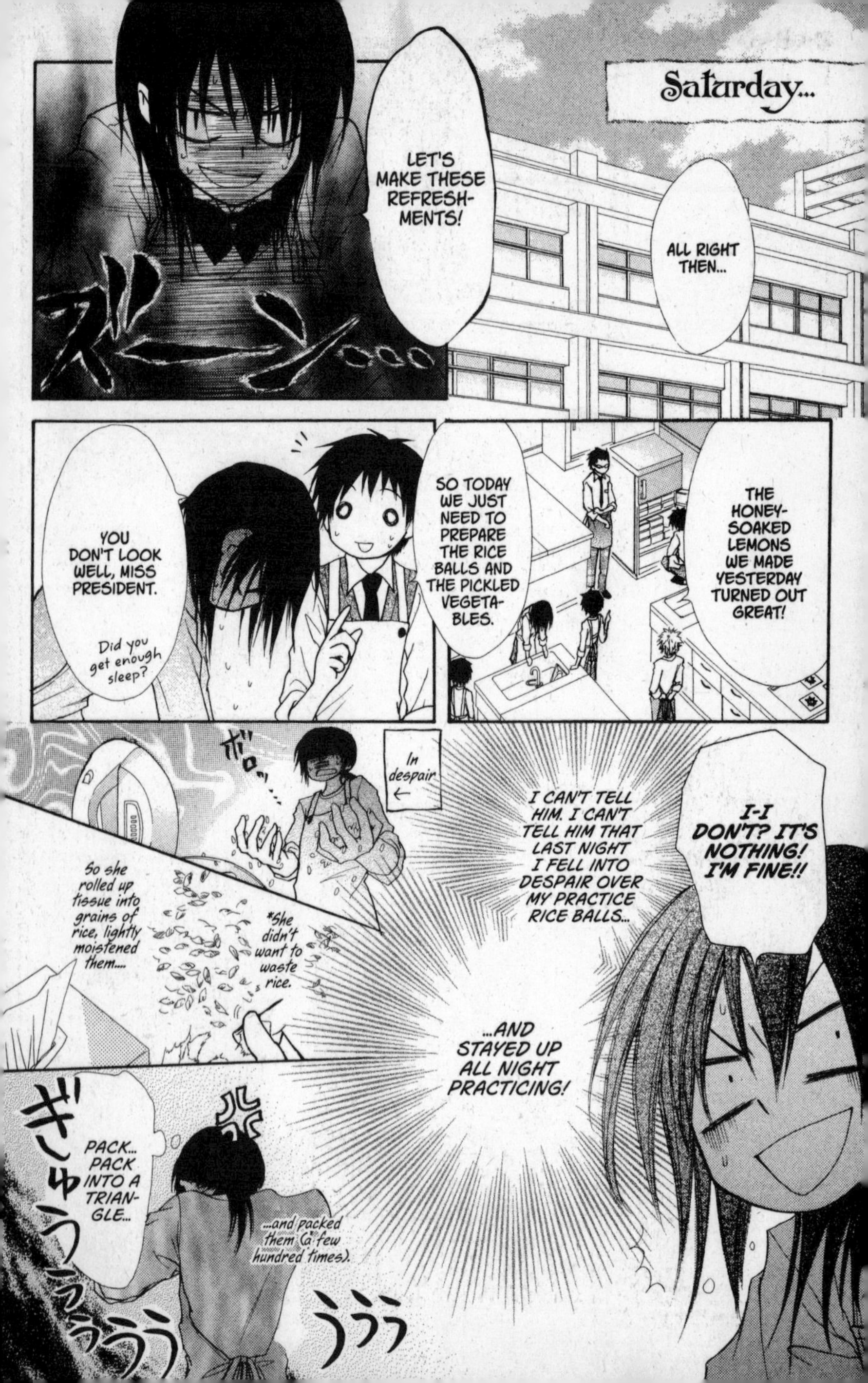
Saturday...
ALL RIGHT THEN...
LET'S MAKE THESE REFRESH-MENTS!
THE HONEY-SOAKED LEMONS WE MADE YESTERDAY TURNED OUT GREAT!
SO TODAY WE JUST NEED TO PREPARE THE RICE BALLS AND THE PICKLED VEGETA-BLES.
YOU DON'T LOOK WELL, MISS PRESIDENT.
Did you get enough sleep?
I-I DON'T? IT'S NOTHING! I'M FINE!!
I CAN'T TELL HIM. I CAN'T TELL HIM THAT LAST NIGHT I FELL INTO DESPAIR OVER MY PRACTICE RICE BALLS...
In despair ←
So she rolled up tissue into grains of rice, lightly moistened them....
*She didn't want to waste rice.
...AND STAYED UP ALL NIGHT PRACTICING!
PACK... PACK INTO A TRIAN-GLE...
...and packed them (a few hundred times).
ぎゅう
ううう

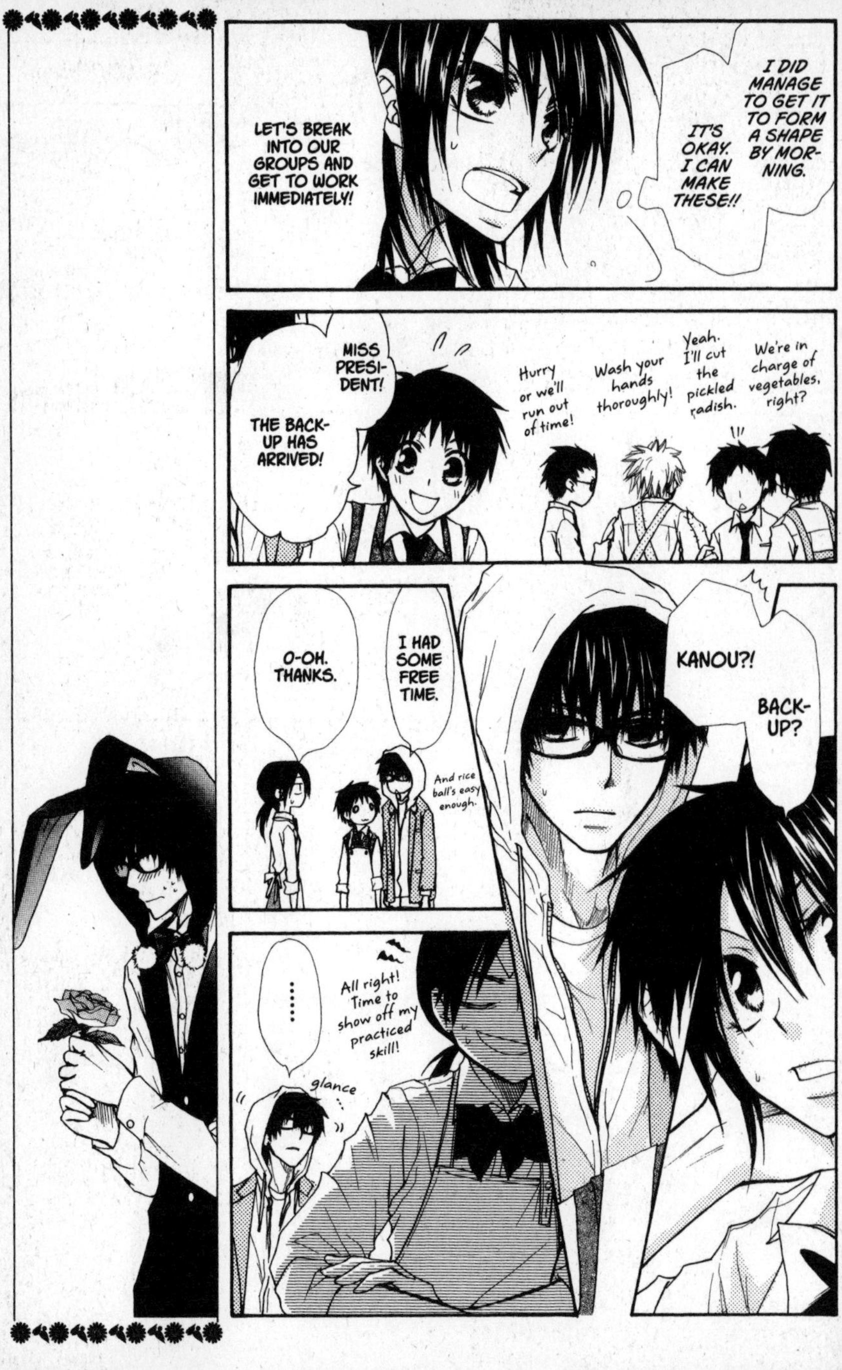
I DID MANAGE TO GET IT TO FORM A SHAPE BY MORNING.
IT'S OKAY. I CAN MAKE THESE!!
LET'S BREAK INTO OUR GROUPS AND GET TO WORK IMMEDIATELY!
We're in charge of vegetables, right?
Yeah. I'll cut the pickled radish.
Wash your hands thoroughly!
Hurry or we'll run out of time!
MISS PRESIDENT!
THE BACK-UP HAS ARRIVED!
KANOU?!
BACK-UP?
I HAD SOME FREE TIME.
O-OH. THANKS.
And rice ball's easy enough.
All right! Time to show off my practiced skill!
......
glance

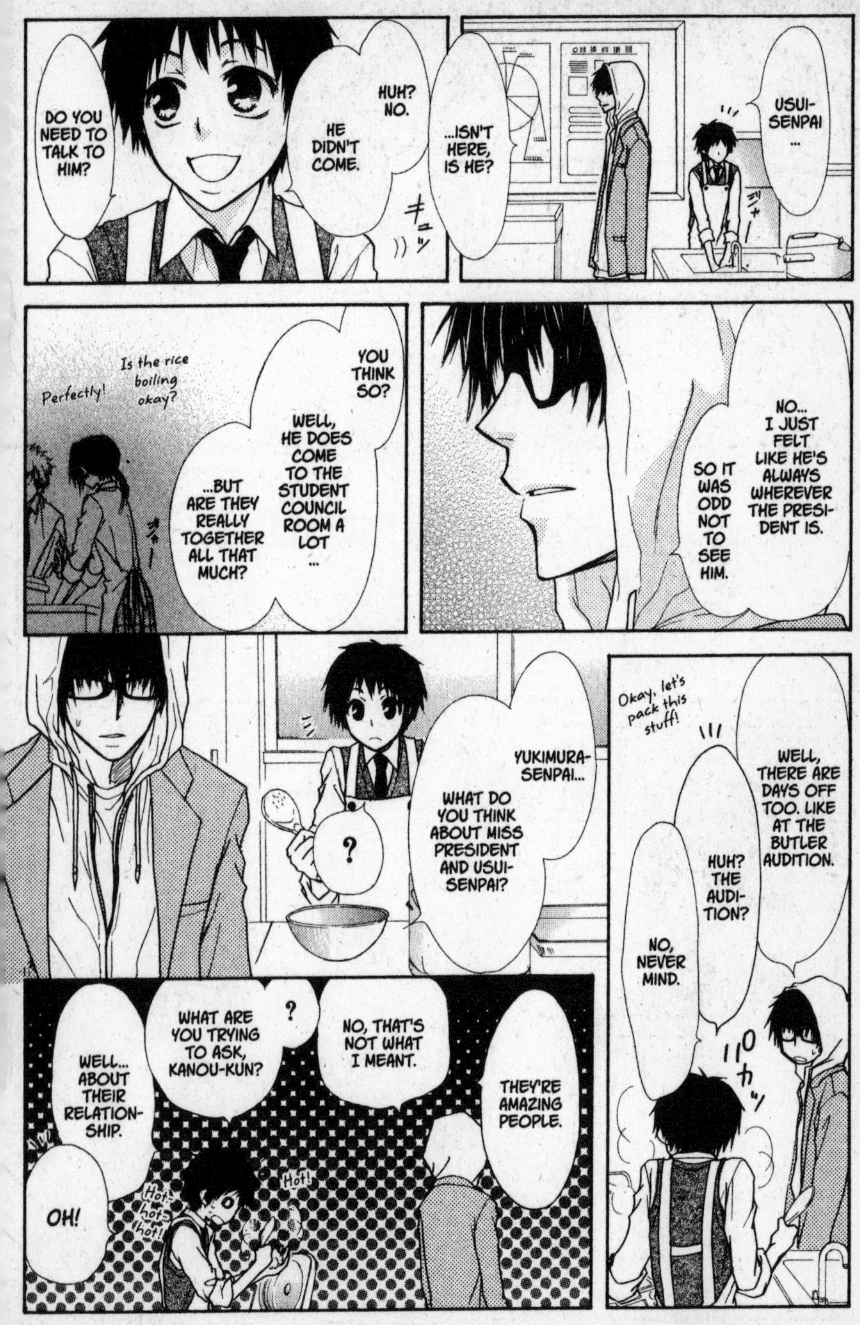
USUI-SENPAI ...
...ISN'T HERE, IS HE?
HUH? NO.
HE DIDN'T COME.
DO YOU NEED TO TALK TO HIM?
NO... I JUST FELT LIKE HE'S ALWAYS WHEREVER THE PRESIDENT IS.
SO IT WAS ODD NOT TO SEE HIM.
YOU THINK SO?
WELL, HE DOES COME TO THE STUDENT COUNCIL ROOM A LOT ...
...BUT ARE THEY REALLY TOGETHER ALL THAT MUCH?
Is the rice boiling okay?
Perfectly!
Okay, let's pack this stuff!
WELL, THERE ARE DAYS OFF TOO. LIKE AT THE BUTLER AUDITION.
HUH? THE AUDITION?
NO, NEVER MIND.
YUKIMURA-SENPAI...
WHAT DO YOU THINK ABOUT MISS PRESIDENT AND USUI-SENPAI?
?
THEY'RE AMAZING PEOPLE.
NO, THAT'S NOT WHAT I MEANT.
?
WHAT ARE YOU TRYING TO ASK, KANOU-KUN?
WELL... ABOUT THEIR RELATIONSHIP.
Hot!
Hot-hots-hot!
OH!

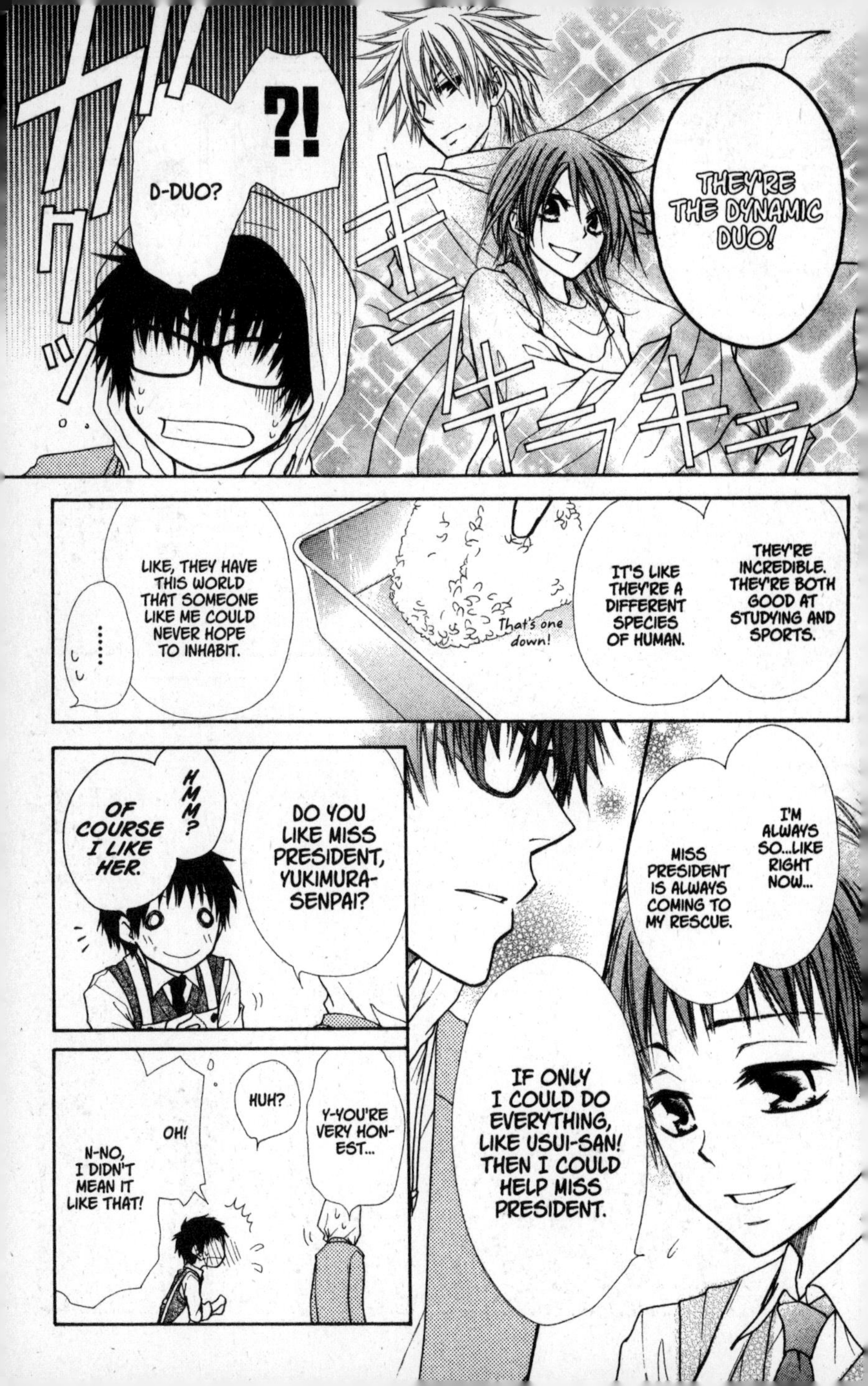
THEY'RE THE DYNAMIC DUO!
?!
D-DUO?
THEY'RE INCREDIBLE. THEY'RE BOTH GOOD AT STUDYING AND SPORTS.
IT'S LIKE THEY'RE A DIFFERENT SPECIES OF HUMAN.
That's one down!
LIKE, THEY HAVE THIS WORLD THAT SOMEONE LIKE ME COULD NEVER HOPE TO INHABIT.
......
I'M ALWAYS SO...LIKE RIGHT NOW...
MISS PRESIDENT IS ALWAYS COMING TO MY RESCUE.
IF ONLY I COULD DO EVERYTHING, LIKE USUI-SAN! THEN I COULD HELP MISS PRESIDENT.
DO YOU LIKE MISS PRESIDENT, YUKIMURA-SENPAI?
HMM?
OF COURSE I LIKE HER.
Y-YOU'RE VERY HON-EST...
HUH?
OH!
N-NO, I DIDN'T MEAN IT LIKE THAT!

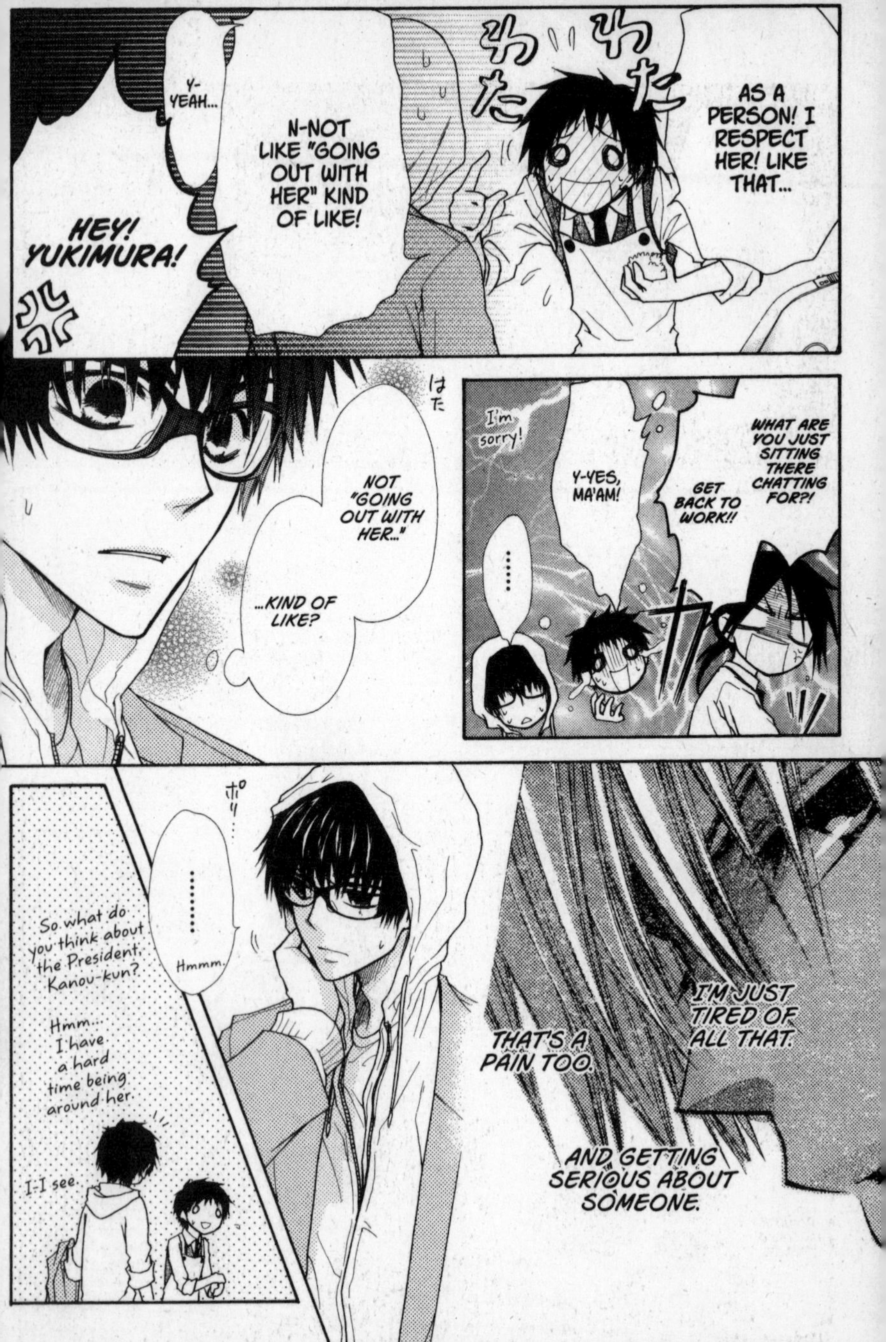
わた わた
AS A PERSON! I RESPECT HER! LIKE THAT...
N-NOT LIKE "GOING OUT WITH HER" KIND OF LIKE!
Y-YEAH...
HEY! YUKIMURA!
WHAT ARE YOU JUST SITTING THERE CHATTING FOR?!
GET BACK TO WORK!!
Y-YES, MA'AM!
I'm sorry!
......
はた
NOT "GOING OUT WITH HER..."
...KIND OF LIKE?
I'M JUST TIRED OF ALL THAT.
THAT'S A PAIN TOO.
AND GETTING SERIOUS ABOUT SOMEONE.
ポリ...
....
Hmmm.
So what do you think about the President, Kanou-kun?
Hmm... I have a hard time being around her.
I-I see.

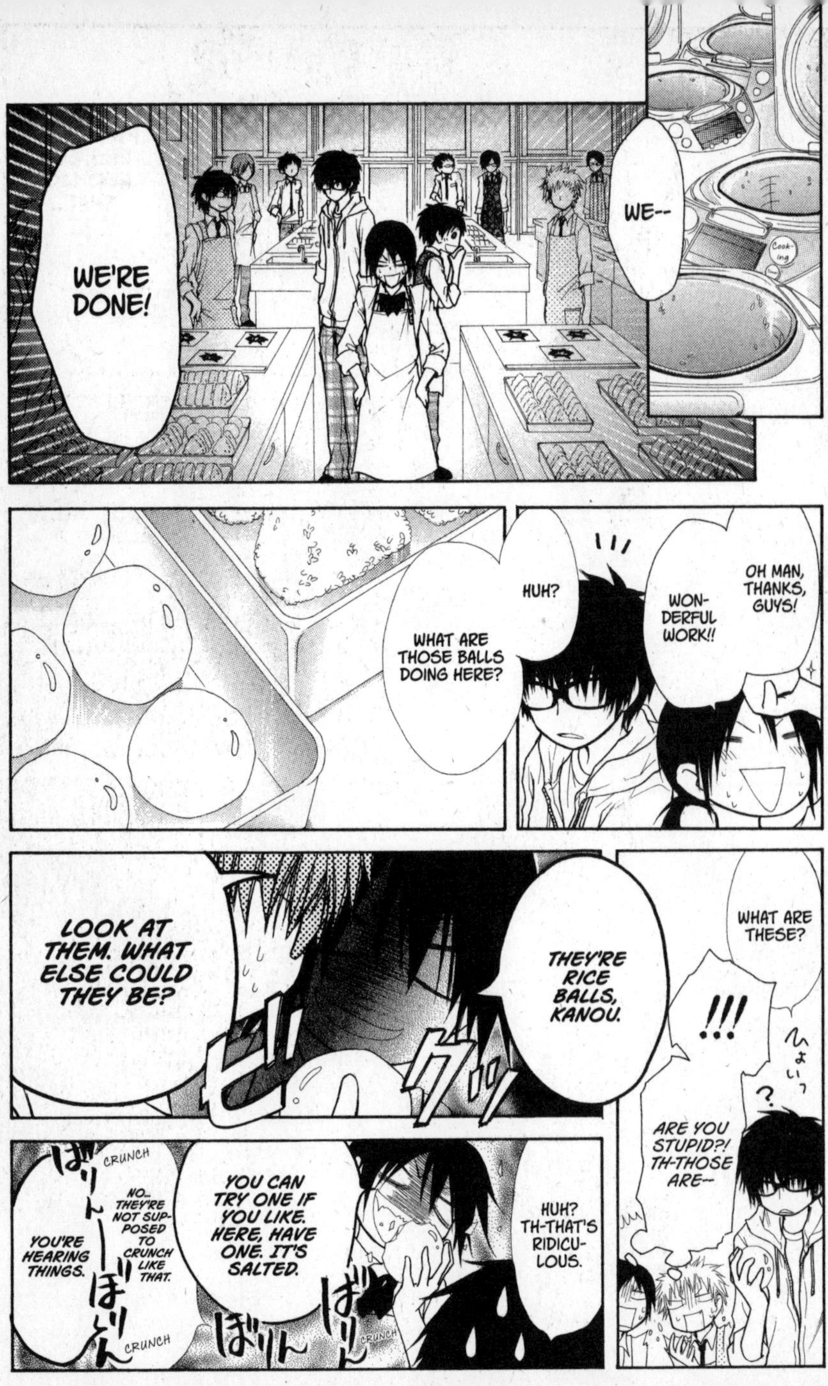
WE--
WE'RE DONE!
OH MAN, THANKS, GUYS!
WON-DERFUL WORK!!
HUH?
WHAT ARE THOSE BALLS DOING HERE?
WHAT ARE THESE?
ひょいっ
!!!
THEY'RE RICE BALLS, KANOU.
LOOK AT THEM. WHAT ELSE COULD THEY BE?
ARE YOU STUPID?! TH-THOSE ARE--
HUH? TH-THAT'S RIDICULOUS.
YOU CAN TRY ONE IF YOU LIKE. HERE, HAVE ONE. IT'S SALTED.
CRUNCH
NO... THEY'RE NOT SUP-POSED TO CRUNCH LIKE THAT.
YOU'RE HEARING THINGS.
CRUNCH
CRUNCH

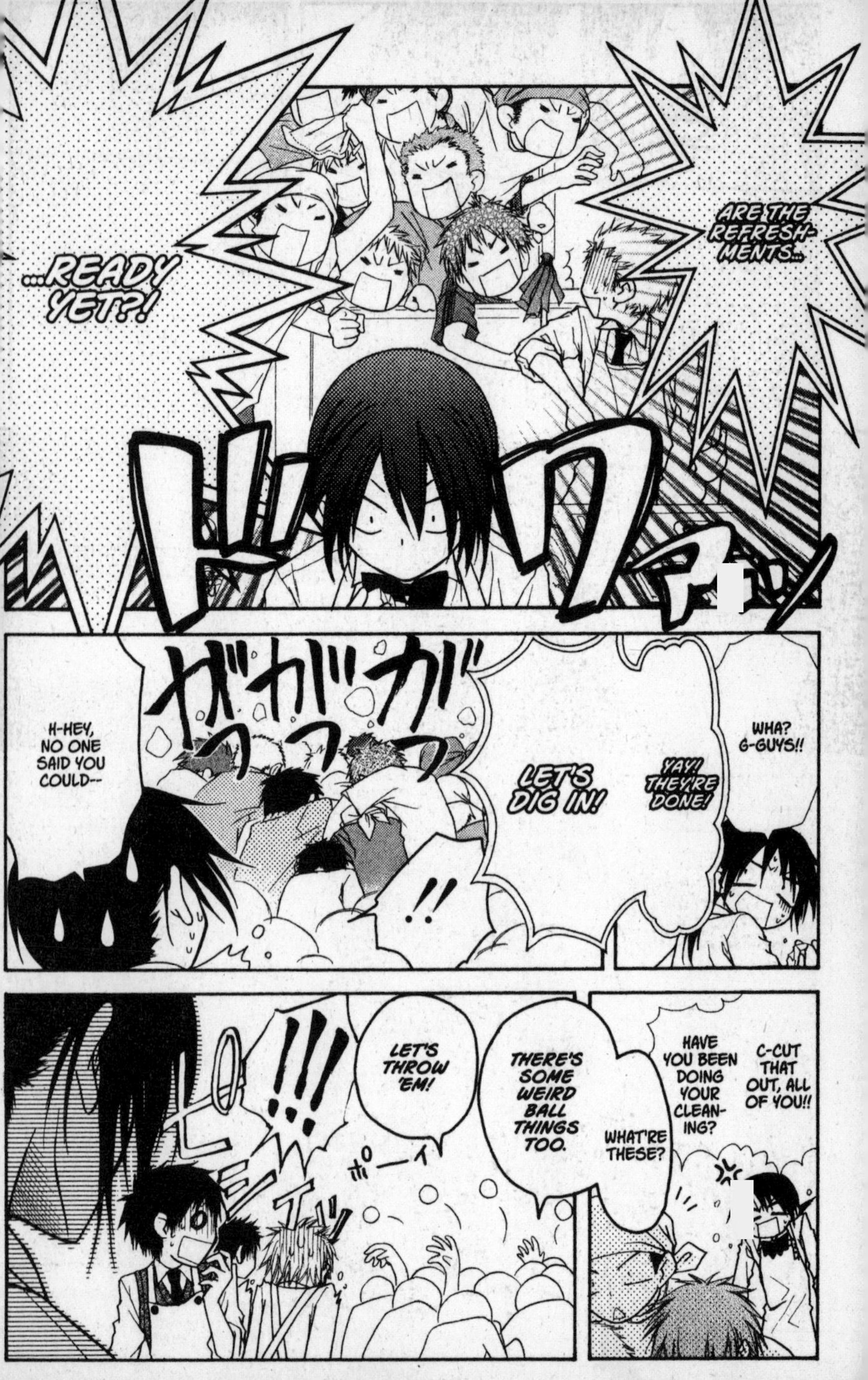
ARE THE REFRESHMENTS...
...READY YET?!
WHA? G-GUYS!!
YAY! THEY'RE DONE!
LET'S DIG IN!
H-HEY, NO ONE SAID YOU COULD--
!!
C-CUT THAT OUT, ALL OF YOU!!
HAVE YOU BEEN DOING YOUR CLEANING?
WHAT'RE THESE?
THERE'S SOME WEIRD BALL THINGS TOO.
LET'S THROW 'EM!
!!!

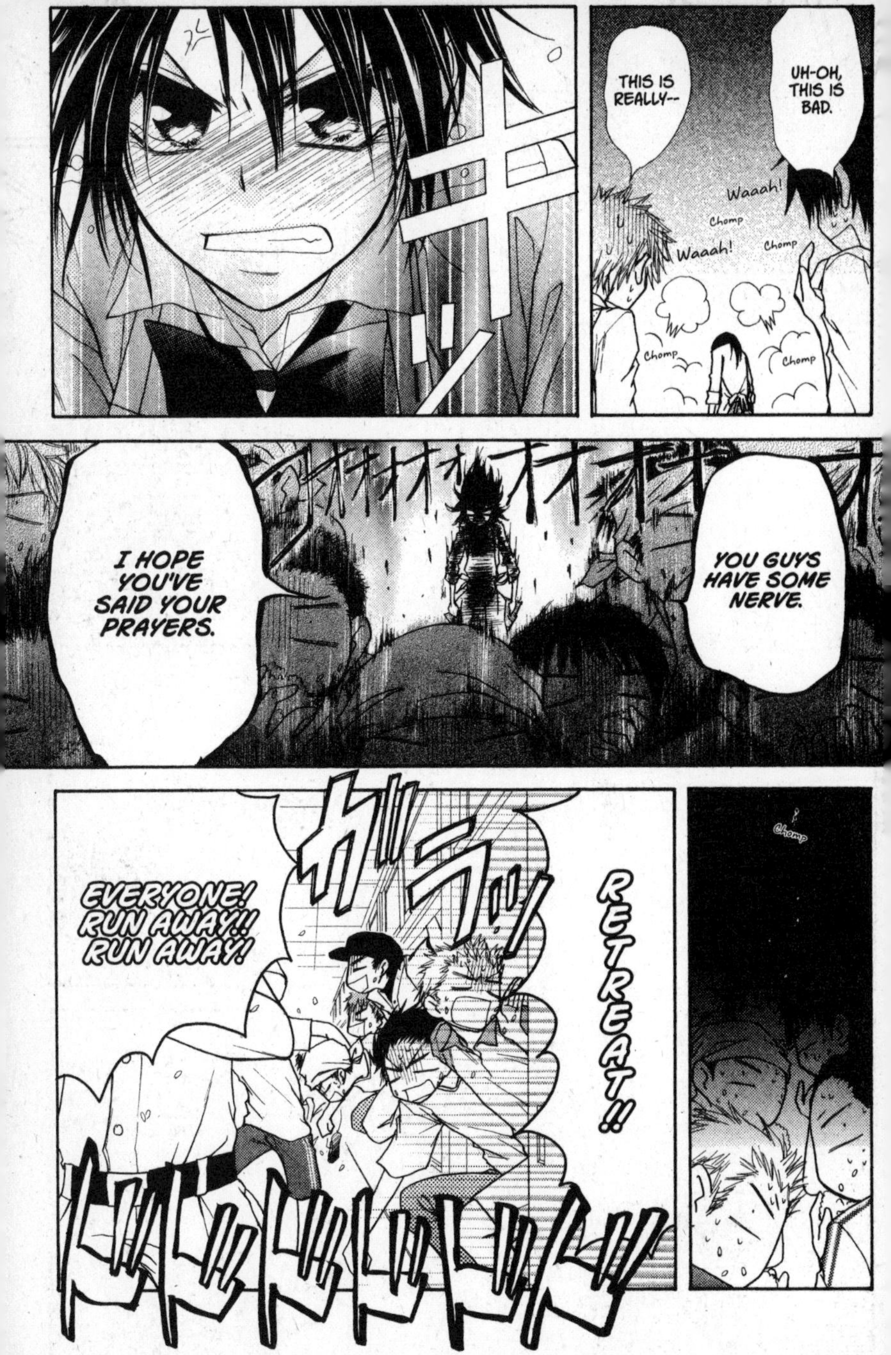
UH-OH, THIS IS BAD.
THIS IS REALLY--
Waaah!
Chomp
Waaah!
Chomp
Chomp
Chomp
YOU GUYS HAVE SOME NERVE.
I HOPE YOU'VE SAID YOUR PRAYERS.
Chomp
RETREAT!!
EVERYONE! RUN AWAY!! RUN AWAY!

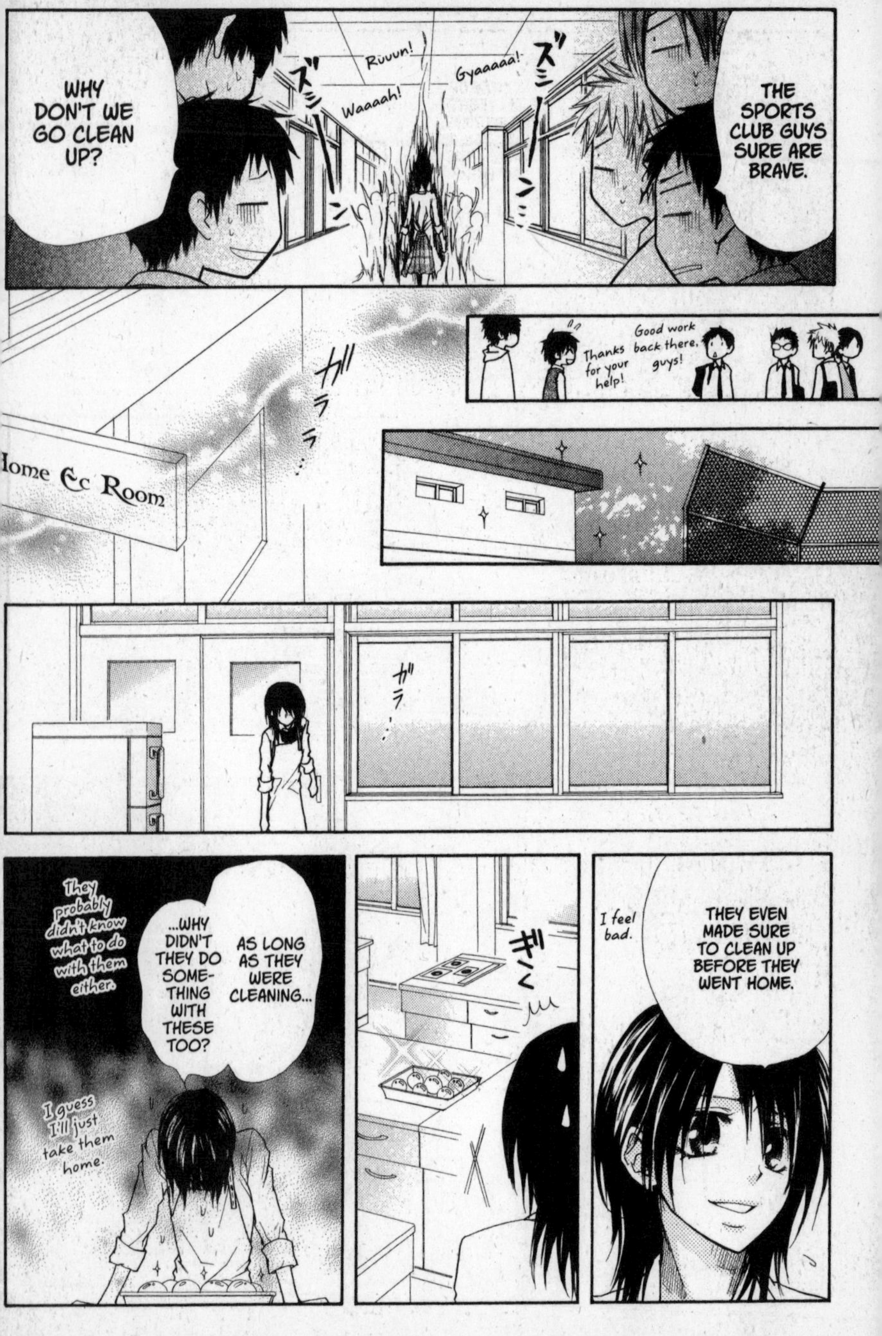
THE SPORTS CLUB GUYS SURE ARE BRAVE.
Gyaaaaa!
Ruuun!
Waaaah!
WHY DON'T WE GO CLEAN UP?
Good work back there, guys!
Thanks for your help!
Home Ec Room
ガララ…
ガラ…
I feel bad.
THEY EVEN MADE SURE TO CLEAN UP BEFORE THEY WENT HOME.
AS LONG AS THEY WERE CLEANING...
...WHY DIDN'T THEY DO SOMETHING WITH THESE TOO?
They probably didn't know what to do with them either.
I guess I'll just take them home.

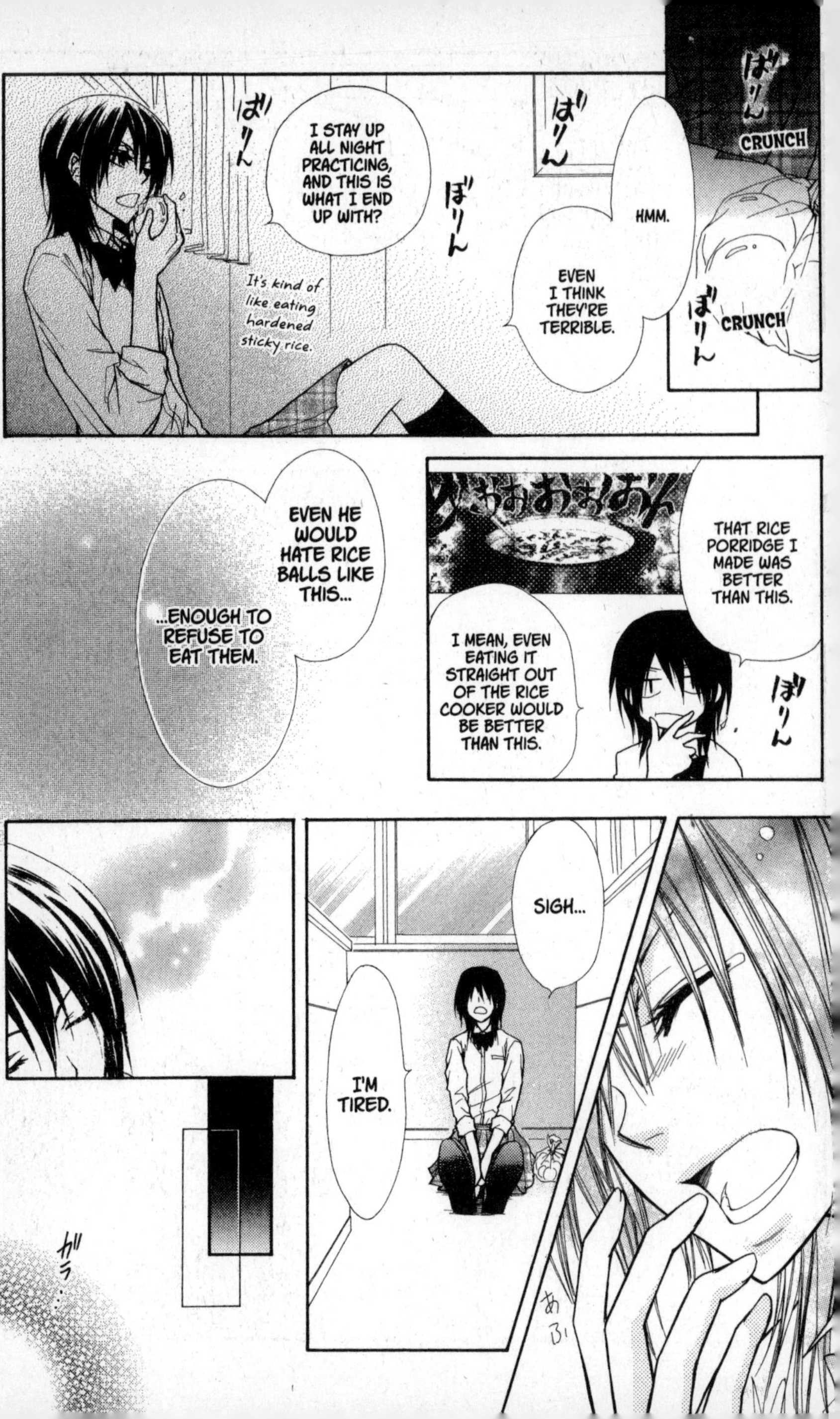
ばりん
CRUNCH
ぼりん
CRUNCH
ばりん
ぼりん
ばりん
HMM.
EVEN I THINK THEY'RE TERRIBLE.
I STAY UP ALL NIGHT PRACTICING, AND THIS IS WHAT I END UP WITH?
It's kind of like eating hardened sticky rice.
THAT RICE PORRIDGE I MADE WAS BETTER THAN THIS.
ぼりん
I MEAN, EVEN EATING IT STRAIGHT OUT OF THE RICE COOKER WOULD BE BETTER THAN THIS.
EVEN HE WOULD HATE RICE BALLS LIKE THIS...
...ENOUGH TO REFUSE TO EAT THEM.
あふ
SIGH...
I'M TIRED.
ガラ…

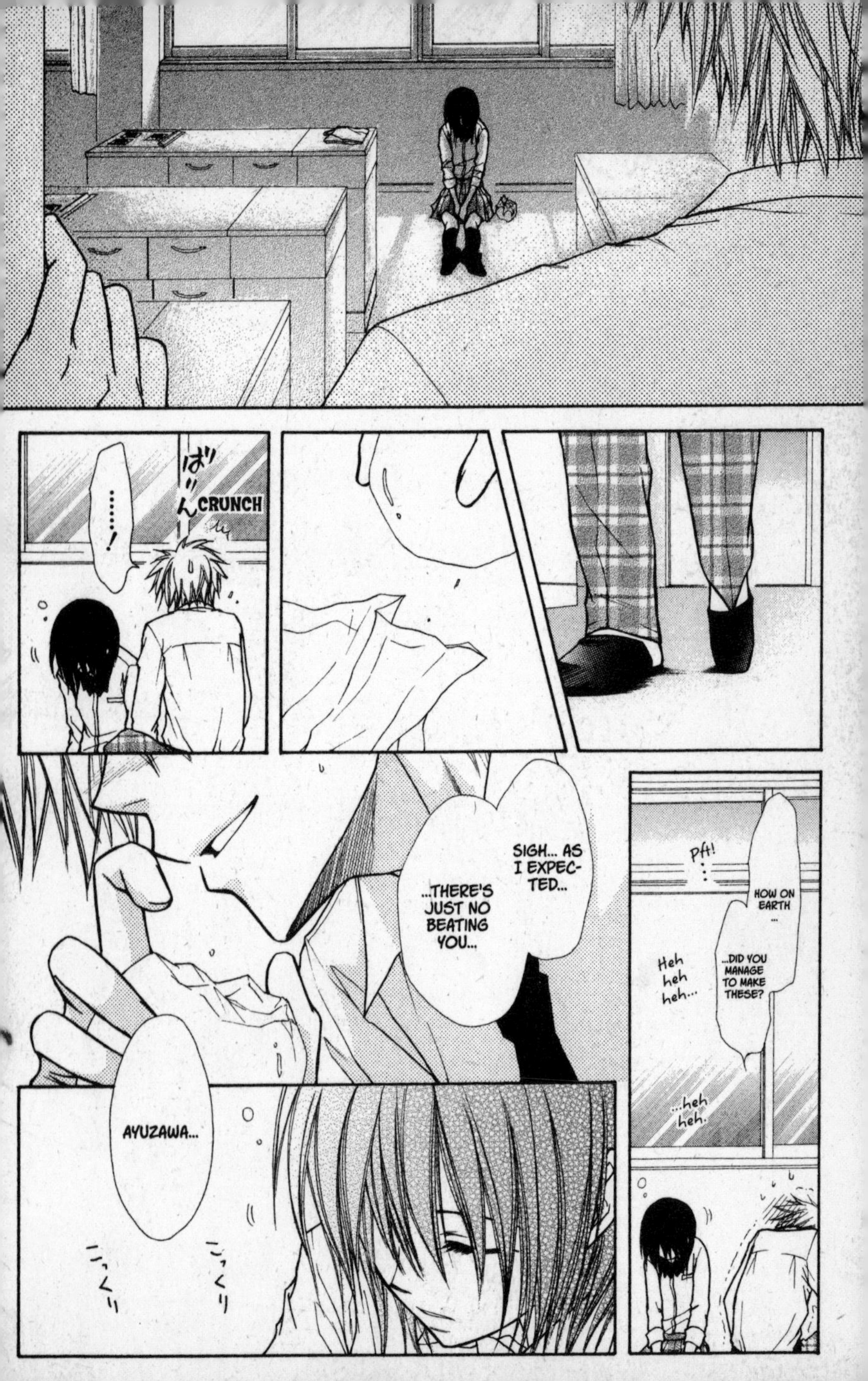
......!
CRUNCH
Pft!
...
HOW ON EARTH ...
...DID YOU MANAGE TO MAKE THESE?
Heh heh heh...
...heh heh.
SIGH... AS I EXPECTED...
...THERE'S JUST NO BEATING YOU...
AYUZAWA...
ごくり
ごくり

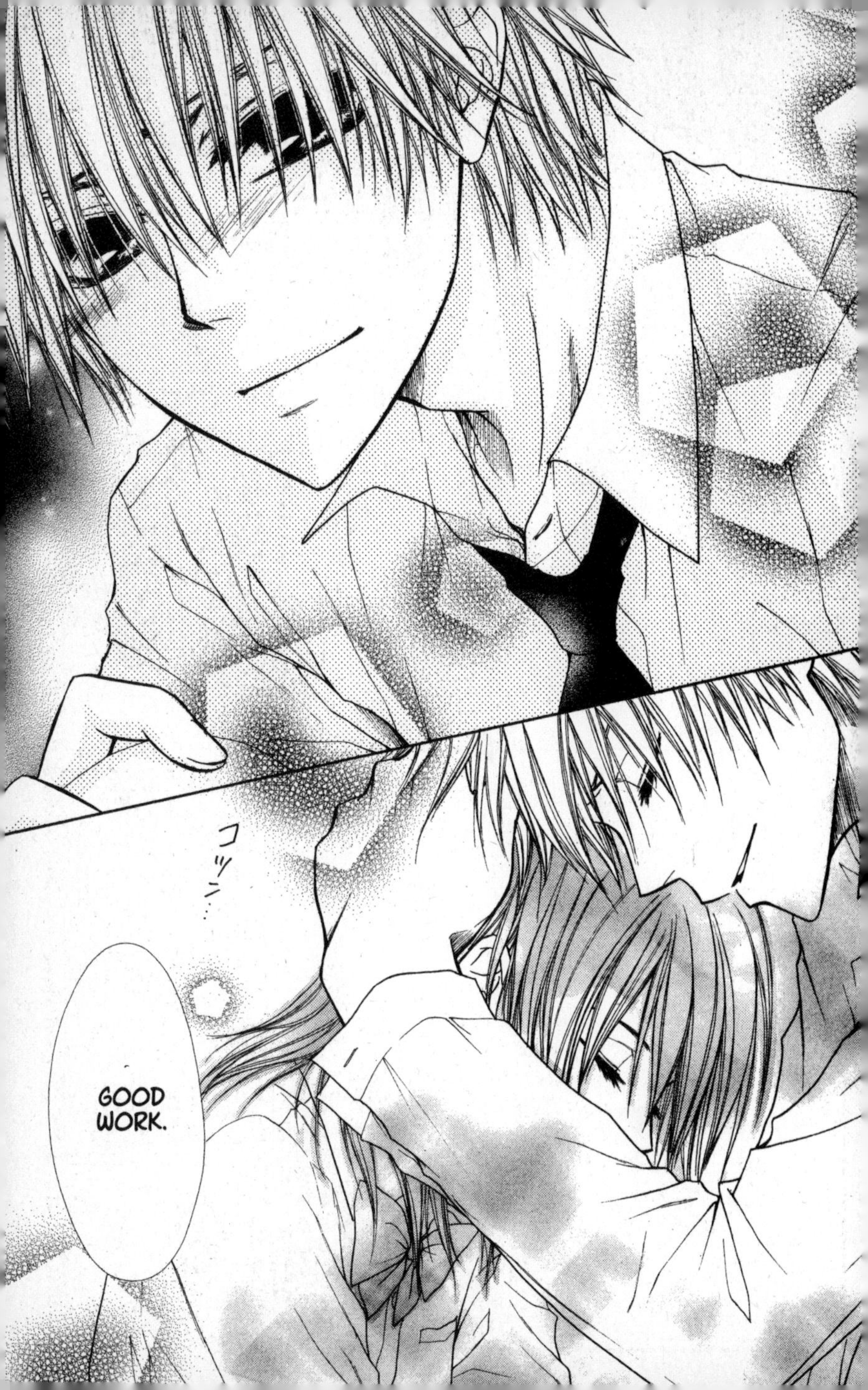
コツン…
GOOD WORK.

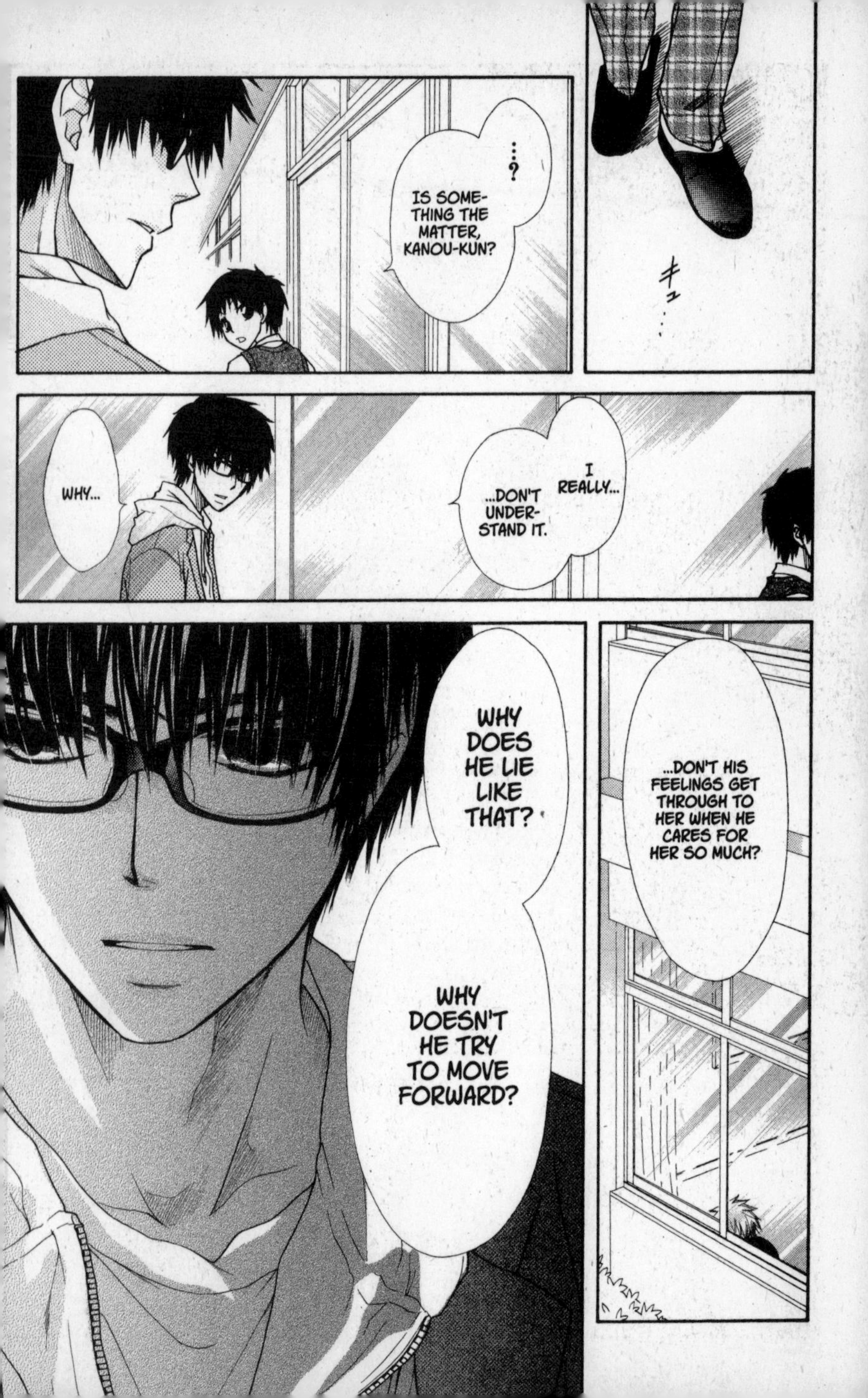
キュ...
...?
IS SOMETHING THE MATTER, KANOU-KUN?
I REALLY...
...DON'T UNDERSTAND IT.
WHY...
...DON'T HIS FEELINGS GET THROUGH TO HER WHEN HE CARES FOR HER SO MUCH?
WHY DOES HE LIE LIKE THAT?
WHY DOESN'T HE TRY TO MOVE FORWARD?

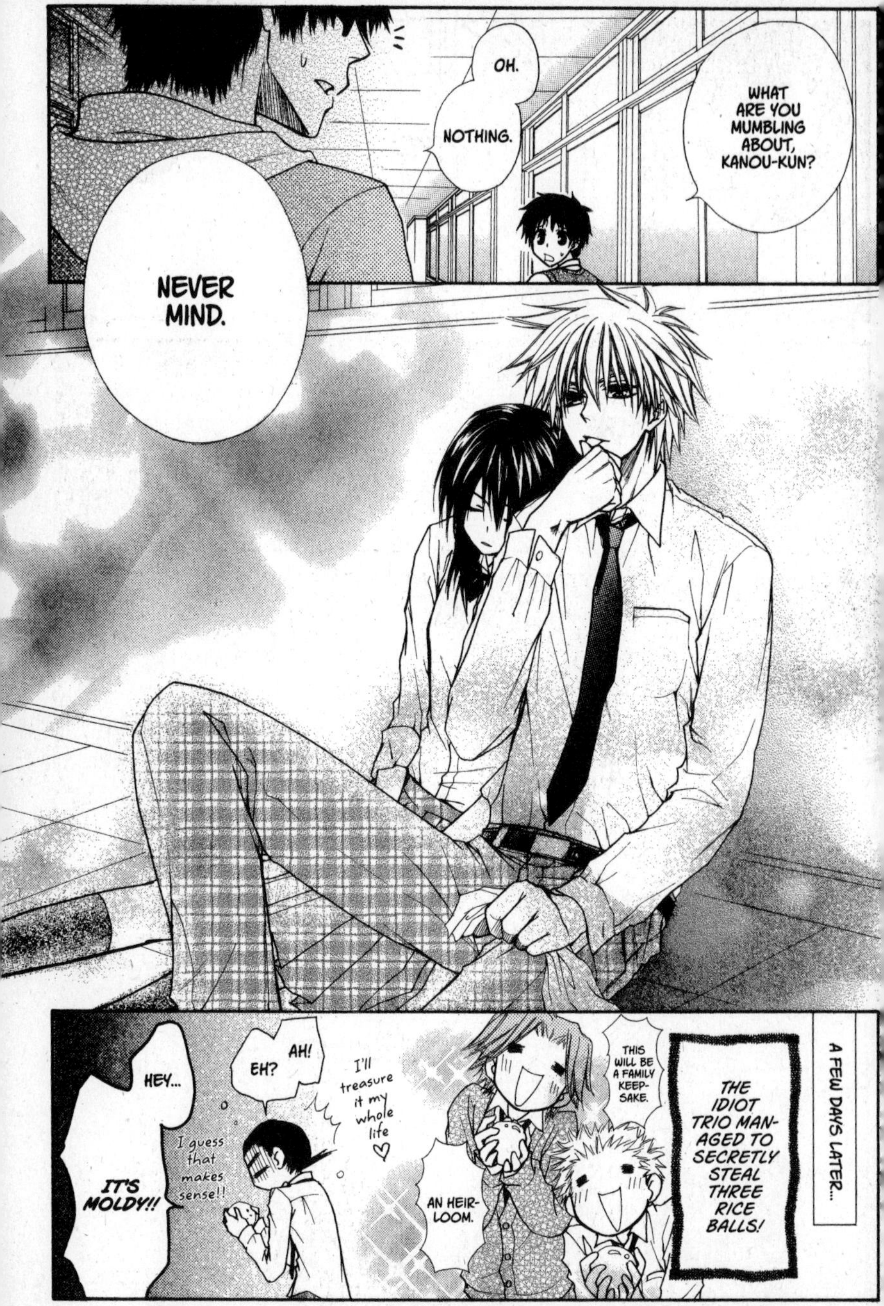
WHAT ARE YOU MUMBLING ABOUT, KANOU-KUN?
OH.
NOTHING.
NEVER MIND.
A FEW DAYS LATER...
THE IDIOT TRIO MAN-AGED TO SECRETLY STEAL THREE RICE BALLS!
THIS WILL BE A FAMILY KEEP-SAKE.
AN HEIR-LOOM.
I'll treasure it my whole life ♥
AH!
EH?
I guess that makes sense!!
HEY...
IT'S MOLDY!!

Q&A time...

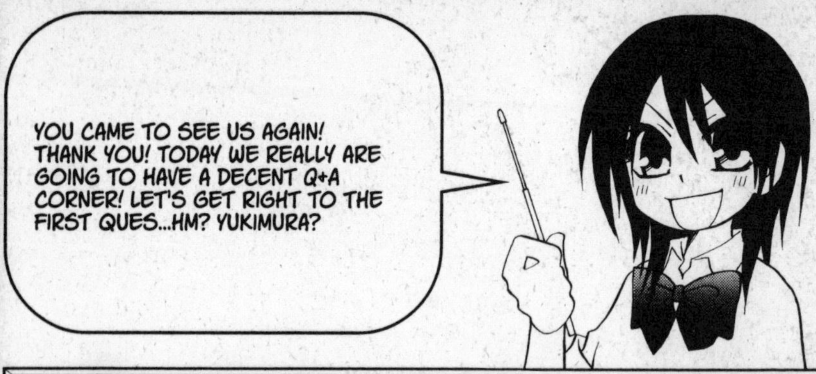
YOU CAME TO SEE US AGAIN! THANK YOU! TODAY WE REALLY ARE GOING TO HAVE A DECENT Q+A CORNER! LET'S GET RIGHT TO THE FIRST QUES...HM? YUKIMURA?

:HELLO, EVERYONE! THIS TIME, I WILL READ THE QUESTIONS FOR MISS PRESIDENT!

:WELL, YOU'RE ENTHUSIASTIC, YUKIMURA! ALL RIGHT, GO AHEAD!

:LEAVE IT TO ME, MISS PRESIDENT. I CHOSE THESE CAREFULLY...HERE'S THE FIRST ONE!

QUESTION 1: WHAT'S YOUR BEST SUBJECT?

:OH, A DECENT QUESTION AT LAST! MY BEST SUBJECT, HUH? WELL, MY NUMBER ONE IS PE. AS FAR AS STUDYING, I THINK I MIGHT BE BETTER AT SCIENCE AND MATH THAN LITERATURE, BUT BASICALLY I'M ABOUT THE SAME AT BOTH.

:THAT'S OUR PRESIDENT. PERFECTION IS STANDARD WITH EVERYTHING, INCLUDING STUDYING! OKAY, NEXT QUESTION!

QUESTION 2: ARE YOU OR HAVE YOU EVER TAKEN LESSONS IN ANYTHING?

:I TOOK A LITTLE AIKIDO IN MIDDLE SCHOOL. A MAN IN MY NEIGHBORHOOD RAN A DOJO, AND HE SAID I NEEDED TO KNOW SELF-DEFENSE AND TAUGHT ME EVEN THOUGH I NEVER ASKED HIM. I LIKE MOVING MY BODY, AND IT REALLY COMES IN HANDY, SO I'M GRATEFUL TO HIM.

:ALTHOUGH IF YOU LIVED A NORMAL LIFE, YOU WOULDN'T HAVE MUCH OPPORTUNITY TO USE IT. B-BUT I GET THE FEELING IT DEFINITELY COMES IN HANDY FOR YOU, MISS PRESIDENT! WELL, NEXT WE HAVE THIS QUESTION!

QUESTION 3: WHAT IS YOUR GRIP STRENGTH?

:HMM...OF COURSE I DON'T REMEMBER THE EXACT NUMBER, BUT I THINK IT WAS ABOUT 50KG IN EACH HAND.

:WHAT?! F-FIFTY...? TH-THAT'S IMPRESSIVE EVEN FOR A BOY! I-I CAN ONLY GRIP ABOUT HALF THAT.

:YOU'RE TOO WEAK, YUKIMURA! YOU'RE A MAN! GO FOR 40!

:TH-THERE'S NO WAY I COULD--YOU'RE JUST TOO INCREDIBLE, MISS PRESIDENT!

:HMM, YOU THINK SO? WELL, OH WELL. THIS WAS AN EXTREMELY DECENT Q+A CORNER! GOOD JOB, YUKIMURA!

:Y-YES, AND WE LEARNED JUST HOW INCREDIBLE YOU REALLY ARE.

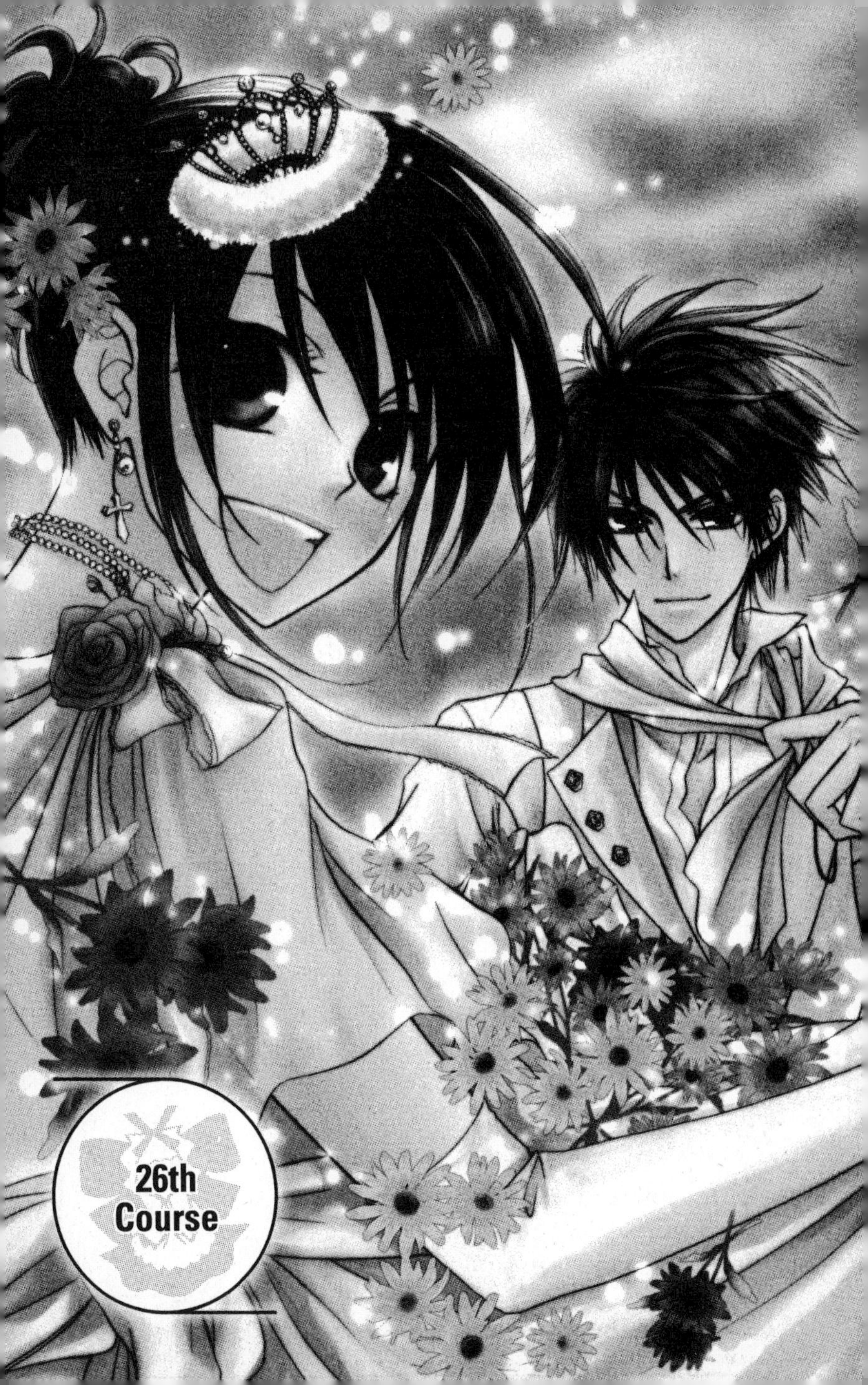
26th
Course

OKAY, HERE IT IS. THE PAINFUL FILLER CORNER. WHAT KIND OF UNSIGHTLY CONTENT WILL WE HAVE THIS TIME? ☆ NOW THEN, TO OUR FIRST POINTLESS QUESTION...

 : H-HEY, HEY!! YOU C-C-CAN'T DO THAT, USUI-SAN!!

 : HUH? WHY ARE YOU HERE, YUKIMURA?

 : *TH-THIS TIME I MADE SURE TO CHOOSE GOOD QUESTIONS!* THE FIRST QUESTION FOR YOU IS...LET'S SEE...HOW DID YOU GET TO BE SO SMART? TELL US HOW YOU STUDY.

QUESTION 4 : WERE YOU BORN A PERVERT, USUI?

 : *I WAS BORN ME.*

 : HEEEEY!! WH-WHAT ARE YOU DOING, ANSWERING A DIFFERENT QUESTION?!

 : HUH? WELL ALL THE QUESTIONS YOU CHOSE ARE COMPLETELY UNINTERESTING. YOU KNOW?
: Y-YOU'RE MEAN, USUI-SAN!!

QUESTION 5 : WHAT PLANET IS USUI FROM?

 : *GOOD QUESTION. IT'S NOT VERY EASY TO GET TO, BUT IF YOU GO TO THE TOP OF A HIGH HILL ON A STARRY NIGHT, GET COMPLETELY NAKED, AND PULL OUT ALL YOUR BODY HAIR, DANCING TO A CHIC RHYTHM, I THINK YOU MIGHT BE ABLE TO GET A FAINT GLIMPSE OF IT.*

 : *WAAAH! THAT WOULD GET YOU ARRESTED!!*

 : HUH? YOU DON'T BELIEVE ME, YUKIMURA? IF YOU THINK I'M LYING, YOU CAN TRY IT AND SEE.

 : *I WILL NOT!!* THERE'S NO WAY I COULD PULL OUT ALL MY BODY HAIR TO A CHIC RHYTHM!!

 : THEN I'LL PULL OUT YOUR HAIR TO A CHIC RHYTHM FOR YOU.

 : UGH, STOP JOKING AROUND--ERK, WHA-WHAT ARE YOU DOING?! STOP! WAAAH! PLEASE DON'T TAKE MY CLOTHES OFF!!!

 : YOU DON'T WANT TO GO THERE, YUKIMURA?

 : *THERE'S NO WAY I WOULD EVER WANT TO GO TO A CRAZY PLANET LIKE THAT!!* (FLEES)

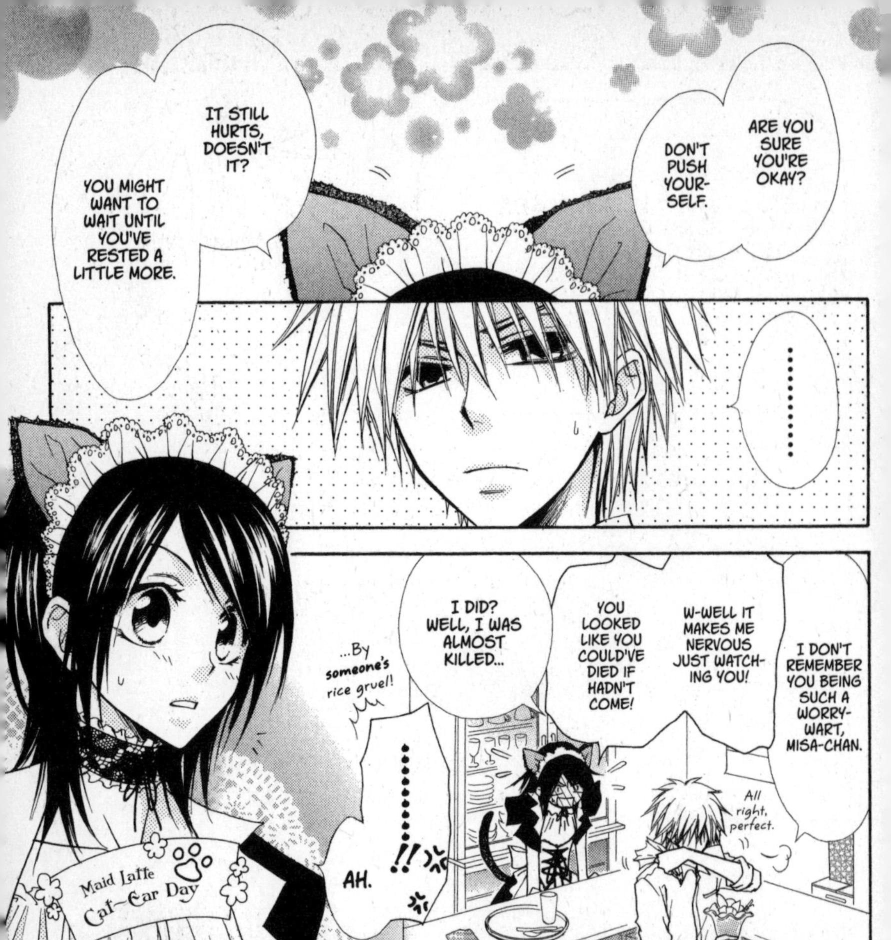
ARE YOU SURE YOU'RE OKAY?
DON'T PUSH YOURSELF.
IT STILL HURTS, DOESN'T IT?
YOU MIGHT WANT TO WAIT UNTIL YOU'VE RESTED A LITTLE MORE.
......
I DON'T REMEMBER YOU BEING SUCH A WORRY-WART, MISA-CHAN.
All right, perfect.
W-WELL IT MAKES ME NERVOUS JUST WATCHING YOU!
YOU LOOKED LIKE YOU COULD'VE DIED IF HADN'T COME!
I DID? WELL, I WAS ALMOST KILLED...
...By someone's rice gruel!
......!!
AH.
Filling in as chef
Maid Latte Cat-Ear Day

Field Trip Question Corner

Question 2

Q. How do we pronounce the second kanji in your name?

A. It's Fujiwara, Fujiwara, FUJIWARA!

It's not Fujihara.

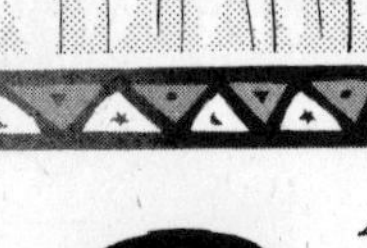

Never thought I'd get that question.

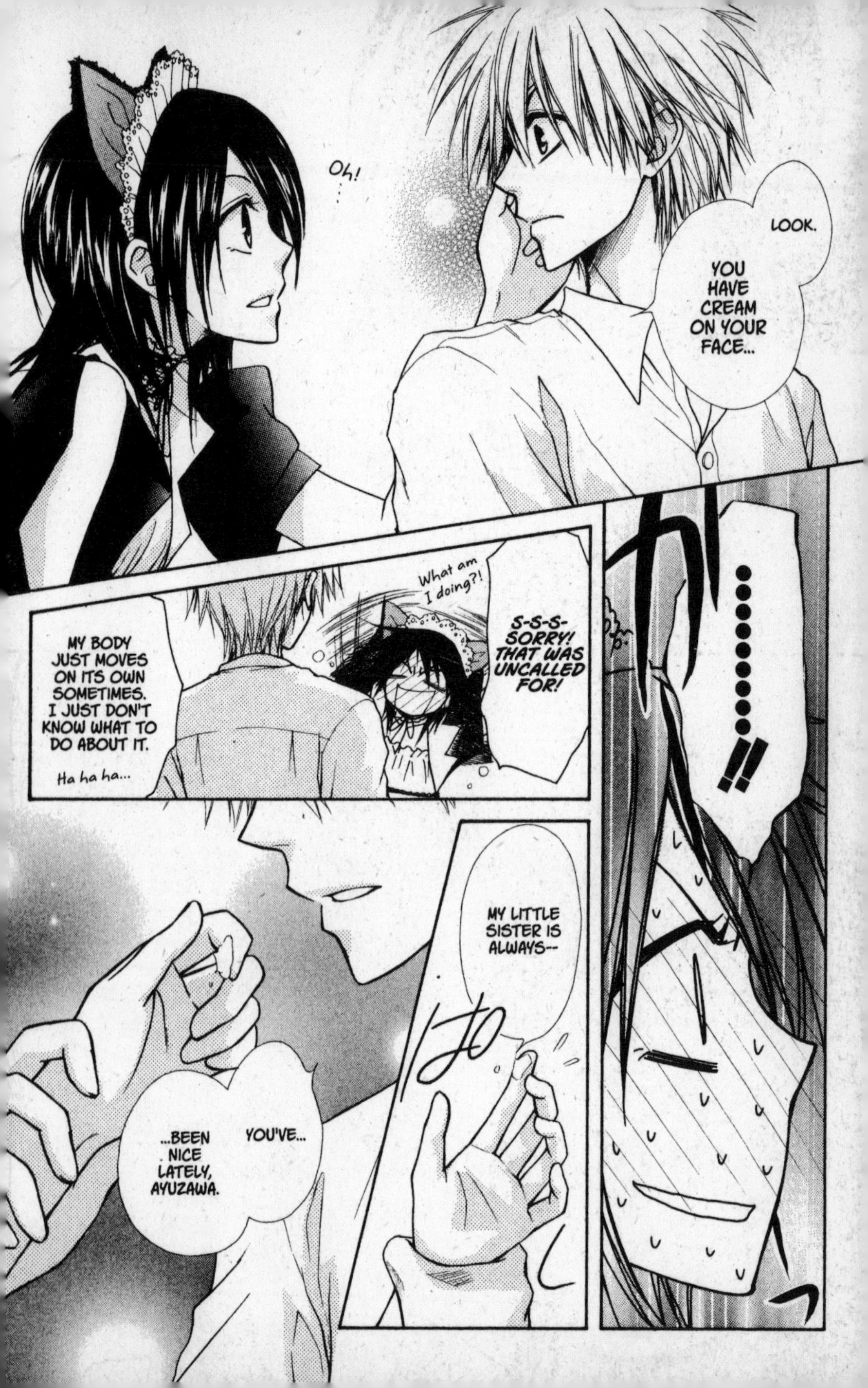
LOOK.
YOU HAVE CREAM ON YOUR FACE...
Oh!
..........!!
S-S-S-SORRY! THAT WAS UNCALLED FOR!
What am I doing?!
MY BODY JUST MOVES ON ITS OWN SOMETIMES. I JUST DON'T KNOW WHAT TO DO ABOUT IT.
Ha ha ha...
MY LITTLE SISTER IS ALWAYS--
YOU'VE...
...BEEN NICE LATELY, AYUZAWA.

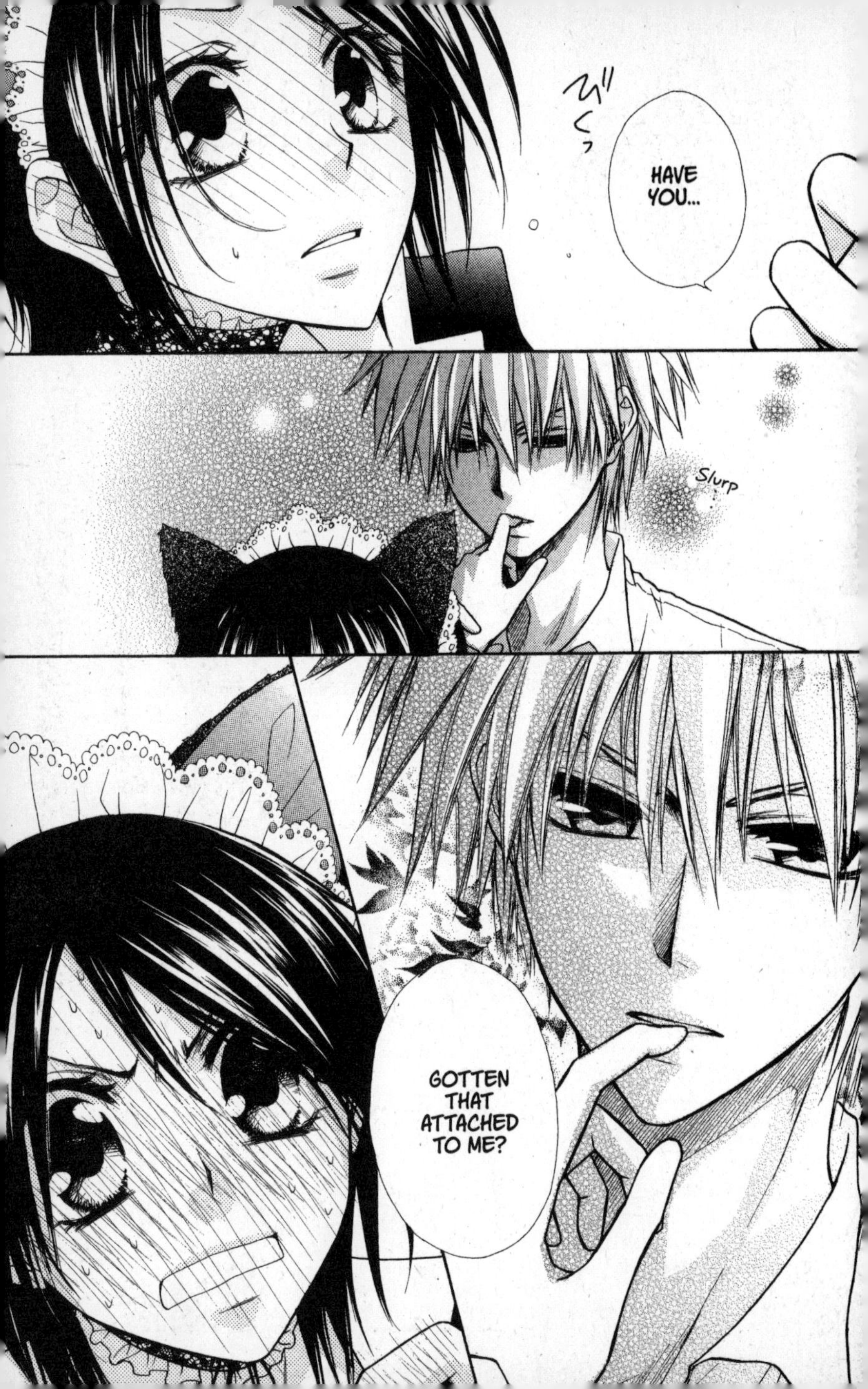
ぴくっ
HAVE YOU...
Slurp
GOTTEN THAT ATTACHED TO ME?

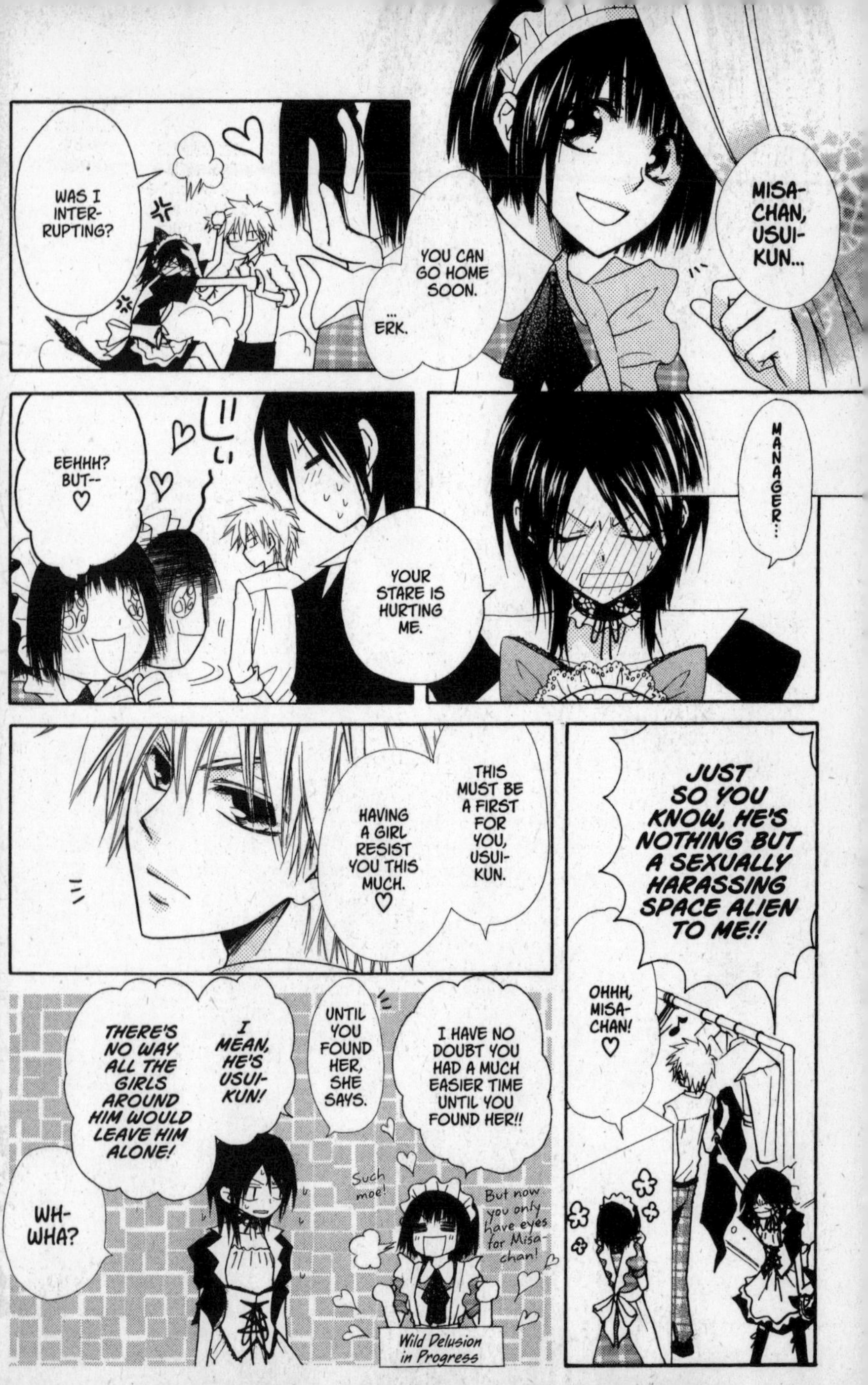
MISA-CHAN, USUI-KUN...
YOU CAN GO HOME SOON.
...ERK.
WAS I INTER-RUPTING?
MANAGER...
EEHHH? BUT--♡
YOUR STARE IS HURTING ME.
JUST SO YOU KNOW, HE'S NOTHING BUT A SEXUALLY HARASSING SPACE ALIEN TO ME!!
OHHH, MISA-CHAN! ♡
THIS MUST BE A FIRST FOR YOU, USUI-KUN.
HAVING A GIRL RESIST YOU THIS MUCH. ♡
I HAVE NO DOUBT YOU HAD A MUCH EASIER TIME UNTIL YOU FOUND HER!!
UNTIL YOU FOUND HER, SHE SAYS.
I MEAN, HE'S USUI-KUN!
THERE'S NO WAY ALL THE GIRLS AROUND HIM WOULD LEAVE HIM ALONE!
WH-WHA?
Such moe!
But now you only have eyes for Misa-chan!
Wild Delusion in Progress

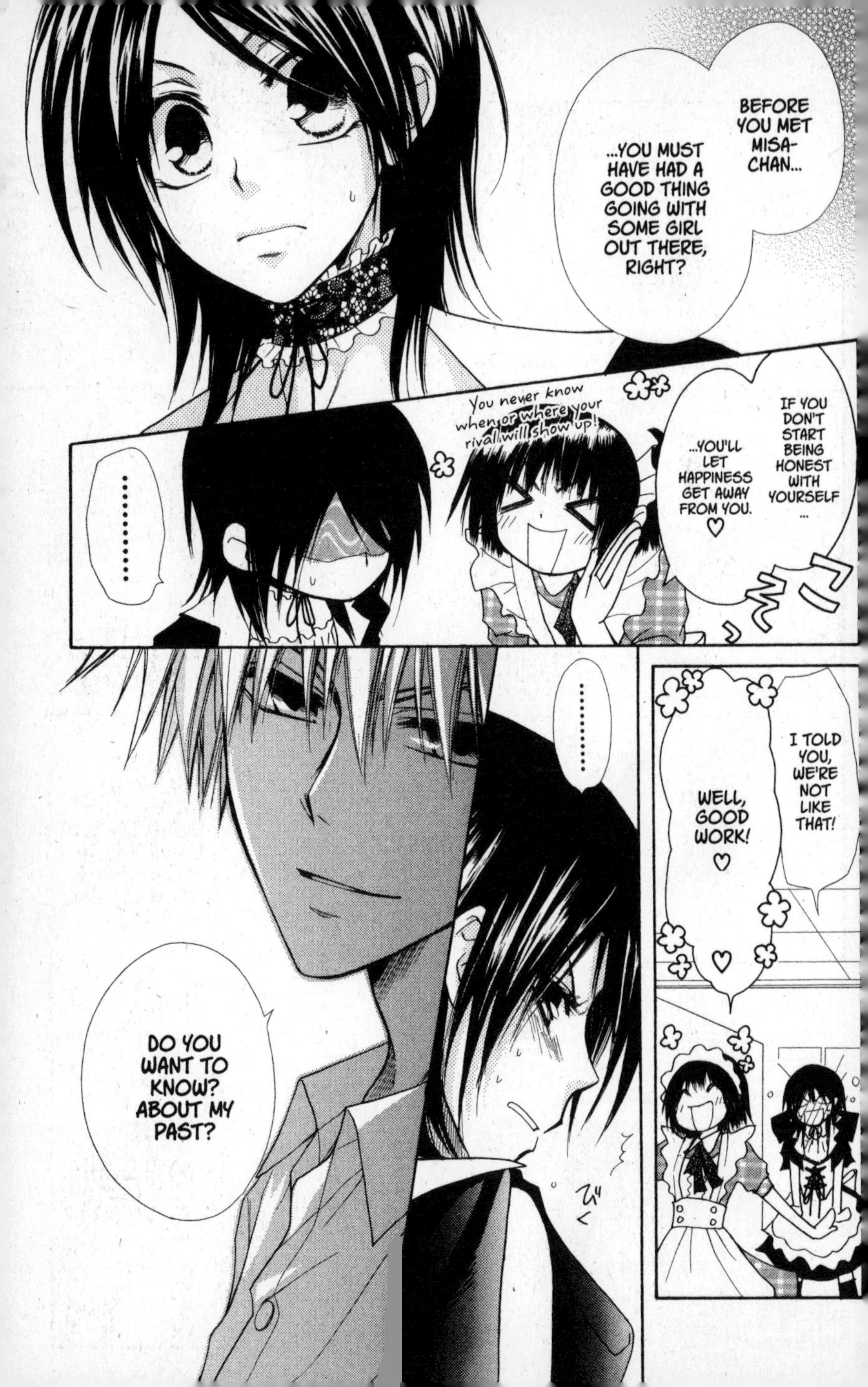
BEFORE YOU MET MISA-CHAN...
...YOU MUST HAVE HAD A GOOD THING GOING WITH SOME GIRL OUT THERE, RIGHT?
IF YOU DON'T START BEING HONEST WITH YOURSELF...
...YOU'LL LET HAPPINESS GET AWAY FROM YOU. ♡
You never know when or where your rival will show up!
....
I TOLD YOU, WE'RE NOT LIKE THAT!
WELL, GOOD WORK! ♡
....
DO YOU WANT TO KNOW? ABOUT MY PAST?

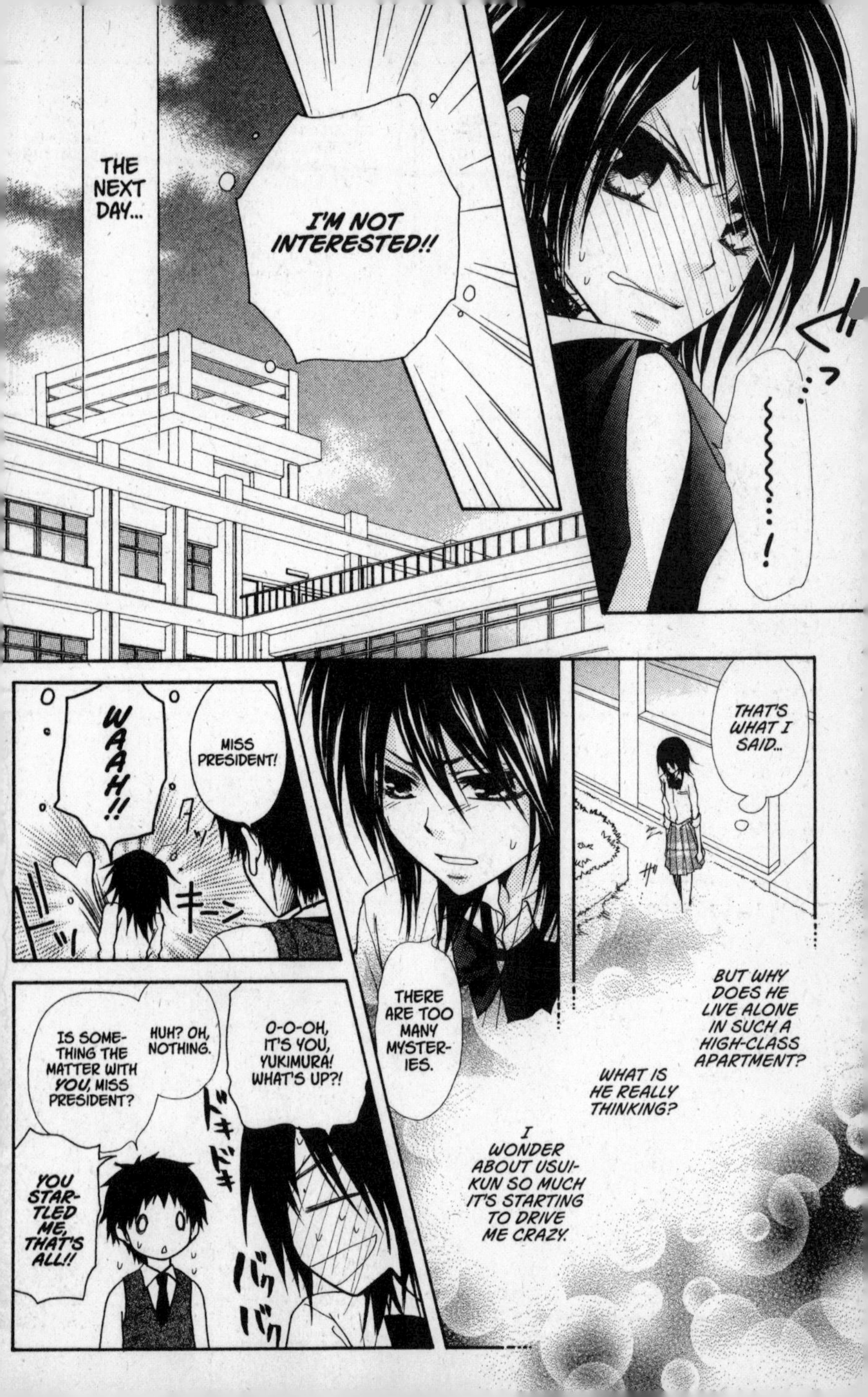
……~~~~……!
I'M NOT INTERESTED!!
THE NEXT DAY...
THAT'S WHAT I SAID...
BUT WHY DOES HE LIVE ALONE IN SUCH A HIGH-CLASS APARTMENT?
WHAT IS HE REALLY THINKING?
I WONDER ABOUT USUI-KUN SO MUCH IT'S STARTING TO DRIVE ME CRAZY.
THERE ARE TOO MANY MYSTERIES.
MISS PRESIDENT!
WAAAH!!
キーン
O-O-OH, IT'S YOU, YUKIMURA! WHAT'S UP?!
ドキドキ
HUH? OH, NOTHING.
IS SOMETHING THE MATTER WITH YOU, MISS PRESIDENT?
バクバク
YOU STARTLED ME, THAT'S ALL!!

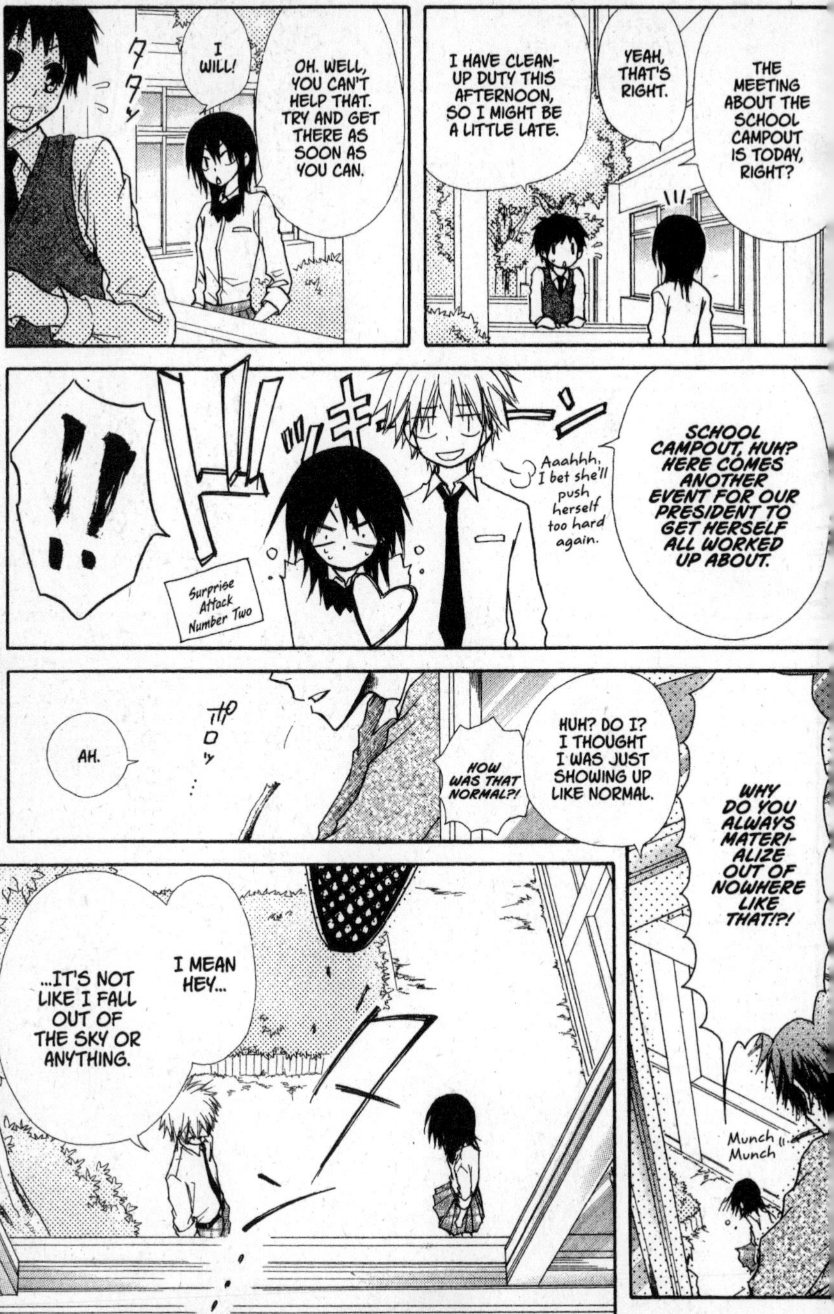
THE MEETING ABOUT THE SCHOOL CAMPOUT IS TODAY, RIGHT?
YEAH, THAT'S RIGHT.
I HAVE CLEAN-UP DUTY THIS AFTERNOON, SO I MIGHT BE A LITTLE LATE.
OH. WELL, YOU CAN'T HELP THAT. TRY AND GET THERE AS SOON AS YOU CAN.
I WILL!
タタタッ
SCHOOL CAMPOUT, HUH? HERE COMES ANOTHER EVENT FOR OUR PRESIDENT TO GET HERSELF ALL WORKED UP ABOUT.
Aaahhh, I bet she'll push herself too hard again.
Surprise Attack Number Two
!!
WHY DO YOU ALWAYS MATERIALIZE OUT OF NOWHERE LIKE THAT!?!
Munch Munch
HUH? DO I? I THOUGHT I WAS JUST SHOWING UP LIKE NORMAL.
HOW WAS THAT NORMAL?!
AH.
I MEAN HEY...
...IT'S NOT LIKE I FALL OUT OF THE SKY OR ANYTHING.

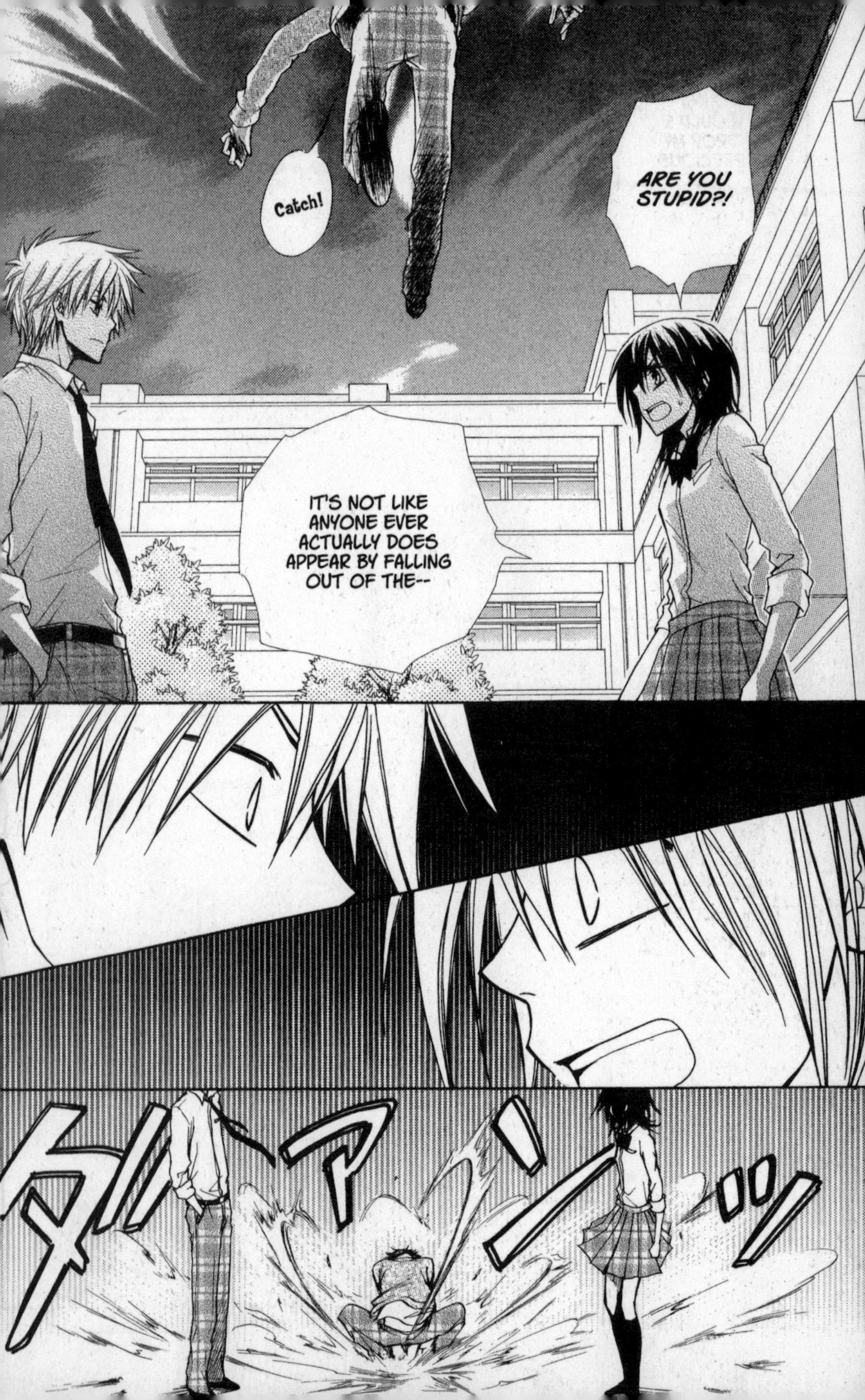
ARE YOU STUPID?!
IT'S NOT LIKE ANYONE EVER ACTUALLY DOES APPEAR BY FALLING OUT OF THE--
Catch!

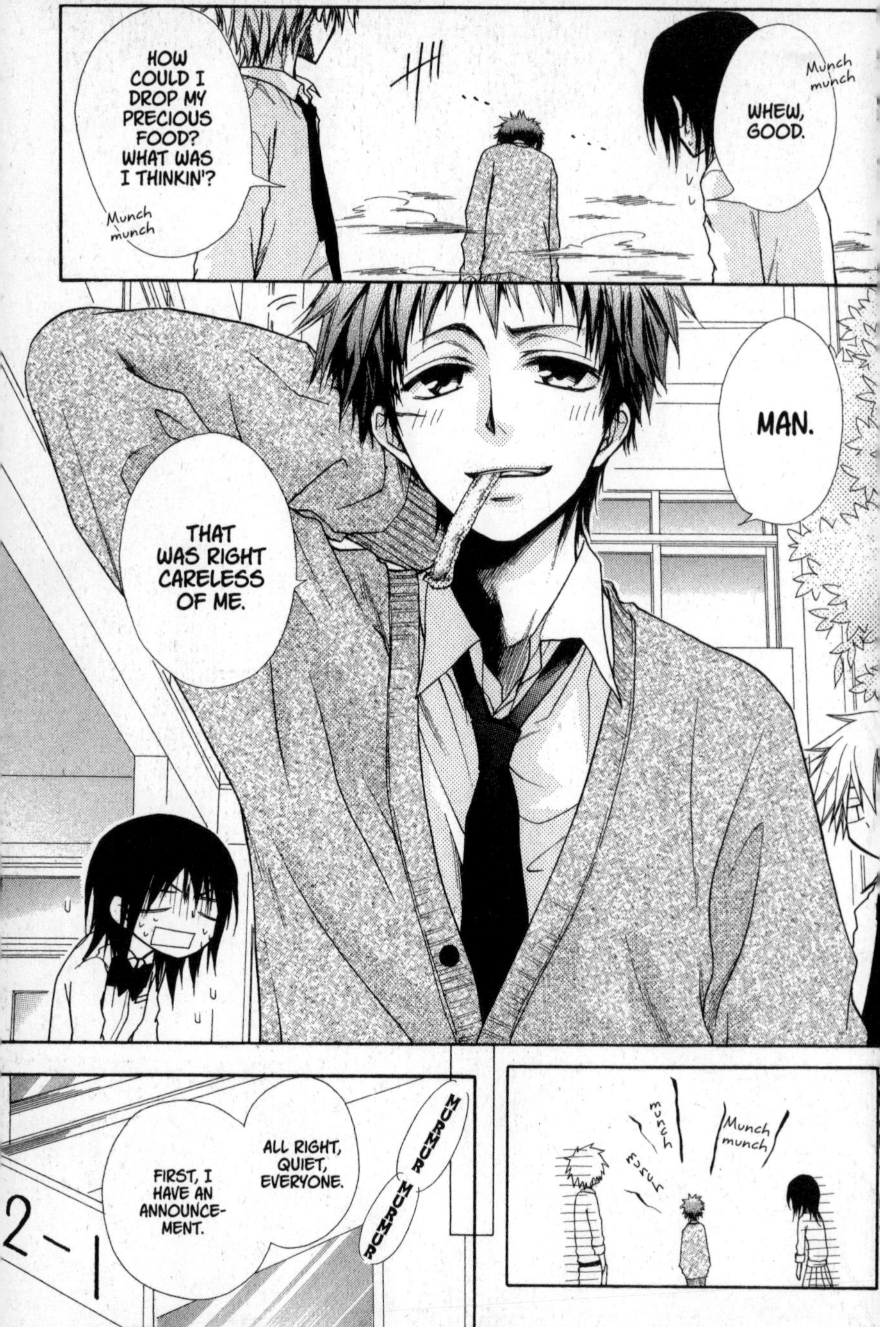
Munch munch
WHEW, GOOD.
HOW COULD I DROP MY PRECIOUS FOOD? WHAT WAS I THINKIN'?
Munch munch
MAN.
THAT WAS RIGHT CARELESS OF ME.
Munch munch
munch
MURMUR MURMUR
ALL RIGHT, QUIET, EVERYONE.
FIRST, I HAVE AN ANNOUNCEMENT.
2-1

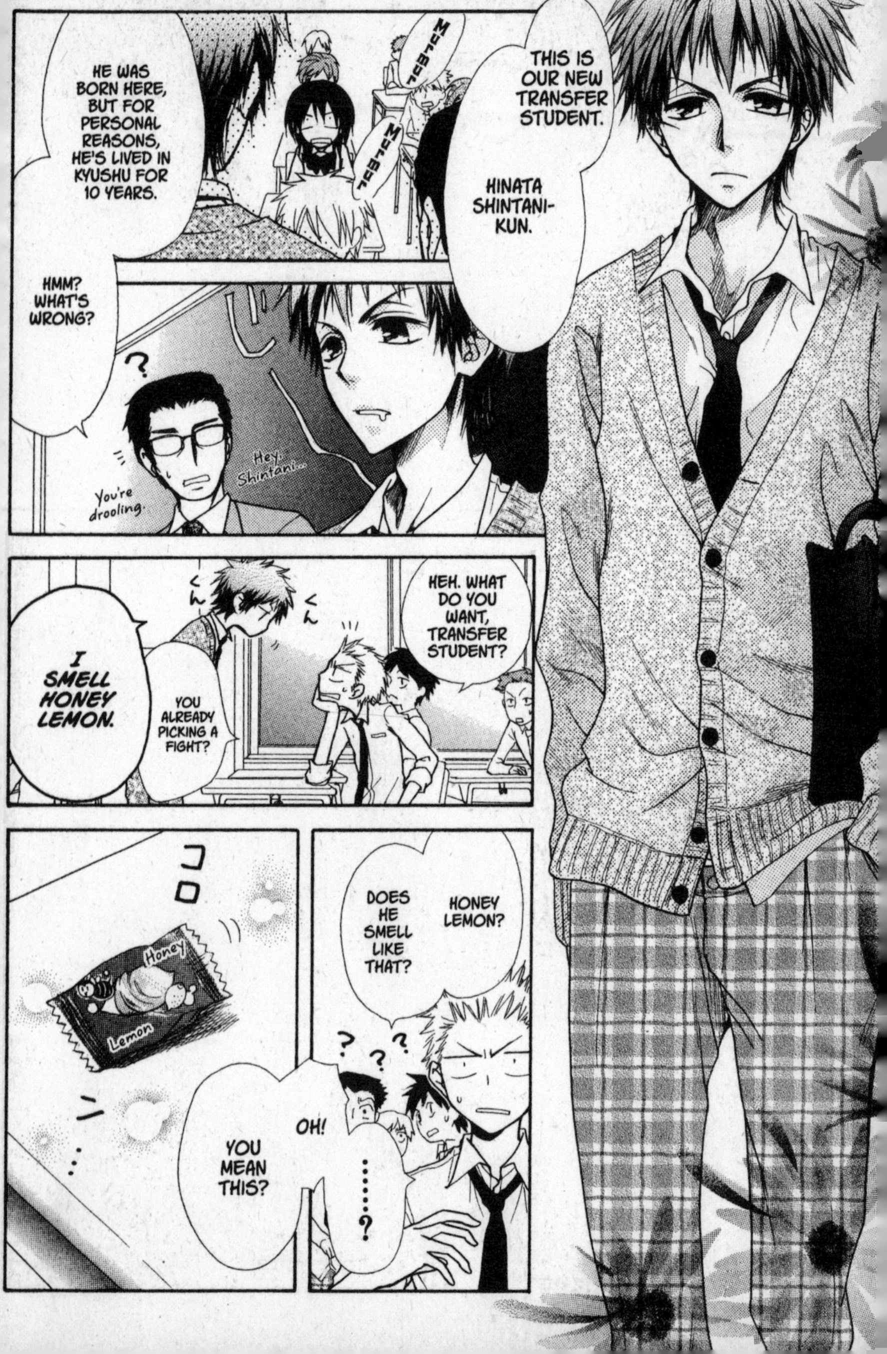
THIS IS OUR NEW TRANSFER STUDENT.
HINATA SHINTANI-KUN.
HE WAS BORN HERE, BUT FOR PERSONAL REASONS, HE'S LIVED IN KYUSHU FOR 10 YEARS.
MUTTER
MUTTER
HMM? WHAT'S WRONG?
Hey, Shintani...
You're drooling.
くん
くん
HEH. WHAT DO YOU WANT, TRANSFER STUDENT?
YOU ALREADY PICKING A FIGHT?
I SMELL HONEY LEMON.
HONEY LEMON?
DOES HE SMELL LIKE THAT?
OH!
YOU MEAN THIS?
......?
コロ
Honey
Lemon

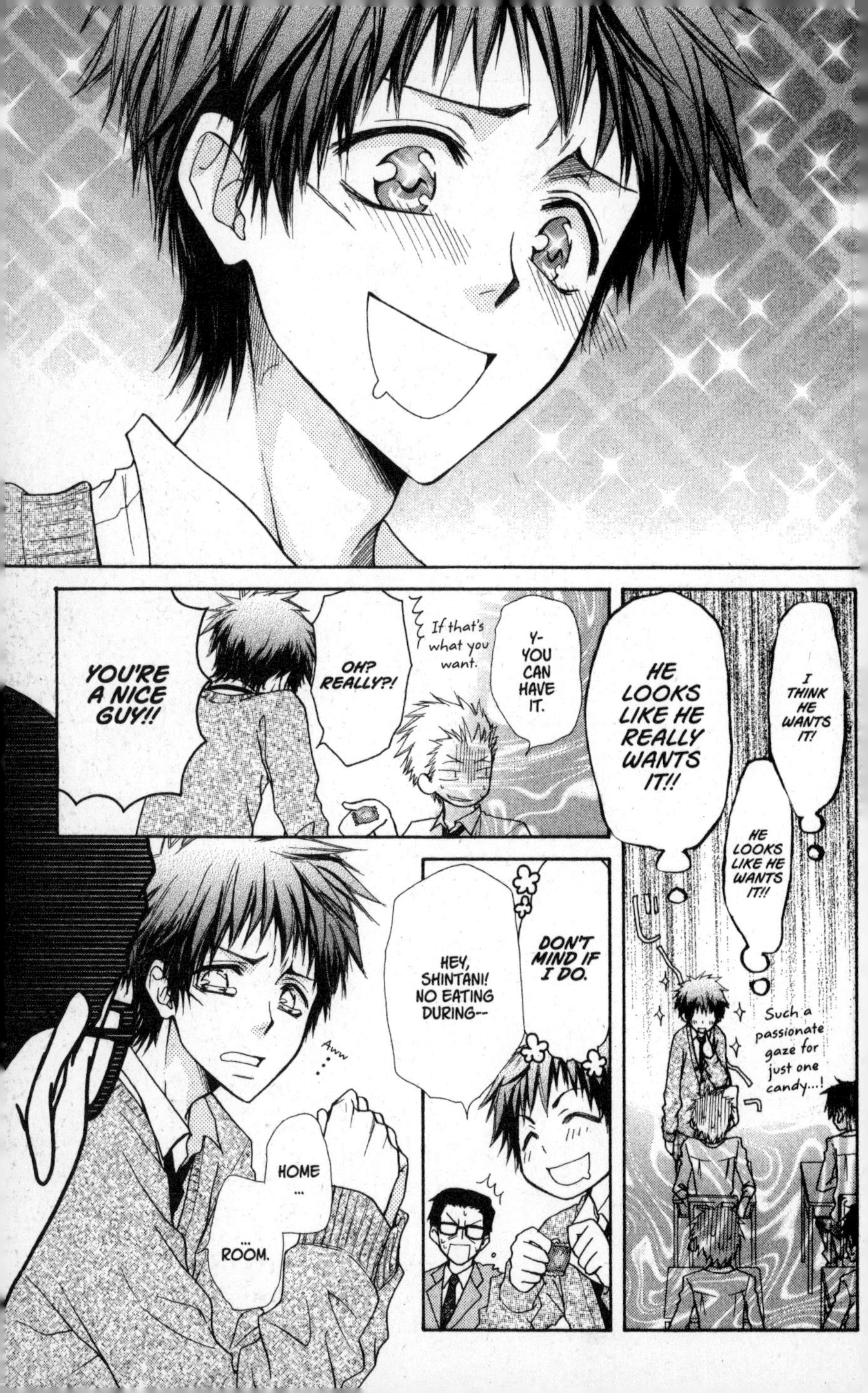
I THINK HE WANTS IT!
HE LOOKS LIKE HE WANTS IT!!
HE LOOKS LIKE HE REALLY WANTS IT!!
Such a passionate gaze for just one candy...!
Y-YOU CAN HAVE IT.
If that's what you want.
OH? REALLY?!
YOU'RE A NICE GUY!!
DON'T MIND IF I DO.
HEY, SHINTANI! NO EATING DURING--
Aww...
HOME...
...ROOM.

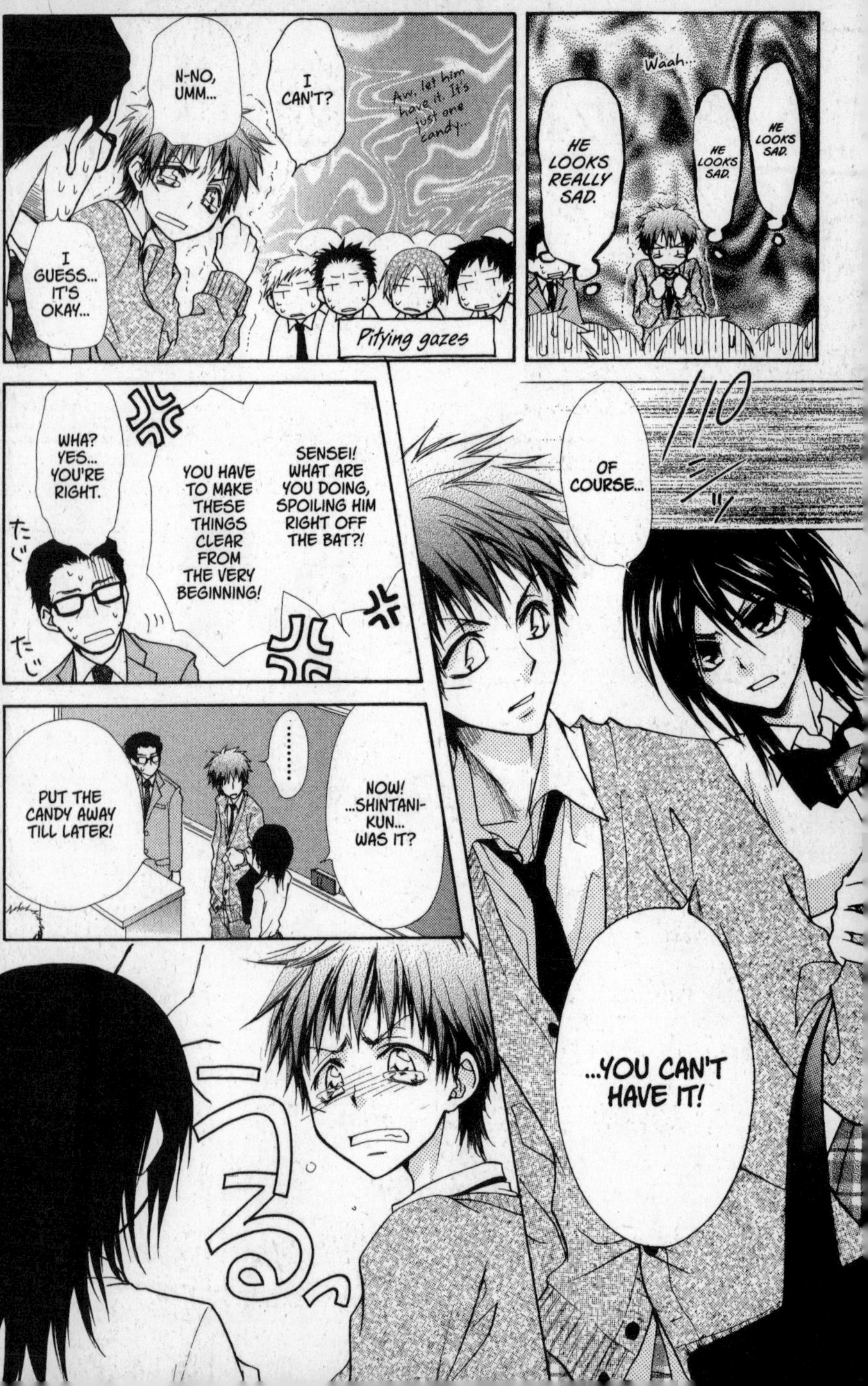
Waah...
HE LOOKS SAD.
HE LOOKS SAD.
HE LOOKS REALLY SAD.
Aw, let him have it. It's just one candy...
I CAN'T?
N-NO, UMM...
I GUESS... IT'S OKAY...
Pitying gazes
OF COURSE...
...YOU CAN'T HAVE IT!
SENSEI! WHAT ARE YOU DOING, SPOILING HIM RIGHT OFF THE BAT?!
YOU HAVE TO MAKE THESE THINGS CLEAR FROM THE VERY BEGINNING!
WHA? YES... YOU'RE RIGHT.
たじ
たじ
NOW! ...SHINTANI-KUN... WAS IT?
....
PUT THE CANDY AWAY TILL LATER!

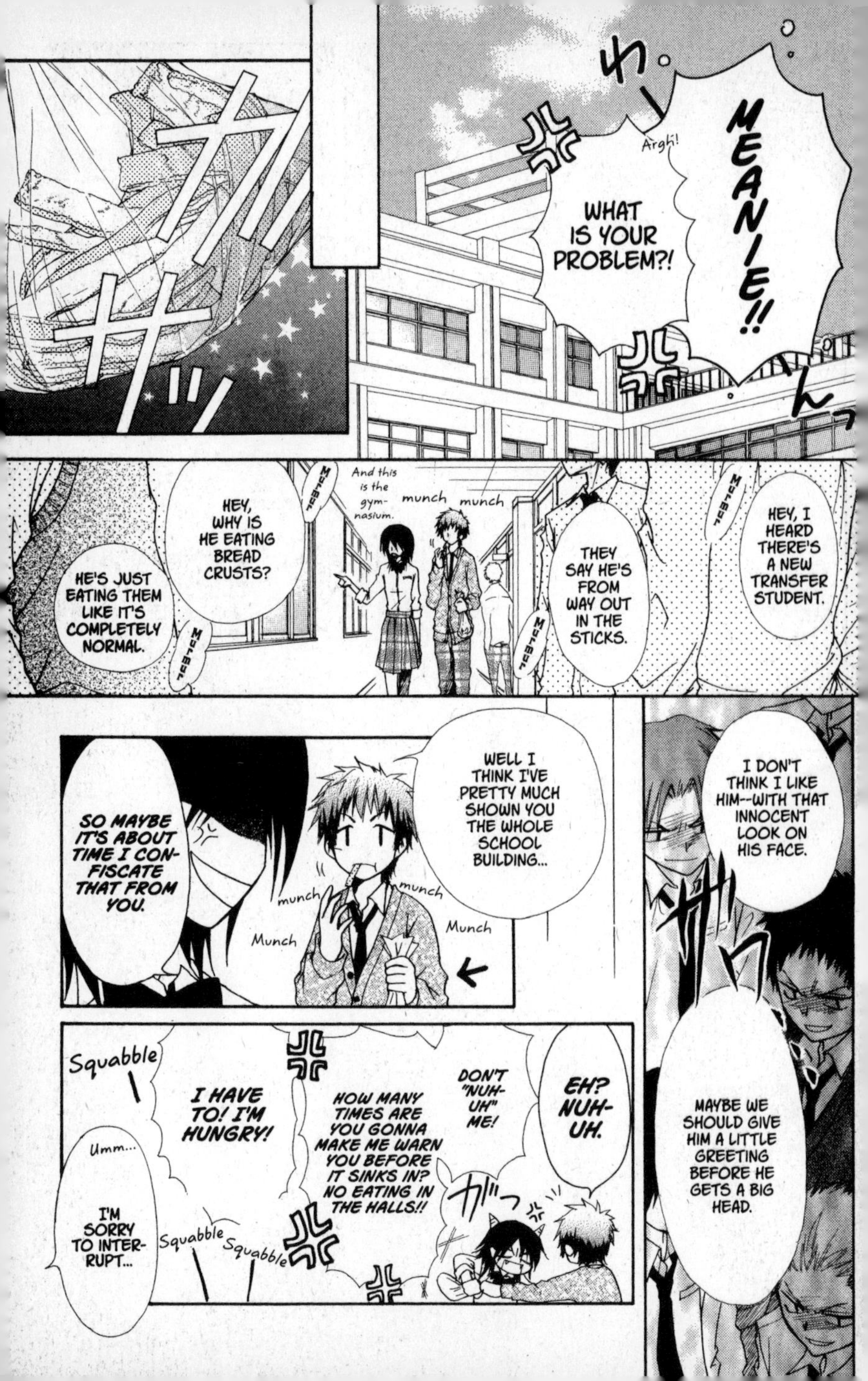
MEANIE!!
WHAT IS YOUR PROBLEM?!
Argh!
HEY, I HEARD THERE'S A NEW TRANSFER STUDENT.
Mutter
THEY SAY HE'S FROM WAY OUT IN THE STICKS.
Mutter
munch munch
And this is the gymnasium.
Mutter
HEY, WHY IS HE EATING BREAD CRUSTS?
HE'S JUST EATING THEM LIKE IT'S COMPLETELY NORMAL.
Mutter
I DON'T THINK I LIKE HIM--WITH THAT INNOCENT LOOK ON HIS FACE.
MAYBE WE SHOULD GIVE HIM A LITTLE GREETING BEFORE HE GETS A BIG HEAD.
WELL I THINK I'VE PRETTY MUCH SHOWN YOU THE WHOLE SCHOOL BUILDING...
munch
Munch
munch
Munch
SO MAYBE IT'S ABOUT TIME I CONFISCATE THAT FROM YOU.
EH? NUH-UH.
DON'T "NUH-UH" ME!
HOW MANY TIMES ARE YOU GONNA MAKE ME WARN YOU BEFORE IT SINKS IN? NO EATING IN THE HALLS!!
I HAVE TO! I'M HUNGRY!
Squabble
Squabble
Squabble
Umm...
I'M SORRY TO INTERRUPT...

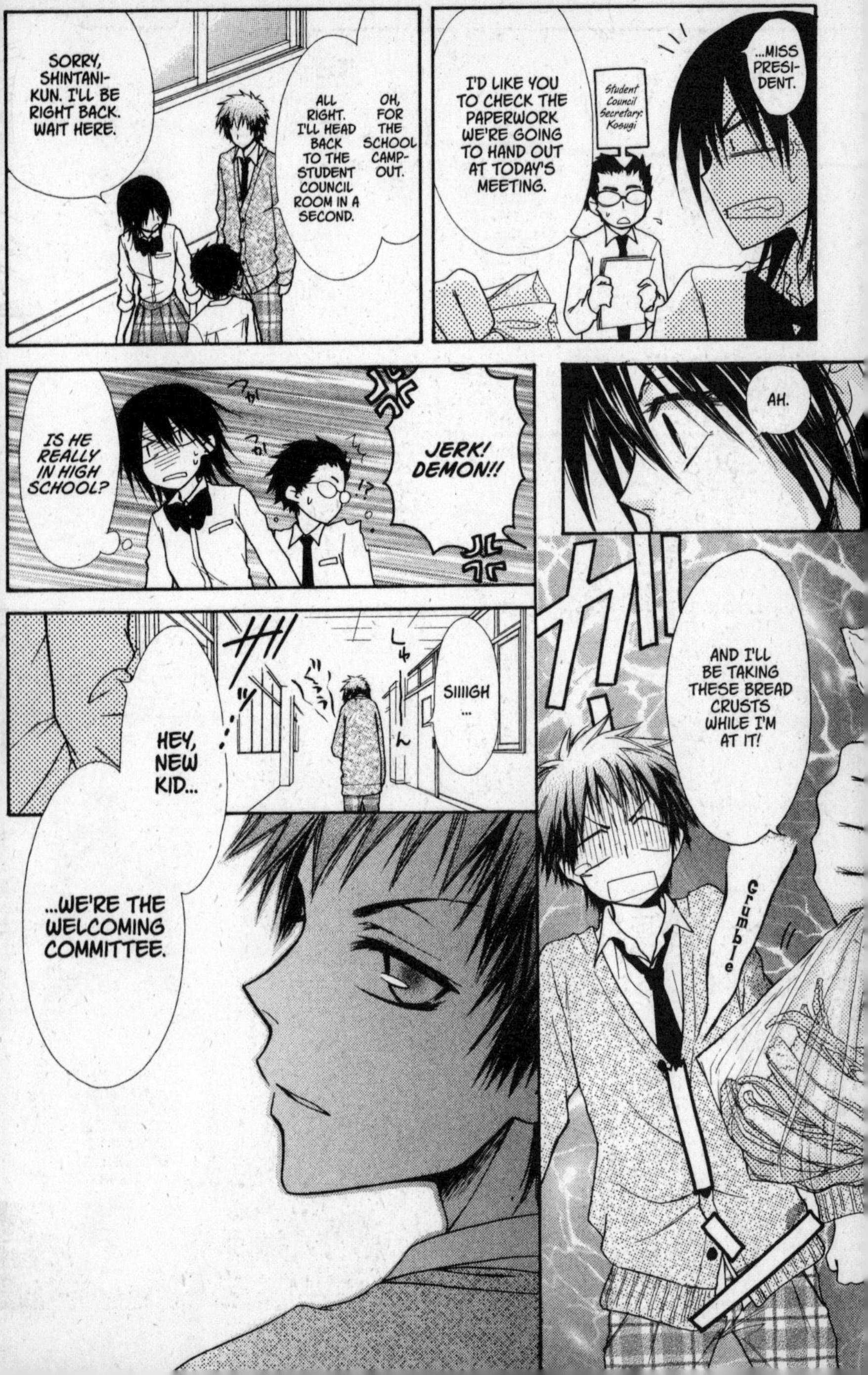
...MISS PRESIDENT.
I'D LIKE YOU TO CHECK THE PAPERWORK WE'RE GOING TO HAND OUT AT TODAY'S MEETING.
Student Council Secretary: Kosugi
OH, FOR THE SCHOOL CAMP-OUT.
ALL RIGHT. I'LL HEAD BACK TO THE STUDENT COUNCIL ROOM IN A SECOND.
SORRY, SHINTANI-KUN. I'LL BE RIGHT BACK. WAIT HERE.
AH.
JERK! DEMON!!
IS HE REALLY IN HIGH SCHOOL?
AND I'LL BE TAKING THESE BREAD CRUSTS WHILE I'M AT IT!
Grumble
SIIIGH ...
HEY, NEW KID...
...WE'RE THE WELCOMING COMMITTEE.

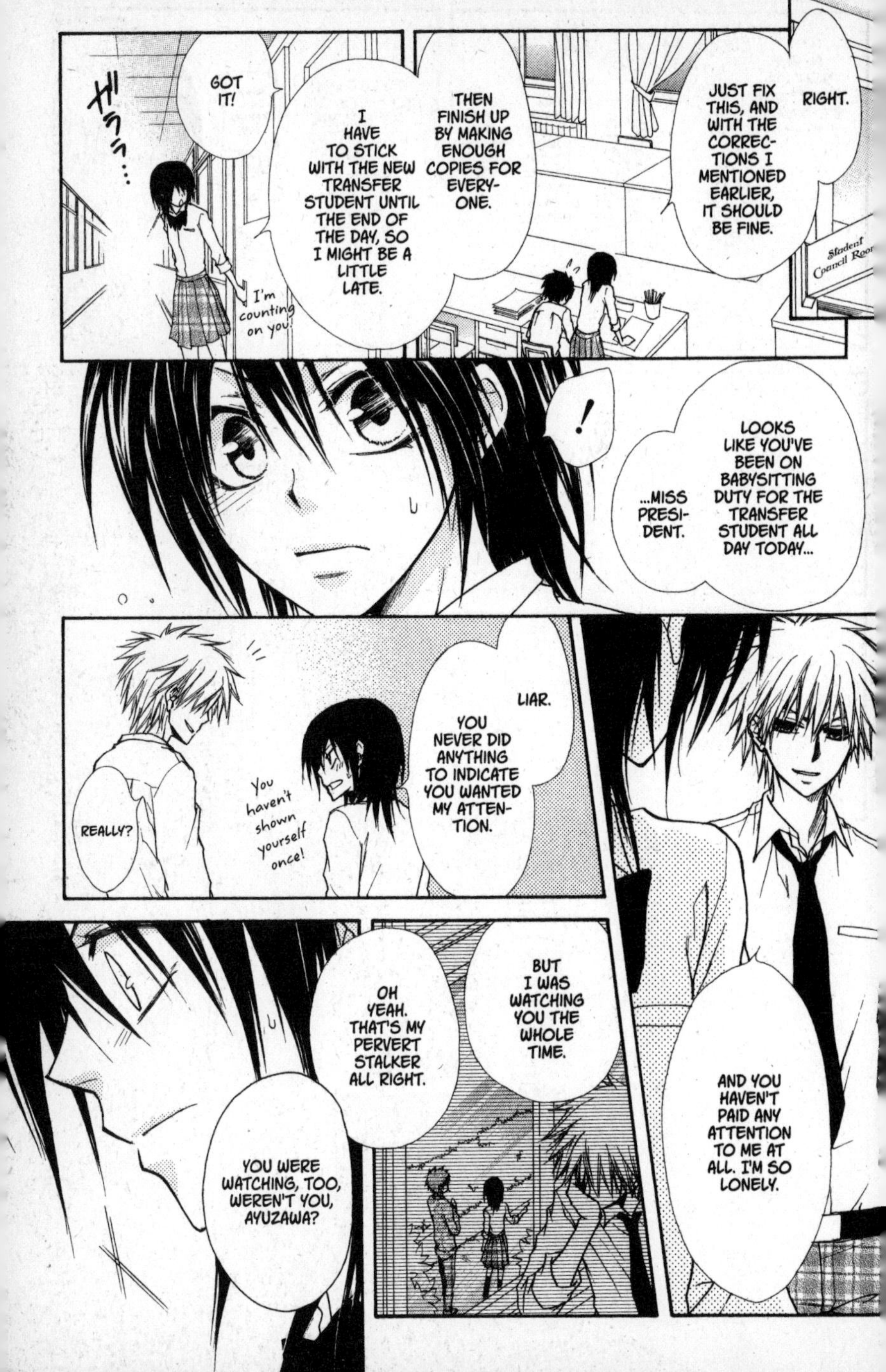
RIGHT.
JUST FIX THIS, AND WITH THE CORRECTIONS I MENTIONED EARLIER, IT SHOULD BE FINE.
Student Council Roo
THEN FINISH UP BY MAKING ENOUGH COPIES FOR EVERYONE.
I HAVE TO STICK WITH THE NEW TRANSFER STUDENT UNTIL THE END OF THE DAY, SO I MIGHT BE A LITTLE LATE.
GOT IT!
ガララ…
I'm counting on you!
LOOKS LIKE YOU'VE BEEN ON BABYSITTING DUTY FOR THE TRANSFER STUDENT ALL DAY TODAY...
...MISS PRESIDENT.
!
AND YOU HAVEN'T PAID ANY ATTENTION TO ME AT ALL. I'M SO LONELY.
LIAR.
YOU NEVER DID ANYTHING TO INDICATE YOU WANTED MY ATTENTION.
You haven't shown yourself once!
REALLY?
BUT I WAS WATCHING YOU THE WHOLE TIME.
OH YEAH. THAT'S MY PERVERT STALKER ALL RIGHT.
YOU WERE WATCHING, TOO, WEREN'T YOU, AYUZAWA?

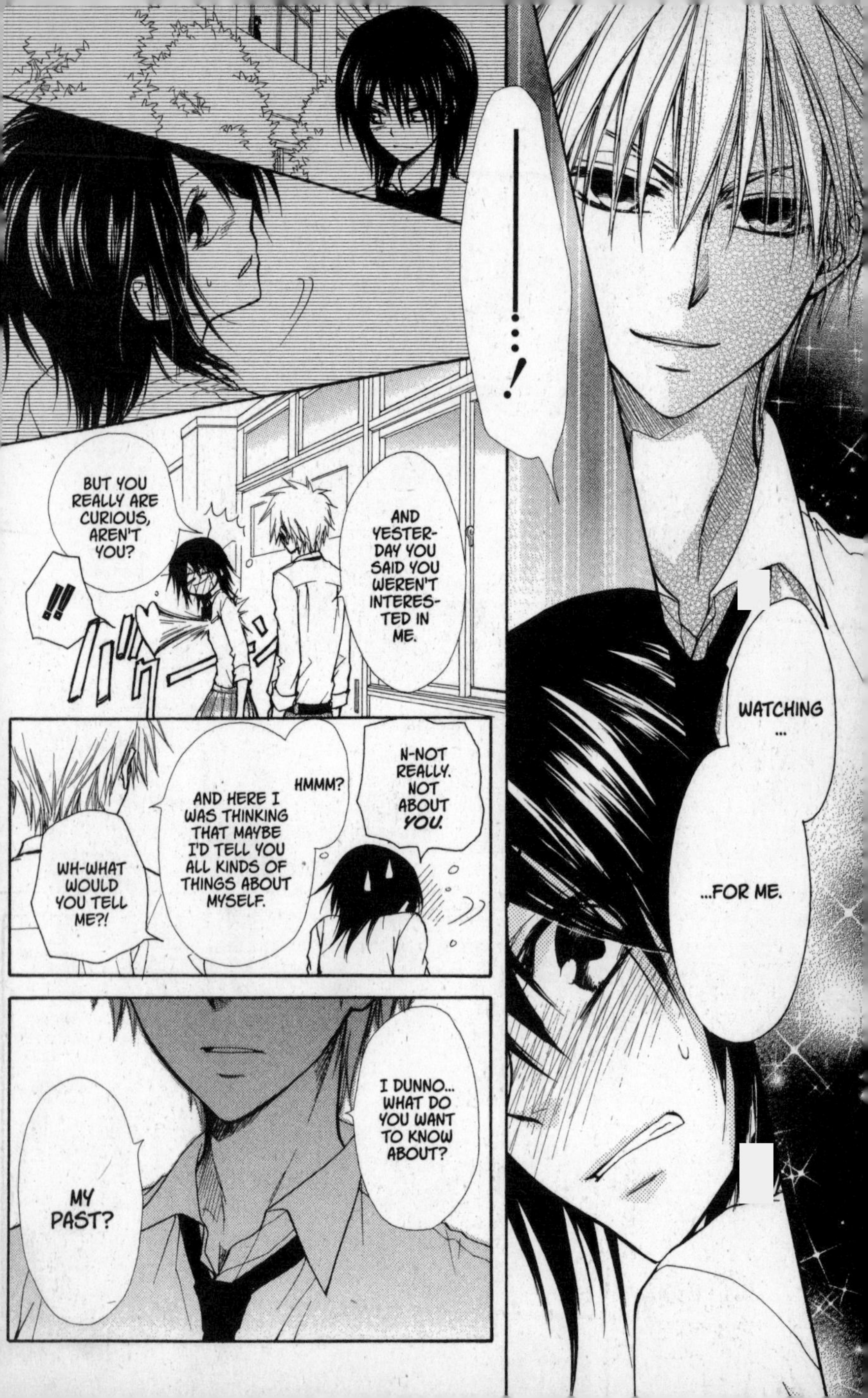

......!
WATCHING...
...FOR ME.
AND YESTERDAY YOU SAID YOU WEREN'T INTERESTED IN ME.
BUT YOU REALLY ARE CURIOUS, AREN'T YOU?
!!
N-NOT REALLY. NOT ABOUT YOU.
HMMM?
AND HERE I WAS THINKING THAT MAYBE I'D TELL YOU ALL KINDS OF THINGS ABOUT MYSELF.
WH-WHAT WOULD YOU TELL ME?!
I DUNNO... WHAT DO YOU WANT TO KNOW ABOUT?
MY PAST?

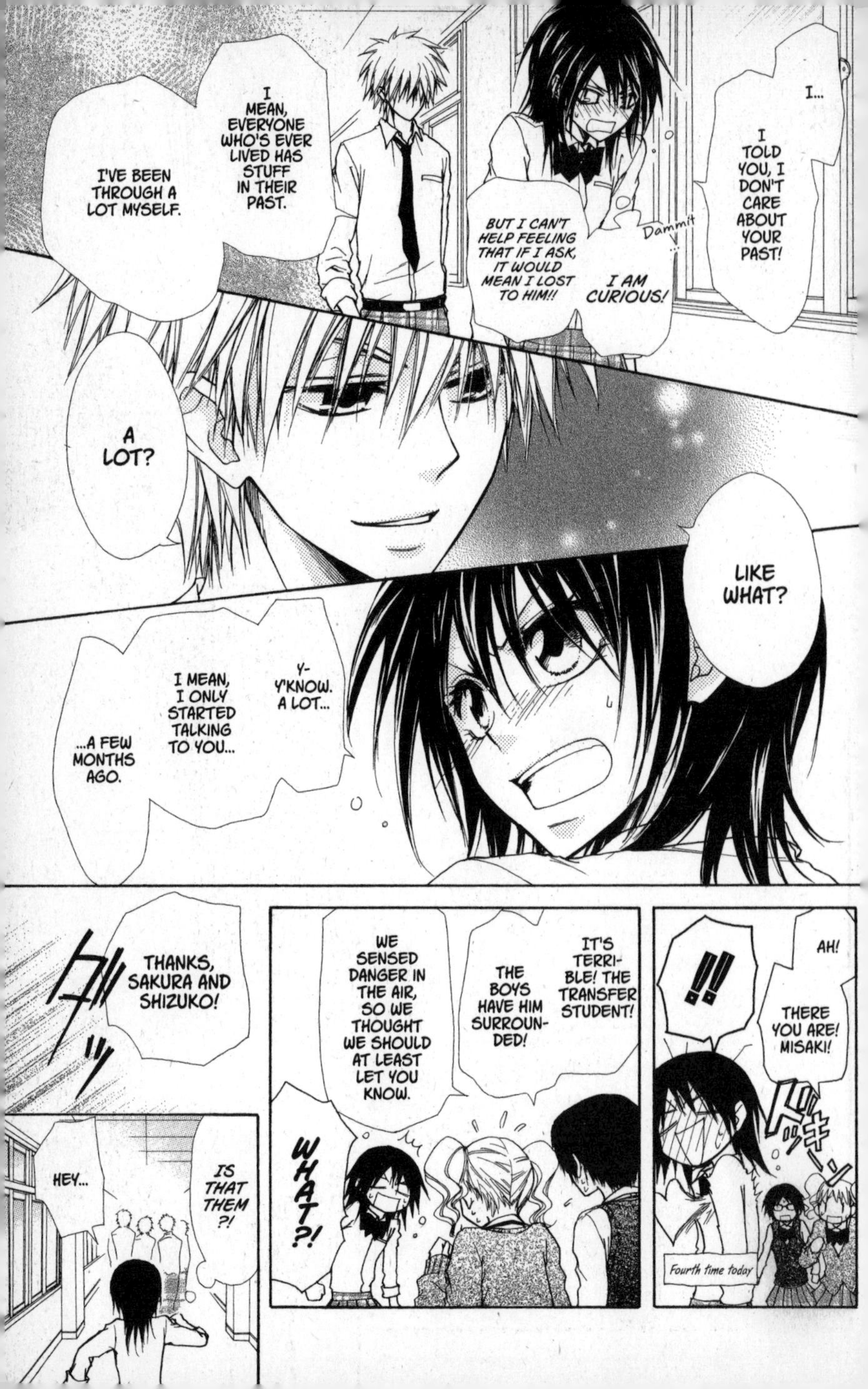
I...
I TOLD YOU, I DON'T CARE ABOUT YOUR PAST!
Dammit...
I AM CURIOUS!
BUT I CAN'T HELP FEELING THAT IF I ASK, IT WOULD MEAN I LOST TO HIM!!
I MEAN, EVERYONE WHO'S EVER LIVED HAS STUFF IN THEIR PAST.
I'VE BEEN THROUGH A LOT MYSELF.
A LOT?
LIKE WHAT?
Y-Y'KNOW. A LOT...
I MEAN, I ONLY STARTED TALKING TO YOU...
...A FEW MONTHS AGO.
AH!
THERE YOU ARE! MISAKI!
!!
Fourth time today
IT'S TERRIBLE! THE TRANSFER STUDENT!
THE BOYS HAVE HIM SURROUNDED!
WE SENSED DANGER IN THE AIR, SO WE THOUGHT WE SHOULD AT LEAST LET YOU KNOW.
WHAT?!
THANKS, SAKURA AND SHIZUKO!
IS THAT THEM?!
HEY...

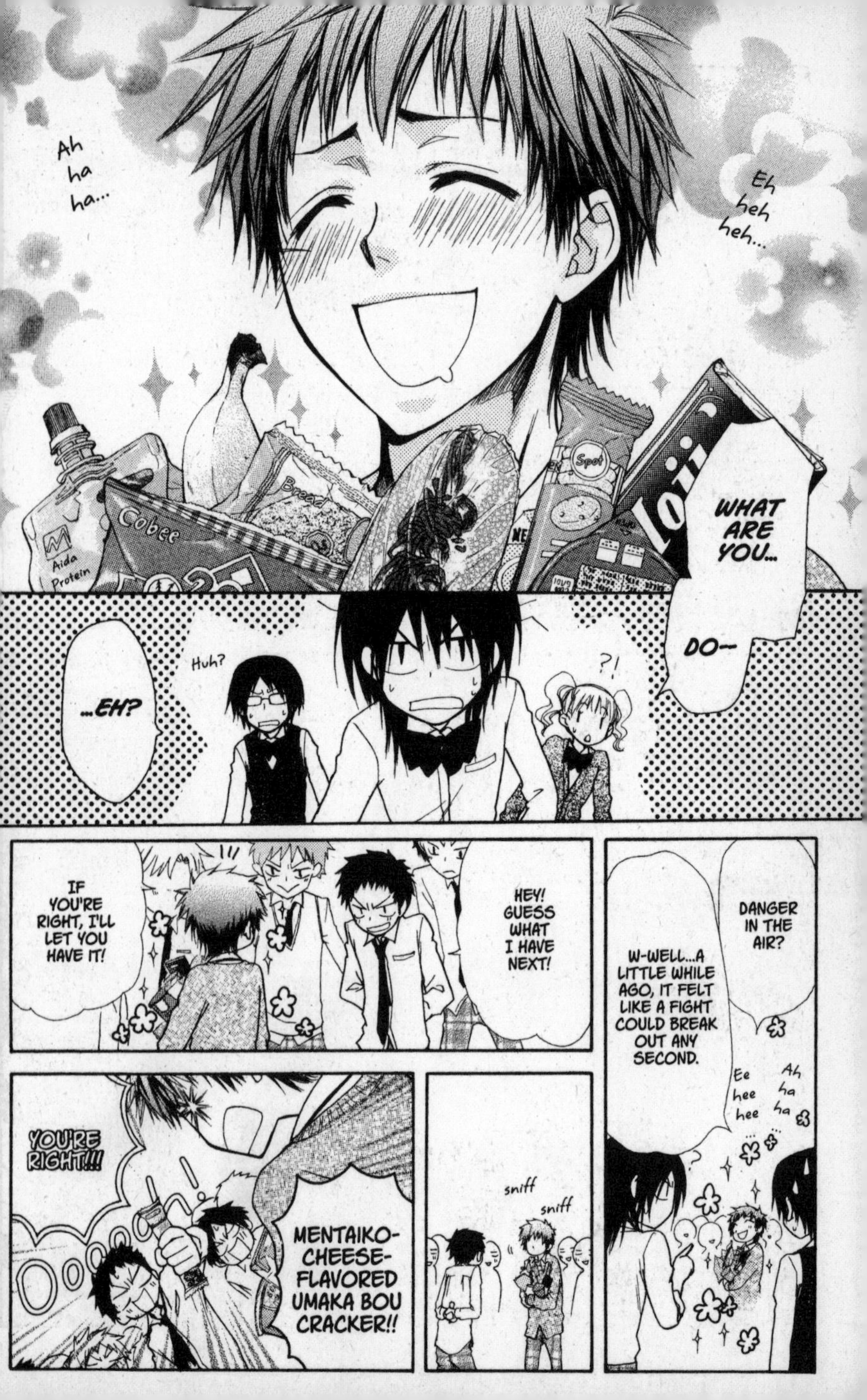
Eh heh heh...
Ah ha ha...
Spot
Bread
Cobee
Aida Protein
WHAT ARE YOU...
DO—
?!
Huh?
...EH?
DANGER IN THE AIR?
W-WELL...A LITTLE WHILE AGO, IT FELT LIKE A FIGHT COULD BREAK OUT ANY SECOND.
Ah ha ha...
Ee hee hee...
HEY! GUESS WHAT I HAVE NEXT!
IF YOU'RE RIGHT, I'LL LET YOU HAVE IT!
sniff
sniff
MENTAIKO-CHEESE-FLAVORED UMAKA BOU CRACKER!!
YOU'RE RIGHT!!!
Ooooo

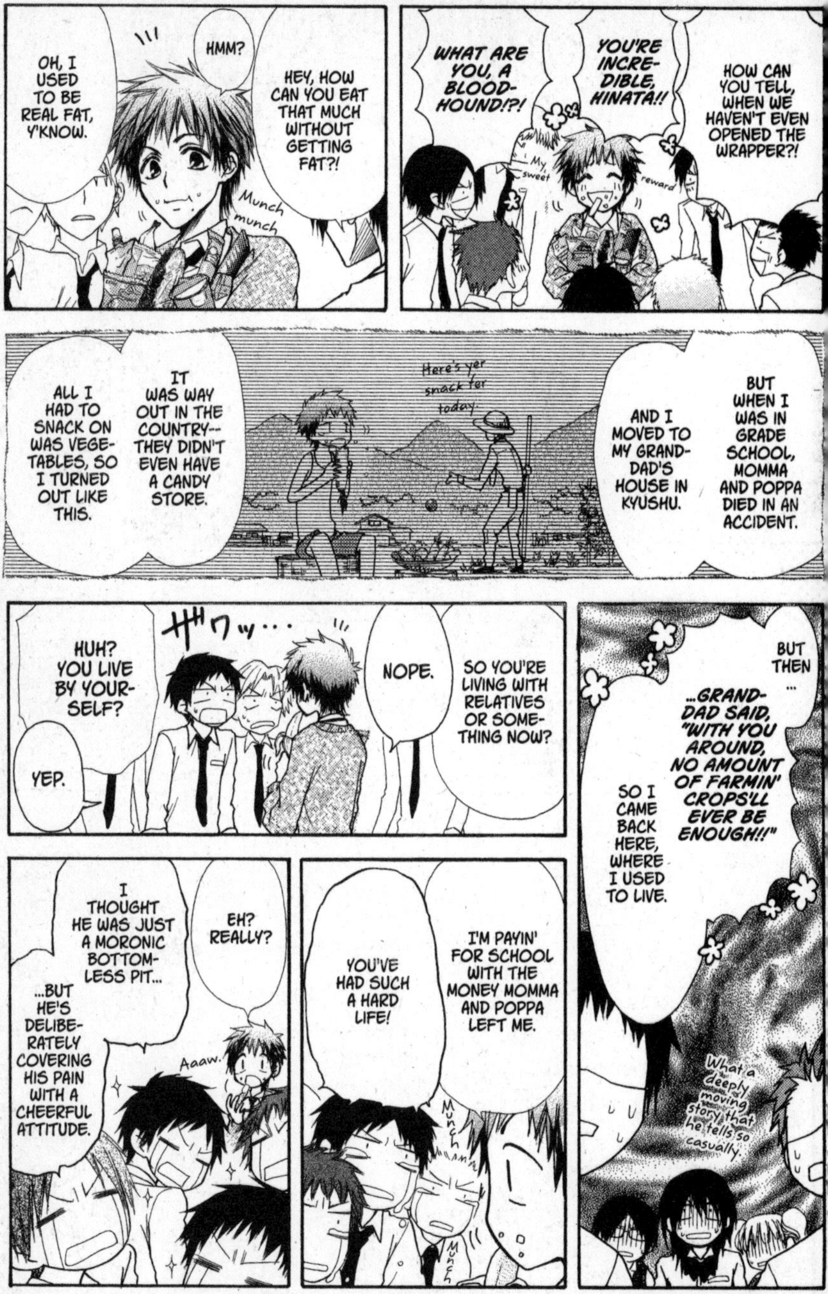
HOW CAN YOU TELL, WHEN WE HAVEN'T EVEN OPENED THE WRAPPER?!
YOU'RE INCREDIBLE, HINATA!!
My sweet
reward
WHAT ARE YOU, A BLOODHOUND!?!
HEY, HOW CAN YOU EAT THAT MUCH WITHOUT GETTING FAT?!
HMM?
Munch munch
OH, I USED TO BE REAL FAT, Y'KNOW.
BUT WHEN I WAS IN GRADE SCHOOL, MOMMA AND POPPA DIED IN AN ACCIDENT.
AND I MOVED TO MY GRANDDAD'S HOUSE IN KYUSHU.
Here's yer snack fer today.
IT WAS WAY OUT IN THE COUNTRY-- THEY DIDN'T EVEN HAVE A CANDY STORE.
ALL I HAD TO SNACK ON WAS VEGETABLES, SO I TURNED OUT LIKE THIS.
BUT THEN...
...GRANDDAD SAID, "WITH YOU AROUND, NO AMOUNT OF FARMIN' CROPS'LL EVER BE ENOUGH!!"
SO I CAME BACK HERE, WHERE I USED TO LIVE.
What a deeply moving story that he tells so casually.
SO YOU'RE LIVING WITH RELATIVES OR SOMETHING NOW?
NOPE.
ザワッ…
HUH? YOU LIVE BY YOURSELF?
YEP.
I'M PAYIN' FOR SCHOOL WITH THE MONEY MOMMA AND POPPA LEFT ME.
YOU'VE HAD SUCH A HARD LIFE!
Munch
Munch
EH? REALLY?
I THOUGHT HE WAS JUST A MORONIC BOTTOMLESS PIT...
Aaaw.
...BUT HE'S DELIBERATELY COVERING HIS PAIN WITH A CHEERFUL ATTITUDE.

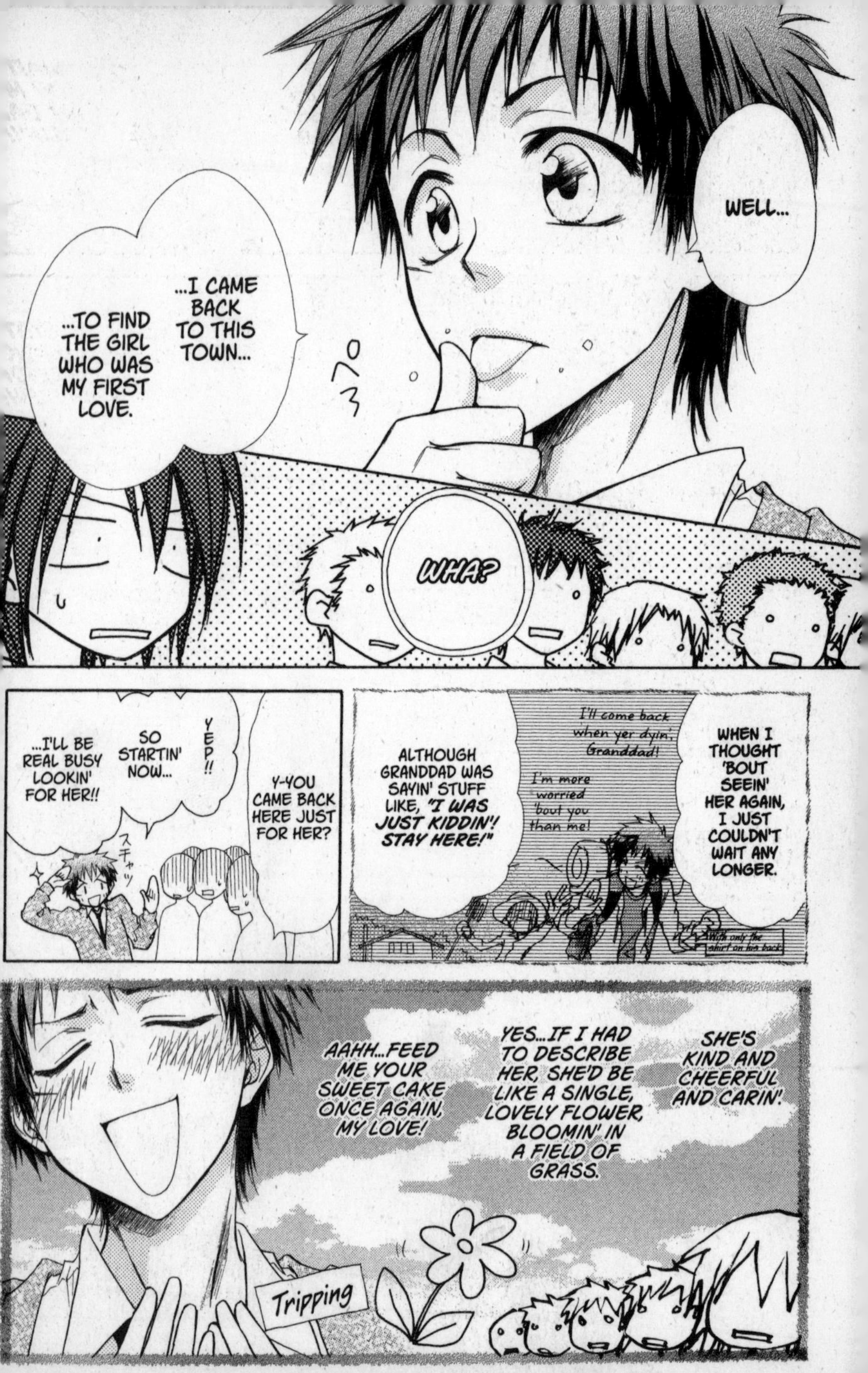
WELL...
...I CAME BACK TO THIS TOWN...
...TO FIND THE GIRL WHO WAS MY FIRST LOVE.
WHA?
WHEN I THOUGHT 'BOUT SEEIN' HER AGAIN, I JUST COULDN'T WAIT ANY LONGER.
I'll come back when yer dyin', Granddad!
I'm more worried 'bout you than me!
ALTHOUGH GRANDDAD WAS SAYIN' STUFF LIKE, "I WAS JUST KIDDIN'! STAY HERE!"
With only the shirt on his back
Y-YOU CAME BACK HERE JUST FOR HER?
YEP!!
SO STARTIN' NOW...
...I'LL BE REAL BUSY LOOKIN' FOR HER!!
スチャッ
SHE'S KIND AND CHEERFUL AND CARIN'.
YES...IF I HAD TO DESCRIBE HER, SHE'D BE LIKE A SINGLE, LOVELY FLOWER, BLOOMIN' IN A FIELD OF GRASS.
AAHH...FEED ME YOUR SWEET CAKE ONCE AGAIN, MY LOVE!
Tripping

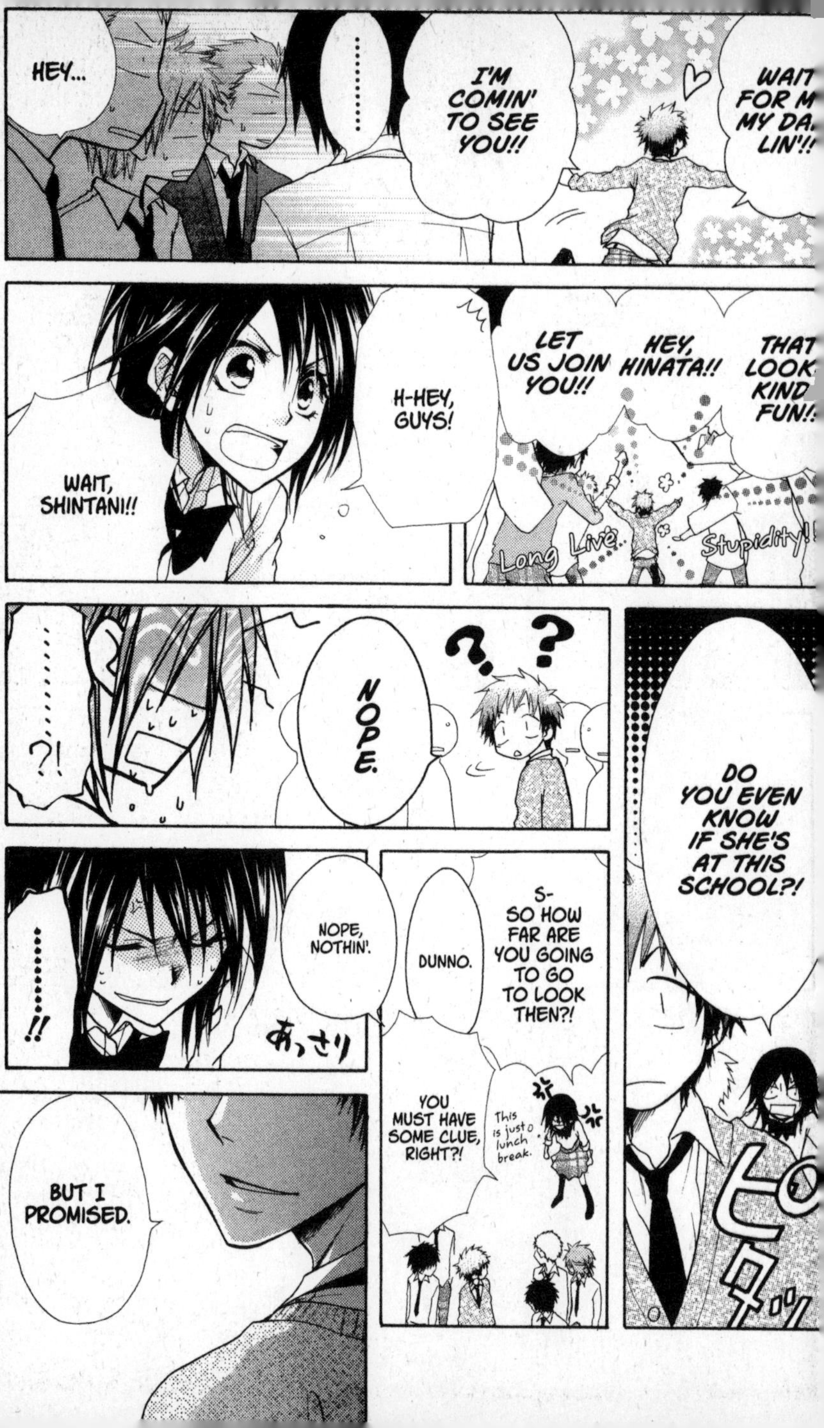

WAIT FOR M MY DA LIN'!!
I'M COMIN' TO SEE YOU!!
......
HEY...
THAT LOOK KIND FUN!!
HEY, HINATA!!
LET US JOIN YOU!!
Long Live Stupidity!!
H-HEY, GUYS!
WAIT, SHINTANI!!
DO YOU EVEN KNOW IF SHE'S AT THIS SCHOOL?!
NOPE.
......?!
S-SO HOW FAR ARE YOU GOING TO GO TO LOOK THEN?!
DUNNO.
YOU MUST HAVE SOME CLUE, RIGHT?!
This is just lunch break.
NOPE, NOTHIN'.
......!!
あっさり
BUT I PROMISED.

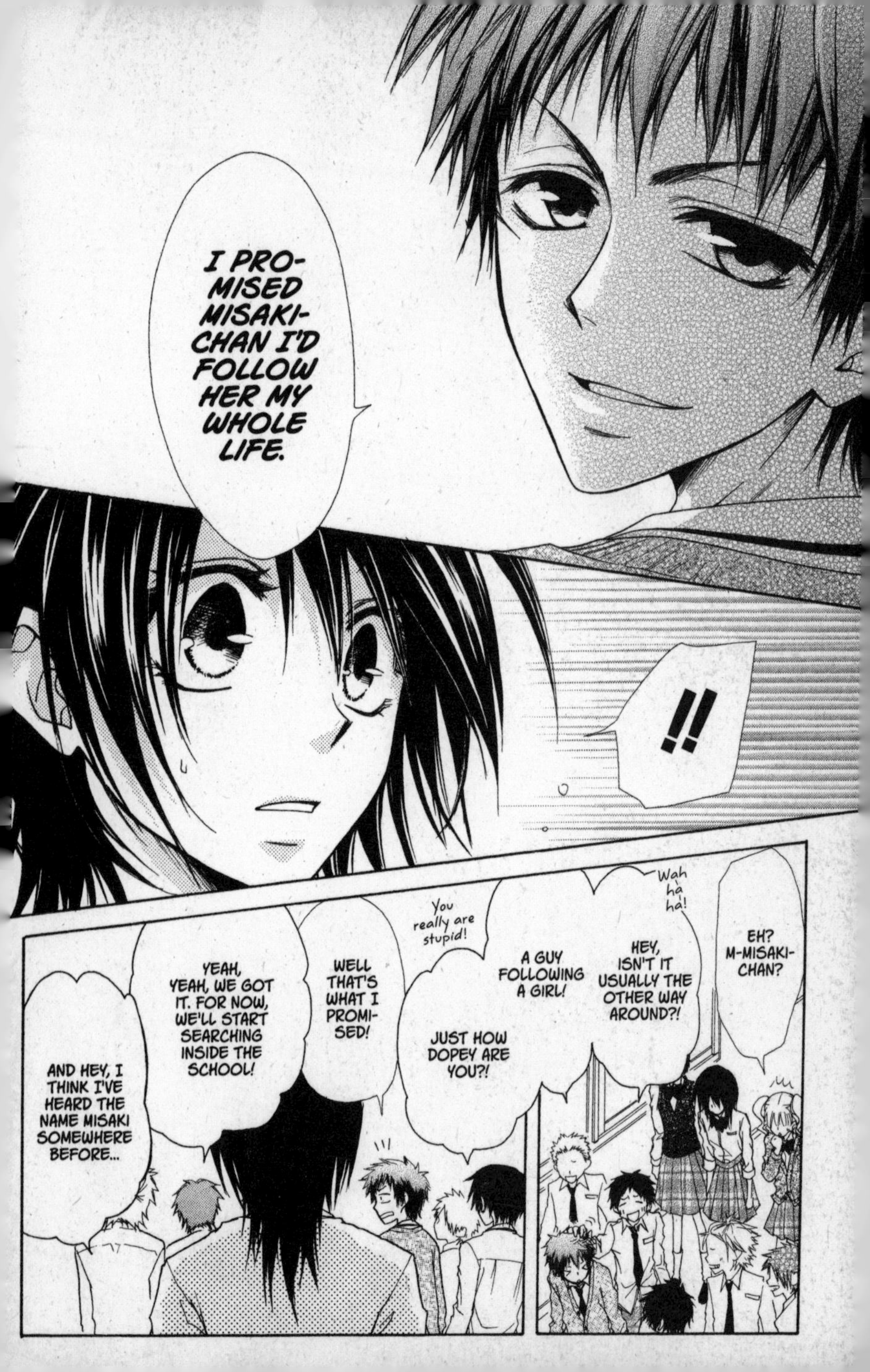

I PROMISED MISAKI-CHAN I'D FOLLOW HER MY WHOLE LIFE.
!!
EH? M-MISAKI-CHAN?
Wah ha ha!
HEY, ISN'T IT USUALLY THE OTHER WAY AROUND?!
A GUY FOLLOWING A GIRL!
You really are stupid!
JUST HOW DOPEY ARE YOU?!
WELL THAT'S WHAT I PROMISED!
YEAH, YEAH, WE GOT IT. FOR NOW, WE'LL START SEARCHING INSIDE THE SCHOOL!
AND HEY, I THINK I'VE HEARD THE NAME MISAKI SOMEWHERE BEFORE...

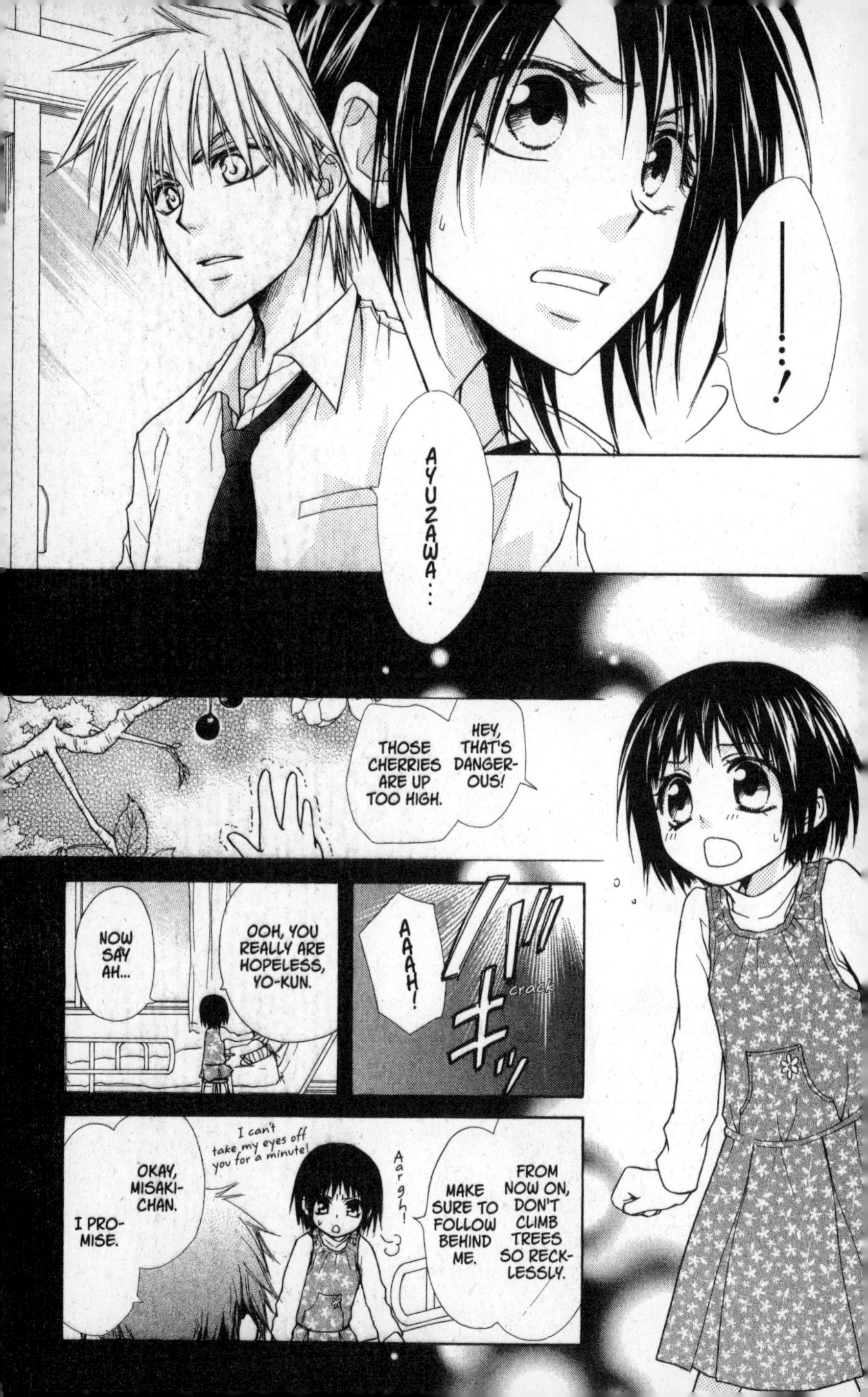
...!
AYUZAWA...
HEY, THAT'S DANGEROUS!
THOSE CHERRIES ARE UP TOO HIGH.
AAAH!
crack
OOH, YOU REALLY ARE HOPELESS, YO-KUN.
NOW SAY AH...
FROM NOW ON, DON'T CLIMB TREES SO RECKLESSLY.
MAKE SURE TO FOLLOW BEHIND ME.
Aargh!
I can't take my eyes off you for a minute!
OKAY, MISAKI-CHAN.
I PROMISE.

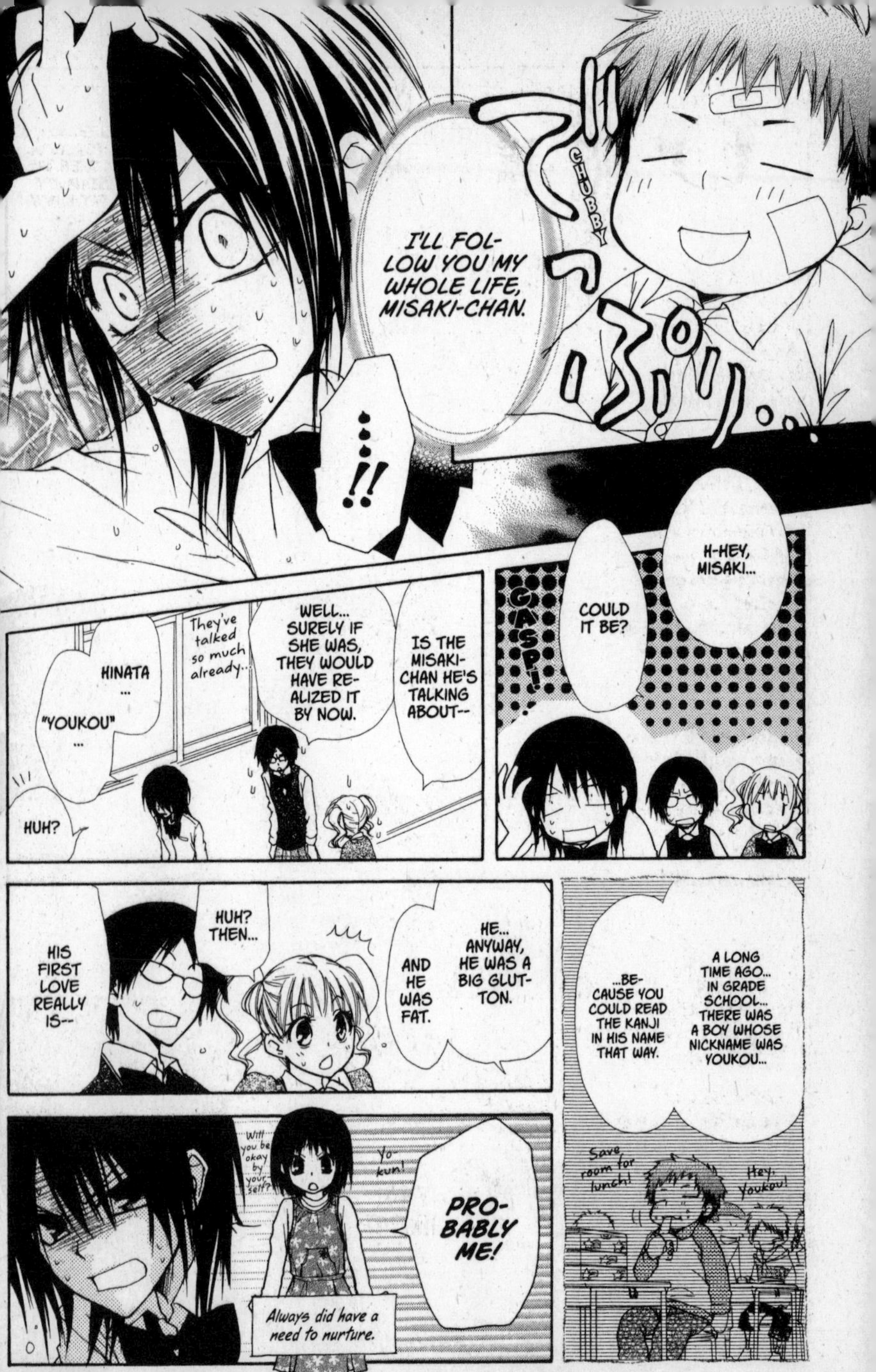
CHUBBY
I'LL FOL-LOW YOU MY WHOLE LIFE, MISAKI-CHAN.
...!!
H-HEY, MISAKI...
COULD IT BE?
GASP!
IS THE MISAKI-CHAN HE'S TALKING ABOUT--
WELL... SURELY IF SHE WAS, THEY WOULD HAVE RE-ALIZED IT BY NOW.
They've talked so much already...
HINATA ... "YOUKOU" ...
HUH?
A LONG TIME AGO... IN GRADE SCHOOL... THERE WAS A BOY WHOSE NICKNAME WAS YOUKOU...
...BE-CAUSE YOU COULD READ THE KANJI IN HIS NAME THAT WAY.
Hey, Youkou!
Save room for lunch!
HE... ANYWAY, HE WAS A BIG GLUT-TON.
AND HE WAS FAT.
HUH? THEN...
HIS FIRST LOVE REALLY IS--
PRO-BABLY ME!
Yo-kun!
Will you be okay by your-self?
Always did have a need to murture.

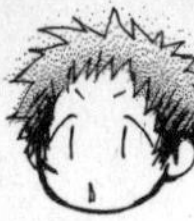

For Hinata's Kyushu dialect, I'm getting guidance from Junmi-sama, the editor who has taken care of me since my debut.

Junmi-sama is from Kyushu, but she's more powerful and unique than my Kansai-born self, and for some reason, she strangely repeated the claim, "Ooita looks out on the Inland Sea, so its dialect is relatively close to Kansai!"

It's true that there are a lot of words that I normally use myself, and if I'm not careful, it turns into normal Kansai dialect, so actually, it's really hard.

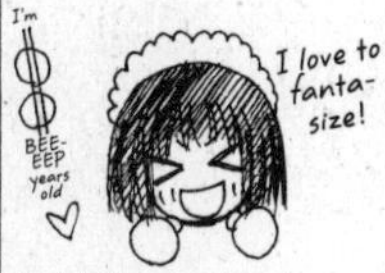
I'm BEE-EEP years old
I love to fantasize!

I didn't mean to at first, but the way things turned out, the manager Satsuki ended up being based on Junmi-sama.

Satsuki started acting like her all on her own...

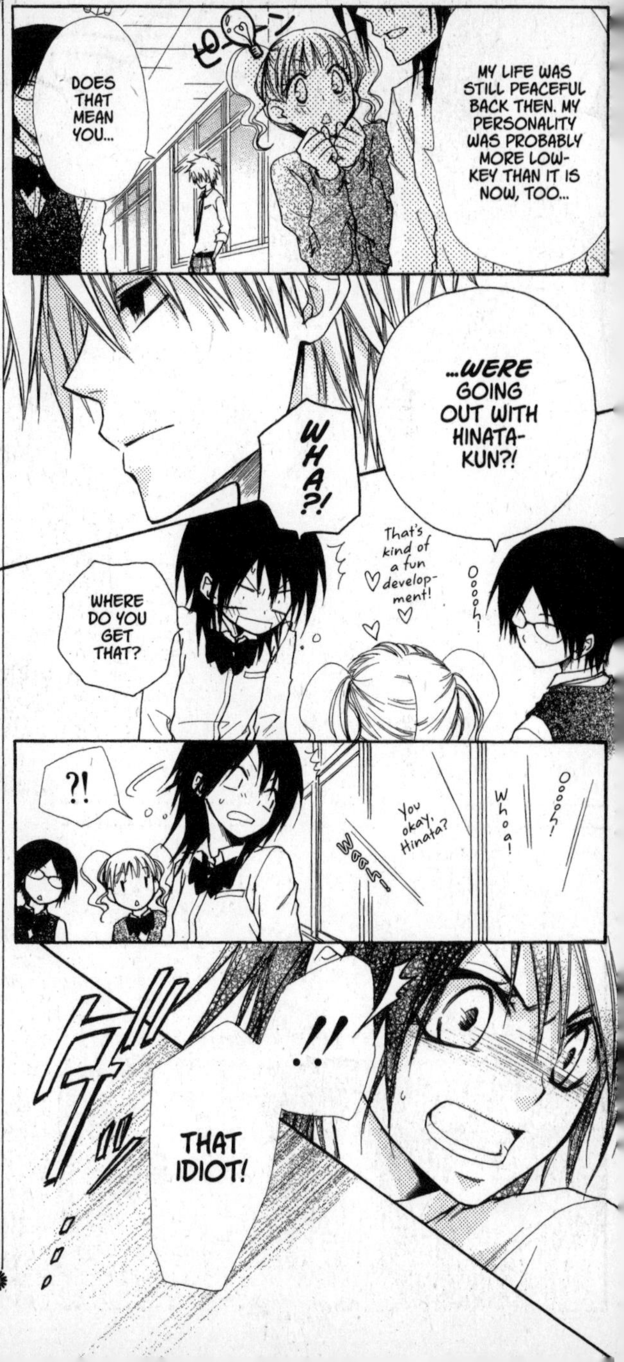
MY LIFE WAS STILL PEACEFUL BACK THEN. MY PERSONALITY WAS PROBABLY MORE LOW-KEY THAN IT IS NOW, TOO...
DOES THAT MEAN YOU...
...WERE GOING OUT WITH HINATA-KUN?!
WHA?!
Ooooh!
That's kind of a fun development!
WHERE DO YOU GET THAT?
Ooooh!
Whoa!
You okay, Hinata?
Woos-
?!
!!
THAT IDIOT!

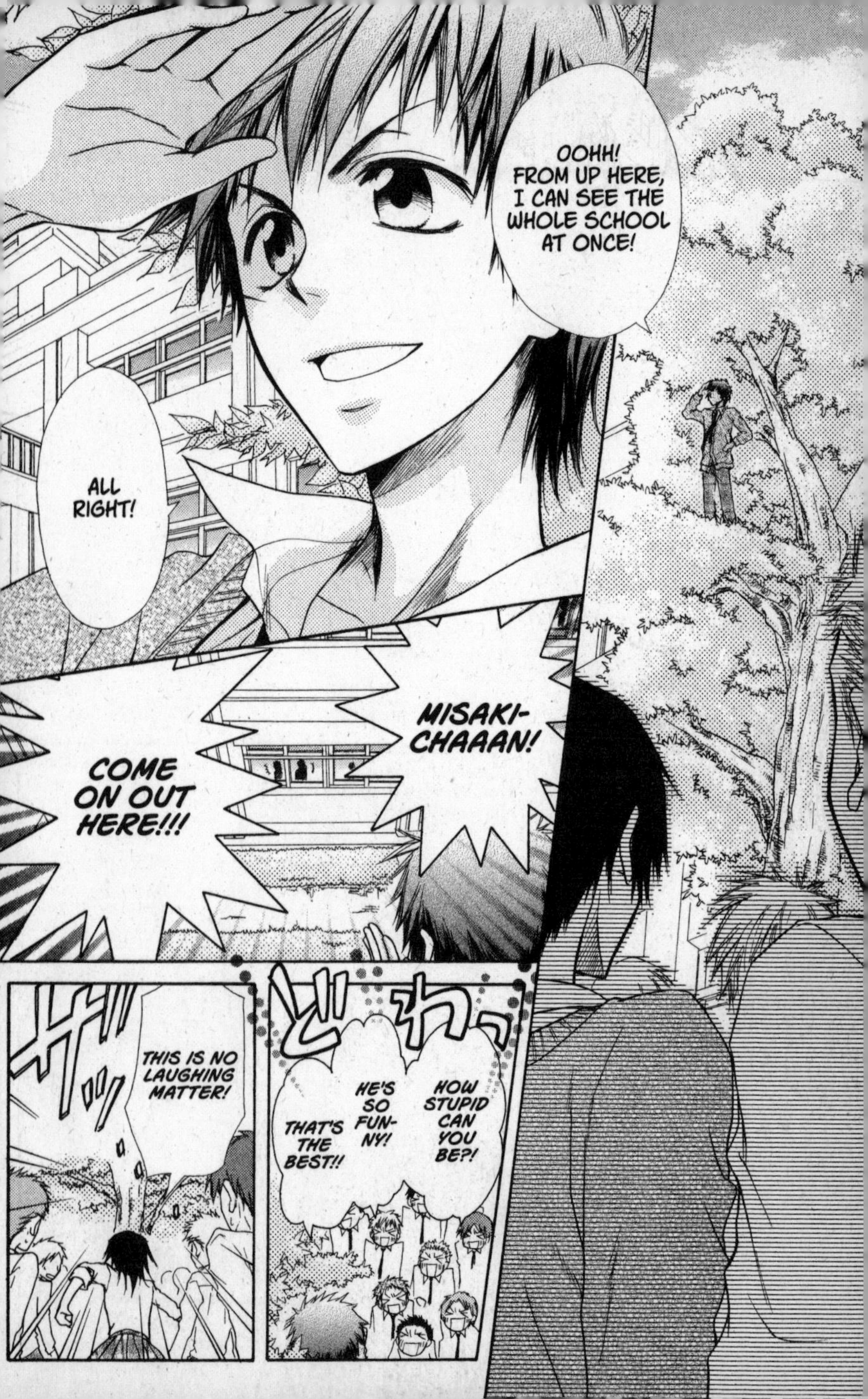
OOHH! FROM UP HERE, I CAN SEE THE WHOLE SCHOOL AT ONCE!
ALL RIGHT!
MISAKI-CHAAAN!
COME ON OUT HERE!!!
どわっ
HOW STUPID CAN YOU BE?!
HE'S SO FUN-NY!
THAT'S THE BEST!!
THIS IS NO LAUGHING MATTER!

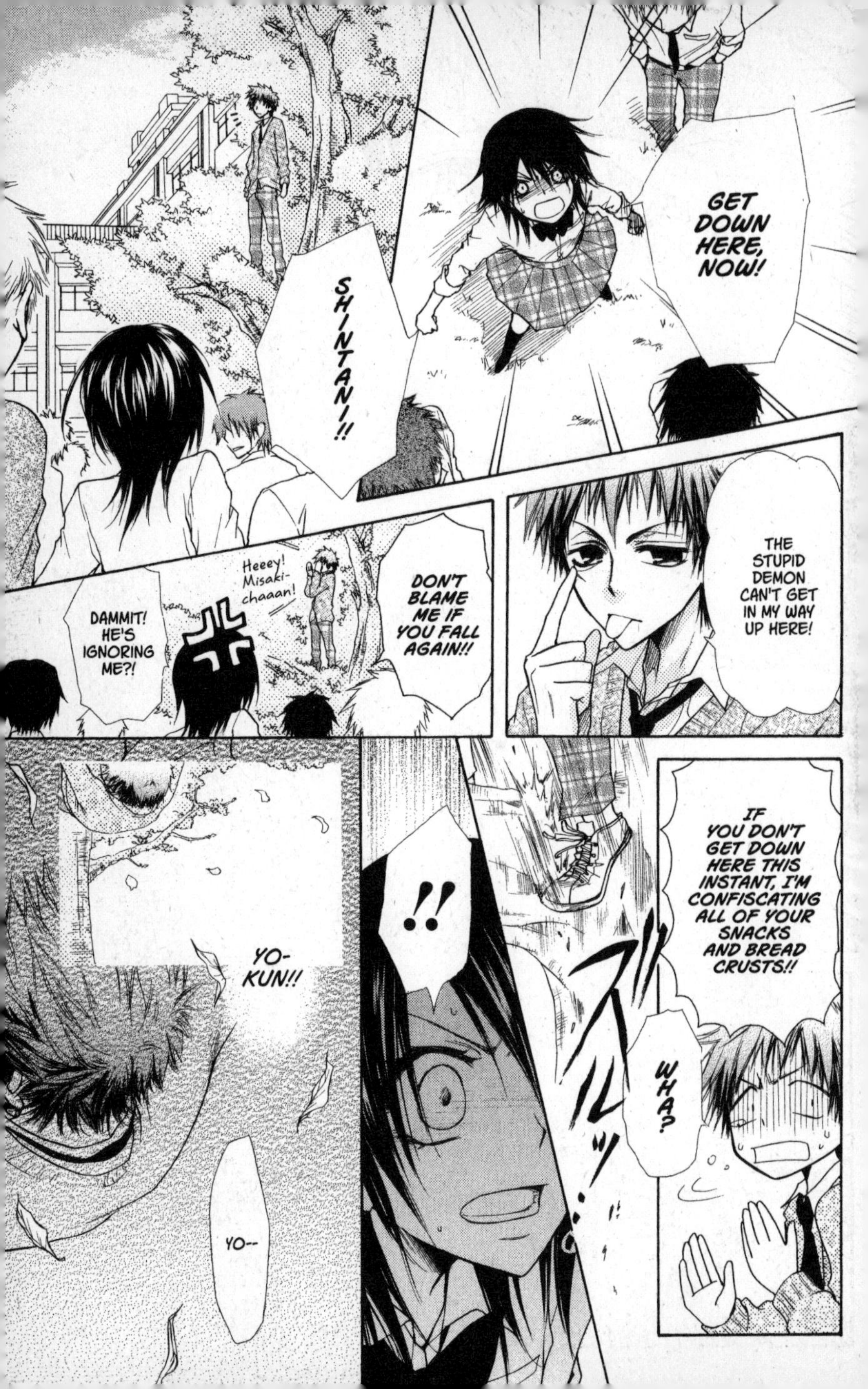
GET DOWN HERE, NOW!
SHINTANI!!
THE STUPID DEMON CAN'T GET IN MY WAY UP HERE!
DON'T BLAME ME IF YOU FALL AGAIN!!
Heeey! Misaki-chaaan!
DAMMIT! HE'S IGNORING ME?!
IF YOU DON'T GET DOWN HERE THIS INSTANT, I'M CONFISCATING ALL OF YOUR SNACKS AND BREAD CRUSTS!!
WHA?
!!
YO-KUN!!
YO--

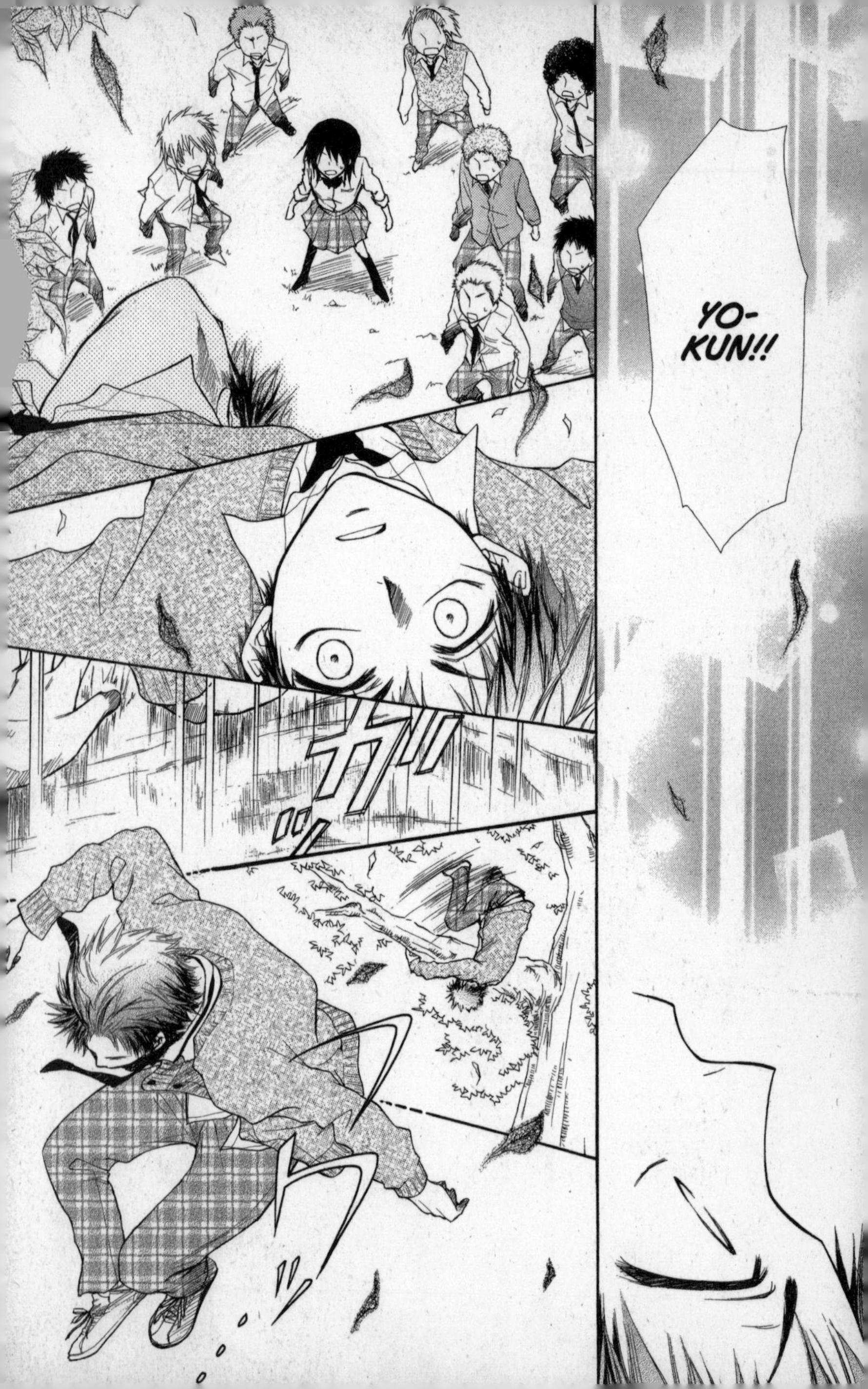
YO-
KUN!!

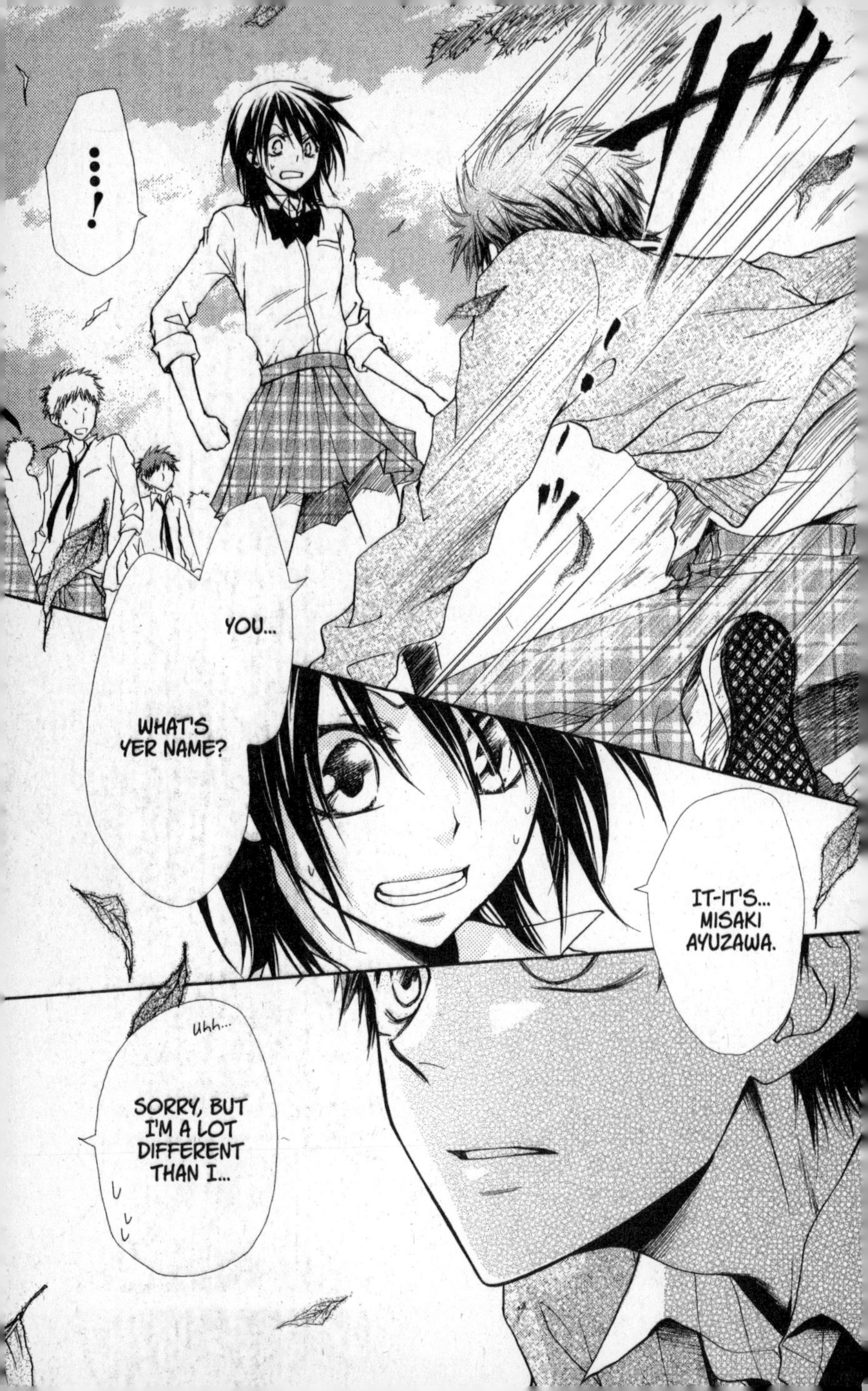

...!
YOU... WHAT'S YER NAME?
IT-IT'S... MISAKI AYUZAWA.
Uhh...
SORRY, BUT I'M A LOT DIFFERENT THAN I...

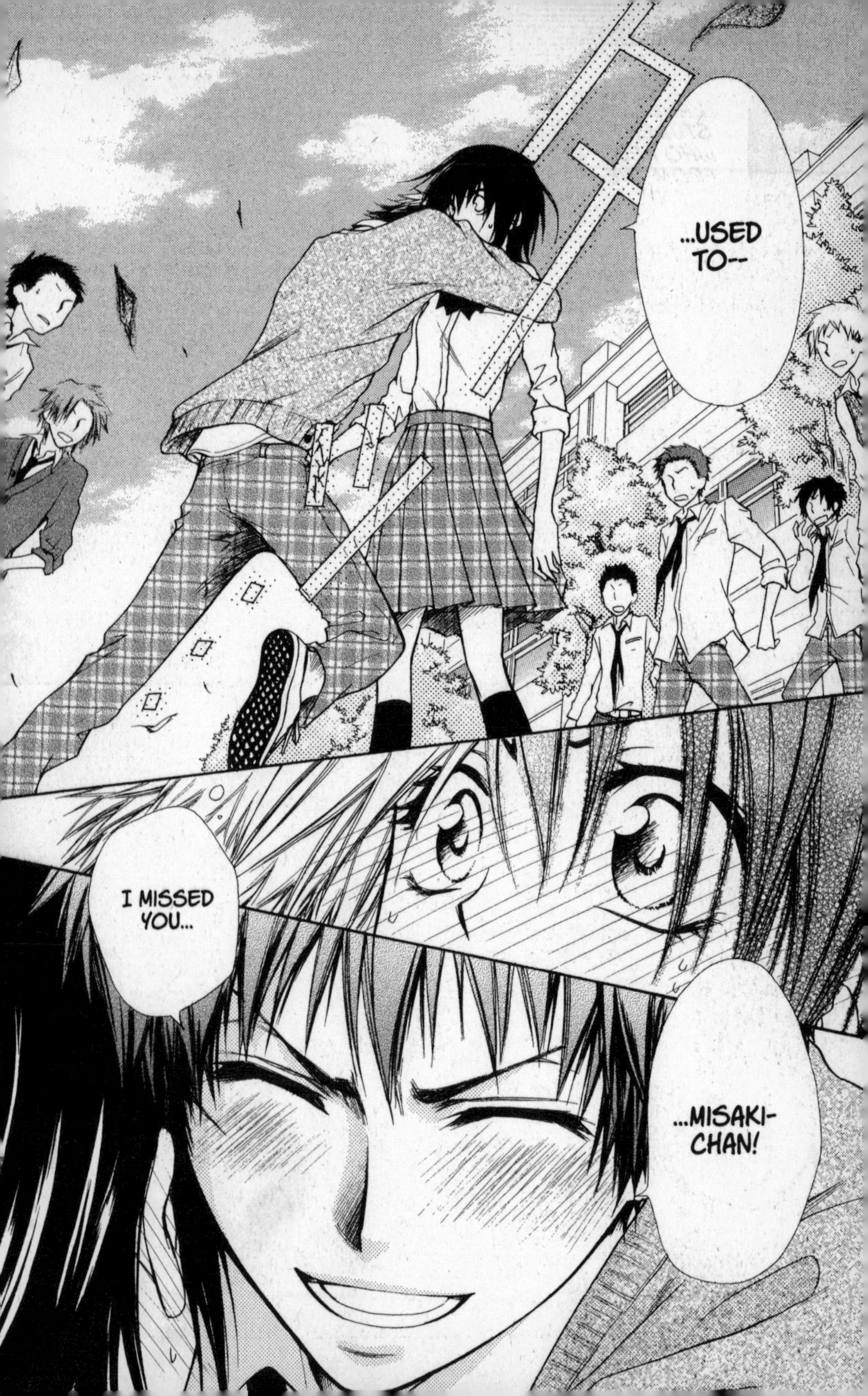
...USED TO--
I MISSED YOU...
...MISAKI-CHAN!

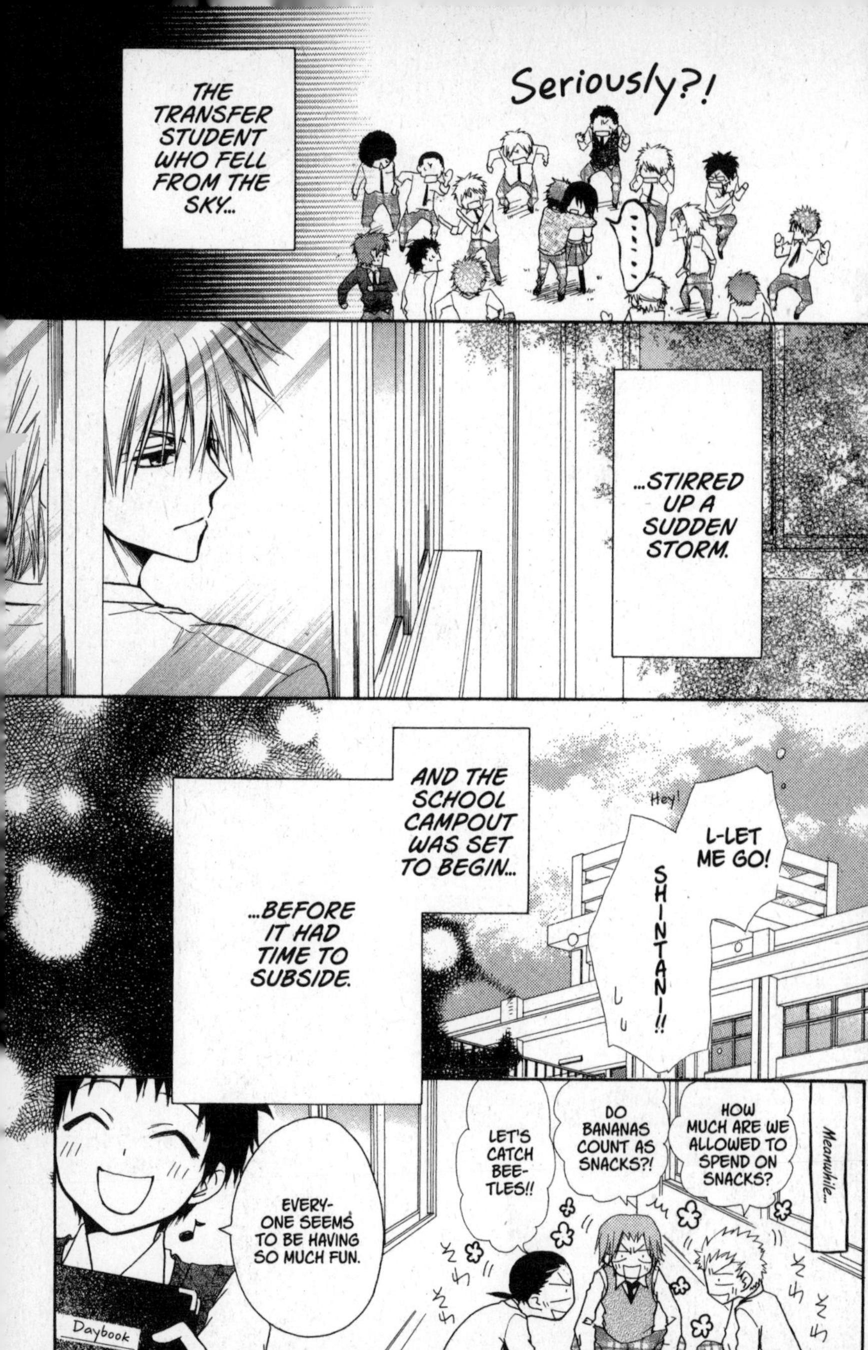
Seriously?!
......
THE TRANSFER STUDENT WHO FELL FROM THE SKY...
...STIRRED UP A SUDDEN STORM.
Hey!
L-LET ME GO!
SHINTANI!!
AND THE SCHOOL CAMPOUT WAS SET TO BEGIN...
...BEFORE IT HAD TIME TO SUBSIDE.
Meanwhile...
HOW MUCH ARE WE ALLOWED TO SPEND ON SNACKS?
DO BANANAS COUNT AS SNACKS?!
LET'S CATCH BEE-TLES!!
EVERY-ONE SEEMS TO BE HAVING SO MUCH FUN.
Daybook

HURRAAH! IT'S FINALLY OUR TURN!!

NO MATTER WHAT ANYONE SAYS, THE FANS DO LOVE US, DON'T THEY SHIROYAN?!

IKKUN...CAN YOU SAY THAT AFTER SEEING THESE QUESTIONS?

WH-WHAT'S WRONG, KUROTATSU?!

QUESTION 6 : ARE THE IDIOT TRIO AND MISAKI IN THE SAME GRADE?

: HEY!!!

: *OF COURSE WE'RE IN THE SAME GRADE! WE'RE SECOND-YEARS! SECOND-YEARS!*

: WE APPEARED REALLY EARLY ON--ON THE FIRST PAGE OF THE FIRST COURSE OF THE FIRST VOLUME, AND STILL, NOBODY RECOGNIZES THESE BASIC FACTS ABOUT US...I BET WE'RE ABOUT AS NOTICEABLE AS THE AIR...

: *HEY! THAT'S DEPRESSING, KUROTATSU!*

: OH! THERE'S ANOTHER QUESTION!

- -

QUESTION 7 : WHO'S THE STRONGEST OF THE THREE IDIOTS?

: *I AM, OF COURSE. THE LEADER, NAOYA SHIROKAWA!!*

: HMM, WELL...YEAH, IF YOU MEAN PHYSICALLY.

: BUT YOU'RE THE WEAKEST WHEN IT COMES TO BRAINS.

: HEY, GUYS! DON'T TALK ABOUT ME LIKE I'M SOME MUSCLE-HEADED MORON!

: WELL, YOU ARE A *HOT-HEADED MUSCLE-HEAD*.

: BUT KUROTATSU'S A *PERVERTED MORON*.

: AND YOU'RE A *CLOSET OTAKU MORON!!*

- -

QUESTION 8 : WHEN I SEE THE IDIOT TRIO, I CRACK UP. *THIS CERTAINLY DOES NOT MEAN THEY HAVE A SOOTHING EFFECT ON ME.

: ......

: ......

: ......HEY...

: *YOU WANNA FIGHT, PUNK!!?!*

: *THAT'S NOT EVEN A QUESTION!!*

: WE REALLY WILL, ALWAYS AND FOREVER, BE THE POOR, PITIFUL IDIOT TRIO.

27th Course
DEMON STUDENT BODY PRESIDENT OF SEIKA HIGH SCHOOL...
Whoooooosh
...MISAKI AYUZAWA.
HER CHILDHOOD FRIEND, HINATA SHINTANI...
I'll follow you my whole life, Misaki-chan.
CHUBBY
Hinata in days gone by
MISAKI-CHAN! ♡
...HAS COME BACK AFTER 10 YEARS OR SO...
...TO BE REUNITED WITH HIS BELOVED MISAKI-CHAN.
FED UP
I said!
DON'T EAT THOSE BREAD CRUSTS IN THE HALLS!!

Question Corner

Question 3

Q. Did you have any school presidents who left an impression on you?

A. When I was in high school, I was secretary on the student council, and I'll never forget the president at the time. He was huge, like a bear. He was a fatherly boy, who was very popular and loved by all. The impact of his looks was incredible. I wonder how he's doing?

Fond memories.

Huh?

But what was his name?

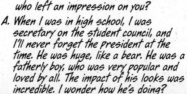

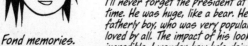

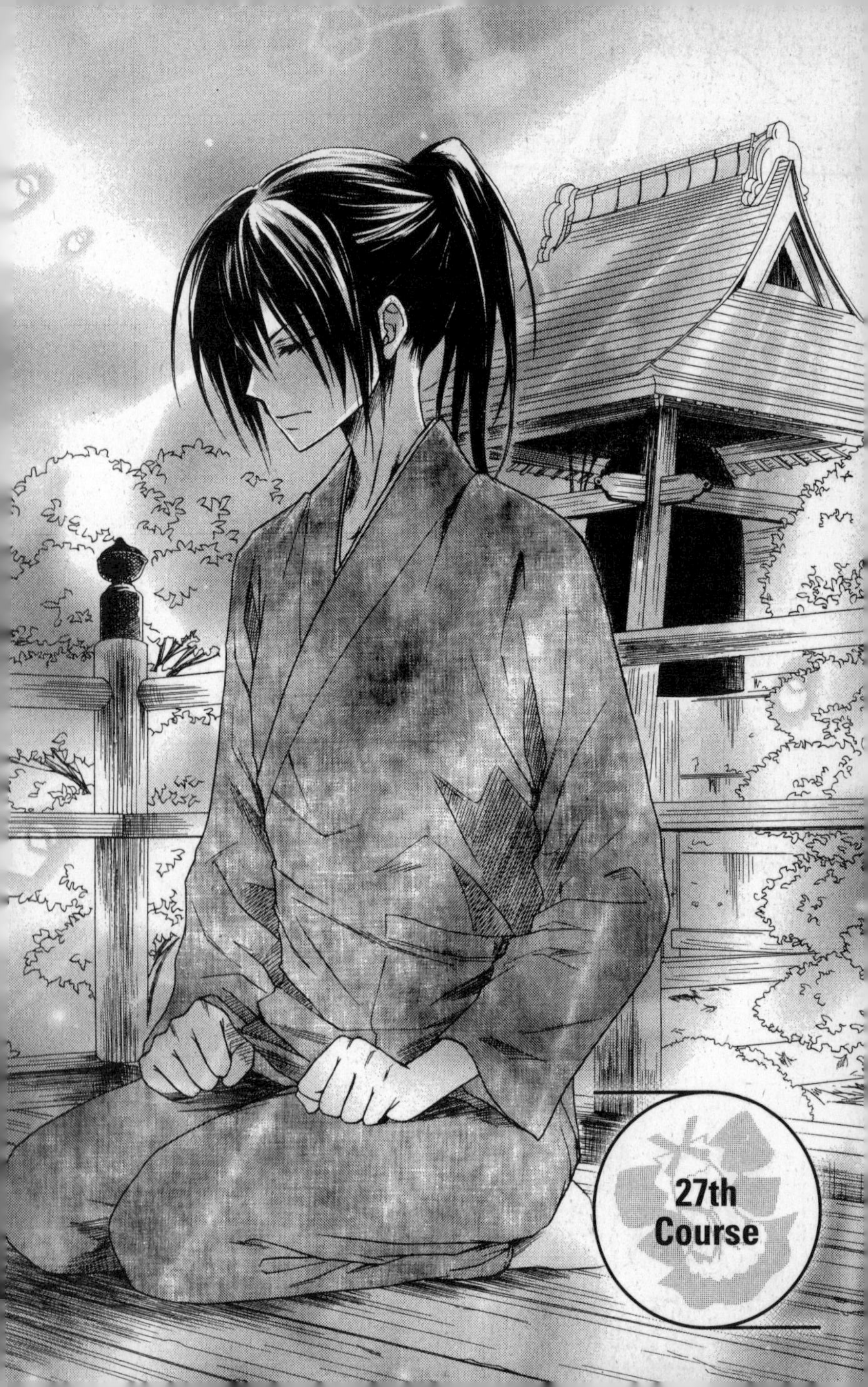
27th
Course

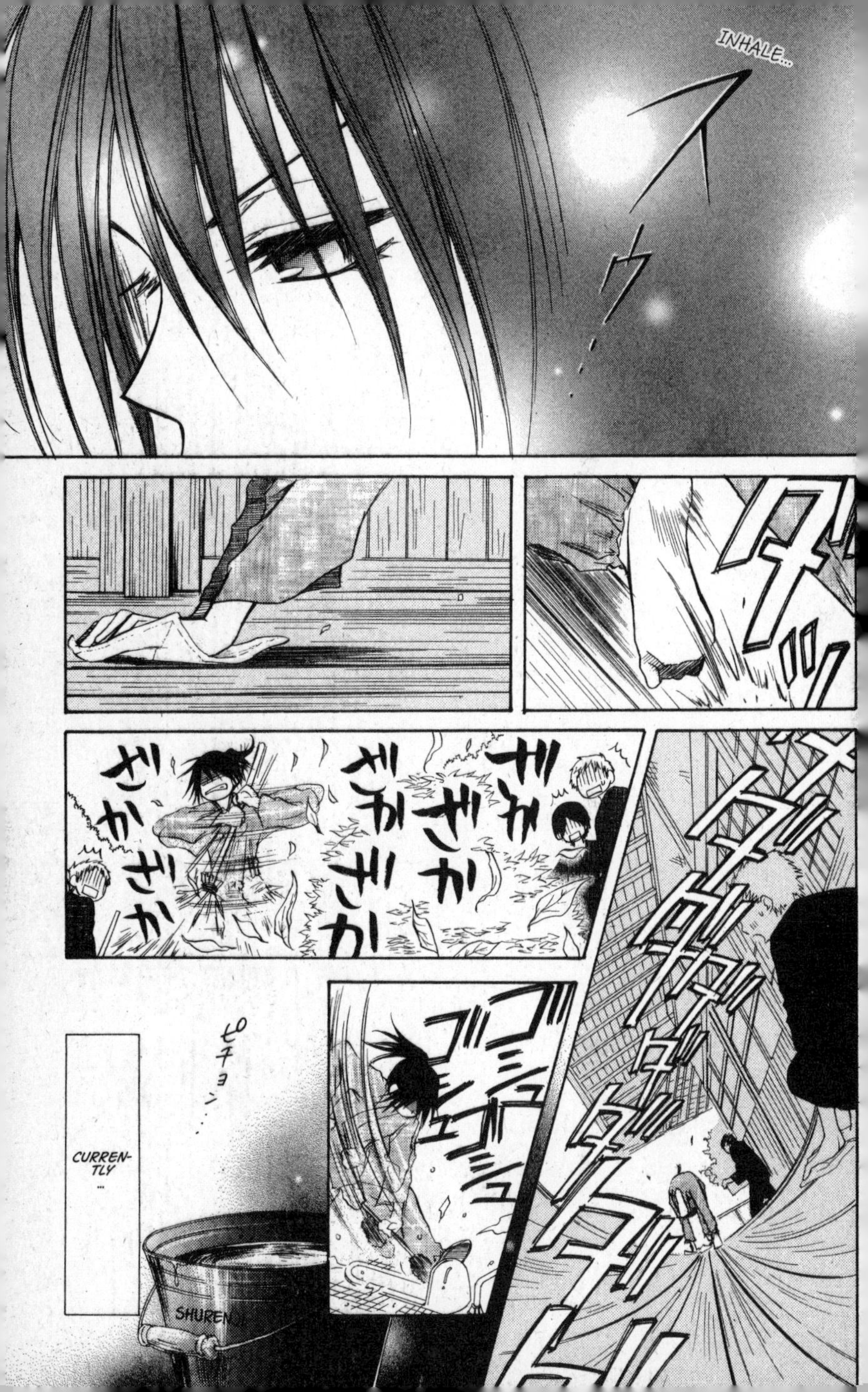
INHALE...
スゥ…
ダッ
ざかざかざかざか
ゴシュゴシュ
ピチョン…
CURRENTLY...
SHUREN...

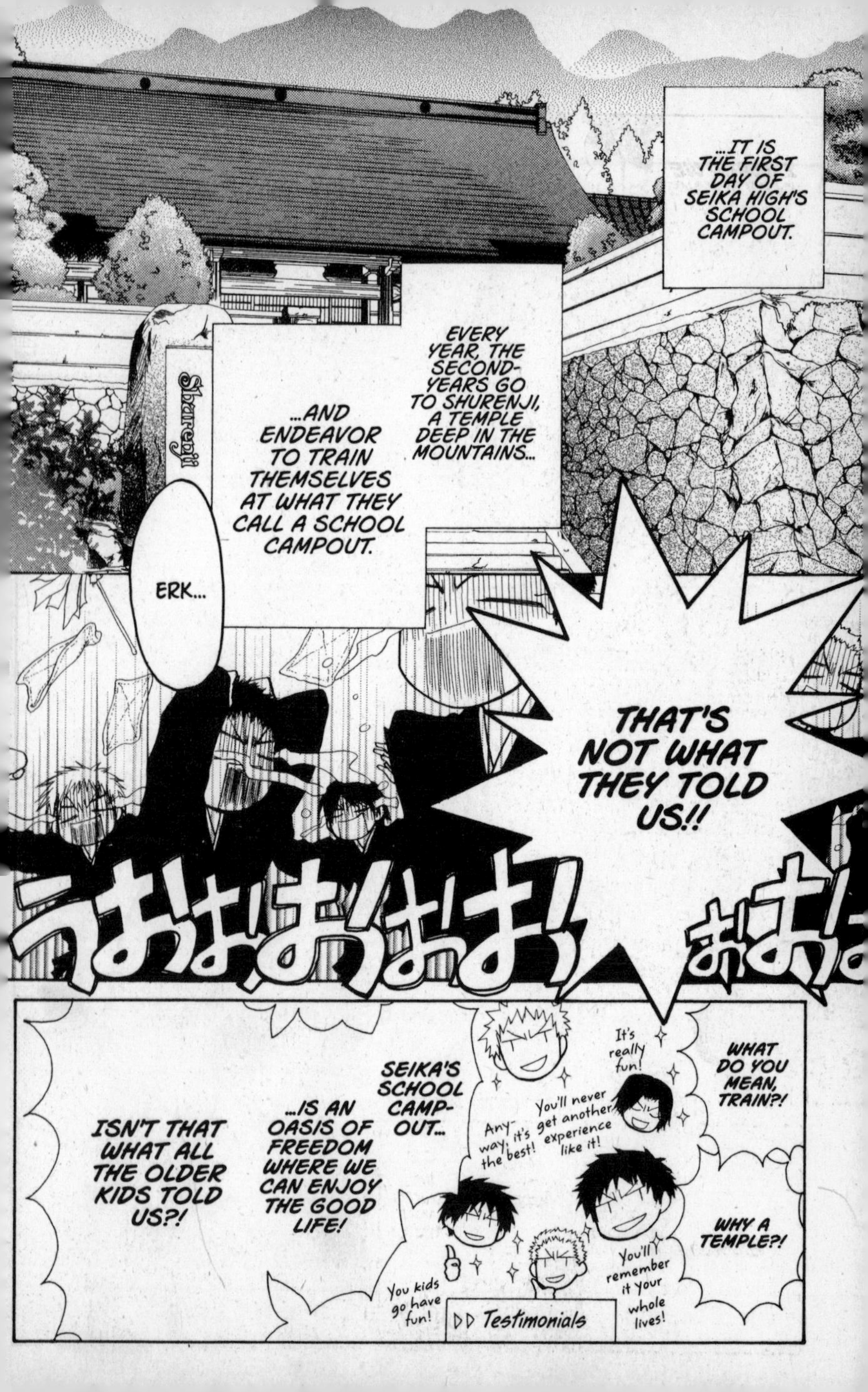

...IT IS THE FIRST DAY OF SEIKA HIGH'S SCHOOL CAMPOUT.
EVERY YEAR, THE SECOND-YEARS GO TO SHURENJI, A TEMPLE DEEP IN THE MOUNTAINS...
...AND ENDEAVOR TO TRAIN THEMSELVES AT WHAT THEY CALL A SCHOOL CAMPOUT.
Shurenji
ERK...
THAT'S NOT WHAT THEY TOLD US!!
WHAT DO YOU MEAN, TRAIN?!
WHY A TEMPLE?!
It's really fun!
You'll never get another experience like it!
Anyway, it's the best!
You'll remember it your whole lives!
You kids go have fun!
Testimonials
SEIKA'S SCHOOL CAMPOUT...
...IS AN OASIS OF FREEDOM WHERE WE CAN ENJOY THE GOOD LIFE!
ISN'T THAT WHAT ALL THE OLDER KIDS TOLD US?!

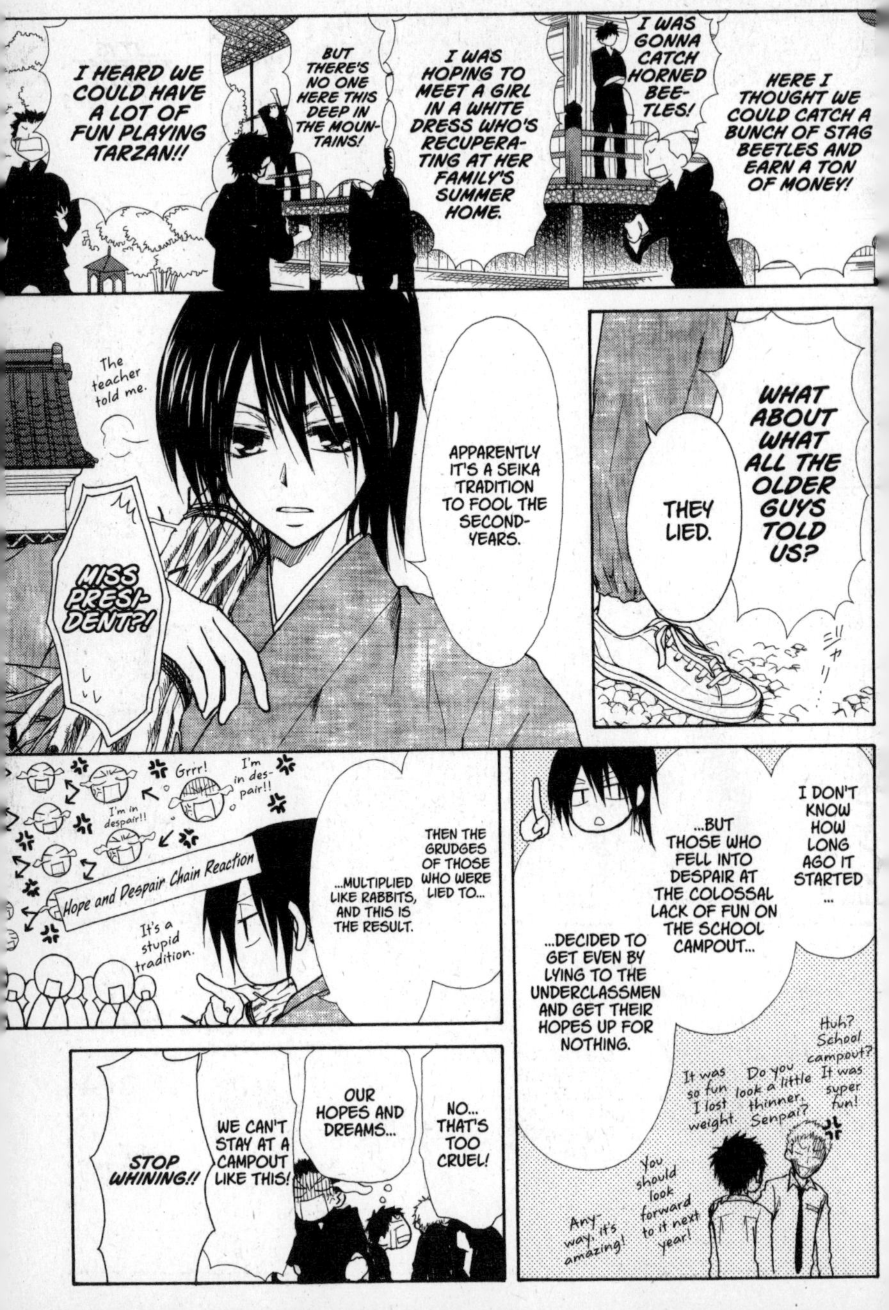

HERE I THOUGHT WE COULD CATCH A BUNCH OF STAG BEETLES AND EARN A TON OF MONEY!
I WAS GONNA CATCH HORNED BEE-TLES!
I WAS HOPING TO MEET A GIRL IN A WHITE DRESS WHO'S RECUPERA-TING AT HER FAMILY'S SUMMER HOME.
BUT THERE'S NO ONE HERE THIS DEEP IN THE MOUN-TAINS!
I HEARD WE COULD HAVE A LOT OF FUN PLAYING TARZAN!!
WHAT ABOUT WHAT ALL THE OLDER GUYS TOLD US?
THEY LIED.
ジャリ
APPARENTLY IT'S A SEIKA TRADITION TO FOOL THE SECOND-YEARS.
The teacher told me.
MISS PRESI-DENT?!
I DON'T KNOW HOW LONG AGO IT STARTED ...
...BUT THOSE WHO FELL INTO DESPAIR AT THE COLOSSAL LACK OF FUN ON THE SCHOOL CAMPOUT...
...DECIDED TO GET EVEN BY LYING TO THE UNDERCLASSMEN AND GET THEIR HOPES UP FOR NOTHING.
Huh? School campout? It was super fun!
Do you look a little thinner, Senpai?
It was so fun I lost weight.
You should look forward to it next year!
Any-way, it's amazing!
THEN THE GRUDGES OF THOSE WHO WERE LIED TO...
...MULTIPLIED LIKE RABBITS, AND THIS IS THE RESULT.
I'm in des-pair!!
Grrr!
I'm in despair!!
Hope and Despair Chain Reaction
It's a stupid tradition.
NO... THAT'S TOO CRUEL!
OUR HOPES AND DREAMS...
WE CAN'T STAY AT A CAMPOUT LIKE THIS!
STOP WHINING!!

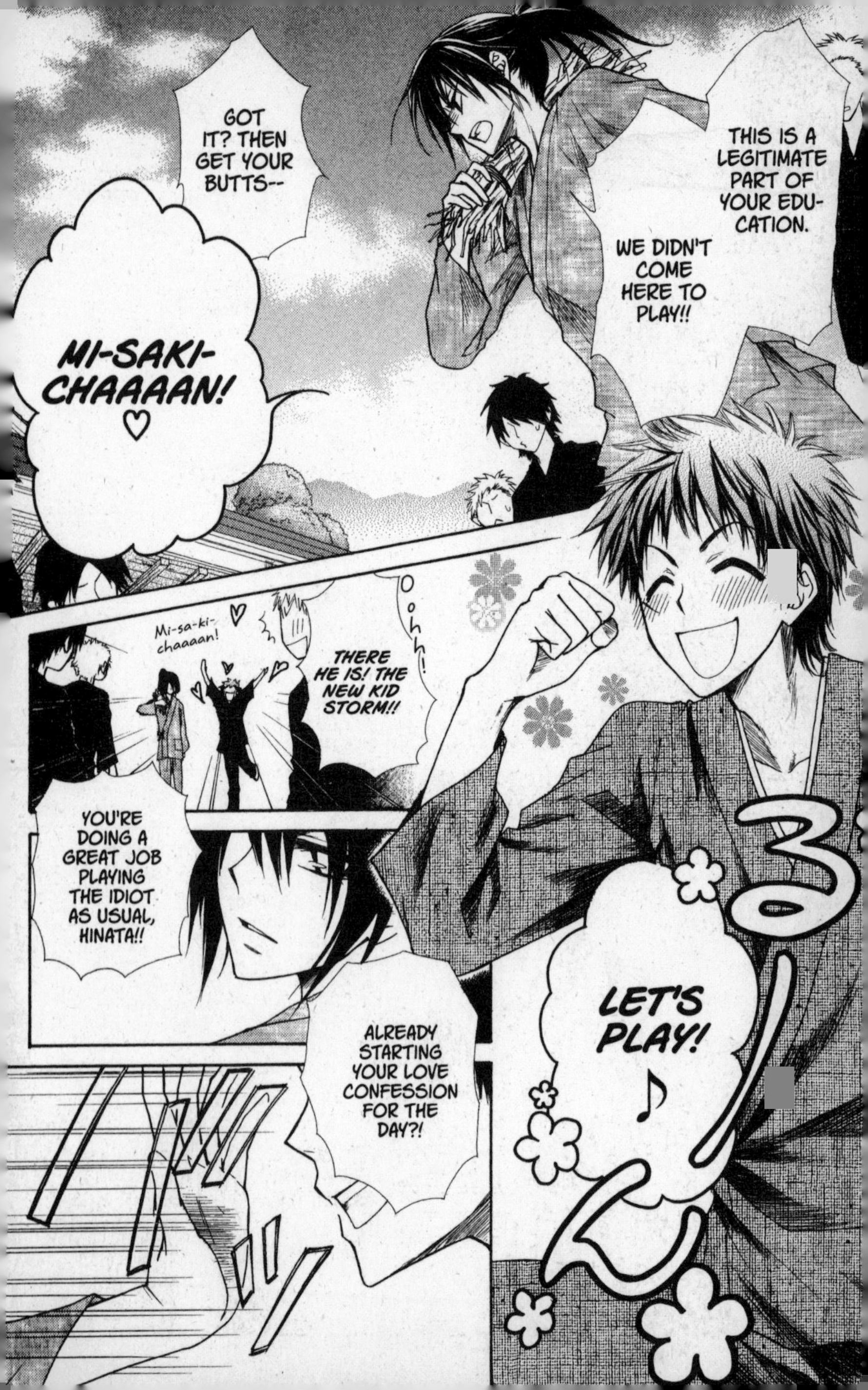
THIS IS A LEGITIMATE PART OF YOUR EDU-CATION.
WE DIDN'T COME HERE TO PLAY!!
GOT IT? THEN GET YOUR BUTTS--
MI-SAKI-CHAAAAN! ♡
LET'S PLAY! ♪
Oohh!
THERE HE IS! THE NEW KID STORM!!
Mi-sa-ki-chaaaan!
YOU'RE DOING A GREAT JOB PLAYING THE IDIOT AS USUAL, HINATA!!
ALREADY STARTING YOUR LOVE CONFESSION FOR THE DAY?!

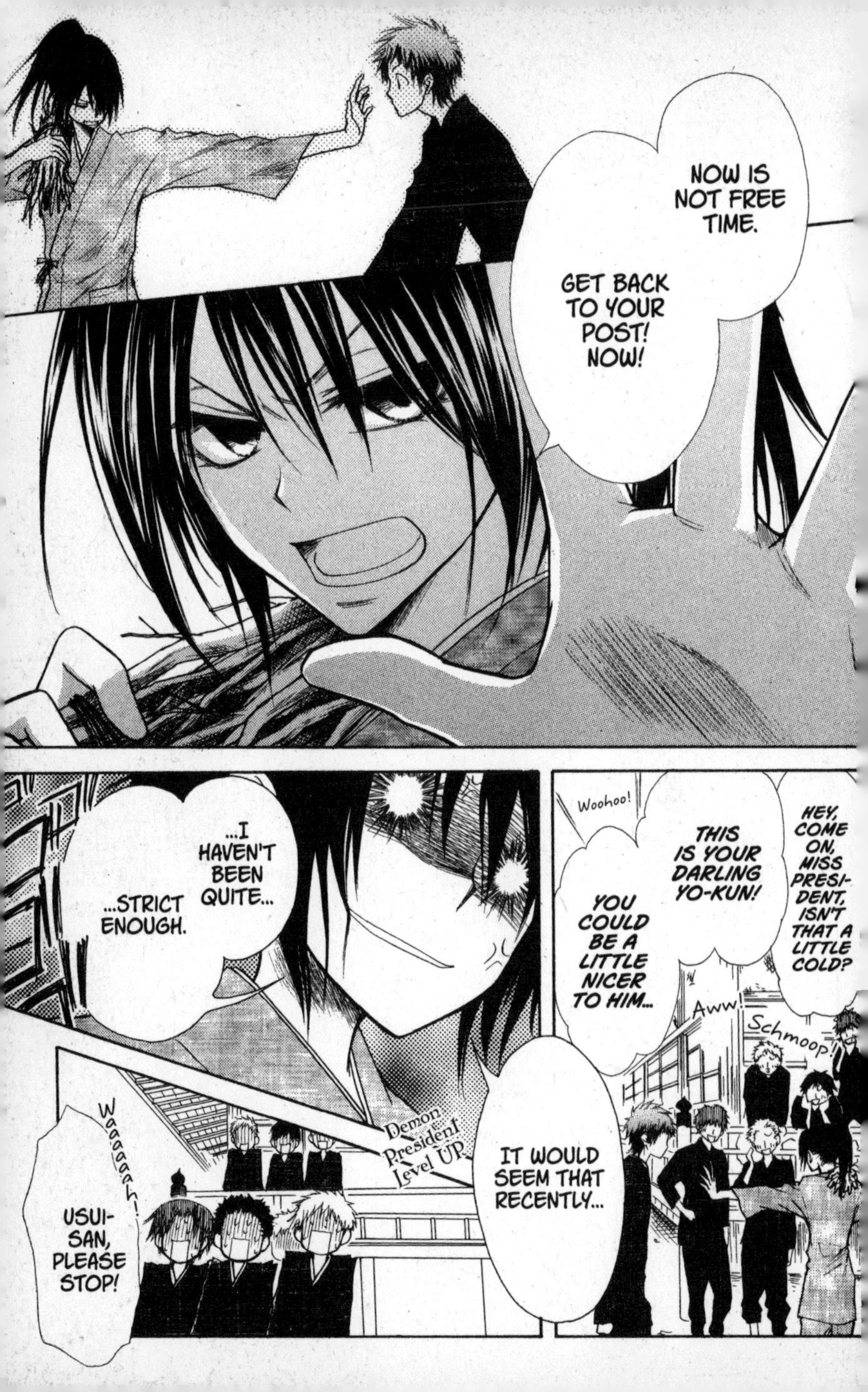
NOW IS NOT FREE TIME.
GET BACK TO YOUR POST! NOW!
HEY, COME ON, MISS PRESIDENT, ISN'T THAT A LITTLE COLD?
Woohoo!
THIS IS YOUR DARLING YO-KUN!
YOU COULD BE A LITTLE NICER TO HIM...
Aww!
Schmoop!
IT WOULD SEEM THAT RECENTLY...
...I HAVEN'T BEEN QUITE...
...STRICT ENOUGH.
Demon President Level UP
Waaaaaah!
USUI-SAN, PLEASE STOP!

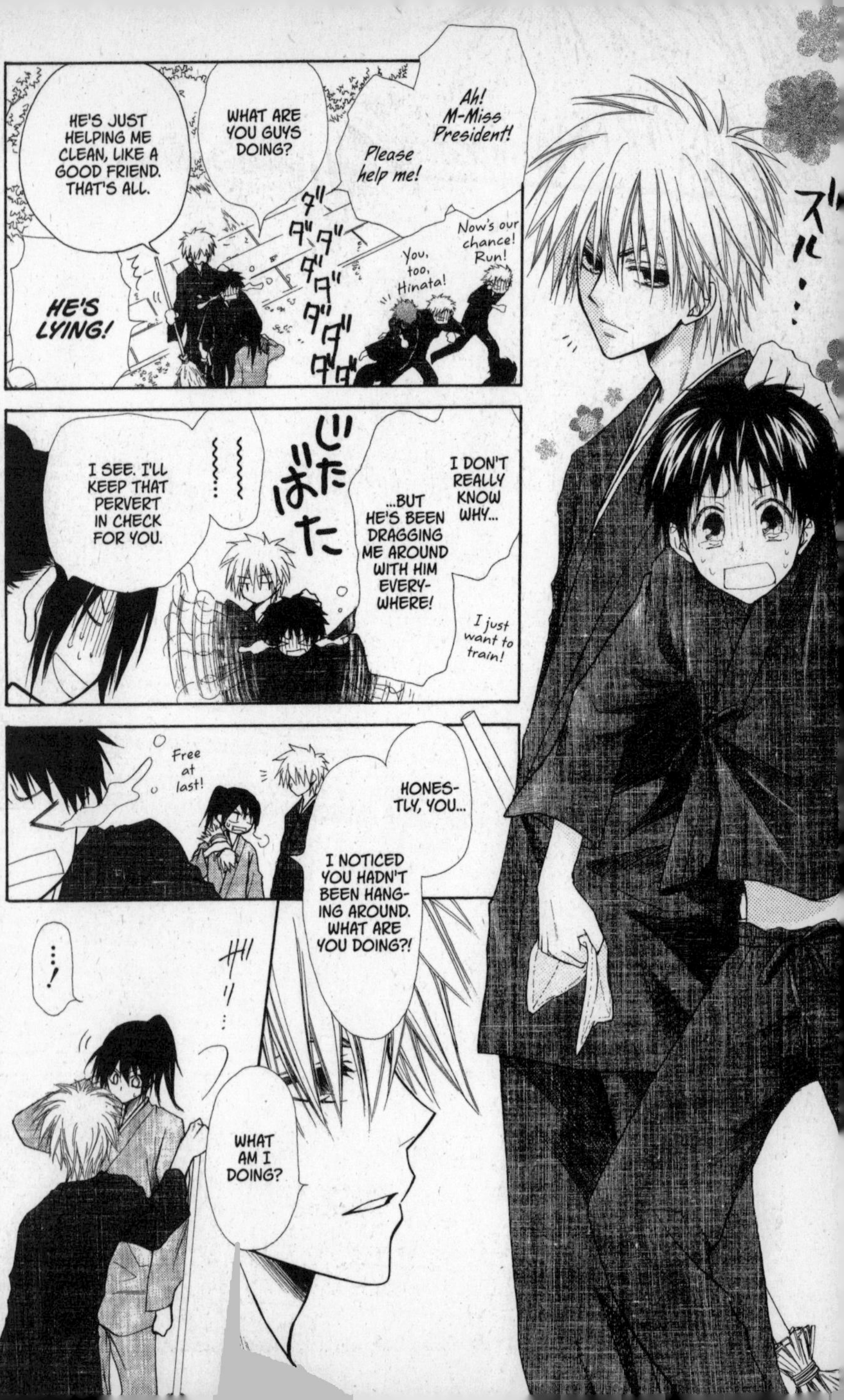
ズル・・・
Ah! M-Miss President!
Please help me!
Now's our chance! Run!
You, too, Hinata!
ダダダダダダダダ
WHAT ARE YOU GUYS DOING?
HE'S JUST HELPING ME CLEAN, LIKE A GOOD FRIEND. THAT'S ALL.
HE'S LYING!
I DON'T REALLY KNOW WHY...
...BUT HE'S BEEN DRAGGING ME AROUND WITH HIM EVERYWHERE!
I just want to train!
じたばた
......
I SEE. I'LL KEEP THAT PERVERT IN CHECK FOR YOU.
HONESTLY, YOU...
Free at last!
I NOTICED YOU HADN'T BEEN HANGING AROUND. WHAT ARE YOU DOING?!
ガリ…
...!
WHAT AM I DOING?

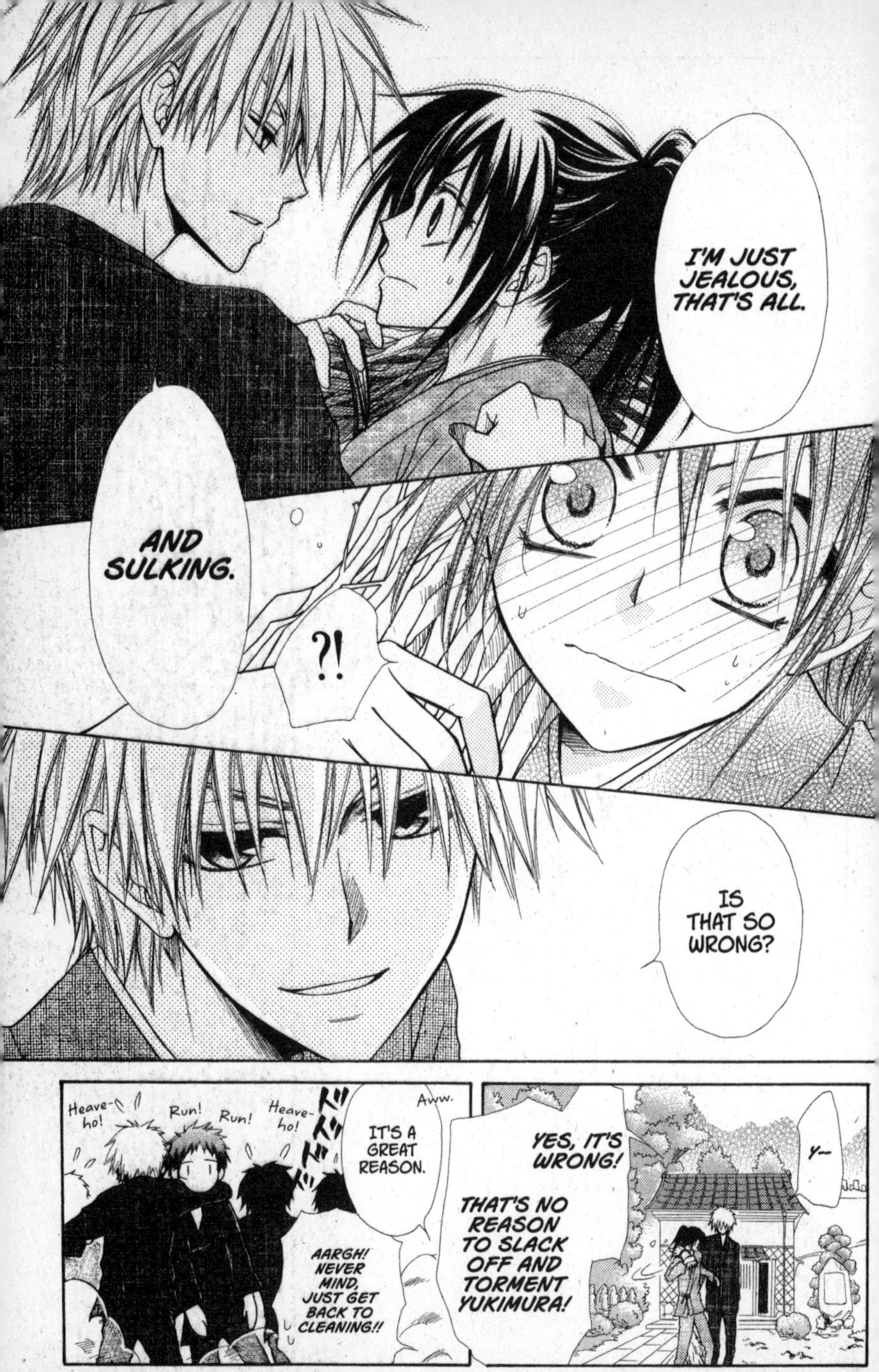

I'M JUST JEALOUS, THAT'S ALL.
AND SULKING.
?!
IS THAT SO WRONG?
Y--
YES, IT'S WRONG!
THAT'S NO REASON TO SLACK OFF AND TORMENT YUKIMURA!
Aww.
IT'S A GREAT REASON.
AARGH! NEVER MIND, JUST GET BACK TO CLEANING!!
Heave-ho!
Run!
Run!
Heave-ho!

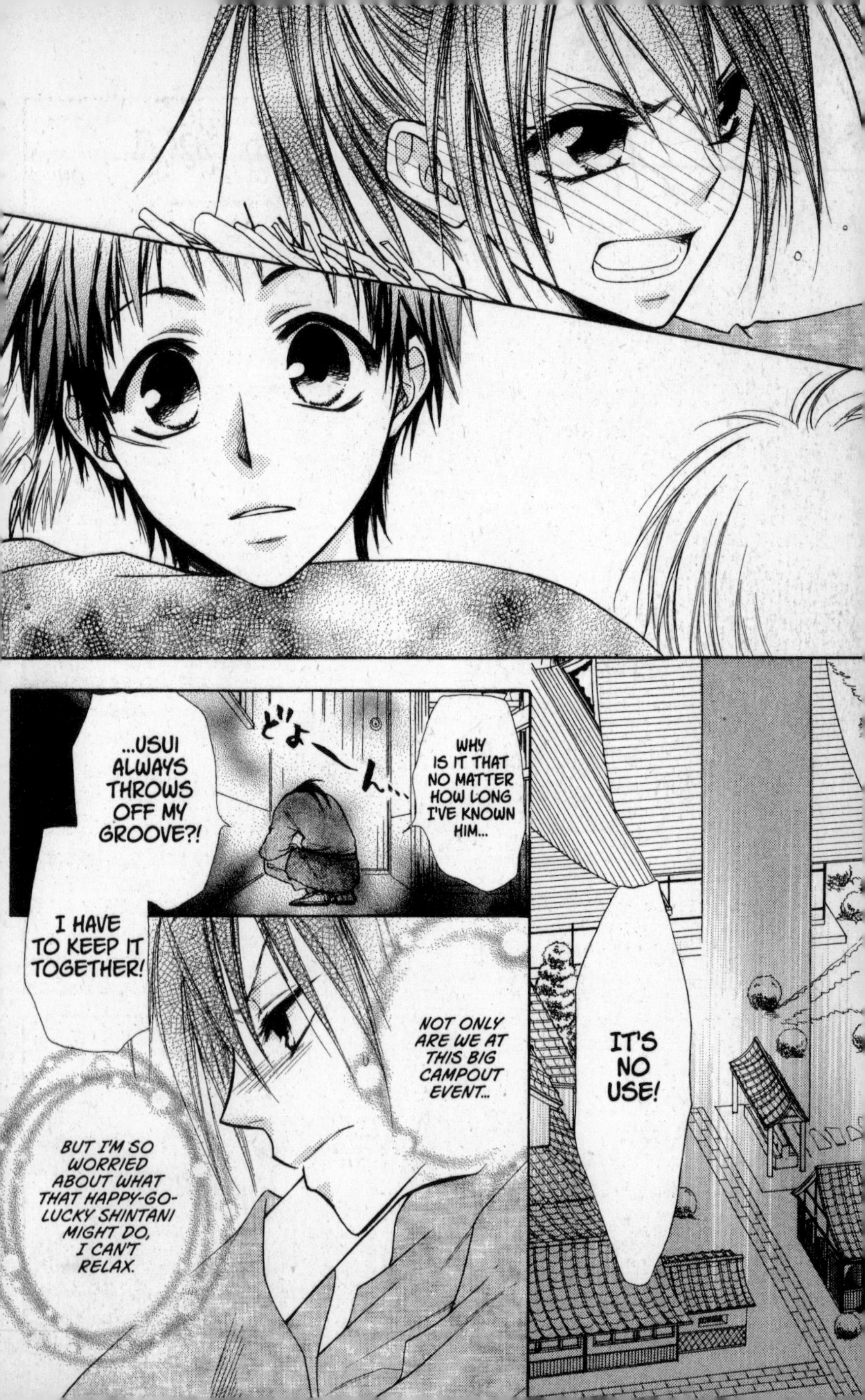
IT'S NO USE!
WHY IS IT THAT NO MATTER HOW LONG I'VE KNOWN HIM...
どよ〜ん...
...USUI ALWAYS THROWS OFF MY GROOVE?!
I HAVE TO KEEP IT TOGETHER!
NOT ONLY ARE WE AT THIS BIG CAMPOUT EVENT...
BUT I'M SO WORRIED ABOUT WHAT THAT HAPPY-GO-LUCKY SHINTANI MIGHT DO, I CAN'T RELAX.

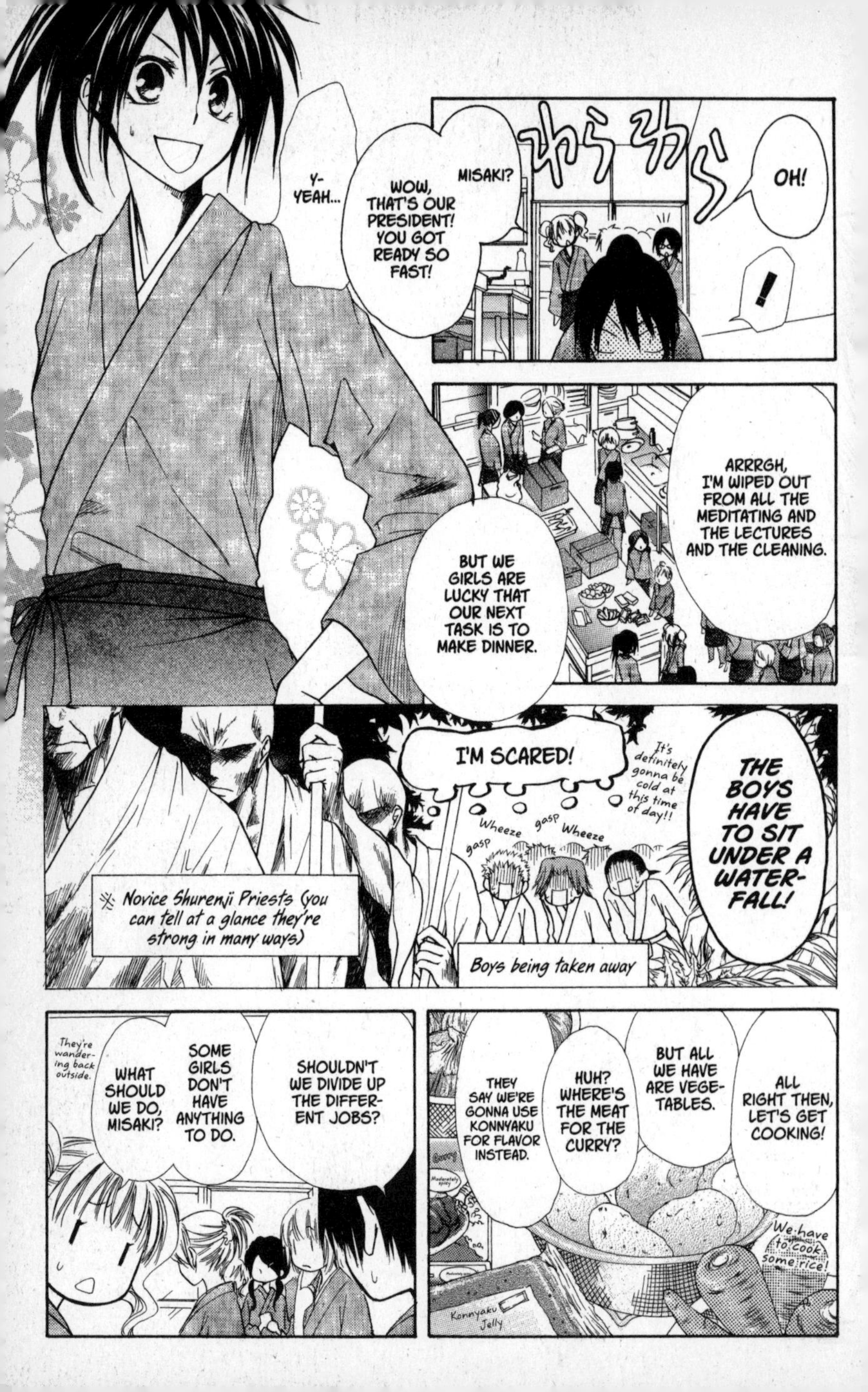
OH!
!
MISAKI?
ARRRGH, I'M WIPED OUT FROM ALL THE MEDITATING AND THE LECTURES AND THE CLEANING.
BUT WE GIRLS ARE LUCKY THAT OUR NEXT TASK IS TO MAKE DINNER.
WOW, THAT'S OUR PRESIDENT! YOU GOT READY SO FAST!
Y-YEAH...
THE BOYS HAVE TO SIT UNDER A WATER-FALL!
It's definitely gonna be cold at this time of day!!
I'M SCARED!
Wheeze gasp Wheeze gasp
※ Novice Shurenji Priests (you can tell at a glance they're strong in many ways)
Boys being taken away
ALL RIGHT THEN, LET'S GET COOKING!
BUT ALL WE HAVE ARE VEGE-TABLES.
HUH? WHERE'S THE MEAT FOR THE CURRY?
THEY SAY WE'RE GONNA USE KONNYAKU FOR FLAVOR INSTEAD.
We have to cook some rice!
Curry
Moderately spicy
Konnyaku Jelly
SHOULDN'T WE DIVIDE UP THE DIFFER-ENT JOBS?
SOME GIRLS DON'T HAVE ANYTHING TO DO.
WHAT SHOULD WE DO, MISAKI?
They're wander-ing back outside.

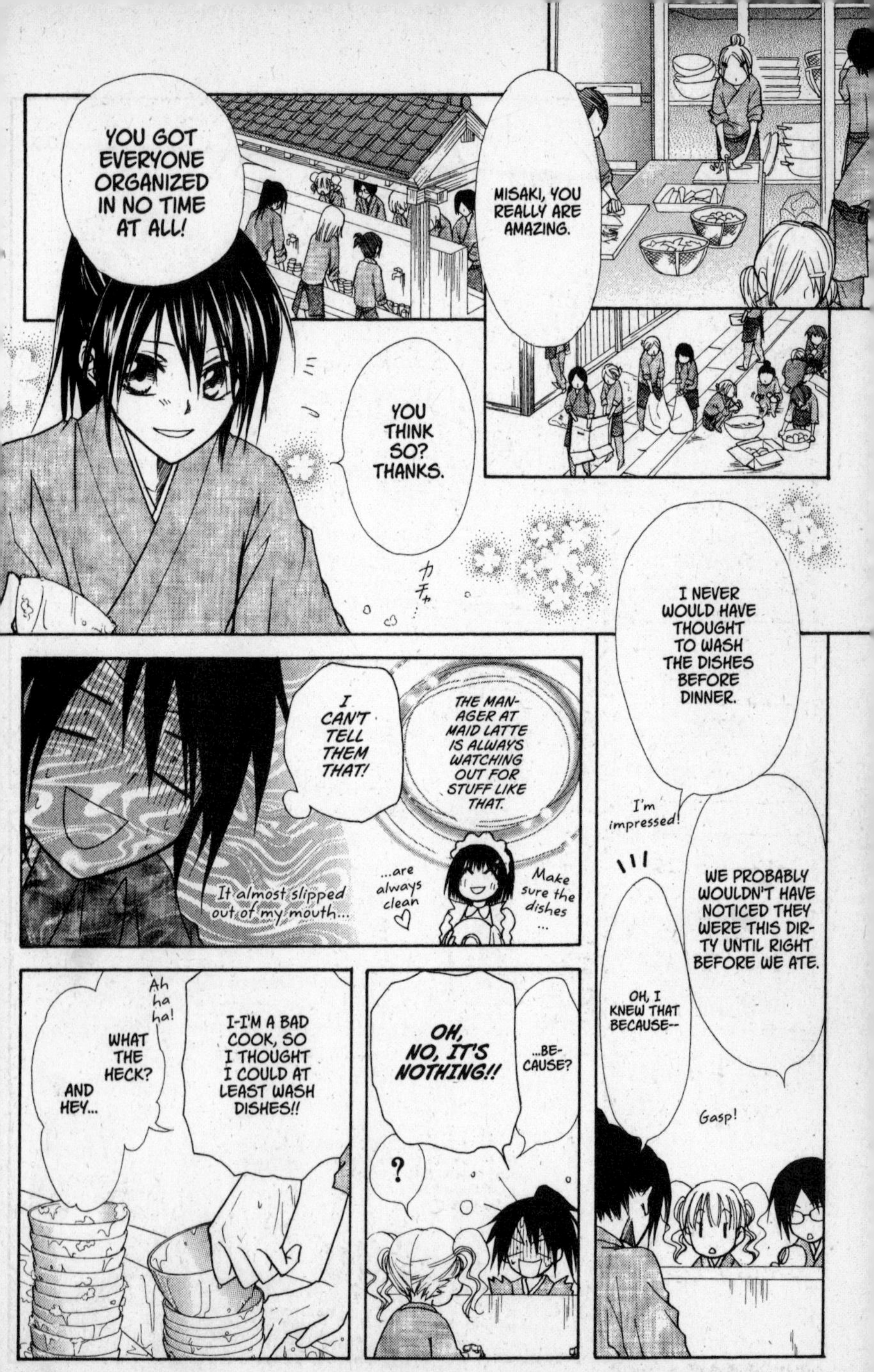
MISAKI, YOU REALLY ARE AMAZING.
YOU GOT EVERYONE ORGANIZED IN NO TIME AT ALL!
YOU THINK SO? THANKS.
カチャ…
I NEVER WOULD HAVE THOUGHT TO WASH THE DISHES BEFORE DINNER.
I'm impressed!
WE PROBABLY WOULDN'T HAVE NOTICED THEY WERE THIS DIRTY UNTIL RIGHT BEFORE WE ATE.
OH, I KNEW THAT BECAUSE--
Gasp!
I CAN'T TELL THEM THAT!
THE MANAGER AT MAID LATTE IS ALWAYS WATCHING OUT FOR STUFF LIKE THAT.
Make sure the dishes...
...are always clean ♡
It almost slipped out of my mouth...
...BECAUSE?
OH, NO, IT'S NOTHING!!
?
I-I'M A BAD COOK, SO I THOUGHT I COULD AT LEAST WASH DISHES!!
Ah ha ha!
WHAT THE HECK?
AND HEY...

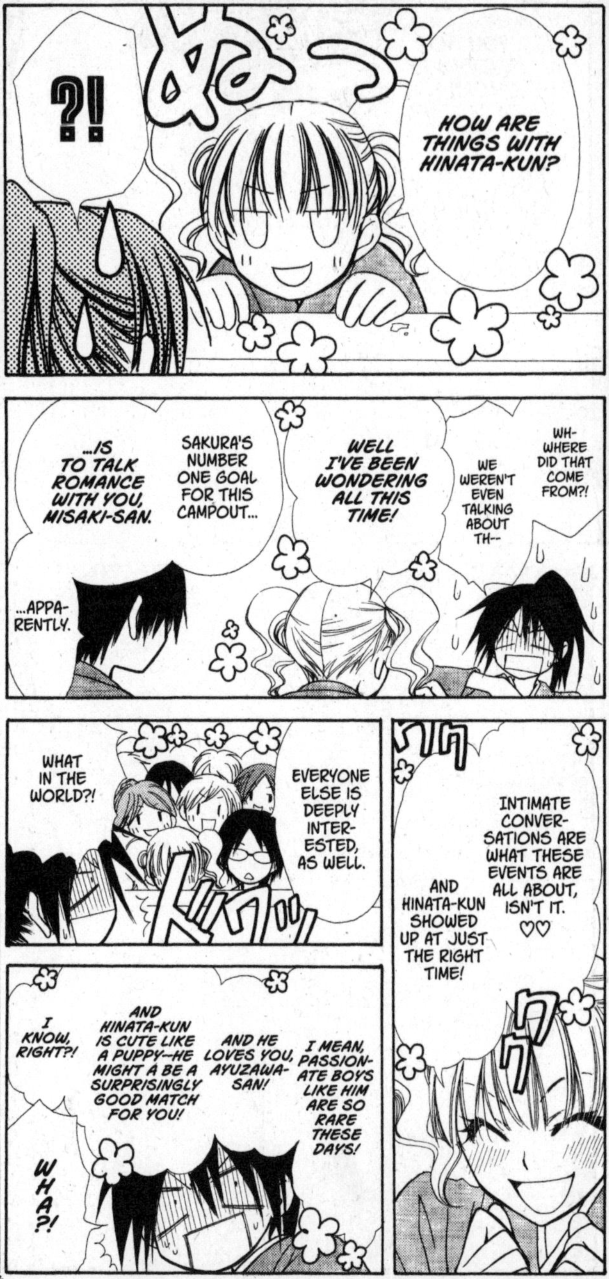
HOW ARE THINGS WITH HINATA-KUN?
ぬっ
?!
WH- WHERE DID THAT COME FROM?!
WE WEREN'T EVEN TALKING ABOUT TH--
WELL I'VE BEEN WONDERING ALL THIS TIME!
SAKURA'S NUMBER ONE GOAL FOR THIS CAMPOUT...
...IS TO TALK ROMANCE WITH YOU, MISAKI-SAN.
...APPARENTLY.
INTIMATE CONVERSATIONS ARE WHAT THESE EVENTS ARE ALL ABOUT, ISN'T IT. ♡♡
AND HINATA-KUN SHOWED UP AT JUST THE RIGHT TIME!
EVERYONE ELSE IS DEEPLY INTERESTED, AS WELL.
WHAT IN THE WORLD?!
I MEAN, PASSIONATE BOYS LIKE HIM ARE SO RARE THESE DAYS!
AND HE LOVES YOU, AYUZAWA-SAN!
AND HINATA-KUN IS CUTE LIKE A PUPPY--HE MIGHT A BE A SURPRISINGLY GOOD MATCH FOR YOU!
I KNOW, RIGHT?!
WHA?!

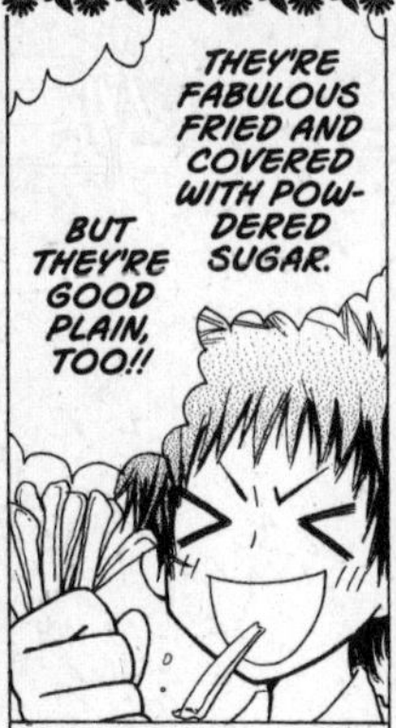
THEY'RE FABULOUS FRIED AND COVERED WITH POWDERED SUGAR.
BUT THEY'RE GOOD PLAIN, TOO!!

Name

Hinata Shintani

Age (Class)

17 (2-1)

Blood Type

AB

Height

177cm (5ft 10in)

Weight

58kg (128 lbs)

Special Skills

I'll eat anything!

Likes

Eating and Misaki-chan

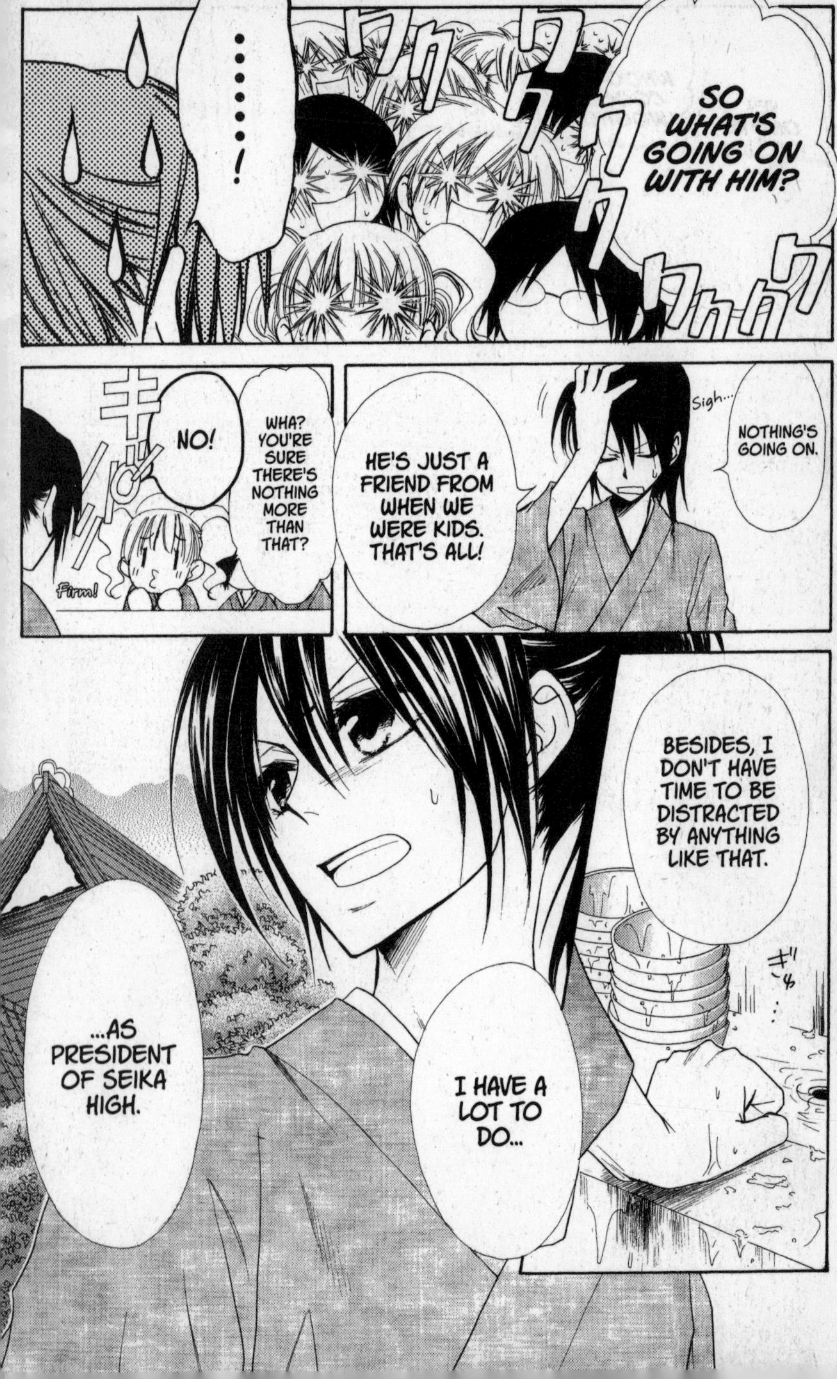
SO WHAT'S GOING ON WITH HIM?
......!
Sigh...
NOTHING'S GOING ON.
HE'S JUST A FRIEND FROM WHEN WE WERE KIDS. THAT'S ALL!
WHA? YOU'RE SURE THERE'S NOTHING MORE THAN THAT?
NO!
Firm!
BESIDES, I DON'T HAVE TIME TO BE DISTRACTED BY ANYTHING LIKE THAT.
I HAVE A LOT TO DO...
...AS PRESIDENT OF SEIKA HIGH.

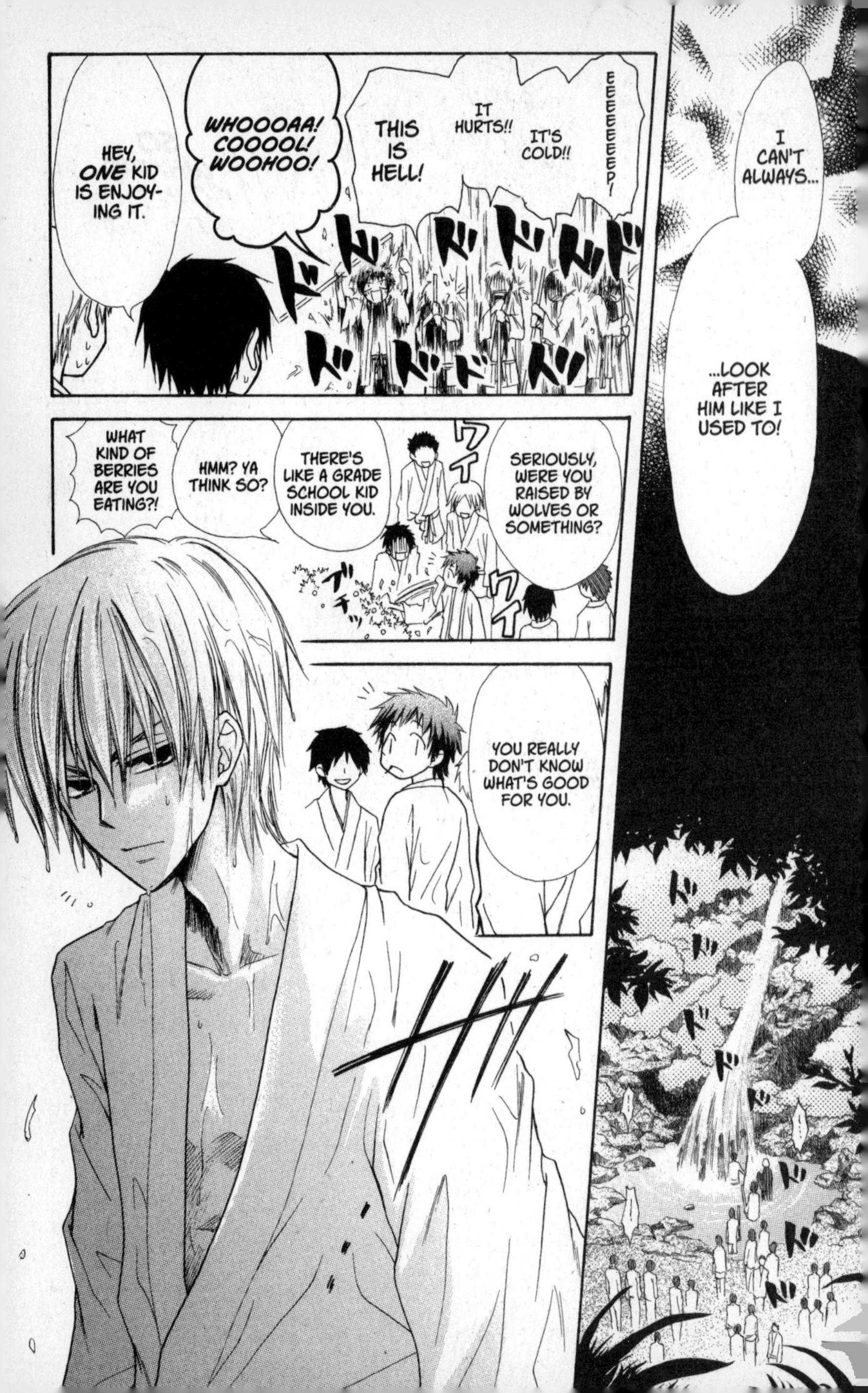
I CAN'T ALWAYS...
...LOOK AFTER HIM LIKE I USED TO!
EEEEEEEEEP!
IT'S COLD!!
IT HURTS!!
THIS IS HELL!
WHOOOAA! COOOOL! WOOHOO!
HEY, ONE KID IS ENJOYING IT.
SERIOUSLY, WERE YOU RAISED BY WOLVES OR SOMETHING?
THERE'S LIKE A GRADE SCHOOL KID INSIDE YOU.
HMM? YA THINK SO?
WHAT KIND OF BERRIES ARE YOU EATING?!
YOU REALLY DON'T KNOW WHAT'S GOOD FOR YOU.

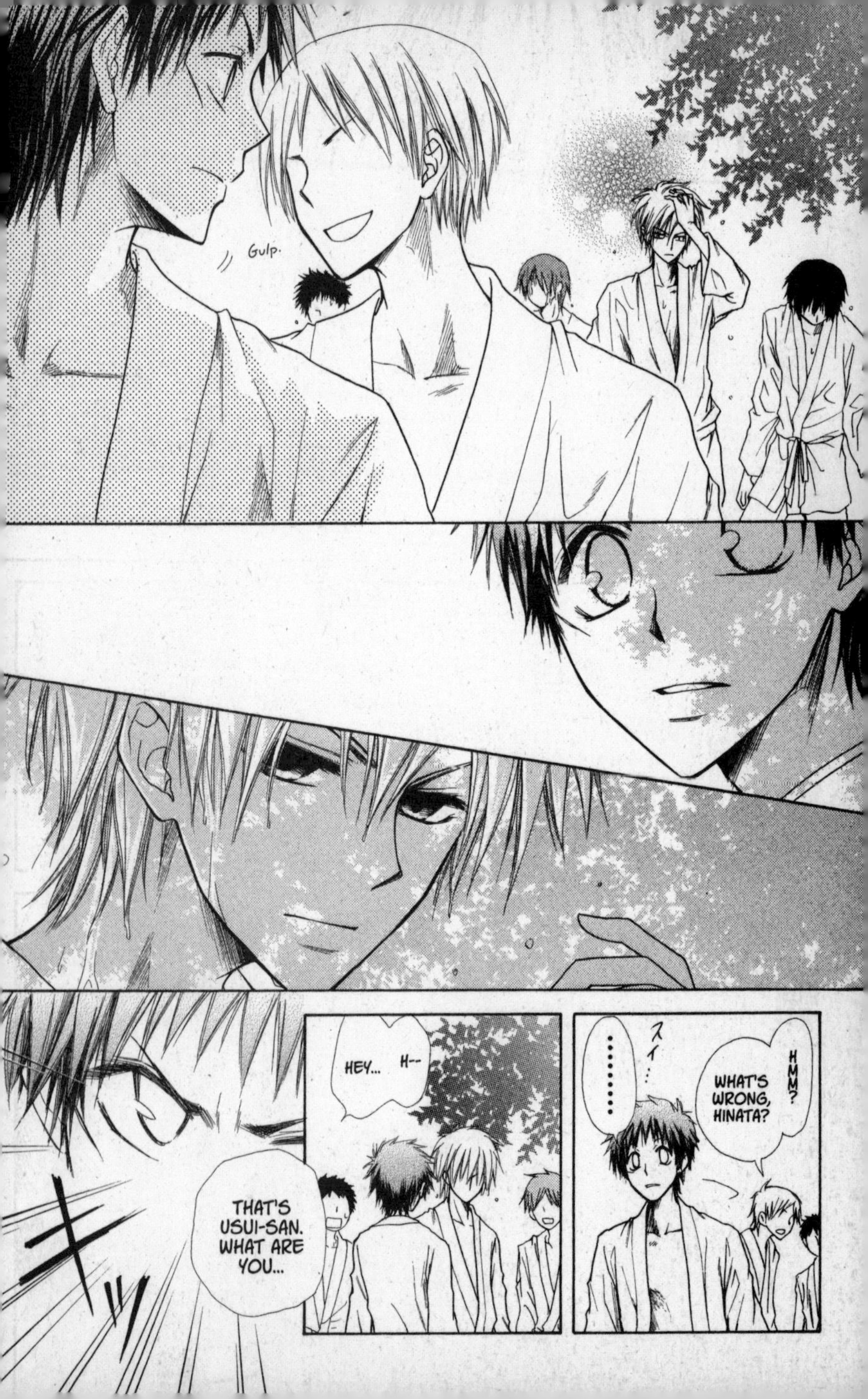
Gulp.
HMM?
WHAT'S WRONG, HINATA?
スイ…
……
HEY... H--
キッ
THAT'S USUI-SAN. WHAT ARE YOU...

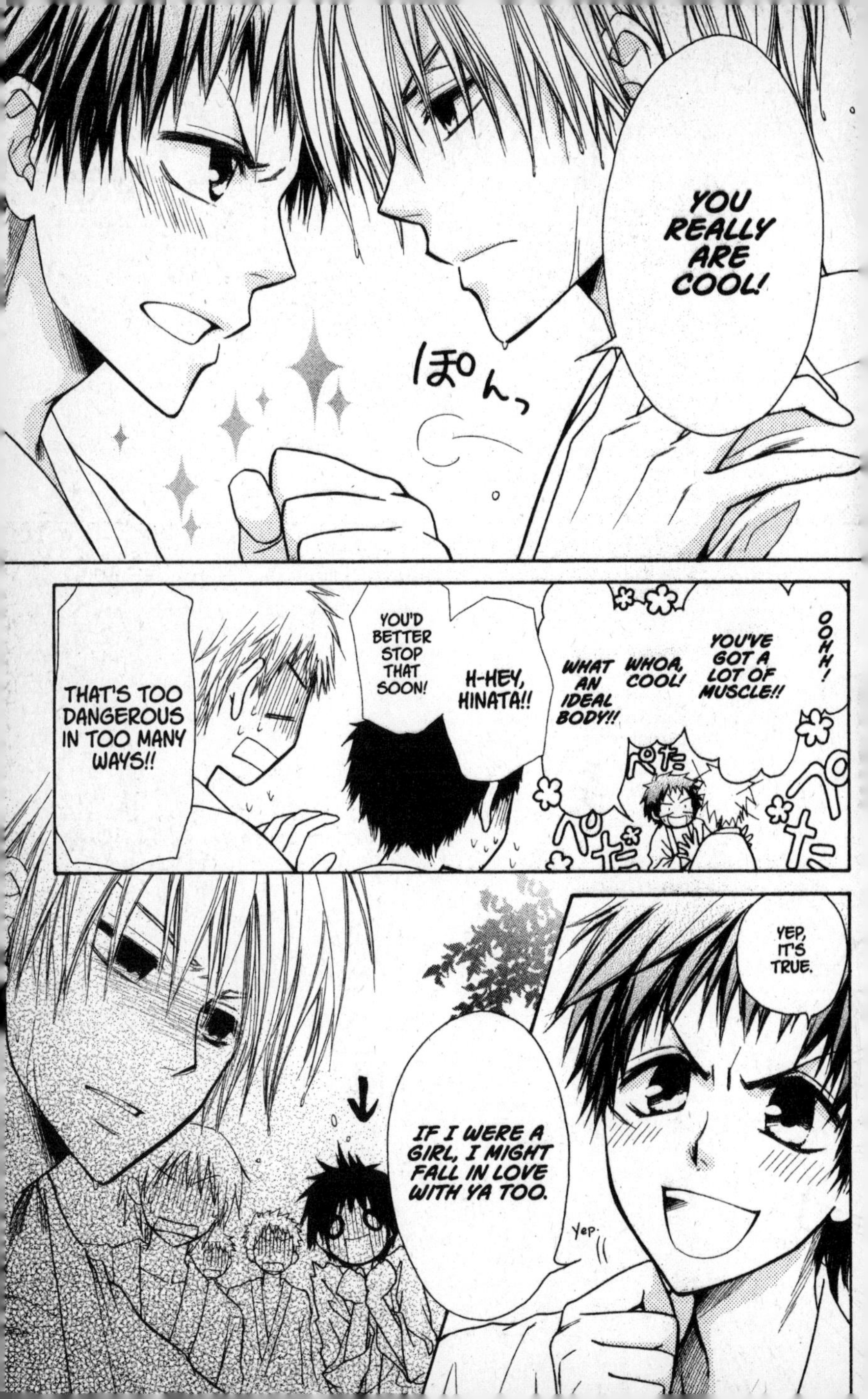
YOU REALLY ARE COOL!
ぽんっ
OOHH!
YOU'VE GOT A LOT OF MUSCLE!!
WHOA, COOL!
WHAT AN IDEAL BODY!!
ぺた ぺた ぺた ぺた
H-HEY, HINATA!!
YOU'D BETTER STOP THAT SOON!
THAT'S TOO DANGEROUS IN TOO MANY WAYS!!
YEP, IT'S TRUE.
IF I WERE A GIRL, I MIGHT FALL IN LOVE WITH YA TOO.
Yep.

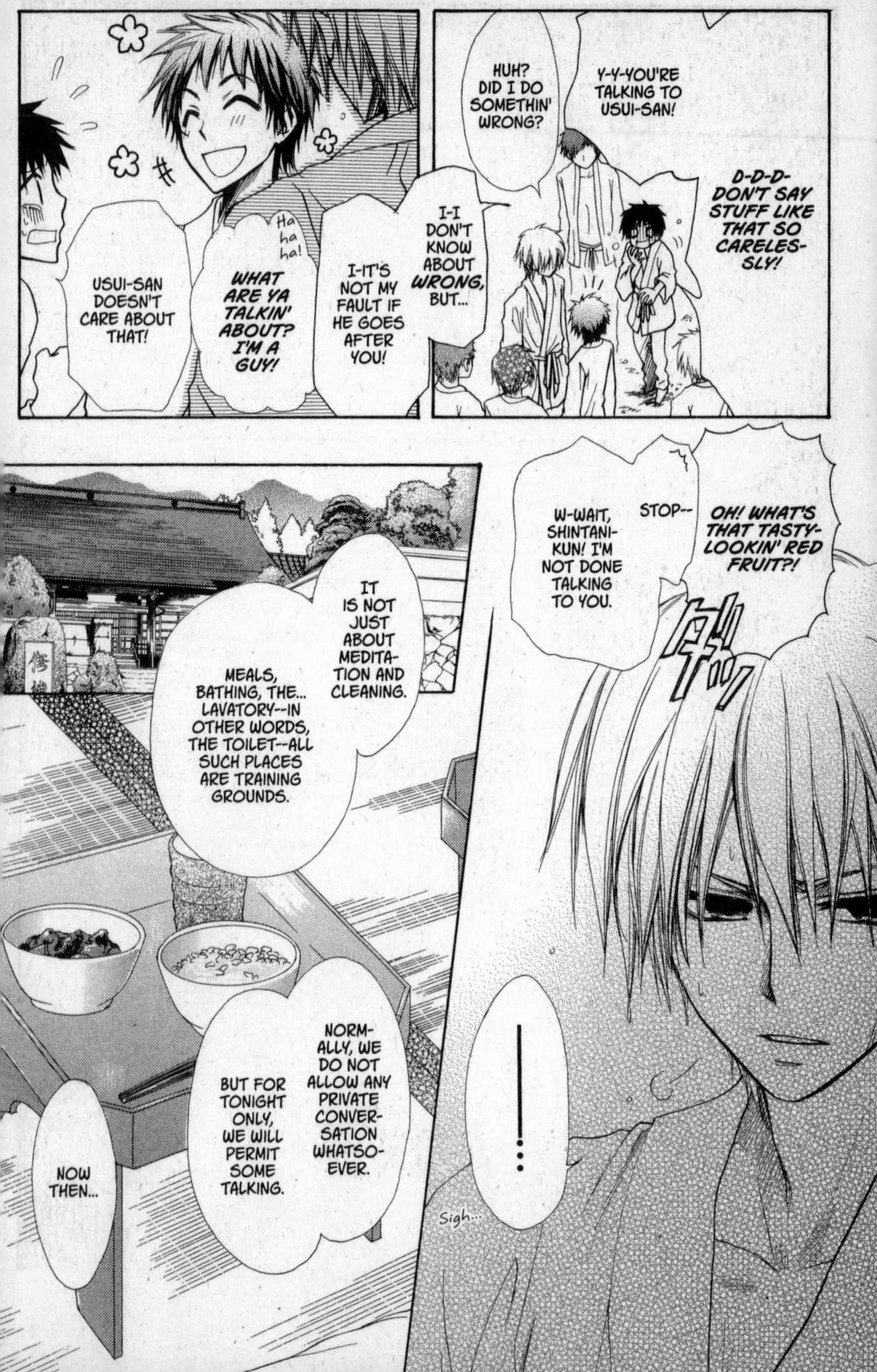
Y-Y-YOU'RE TALKING TO USUI-SAN!
HUH? DID I DO SOMETHIN' WRONG?
D-D-D-DON'T SAY STUFF LIKE THAT SO CARELESSLY!
I-I DON'T KNOW ABOUT WRONG, BUT...
I-IT'S NOT MY FAULT IF HE GOES AFTER YOU!
Ha ha ha!
WHAT ARE YA TALKIN' ABOUT? I'M A GUY!
USUI-SAN DOESN'T CARE ABOUT THAT!
OH! WHAT'S THAT TASTY-LOOKIN' RED FRUIT?!
STOP--
W-WAIT, SHINTANI-KUN! I'M NOT DONE TALKING TO YOU.
......
Sigh...
IT IS NOT JUST ABOUT MEDITATION AND CLEANING.
MEALS, BATHING, THE... LAVATORY--IN OTHER WORDS, THE TOILET--ALL SUCH PLACES ARE TRAINING GROUNDS.
NORMALLY, WE DO NOT ALLOW ANY PRIVATE CONVERSATION WHATSOEVER.
BUT FOR TONIGHT ONLY, WE WILL PERMIT SOME TALKING.
NOW THEN...

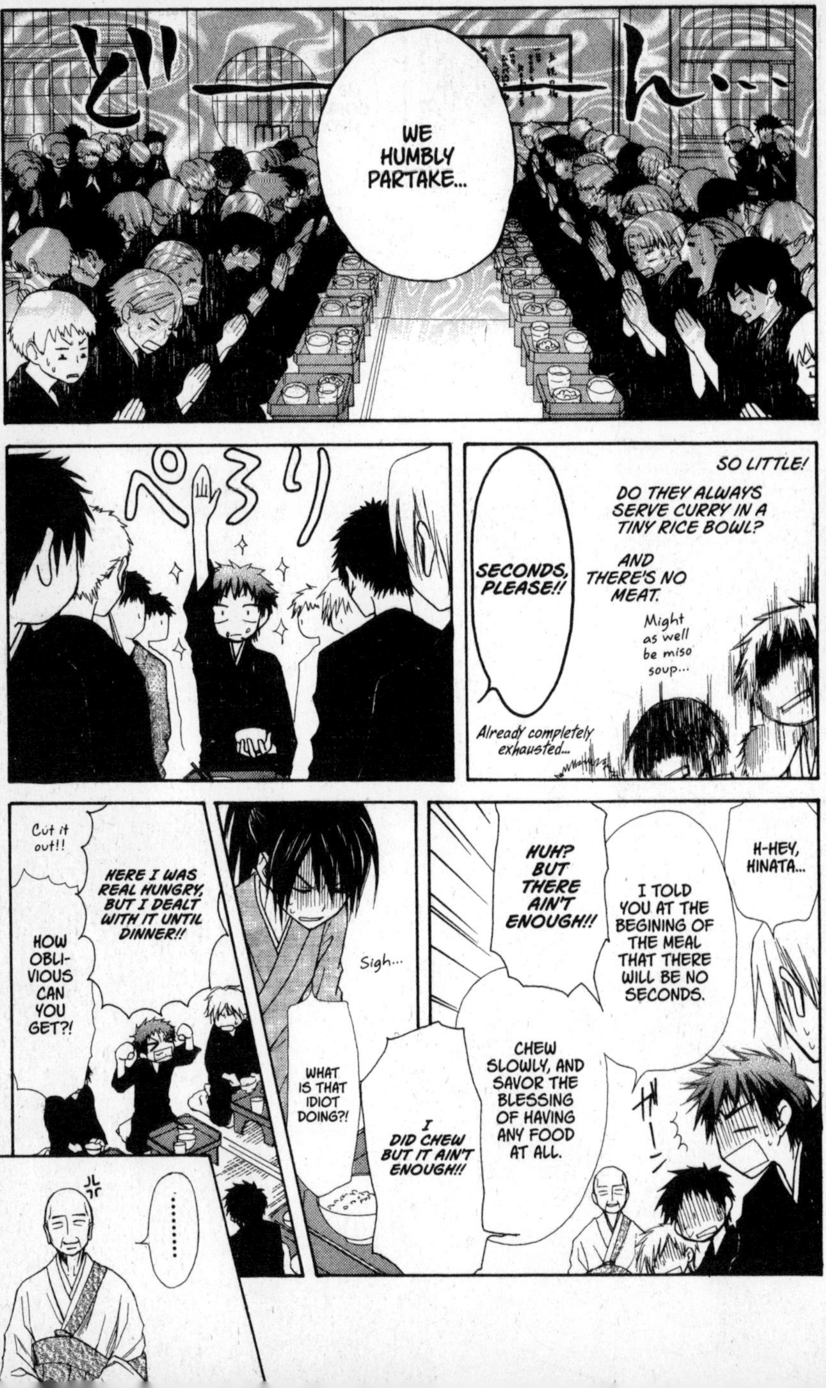
WE HUMBLY PARTAKE...
SO LITTLE!
DO THEY ALWAYS SERVE CURRY IN A TINY RICE BOWL?
AND THERE'S NO MEAT.
Might as well be miso soup...
SECONDS, PLEASE!!
Already completely exhausted...
ぺろり
H-HEY, HINATA...
I TOLD YOU AT THE BEGINING OF THE MEAL THAT THERE WILL BE NO SECONDS.
HUH? BUT THERE AIN'T ENOUGH!!
CHEW SLOWLY, AND SAVOR THE BLESSING OF HAVING ANY FOOD AT ALL.
I DID CHEW BUT IT AIN'T ENOUGH!!
Sigh...
WHAT IS THAT IDIOT DOING?!
HERE I WAS REAL HUNGRY, BUT I DEALT WITH IT UNTIL DINNER!!
Cut it out!!
HOW OBLIVIOUS CAN YOU GET?!
......

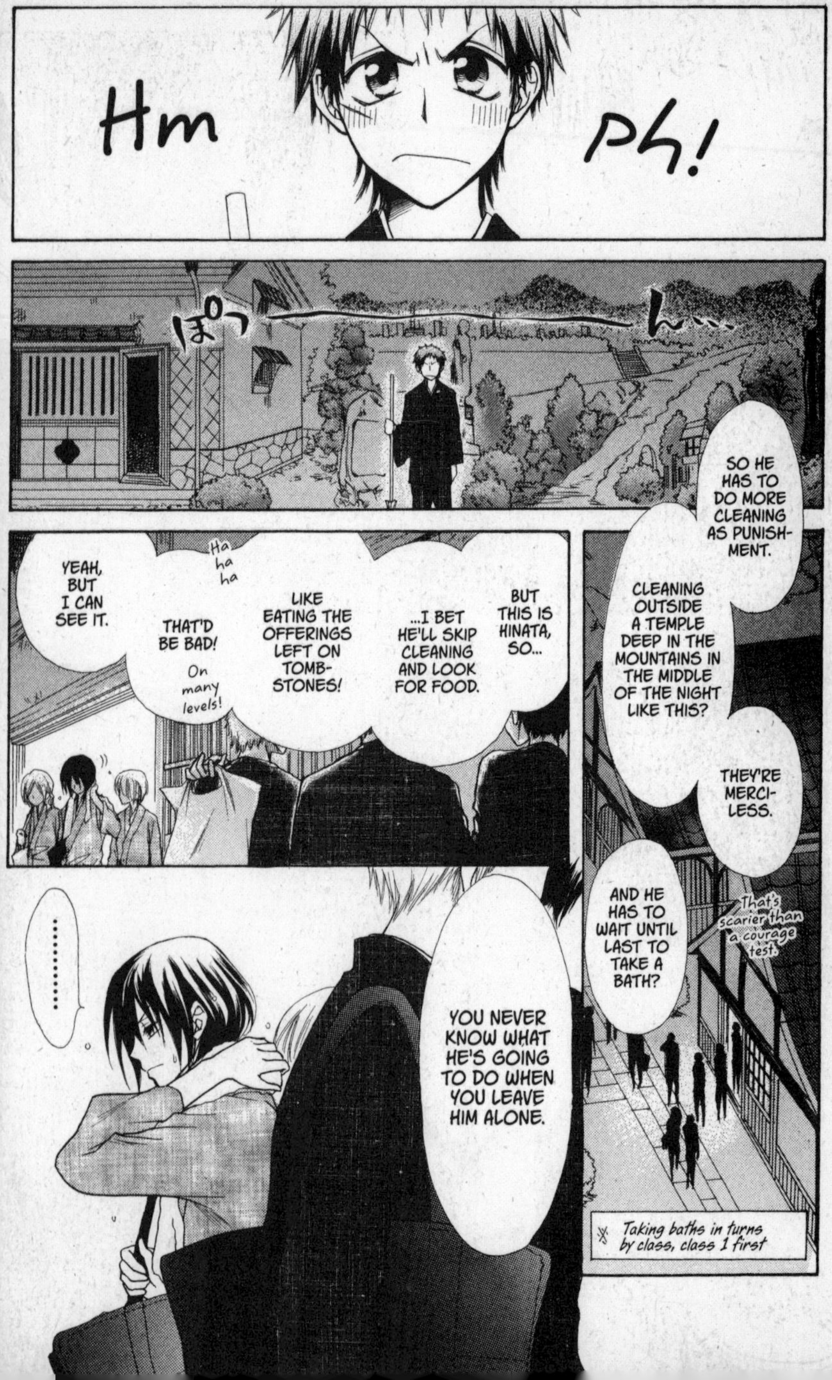
Hm
ph!
ぽつ———ん...
SO HE HAS TO DO MORE CLEANING AS PUNISH-MENT.
CLEANING OUTSIDE A TEMPLE DEEP IN THE MOUNTAINS IN THE MIDDLE OF THE NIGHT LIKE THIS?
THEY'RE MERCI-LESS.
AND HE HAS TO WAIT UNTIL LAST TO TAKE A BATH?
That's scarier than a courage test.
※ Taking baths in turns by class, class 1 first
BUT THIS IS HINATA, SO...
...I BET HE'LL SKIP CLEANING AND LOOK FOR FOOD.
LIKE EATING THE OFFERINGS LEFT ON TOMB-STONES!
Ha ha ha
THAT'D BE BAD!
On many levels!
YEAH, BUT I CAN SEE IT.
YOU NEVER KNOW WHAT HE'S GOING TO DO WHEN YOU LEAVE HIM ALONE.
......

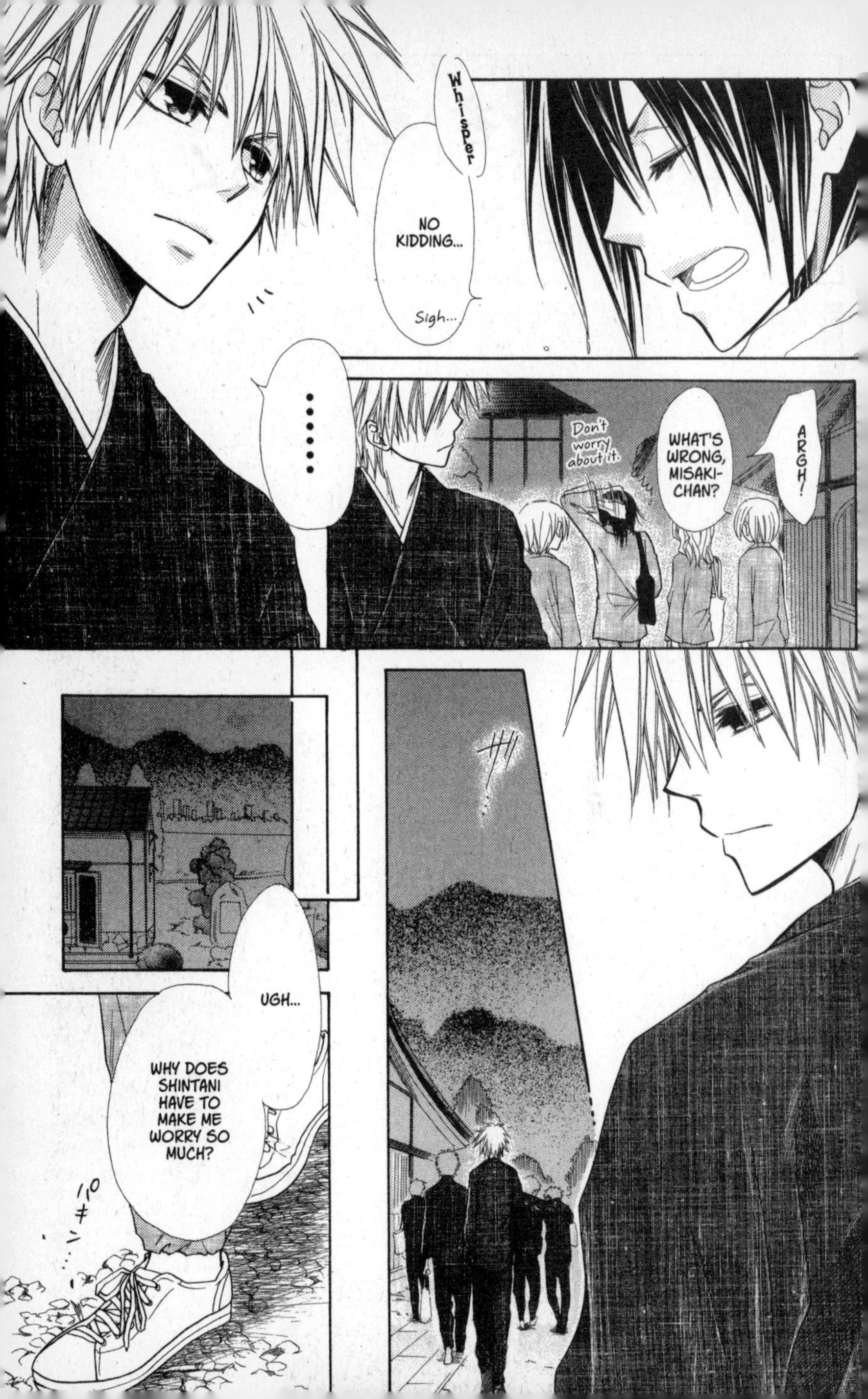

Whisper
NO KIDDING...
Sigh...
......
ARGH!
WHAT'S WRONG, MISAKI-CHAN?
Don't worry about it.
UGH...
WHY DOES SHINTANI HAVE TO MAKE ME WORRY SO MUCH?

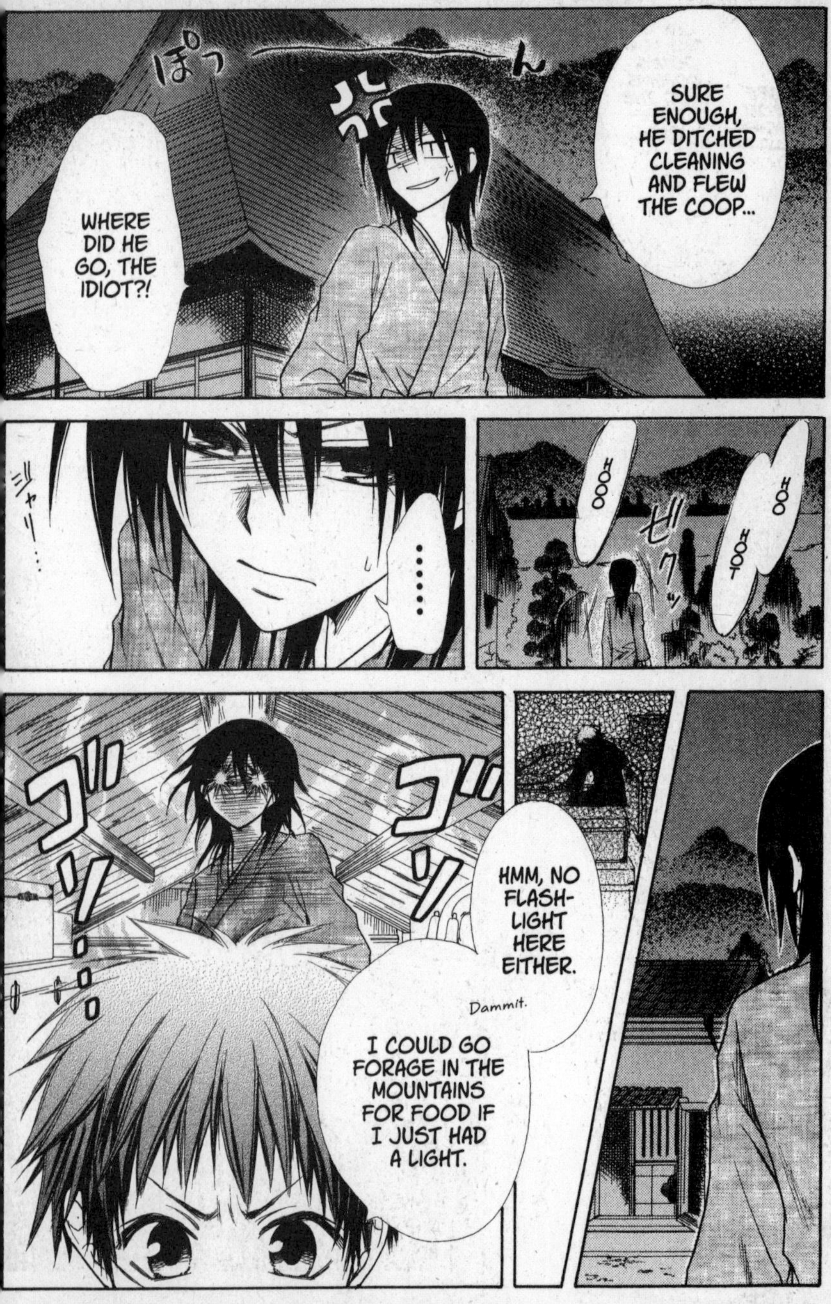
ぽっ———ん
SURE ENOUGH, HE DITCHED CLEANING AND FLEW THE COOP...
WHERE DID HE GO, THE IDIOT?!
HOO HOOT
HOOO
ギクッ
ジャリ…
......
ゴゴゴ…
HMM, NO FLASH-LIGHT HERE EITHER.
Dammit.
I COULD GO FORAGE IN THE MOUNTAINS FOR FOOD IF I JUST HAD A LIGHT.

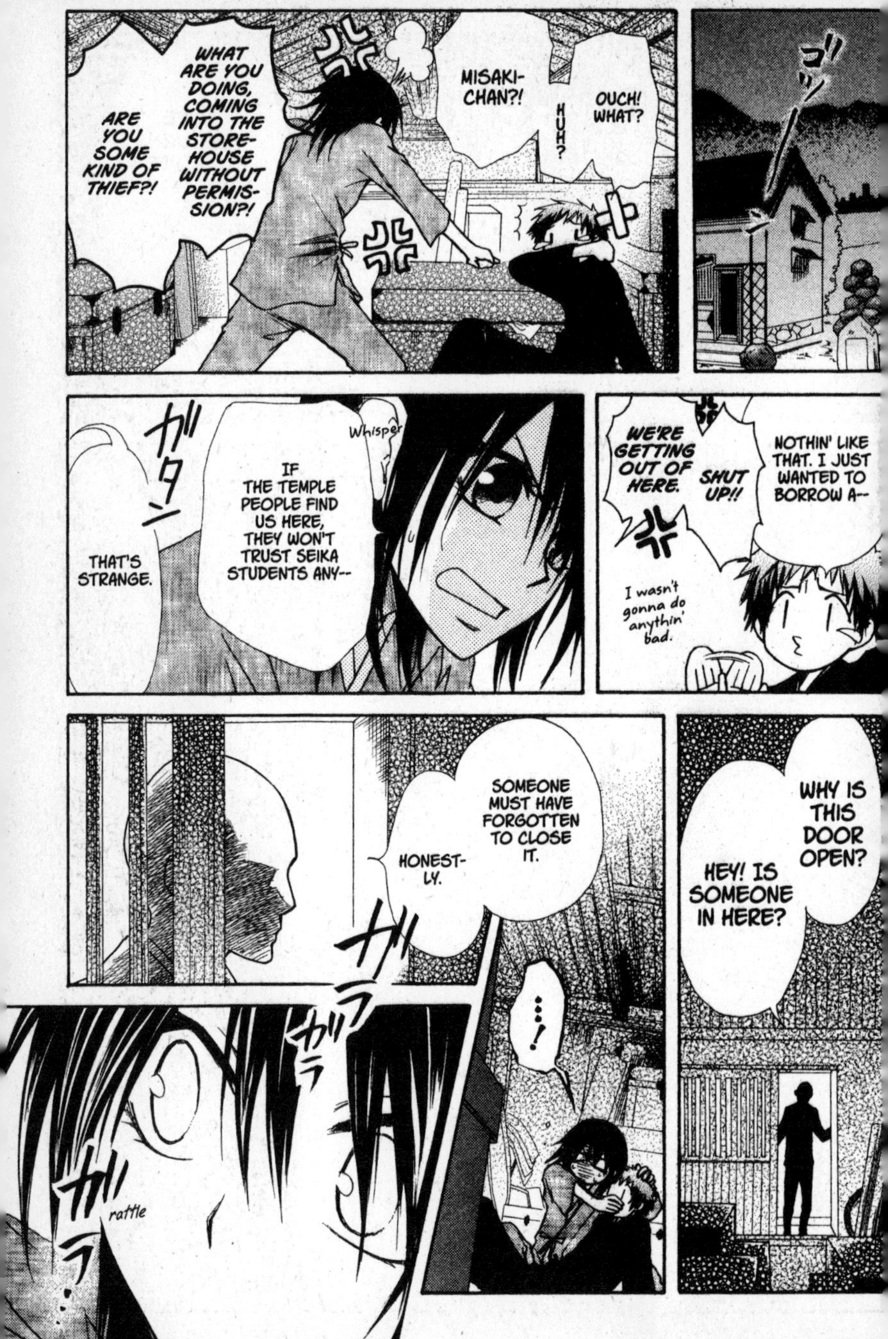
OUCH! WHAT?
HUH?
MISAKI-CHAN?!
WHAT ARE YOU DOING, COMING INTO THE STOREHOUSE WITHOUT PERMISSION?!
ARE YOU SOME KIND OF THIEF?!
NOTHIN' LIKE THAT. I JUST WANTED TO BORROW A--
SHUT UP!!
WE'RE GETTING OUT OF HERE.
I wasn't gonna do anythin' bad.
Whisper
IF THE TEMPLE PEOPLE FIND US HERE, THEY WON'T TRUST SEIKA STUDENTS ANY--
THAT'S STRANGE.
WHY IS THIS DOOR OPEN?
HEY! IS SOMEONE IN HERE?
SOMEONE MUST HAVE FORGOTTEN TO CLOSE IT.
HONEST-LY.
...!
rattle

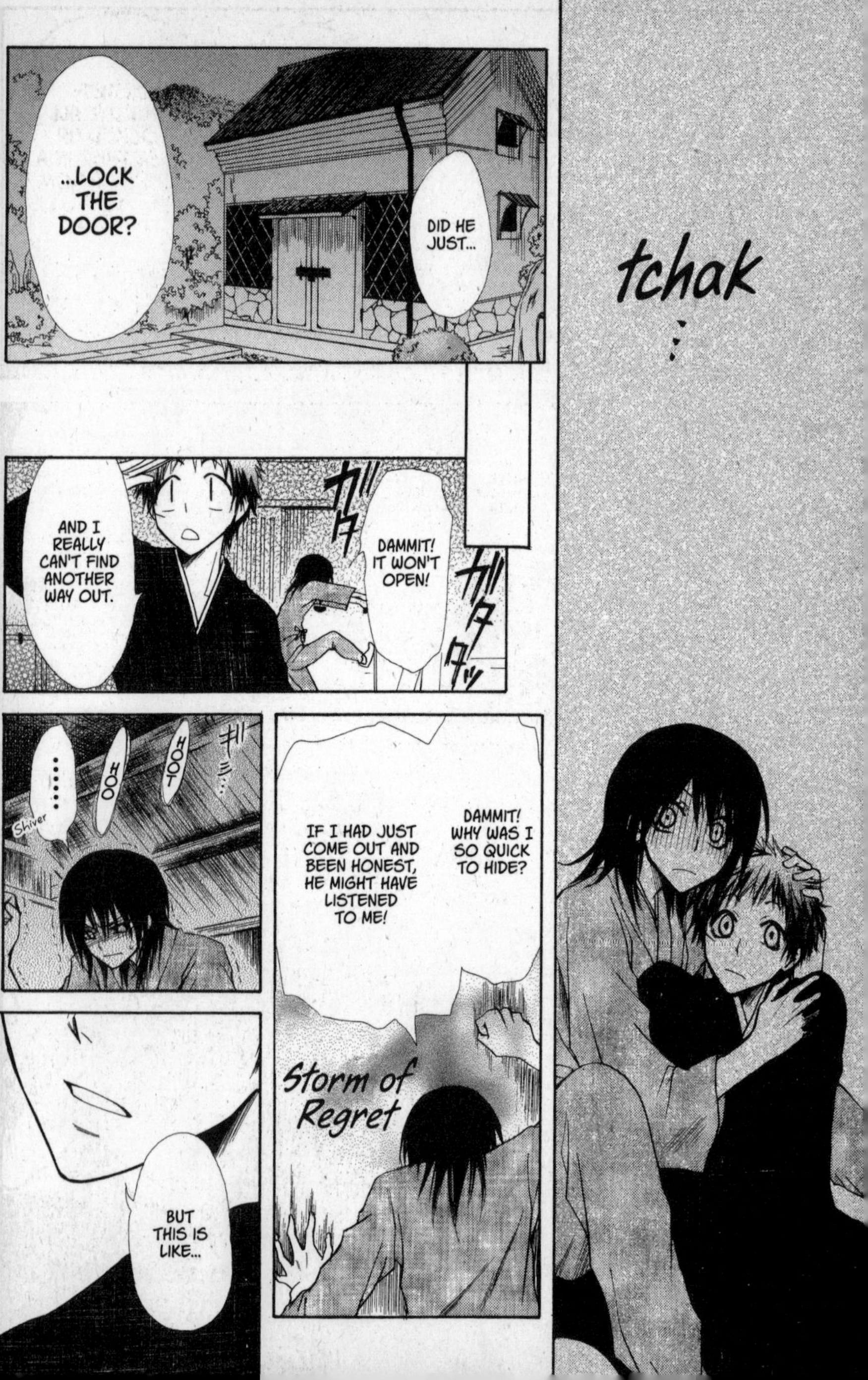
tchak
DID HE JUST...
...LOCK THE DOOR?
DAMMIT! IT WON'T OPEN!
AND I REALLY CAN'T FIND ANOTHER WAY OUT.
DAMMIT! WHY WAS I SO QUICK TO HIDE?
IF I HAD JUST COME OUT AND BEEN HONEST, HE MIGHT HAVE LISTENED TO ME!
Storm of Regret
HOOT
HOO
......
Shiver
BUT THIS IS LIKE...

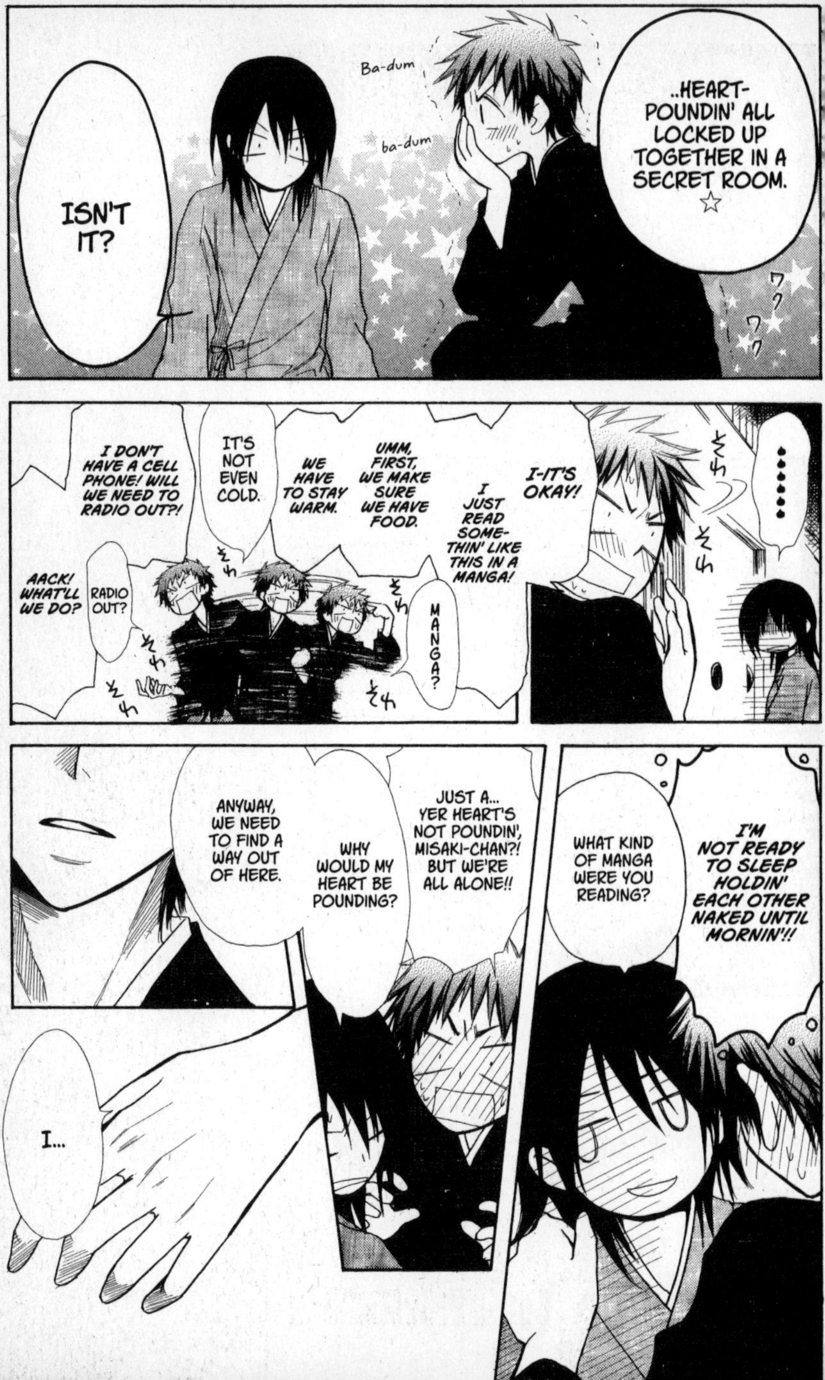
..HEART-POUNDIN' ALL LOCKED UP TOGETHER IN A SECRET ROOM. ☆
Ba-dum
ba-dum
ワクワク
ISN'T IT?
......
I-IT'S OKAY!
I JUST READ SOME-THIN' LIKE THIS IN A MANGA!
UMM, FIRST, WE MAKE SURE WE HAVE FOOD.
WE HAVE TO STAY WARM.
IT'S NOT EVEN COLD.
I DON'T HAVE A CELL PHONE! WILL WE NEED TO RADIO OUT?!
MANGA?
RADIO OUT?
AACK! WHAT'LL WE DO?
I'M NOT READY TO SLEEP HOLDIN' EACH OTHER NAKED UNTIL MORNIN'!!
WHAT KIND OF MANGA WERE YOU READING?
JUST A... YER HEART'S NOT POUNDIN', MISAKI-CHAN?! BUT WE'RE ALL ALONE!!
WHY WOULD MY HEART BE POUNDING?
ANYWAY, WE NEED TO FIND A WAY OUT OF HERE.
I...

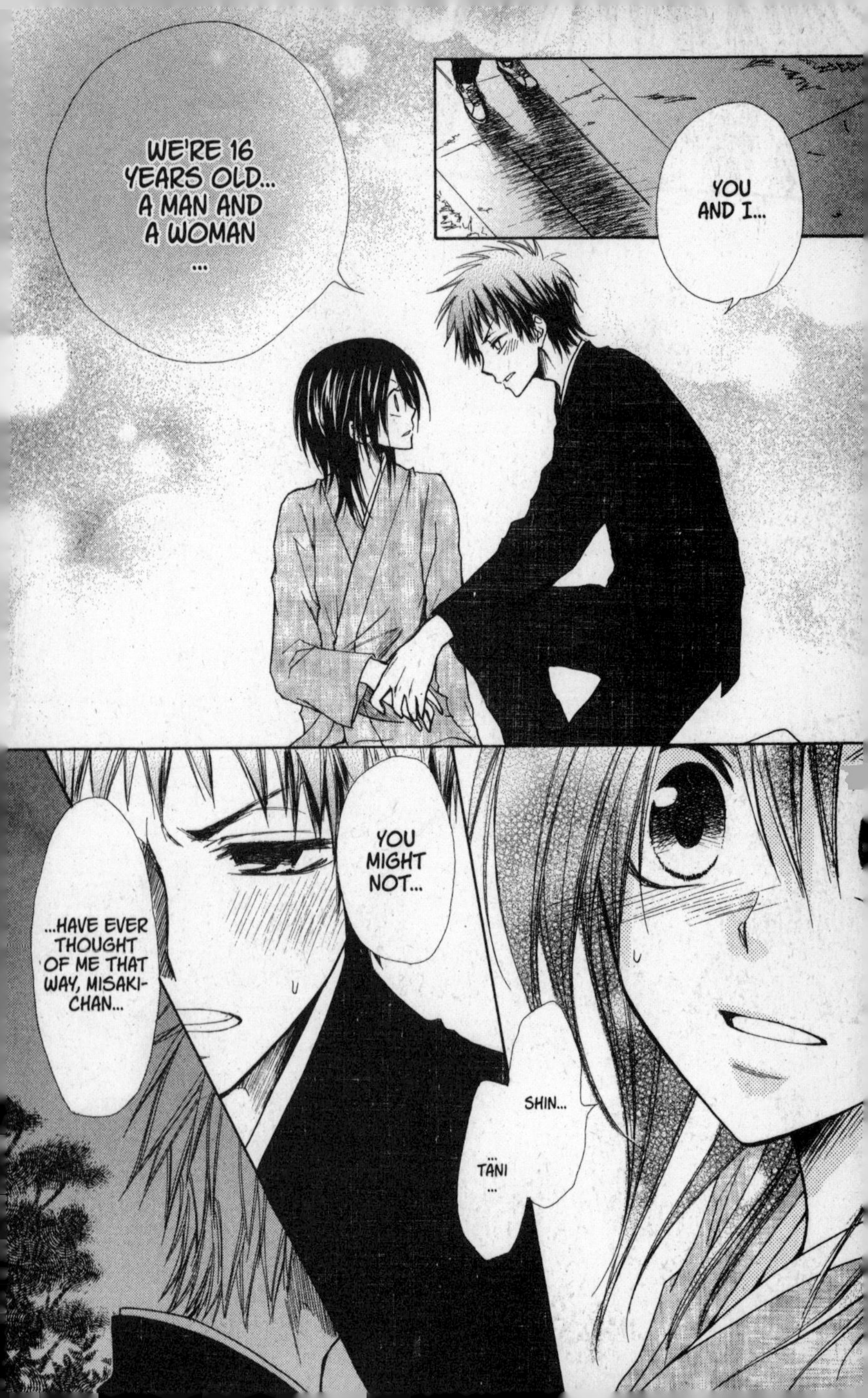
YOU AND I...
WE'RE 16 YEARS OLD... A MAN AND A WOMAN ...
YOU MIGHT NOT...
...HAVE EVER THOUGHT OF ME THAT WAY, MISAKI-CHAN...
SHIN...
...TANI ...

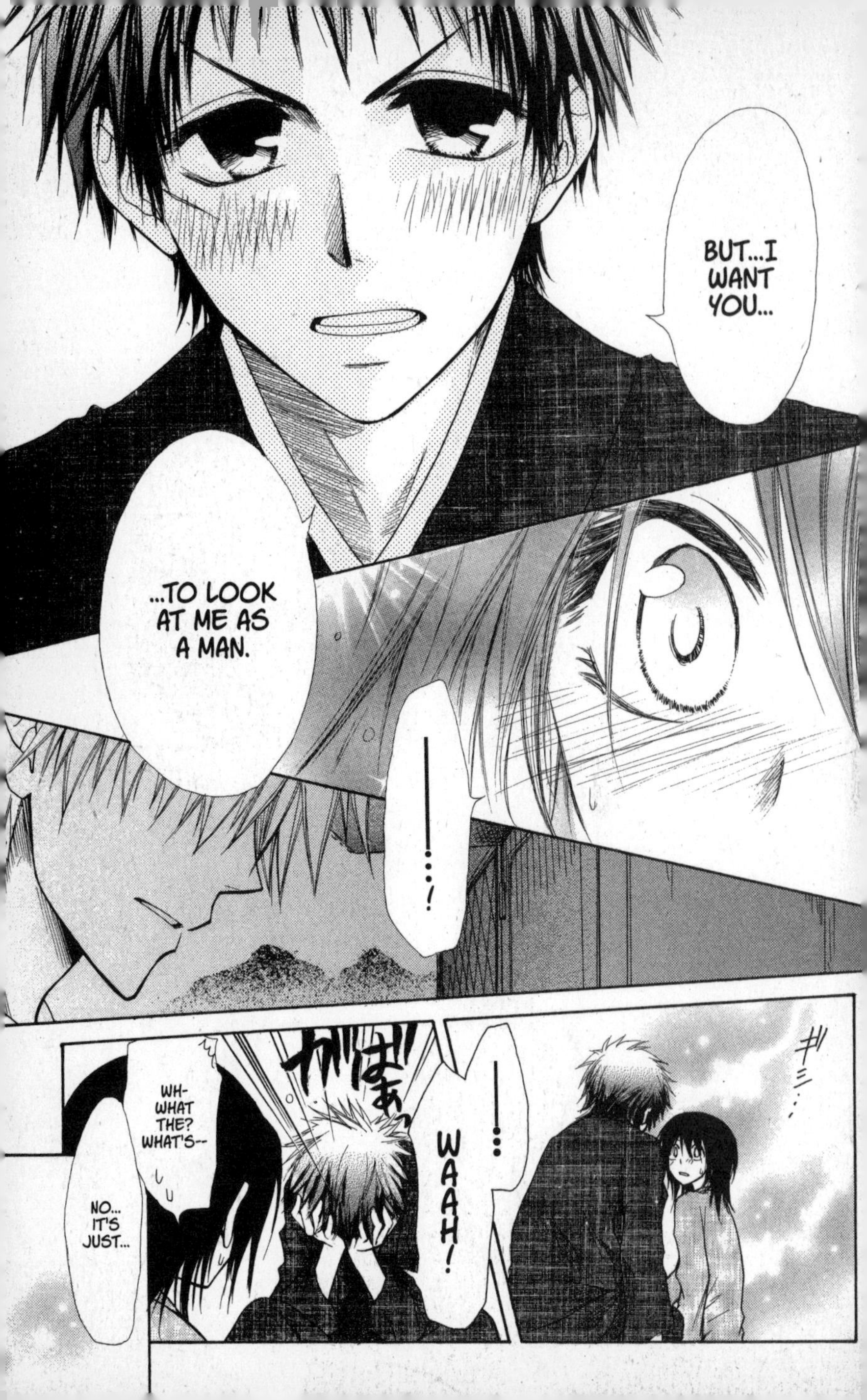
BUT...I WANT YOU...
...TO LOOK AT ME AS A MAN.
—...!
—...
WAAH!
WH-WHAT THE? WHAT'S--
NO... IT'S JUST...

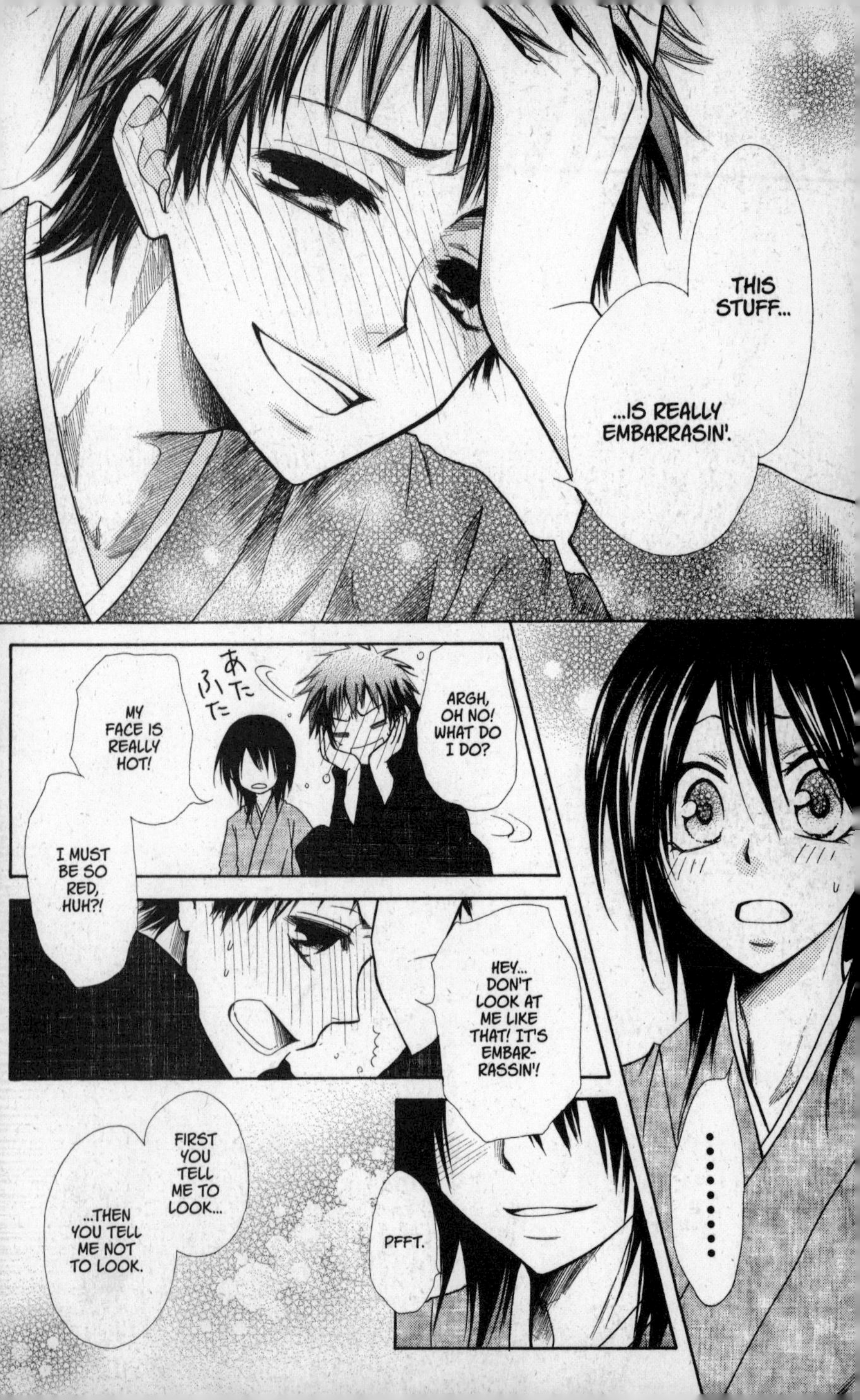

THIS STUFF...
...IS REALLY EMBARRASIN'.
......
ARGH, OH NO! WHAT DO I DO?
あたふた
MY FACE IS REALLY HOT!
I MUST BE SO RED, HUH?!
HEY... DON'T LOOK AT ME LIKE THAT! IT'S EMBAR-RASSIN'!
PFFT.
FIRST YOU TELL ME TO LOOK...
...THEN YOU TELL ME NOT TO LOOK.

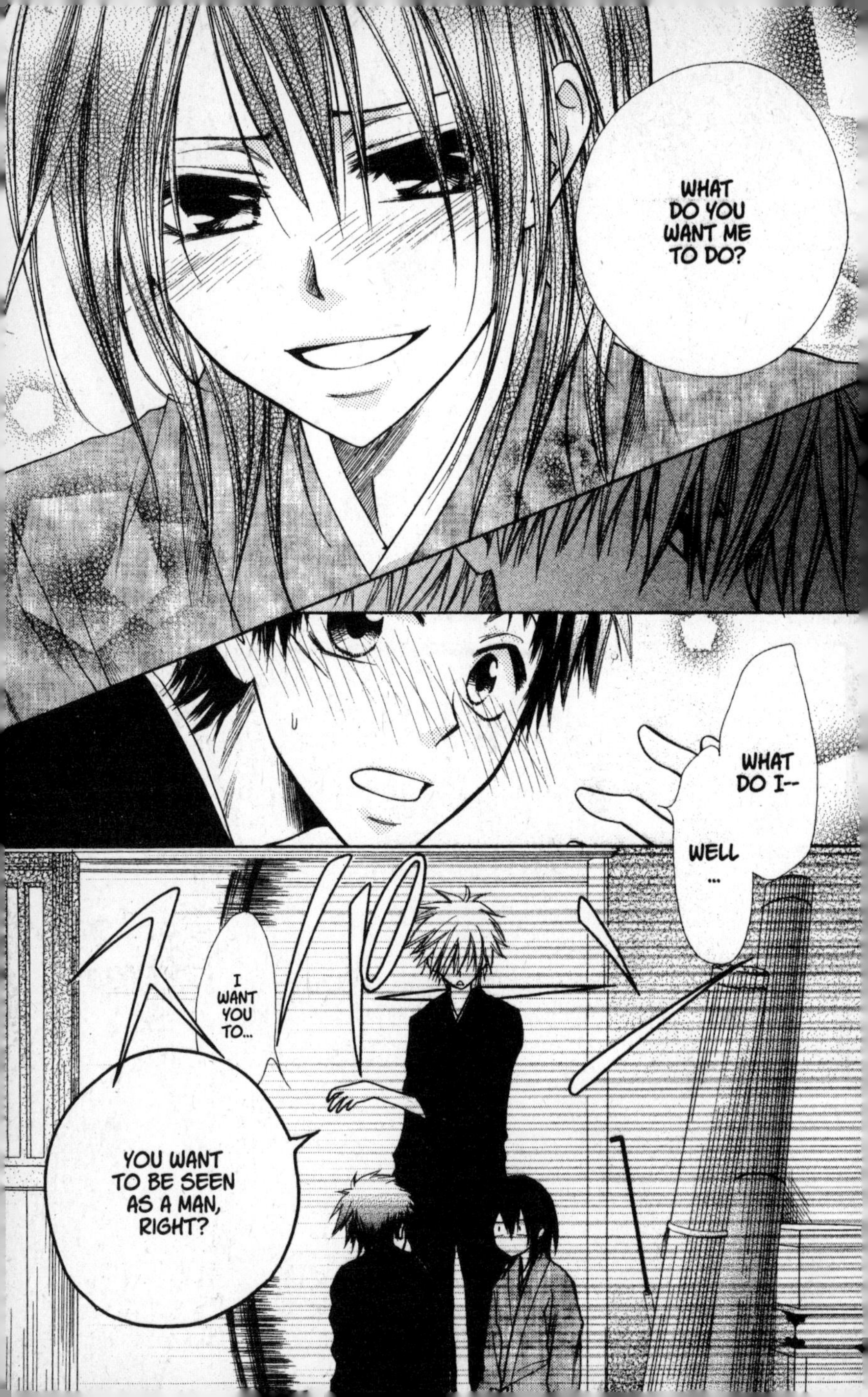
WHAT DO YOU WANT ME TO DO?
WHAT DO I--
WELL ...
I WANT YOU TO...
YOU WANT TO BE SEEN AS A MAN, RIGHT?

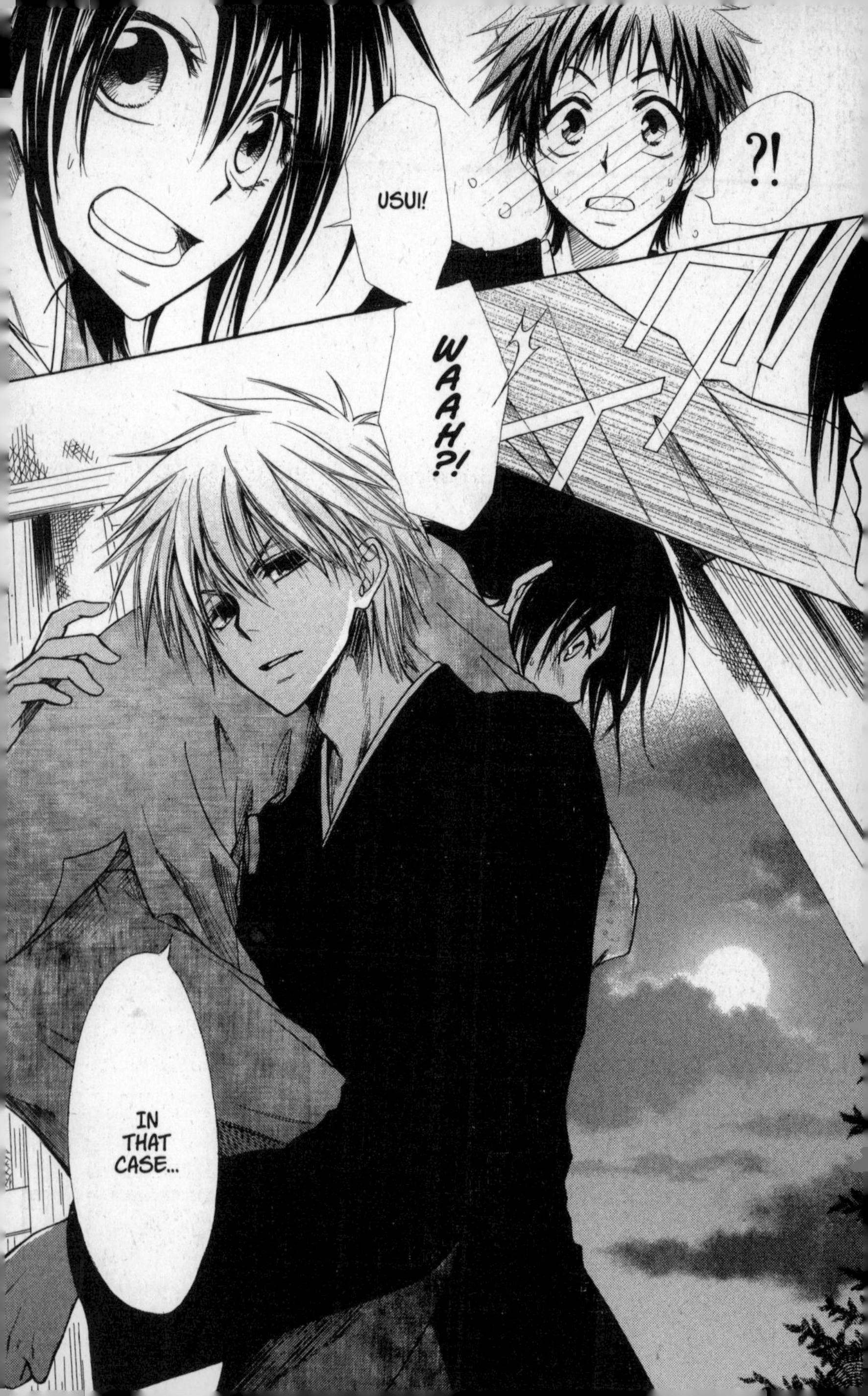
?!
USUI!
WAAAH?!
IN THAT CASE...

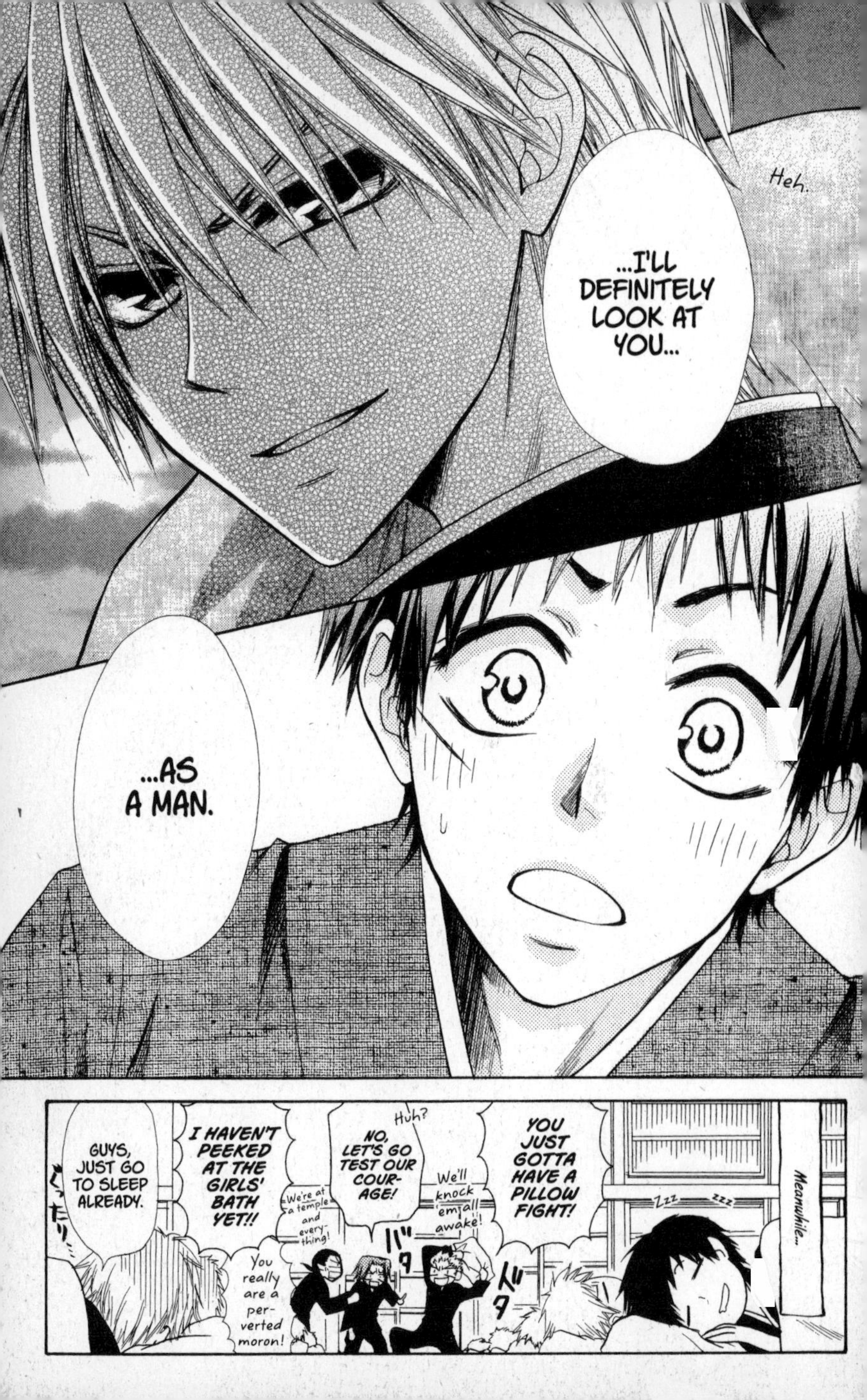
Heh.
...I'LL DEFINITELY LOOK AT YOU...
...AS A MAN.
Meanwhile...
YOU JUST GOTTA HAVE A PILLOW FIGHT!
Zzz
zzz
We'll knock 'em all awake!
Huh?
NO, LET'S GO TEST OUR COURAGE!
We're at a temple and everything!
I HAVEN'T PEEKED AT THE GIRLS' BATH YET!!
You really are a perverted moron!
GUYS, JUST GO TO SLEEP ALREADY.

OH NO! WHAT'S THIS, WHAT'S THIS?! A QUESTION AND ANSWER CORNER?! YOU WANT TO KNOW ABOUT MAID LATTE, RIGHT?! I'M SO HAPPY! I'M THE MANAGER, SATSUKI-SAN, AND I'LL BE HAPPY TO TELL YOU ANYTHING YOU WANT TO KNOW!!

QUESTION 9: WHAT IS THE MENU LIKE AT MAID LATTE?

· GOOD QUESTION. WELL, NO MATTER WHAT, FIRST, I HAVE TO MENTION THE *CUTESY-WUTESY RICE OMELET!* OTHER THAN THAT, WE HAVE AN ASSORTMENT OF LIGHT ENTREES LIKE PASTA AND SANDWICHES. WE EMPHASIZE *TASTE* OVER *ORIGINALITY* SO EVERYONE CAN ENJOY THEIR FOOD WITHOUT WORRYING ABOUT WHAT IT'LL TASTE LIKE. OF COURSE, WE ALSO HAVE SWEETS LIKE PARFAITS, CAKE, AND SOME EXTRAORDINARILY ADORABLE ICE CREAM PLATES. FOR DRINKS, WE HAVE COFFEE, TEA, AND SOFT DRINKS. WE DON'T SERVE ALCOHOL. BUT TO MAKE UP FOR IT, WE HAVE A *WIDE VARIETY OF TEAS*. I WOULD DEFINITELY RECOMMEND SOME DELICIOUS TEA TO GO WITH YOUR ENTREE AND DESSERT! ☆ THAT ABOUT DESCRIBES THE BASIC MENU, BUT *WHEN WE HAVE EVENTS, WE HAVE SPECIAL MENUS*. FOOD TO GO WITH THE SEASON, SOMETHING MADE PERSONALLY BY OUR MAIDS...THINGS YOU CAN LOOK FORWARD TO ON THOSE SPECIAL DAYS. ♡

QUESTION 10: WHO IS THE MOST POPULAR AT MAID LATTE?

: HMM, GOOD QUESTION...IT'S OUR POLICY NOT TO ASSIGN POPULARITY RANKS, SO IT'S NOT LIKE I CAN GIVE YOU A PRECISE ANSWER, BUT...FOR EXAMPLE, *HONOKA-CHAN* IS A *SOOTHING TYPE*, SO SHE'S POPULAR WITH A WIDE RANGE OF REGULAR CUSTOMERS AS WELL AS FIRST-TIMERS. SHE'S ALSO *EQUIPPED WITH ENOUGH DEEP KNOWLEDGE* TO HAVE A PLEASANT CONVERSATION WITH ANYONE. SHE'S A VERY RESOURCEFUL MAID. *ERIKA-CHAN* ATTRACTS PEOPLE WITH *HER NICE BODY* AND *BIG HEART*, AND *SUBARU-CHAN* HAS A LOYAL FOLLOWING AS A *TRADITIONAL MAID*. WE HAVE MANY OTHER CHARMING GIRLS, BUT I SUPPOSE THOSE THREE HAVE A STRONG PRESENCE BECAUSE THEY SPEND SO MUCH TIME AT THE CAFE. *MISA-CHAN* IS AN EVEN MATCH FOR THOSE THREE VETERANS, HOWEVER! THERE WAS A TIME AT THE BEGINNING WHEN SHE WASN'T MAKING MUCH PROGRESS, BUT SHE *LEARNS QUICKLY*, AND SHE'S A *HARD WORKER*, SO SHE QUICKLY BECAME A FINE MAID. OH! WE'RE DONE ALREADY?! THAT'S TOO BAD. I'VE HARDLY TOLD YOU ANYTHING! ASK ME ANOTHER QUESTION SOME TIME!

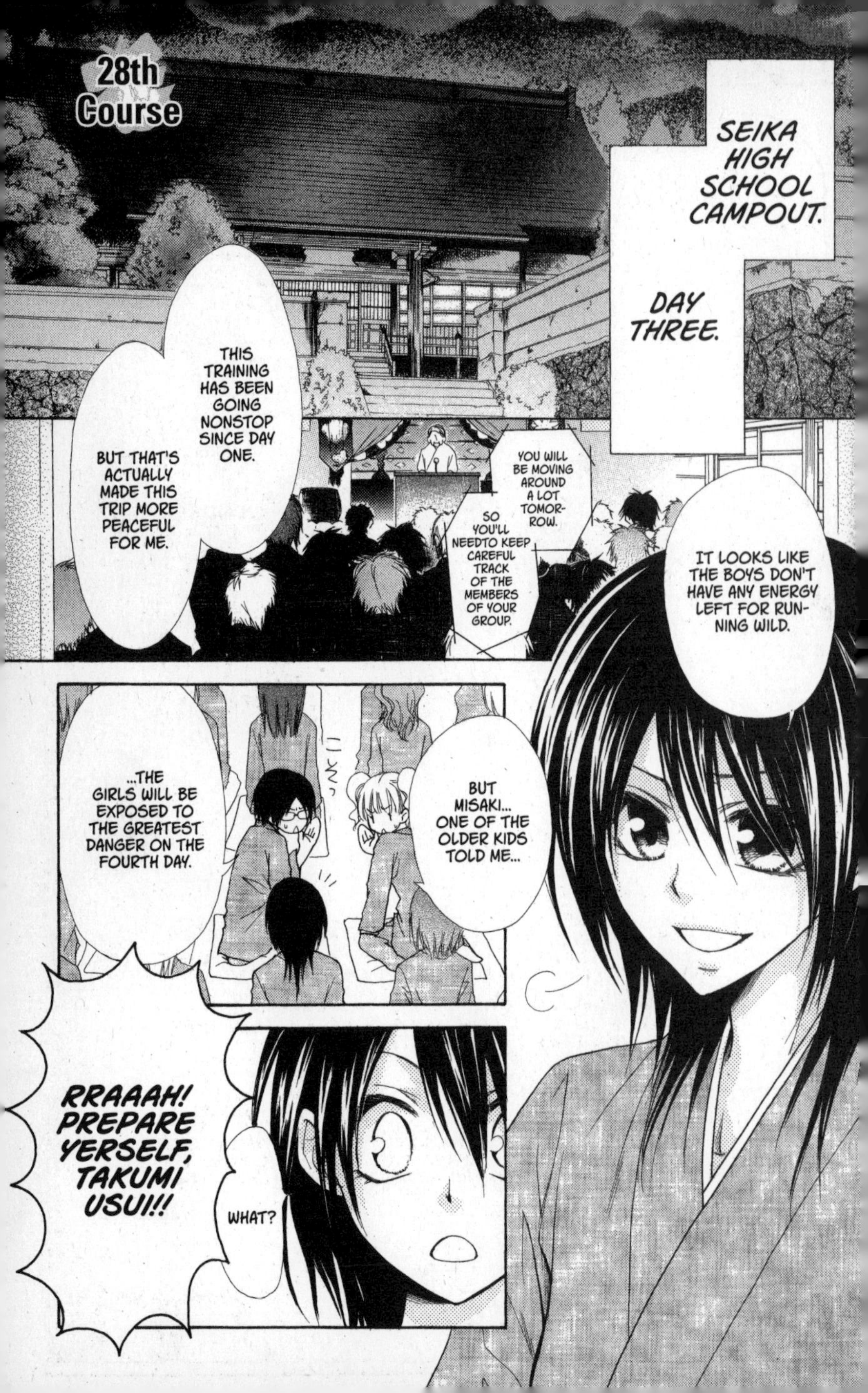
28th Course
SEIKA HIGH SCHOOL CAMPOUT.
DAY THREE.
YOU WILL BE MOVING AROUND A LOT TOMORROW.
SO YOU'LL NEEDTO KEEP CAREFUL TRACK OF THE MEMBERS OF YOUR GROUP.
THIS TRAINING HAS BEEN GOING NONSTOP SINCE DAY ONE.
BUT THAT'S ACTUALLY MADE THIS TRIP MORE PEACEFUL FOR ME.
IT LOOKS LIKE THE BOYS DON'T HAVE ANY ENERGY LEFT FOR RUNNING WILD.
BUT MISAKI... ONE OF THE OLDER KIDS TOLD ME...
...THE GIRLS WILL BE EXPOSED TO THE GREATEST DANGER ON THE FOURTH DAY.
WHAT?
RRAAAH! PREPARE YERSELF, TAKUMI USUI!!

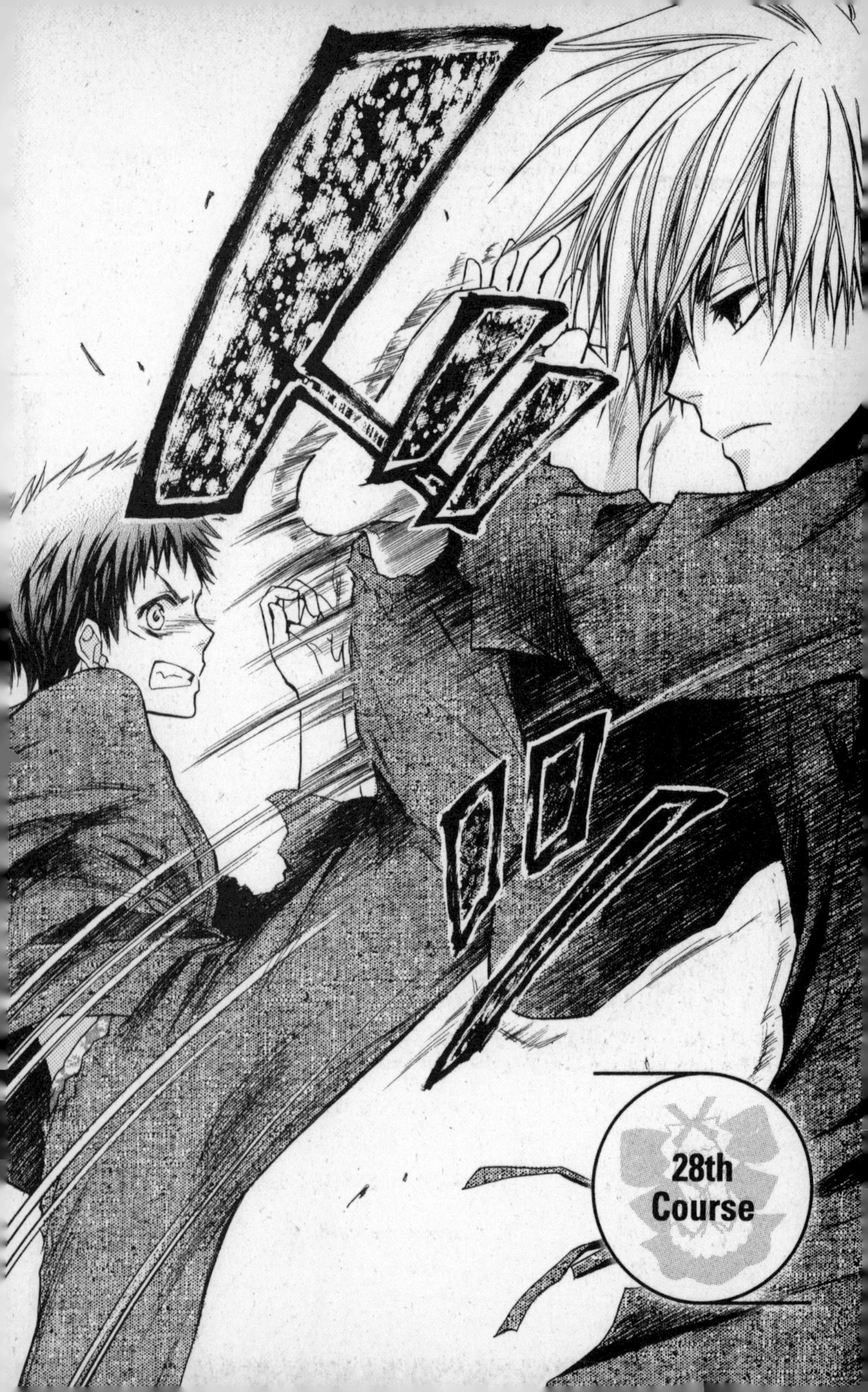
28th
Course

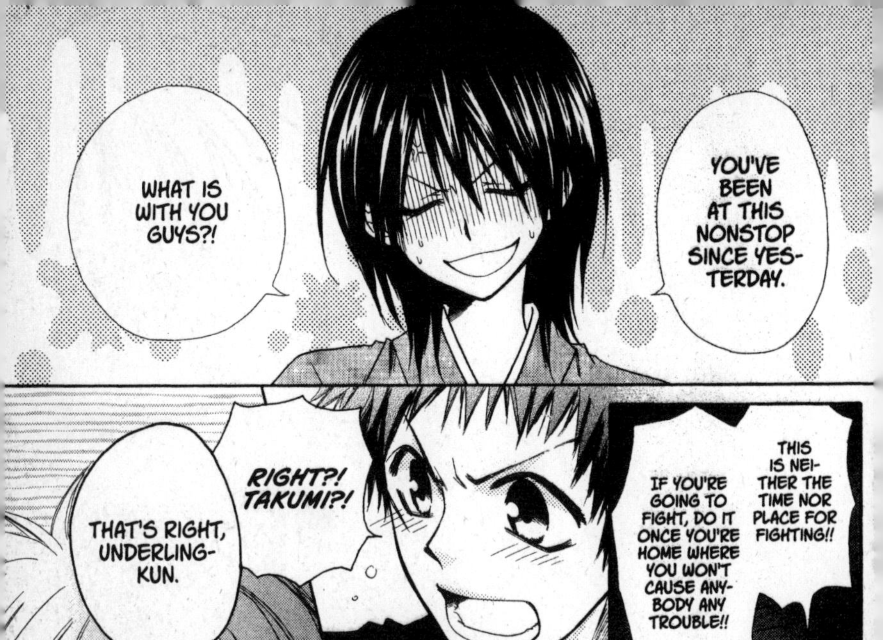
YOU'VE BEEN AT THIS NONSTOP SINCE YES-TERDAY.
WHAT IS WITH YOU GUYS?!
THIS IS NEI-THER THE TIME NOR PLACE FOR FIGHTING!!
IF YOU'RE GOING TO FIGHT, DO IT ONCE YOU'RE HOME WHERE YOU WON'T CAUSE ANY-BODY ANY TROUBLE!!
THIS AIN'T A FIGHT!
THIS IS A PASSIONATE DIALOGUE BETWEEN MEN!!
RIGHT?! TAKUMI?!
THAT'S RIGHT, UNDERLING-KUN.

Question Corner

Question 4

Q. Who thinks up all of Usui's moronic lines?

A. That would be me. Why?

I'm sure that's a compliment.

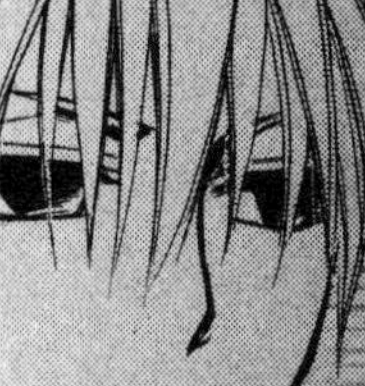

Long live stupidity!!

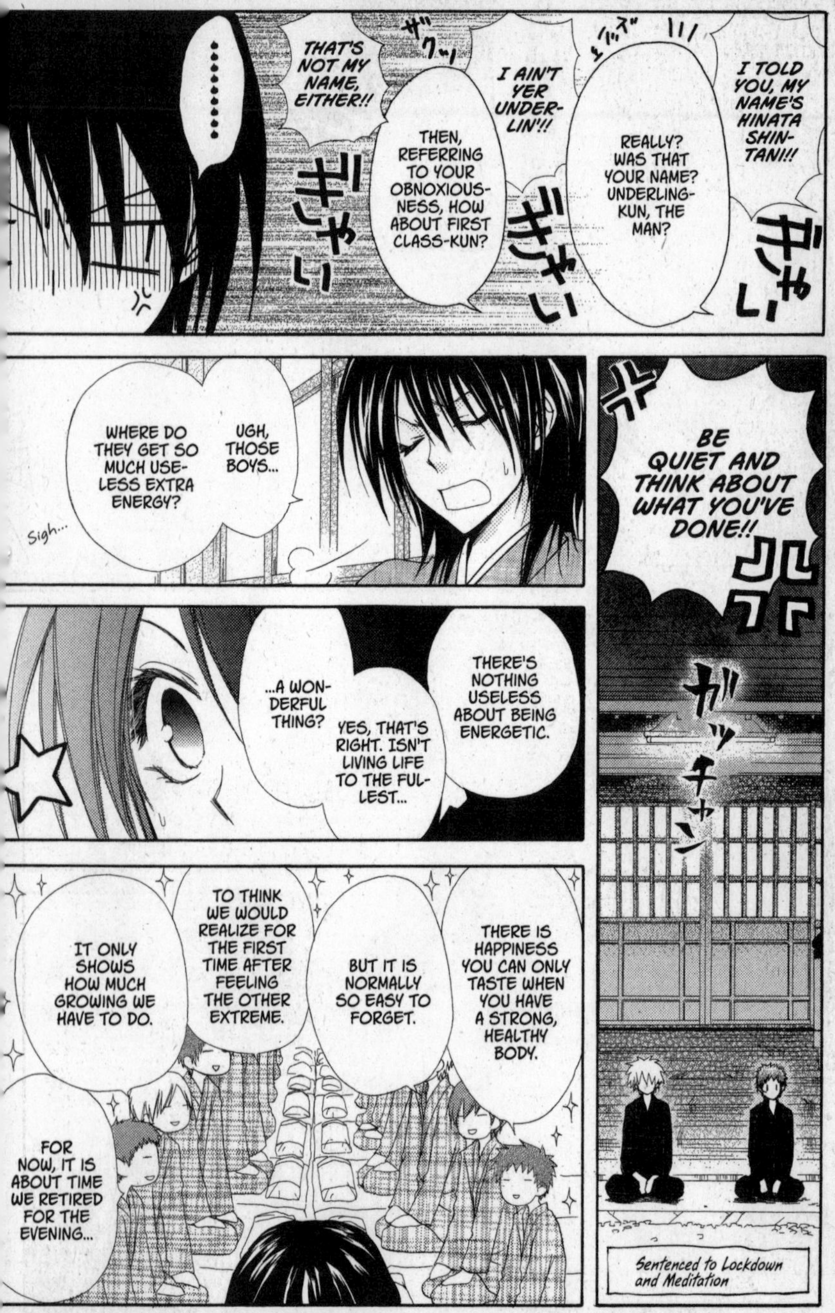
I TOLD YOU, MY NAME'S HINATA SHIN-TANI!!
REALLY? WAS THAT YOUR NAME? UNDERLING-KUN, THE MAN?
I AIN'T YER UNDER-LIN'!!
THEN, REFERRING TO YOUR OBNOXIOUS-NESS, HOW ABOUT FIRST CLASS-KUN?
THAT'S NOT MY NAME, EITHER!!
....
BE QUIET AND THINK ABOUT WHAT YOU'VE DONE!!
Sentenced to Lockdown and Meditation
UGH, THOSE BOYS...
WHERE DO THEY GET SO MUCH USE-LESS EXTRA ENERGY?
Sigh...
THERE'S NOTHING USELESS ABOUT BEING ENERGETIC.
YES, THAT'S RIGHT. ISN'T LIVING LIFE TO THE FUL-LEST...
...A WON-DERFUL THING?
THERE IS HAPPINESS YOU CAN ONLY TASTE WHEN YOU HAVE A STRONG, HEALTHY BODY.
BUT IT IS NORMALLY SO EASY TO FORGET.
TO THINK WE WOULD REALIZE FOR THE FIRST TIME AFTER FEELING THE OTHER EXTREME.
IT ONLY SHOWS HOW MUCH GROWING WE HAVE TO DO.
FOR NOW, IT IS ABOUT TIME WE RETIRED FOR THE EVENING...

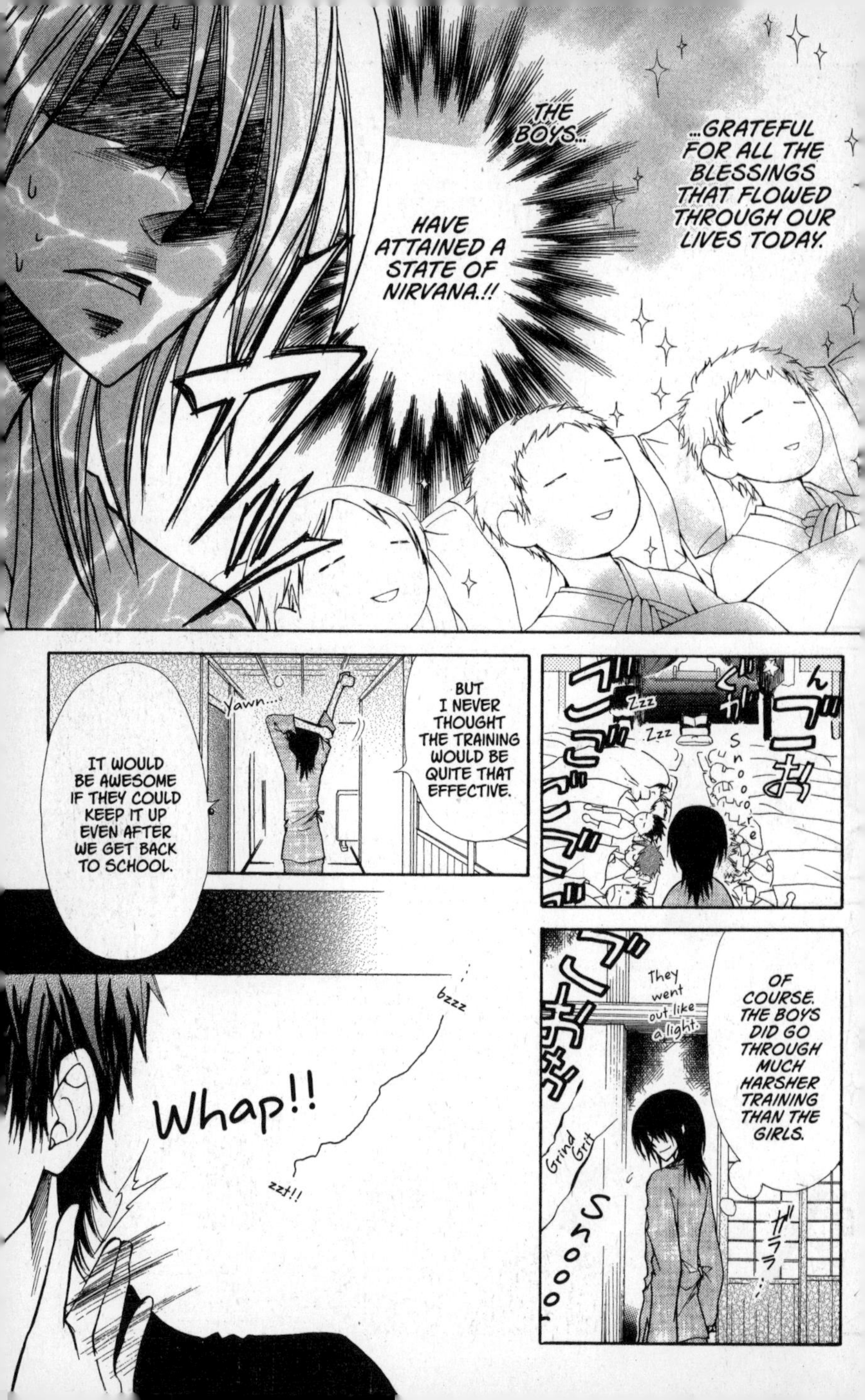
...GRATEFUL FOR ALL THE BLESSINGS THAT FLOWED THROUGH OUR LIVES TODAY.
THE BOYS...
HAVE ATTAINED A STATE OF NIRVANA.!!
Zzz
Zzz
Snooore
Yawn...
BUT I NEVER THOUGHT THE TRAINING WOULD BE QUITE THAT EFFECTIVE.
IT WOULD BE AWESOME IF THEY COULD KEEP IT UP EVEN AFTER WE GET BACK TO SCHOOL.
OF COURSE. THE BOYS DID GO THROUGH MUCH HARSHER TRAINING THAN THE GIRLS.
They went out like a light.
Grind Grit
Snoooo...
bzzz
Whap!!
zzt!!

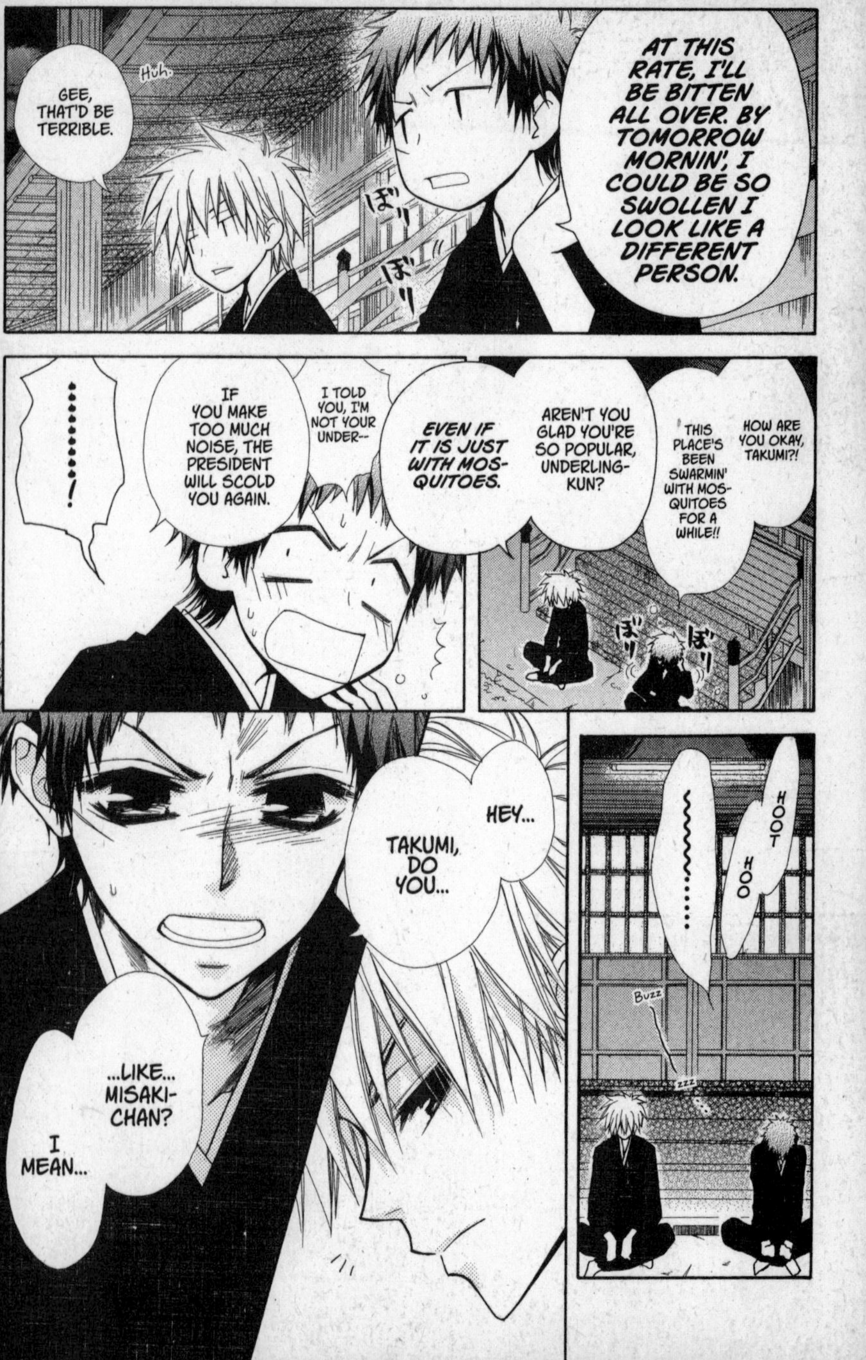
AT THIS RATE, I'LL BE BITTEN ALL OVER. BY TOMORROW MORNIN', I COULD BE SO SWOLLEN I LOOK LIKE A DIFFERENT PERSON.
ぼり
ぼり
Huh.
GEE, THAT'D BE TERRIBLE.
HOW ARE YOU OKAY, TAKUMI?!
THIS PLACE'S BEEN SWARMIN' WITH MOS-QUITOES FOR A WHILE!!
ぼり
ぼり
AREN'T YOU GLAD YOU'RE SO POPULAR, UNDERLING-KUN?
EVEN IF IT IS JUST WITH MOS-QUITOES.
I TOLD YOU, I'M NOT YOUR UNDER--
IF YOU MAKE TOO MUCH NOISE, THE PRESIDENT WILL SCOLD YOU AGAIN.
.........!
HOOT
HOO
~~~......
Buzz
zzz
HEY...
TAKUMI, DO YOU...
...LIKE... MISAKI-CHAN?
I MEAN...
~~~

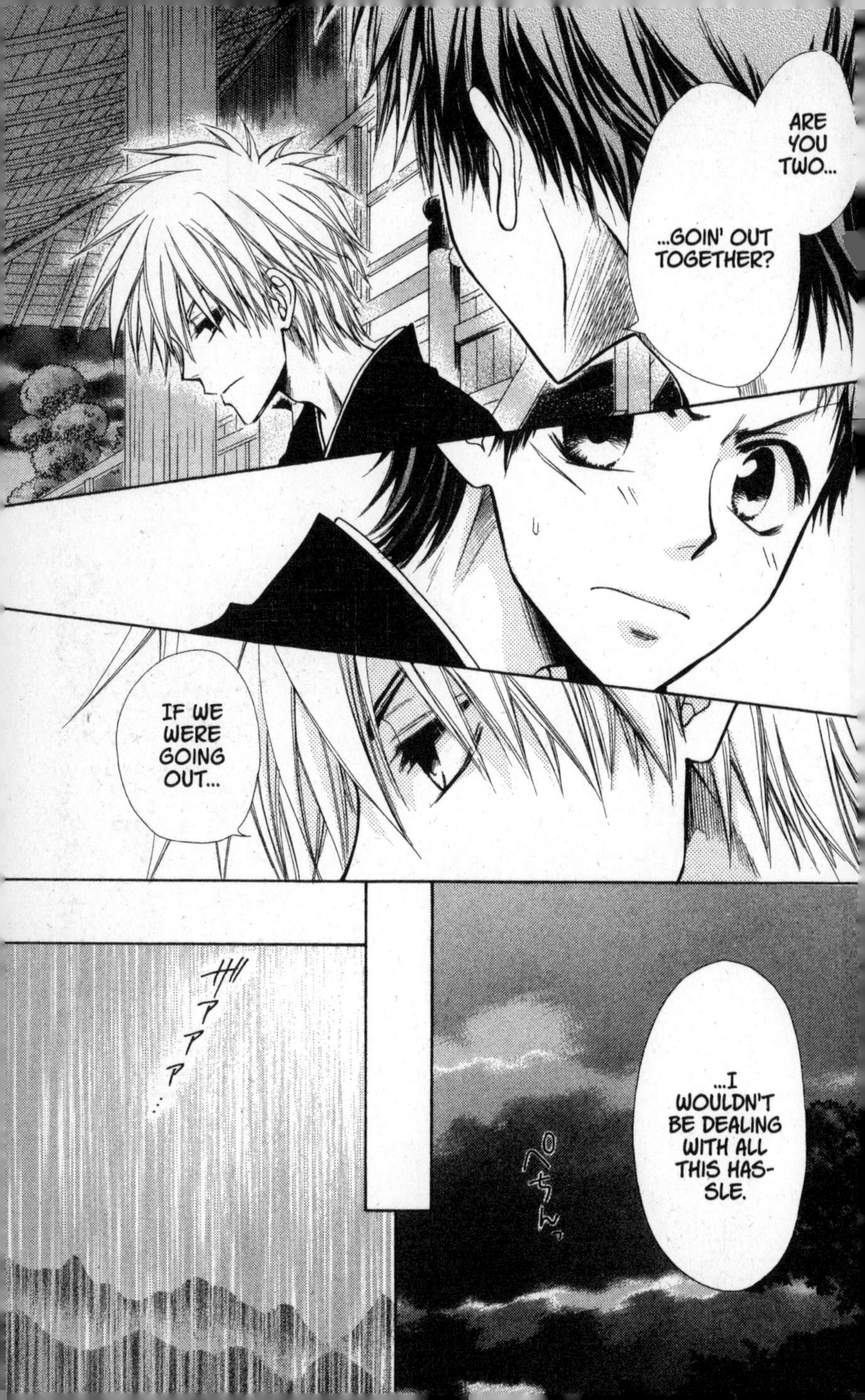
ARE YOU TWO...
...GOIN' OUT TOGETHER?
IF WE WERE GOING OUT...
...I WOULDN'T BE DEALING WITH ALL THIS HAS-SLE.
ぺちん
ザァァァ…

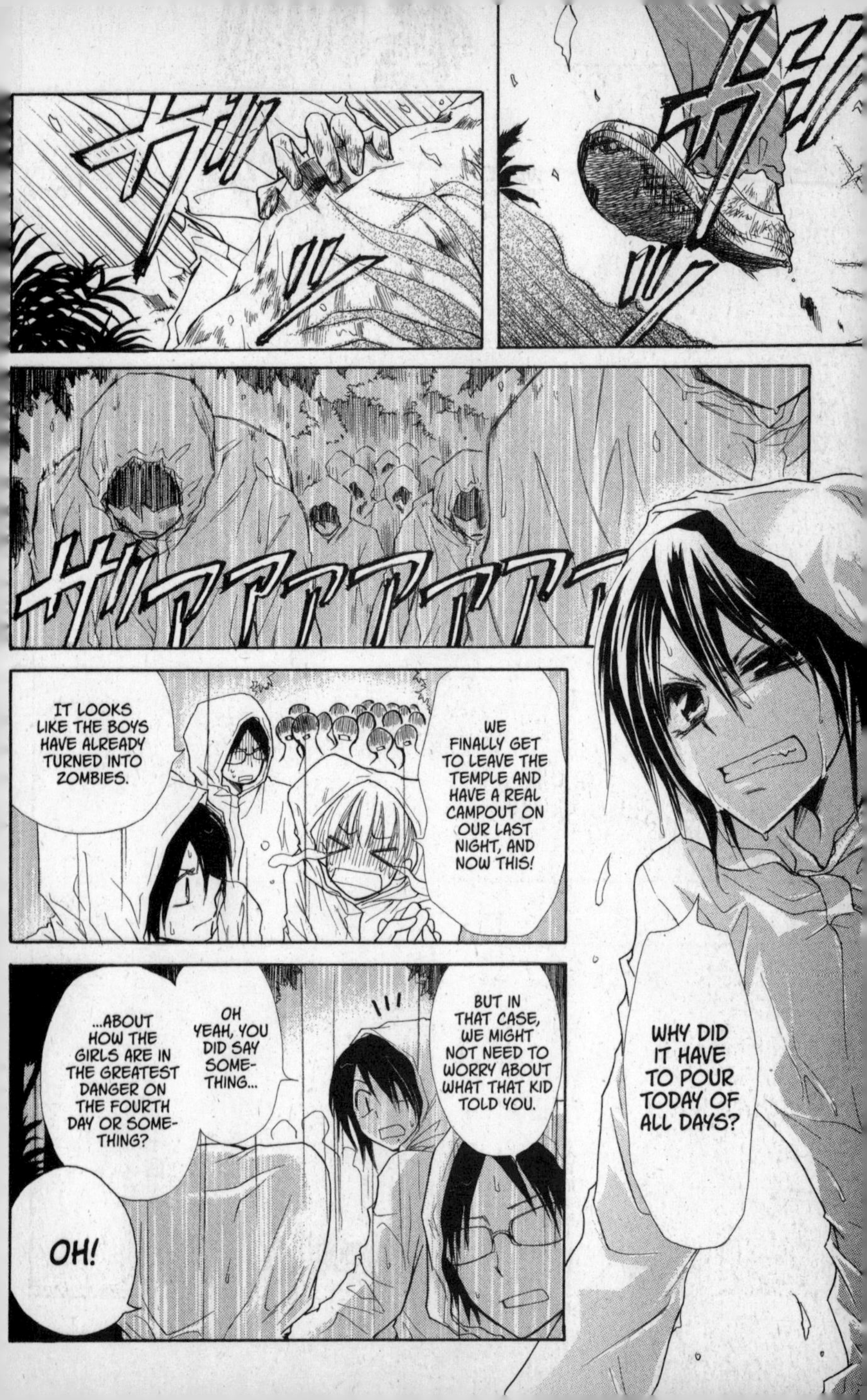
WHY DID IT HAVE TO POUR TODAY OF ALL DAYS?
WE FINALLY GET TO LEAVE THE TEMPLE AND HAVE A REAL CAMPOUT ON OUR LAST NIGHT, AND NOW THIS!
IT LOOKS LIKE THE BOYS HAVE ALREADY TURNED INTO ZOMBIES.
BUT IN THAT CASE, WE MIGHT NOT NEED TO WORRY ABOUT WHAT THAT KID TOLD YOU.
OH YEAH, YOU DID SAY SOME-THING...
...ABOUT HOW THE GIRLS ARE IN THE GREATEST DANGER ON THE FOURTH DAY OR SOME-THING?
OH!

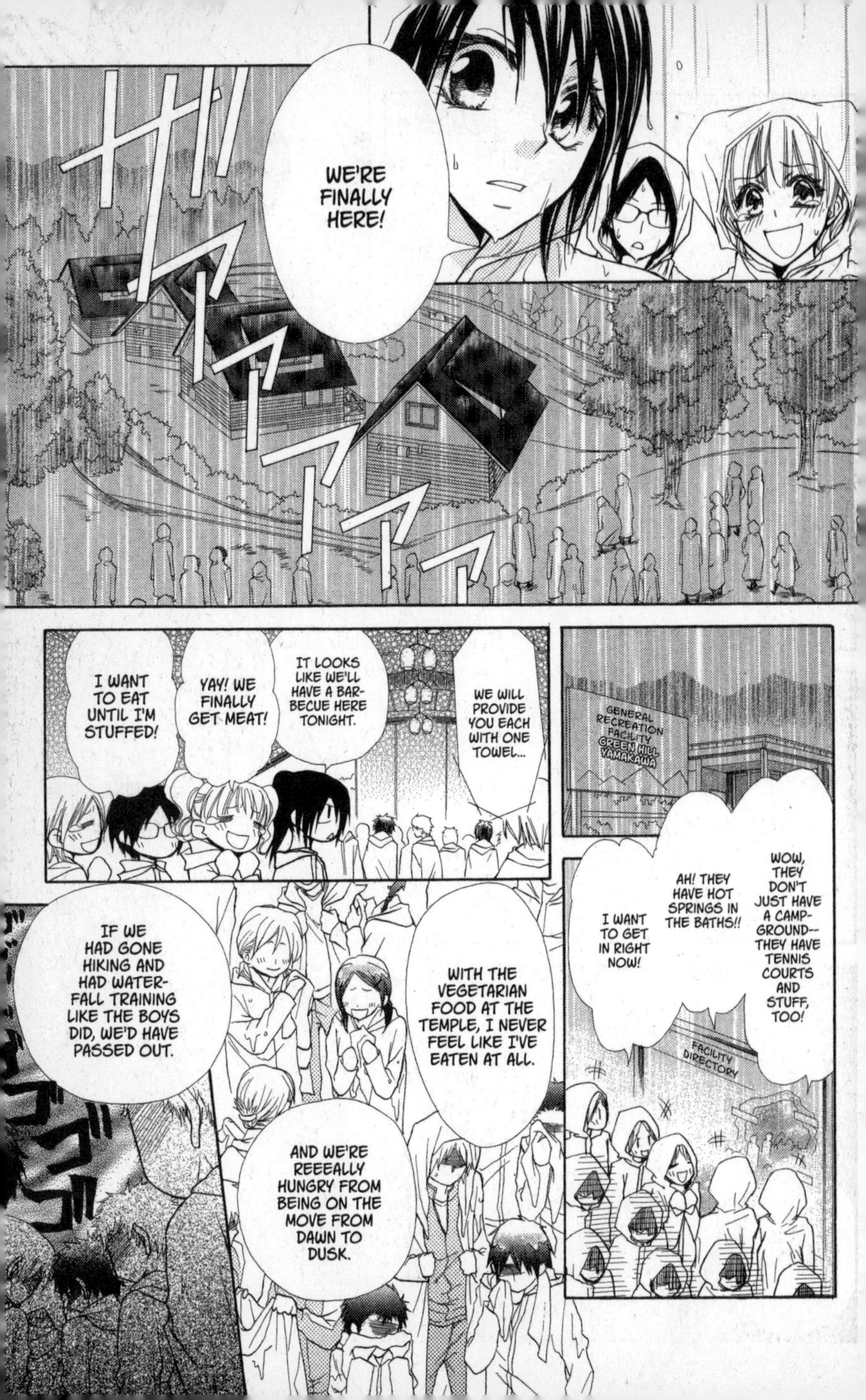
WE'RE FINALLY HERE!
GENERAL RECREATION FACILITY GREEN HILL YAMAKAWA
WE WILL PROVIDE YOU EACH WITH ONE TOWEL...
IT LOOKS LIKE WE'LL HAVE A BAR-BECUE HERE TONIGHT.
YAY! WE FINALLY GET MEAT!
I WANT TO EAT UNTIL I'M STUFFED!
WOW, THEY DON'T JUST HAVE A CAMP-GROUND--THEY HAVE TENNIS COURTS AND STUFF, TOO!
AH! THEY HAVE HOT SPRINGS IN THE BATHS!!
I WANT TO GET IN RIGHT NOW!
FACILITY DIRECTORY
WITH THE VEGETARIAN FOOD AT THE TEMPLE, I NEVER FEEL LIKE I'VE EATEN AT ALL.
IF WE HAD GONE HIKING AND HAD WATER-FALL TRAINING LIKE THE BOYS DID, WE'D HAVE PASSED OUT.
AND WE'RE REEEALLY HUNGRY FROM BEING ON THE MOVE FROM DAWN TO DUSK.

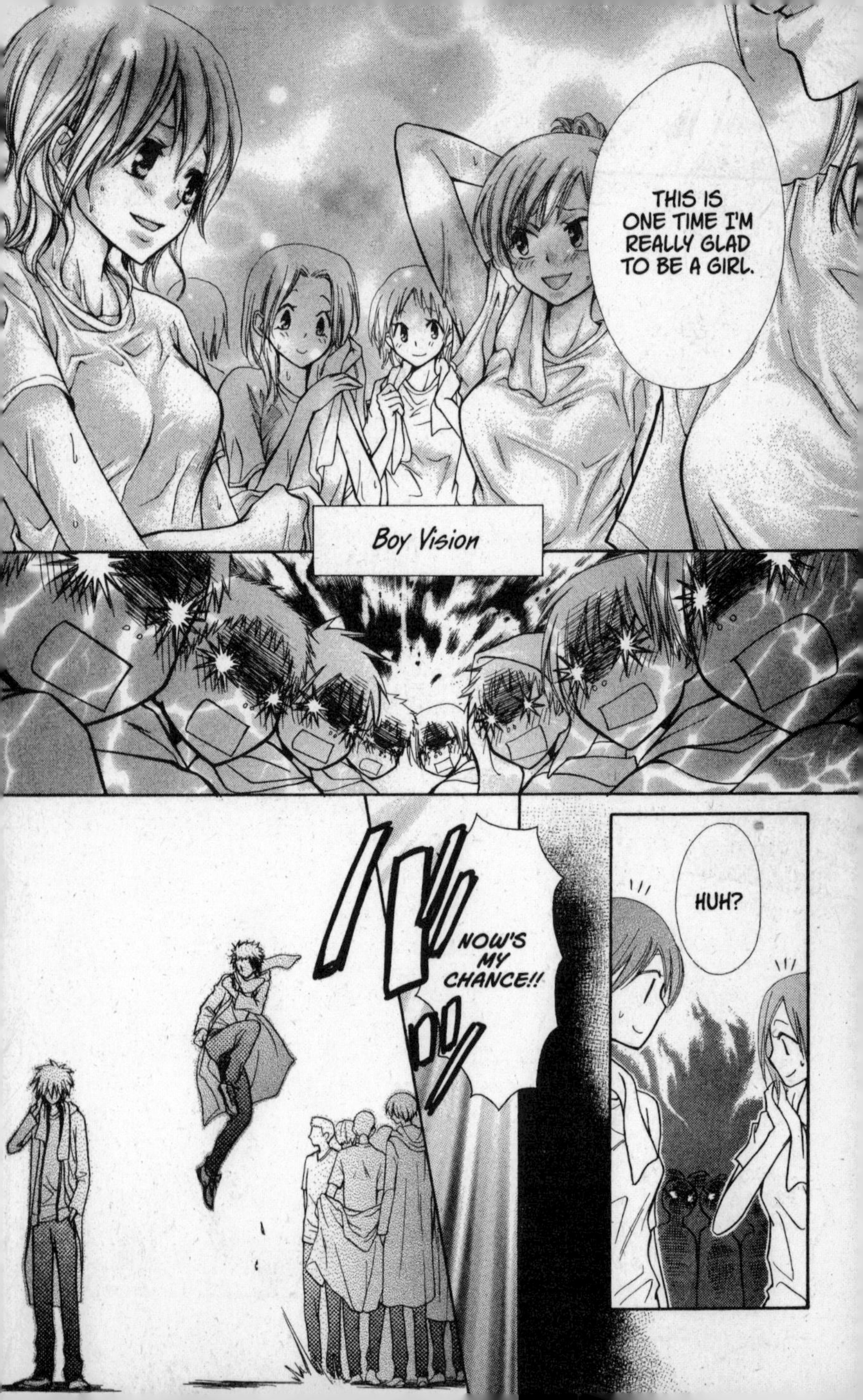
THIS IS ONE TIME I'M REALLY GLAD TO BE A GIRL.
Boy Vision
HUH?
NOW'S MY CHANCE!!

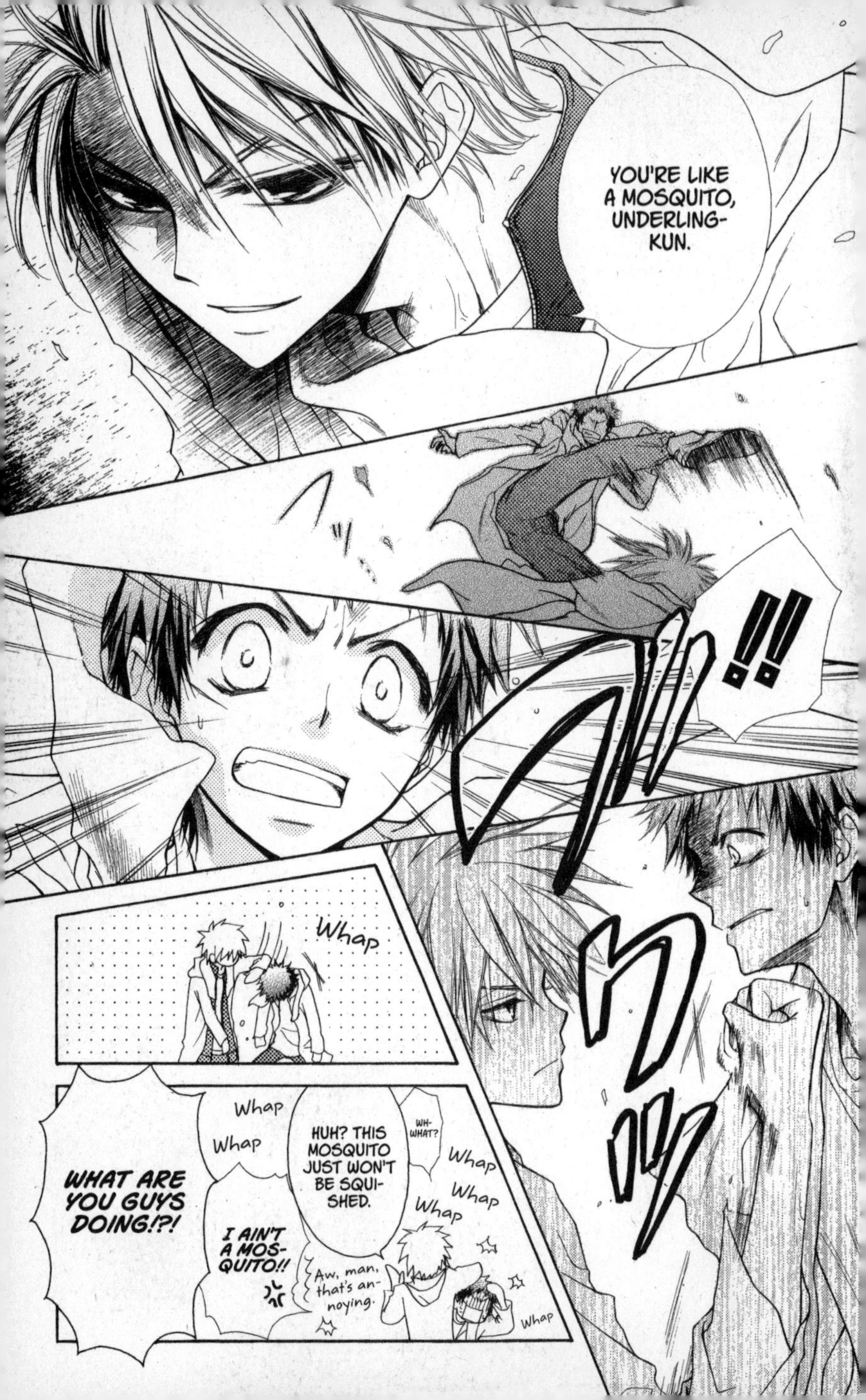
YOU'RE LIKE A MOSQUITO, UNDERLING-KUN.
!!
Whap
Whap
Whap
Whap
Whap
WH-WHAT?
HUH? THIS MOSQUITO JUST WON'T BE SQUISHED.
Whap
Whap
Aw, man, that's annoying.
I AIN'T A MOSQUITO!!
WHAT ARE YOU GUYS DOING!?!

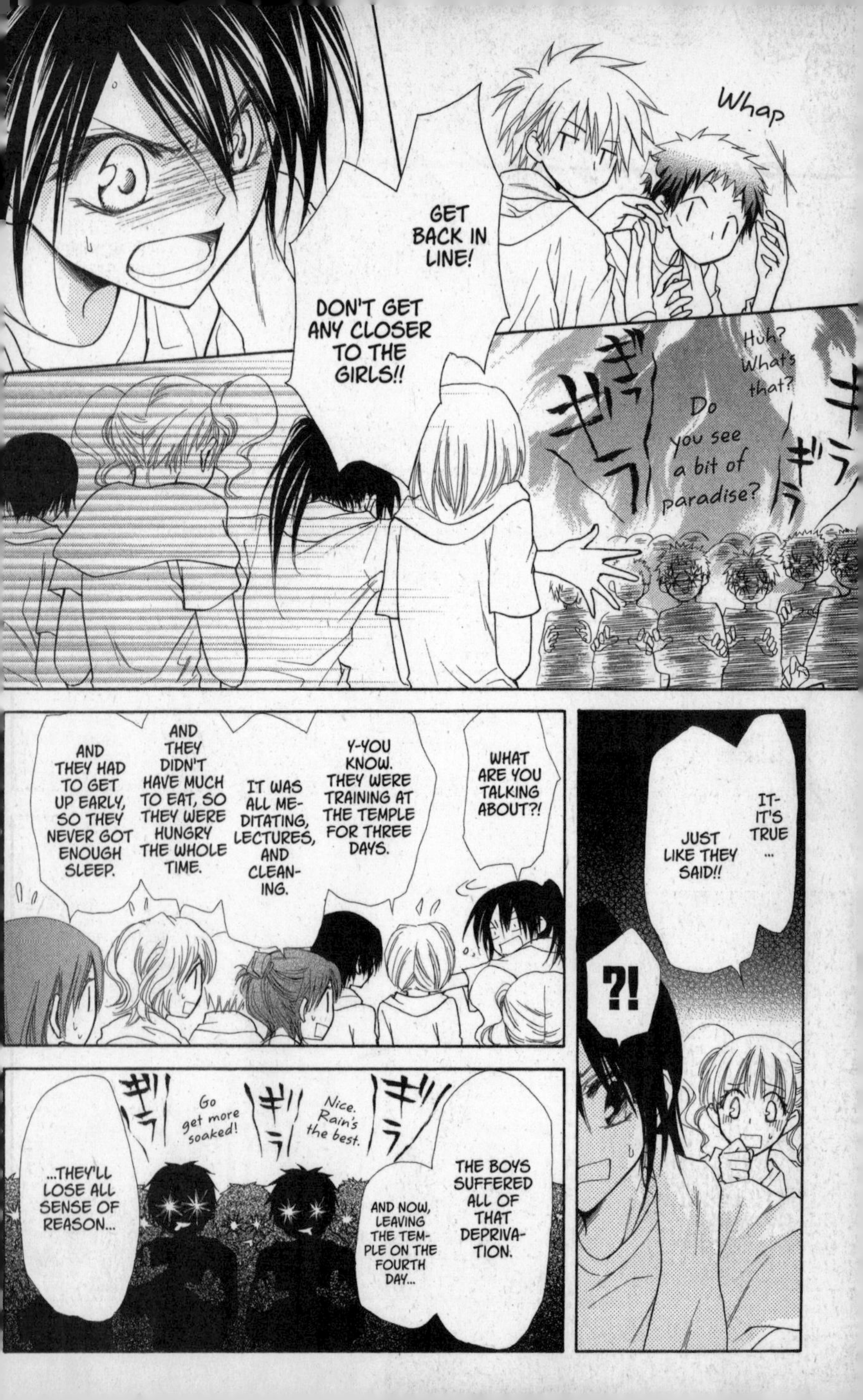
Whap
GET BACK IN LINE!
DON'T GET ANY CLOSER TO THE GIRLS!!
ギラ
Huh? What's that?
Do you see a bit of paradise?
ギラ
ギラ
ギラ
IT- IT'S TRUE ...
JUST LIKE THEY SAID!!
?!
WHAT ARE YOU TALKING ABOUT?!
Y-YOU KNOW. THEY WERE TRAINING AT THE TEMPLE FOR THREE DAYS.
IT WAS ALL ME-DITATING, LECTURES, AND CLEAN-ING.
AND THEY DIDN'T HAVE MUCH TO EAT, SO THEY WERE HUNGRY THE WHOLE TIME.
AND THEY HAD TO GET UP EARLY, SO THEY NEVER GOT ENOUGH SLEEP.
THE BOYS SUFFERED ALL OF THAT DEPRIVA-TION.
AND NOW, LEAVING THE TEM-PLE ON THE FOURTH DAY...
ギラ
Nice. Rain's the best.
ギラ
Go get more soaked!
ギラ
...THEY'LL LOSE ALL SENSE OF REASON...

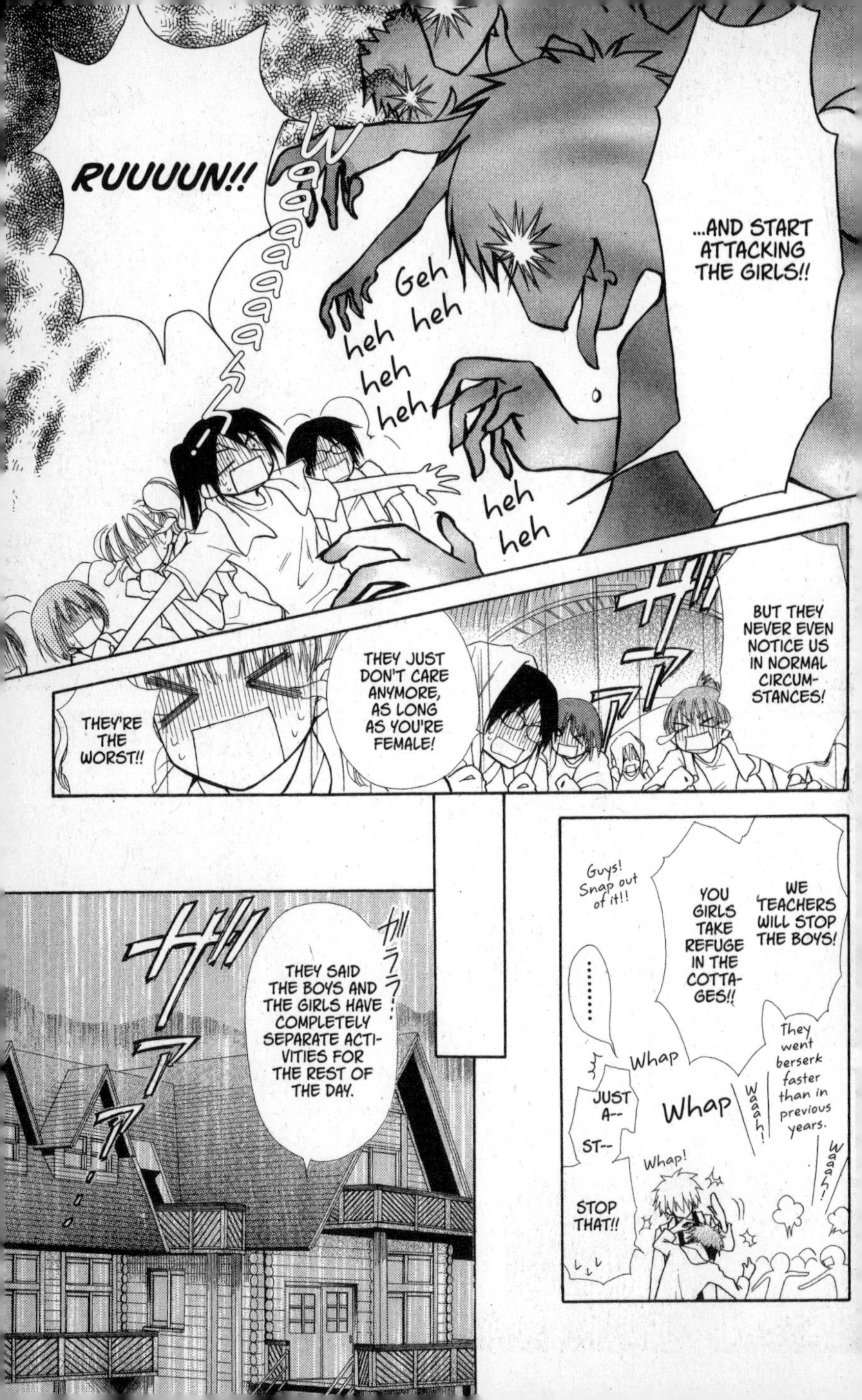
...AND START ATTACKING THE GIRLS!!
Geh heh heh heh heh heh heh
RUUUUN!!
Waaaaaaaaah!
BUT THEY NEVER EVEN NOTICE US IN NORMAL CIRCUM-STANCES!
THEY JUST DON'T CARE ANYMORE, AS LONG AS YOU'RE FEMALE!
THEY'RE THE WORST!!
WE TEACHERS WILL STOP THE BOYS!
YOU GIRLS TAKE REFUGE IN THE COTTA-GES!!
Guys! Snap out of it!!
......
They went berserk faster than in previous years.
Whap
Whap
Waaah!
JUST A--
ST--
Whap!
Waaah!
STOP THAT!!
THEY SAID THE BOYS AND THE GIRLS HAVE COMPLETELY SEPARATE ACTI-VITIES FOR THE REST OF THE DAY.

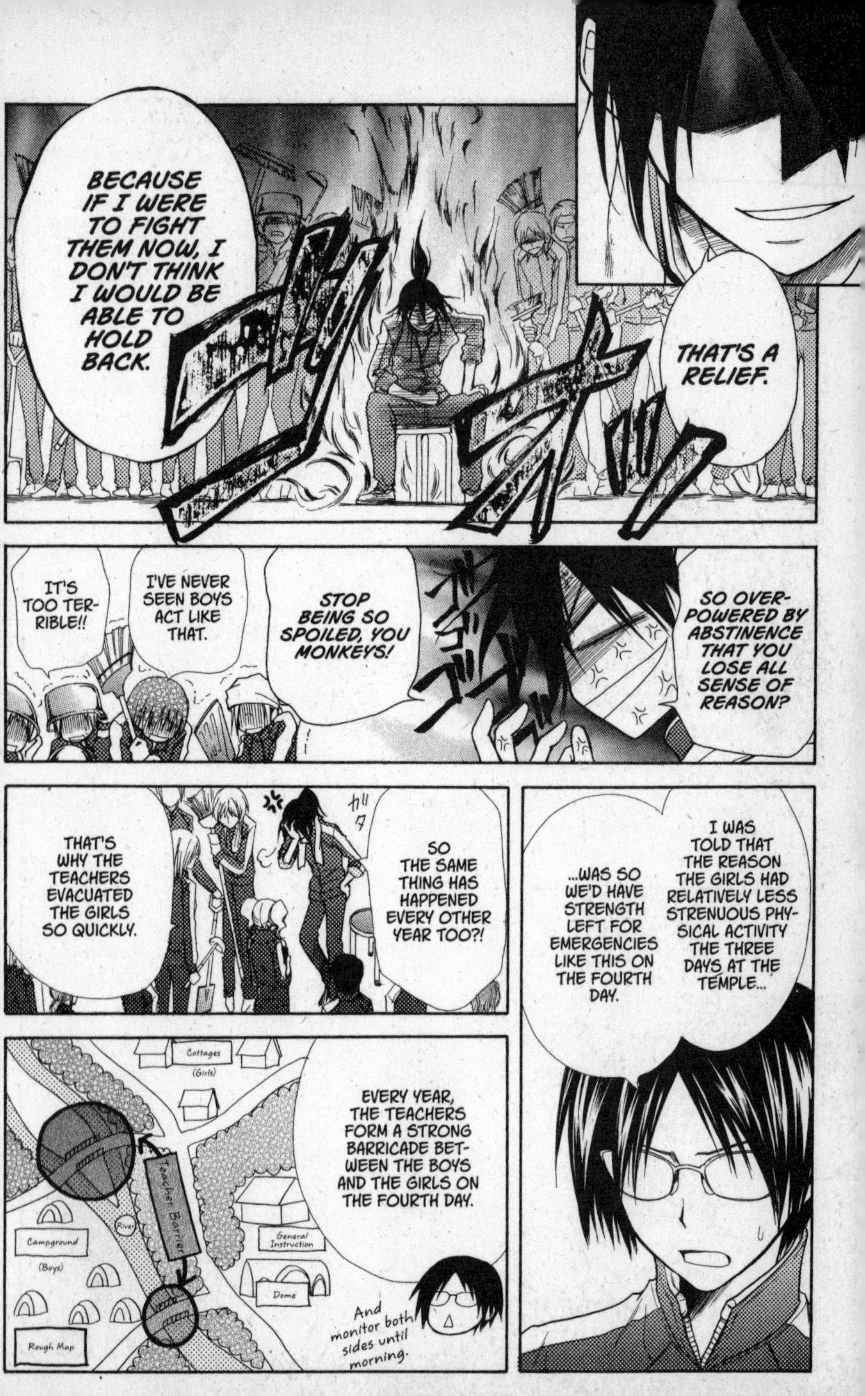
THAT'S A RELIEF.
BECAUSE IF I WERE TO FIGHT THEM NOW, I DON'T THINK I WOULD BE ABLE TO HOLD BACK.
SO OVER-POWERED BY ABSTINENCE THAT YOU LOSE ALL SENSE OF REASON?
STOP BEING SO SPOILED, YOU MONKEYS!
I'VE NEVER SEEN BOYS ACT LIKE THAT.
IT'S TOO TER-RIBLE!!
I WAS TOLD THAT THE REASON THE GIRLS HAD RELATIVELY LESS STRENUOUS PHY-SICAL ACTIVITY THE THREE DAYS AT THE TEMPLE...
...WAS SO WE'D HAVE STRENGTH LEFT FOR EMERGENCIES LIKE THIS ON THE FOURTH DAY.
SO THE SAME THING HAS HAPPENED EVERY OTHER YEAR TOO?!
THAT'S WHY THE TEACHERS EVACUATED THE GIRLS SO QUICKLY.
EVERY YEAR, THE TEACHERS FORM A STRONG BARRICADE BET-WEEN THE BOYS AND THE GIRLS ON THE FOURTH DAY.
Cottages
(Girls)
Teacher Barrier
River
Campground
(Boys)
General Instruction
Dome
Rough Map
And monitor both sides until morning.

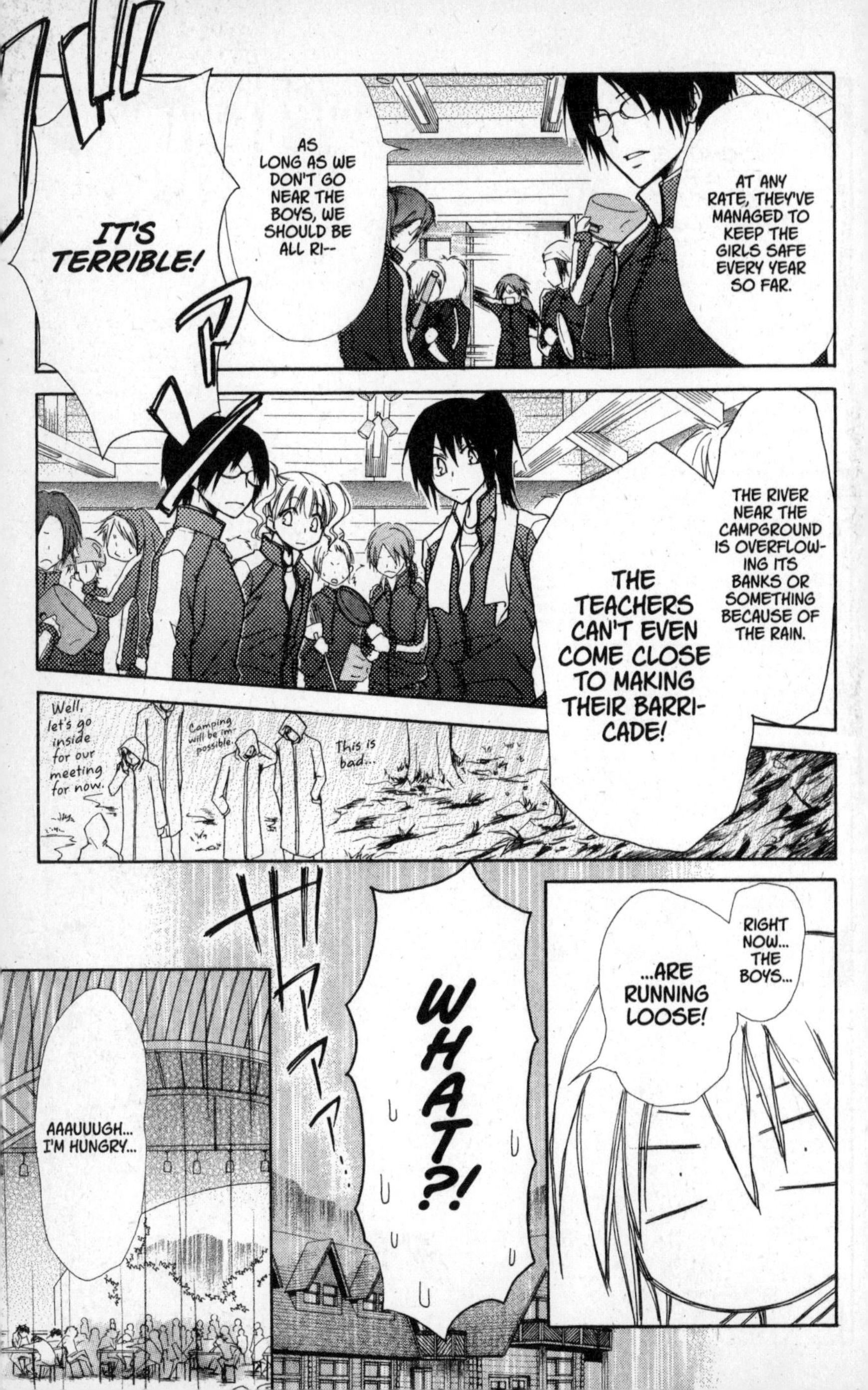
AT ANY RATE, THEY'VE MANAGED TO KEEP THE GIRLS SAFE EVERY YEAR SO FAR.
AS LONG AS WE DON'T GO NEAR THE BOYS, WE SHOULD BE ALL RI--
IT'S TERRIBLE!
THE RIVER NEAR THE CAMPGROUND IS OVERFLOWING ITS BANKS OR SOMETHING BECAUSE OF THE RAIN.
THE TEACHERS CAN'T EVEN COME CLOSE TO MAKING THEIR BARRICADE!
This is bad...
Camping will be impossible.
Well, let's go inside for our meeting for now.
RIGHT NOW... THE BOYS...
...ARE RUNNING LOOSE!
WHAT?!
AAAUUUGH... I'M HUNGRY...

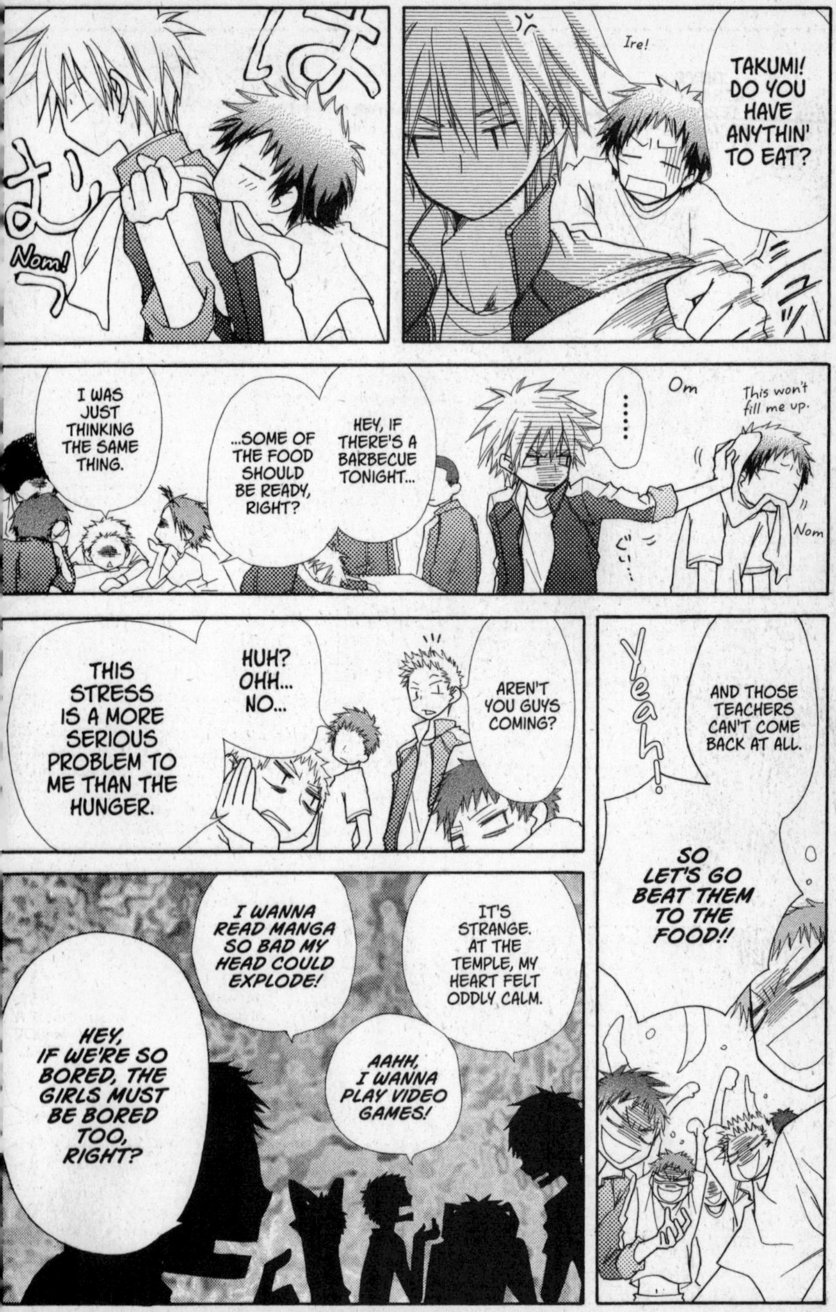

TAKUMI! DO YOU HAVE ANYTHIN' TO EAT?
Ire!
Nom!
This won't fill me up.
Om
Nom
......
HEY, IF THERE'S A BARBECUE TONIGHT...
...SOME OF THE FOOD SHOULD BE READY, RIGHT?
I WAS JUST THINKING THE SAME THING.
AND THOSE TEACHERS CAN'T COME BACK AT ALL.
Yeah!
SO LET'S GO BEAT THEM TO THE FOOD!!
AREN'T YOU GUYS COMING?
HUH? OHH... NO...
THIS STRESS IS A MORE SERIOUS PROBLEM TO ME THAN THE HUNGER.
IT'S STRANGE. AT THE TEMPLE, MY HEART FELT ODDLY CALM.
I WANNA READ MANGA SO BAD MY HEAD COULD EXPLODE!
AAHH, I WANNA PLAY VIDEO GAMES!
HEY, IF WE'RE SO BORED, THE GIRLS MUST BE BORED TOO, RIGHT?

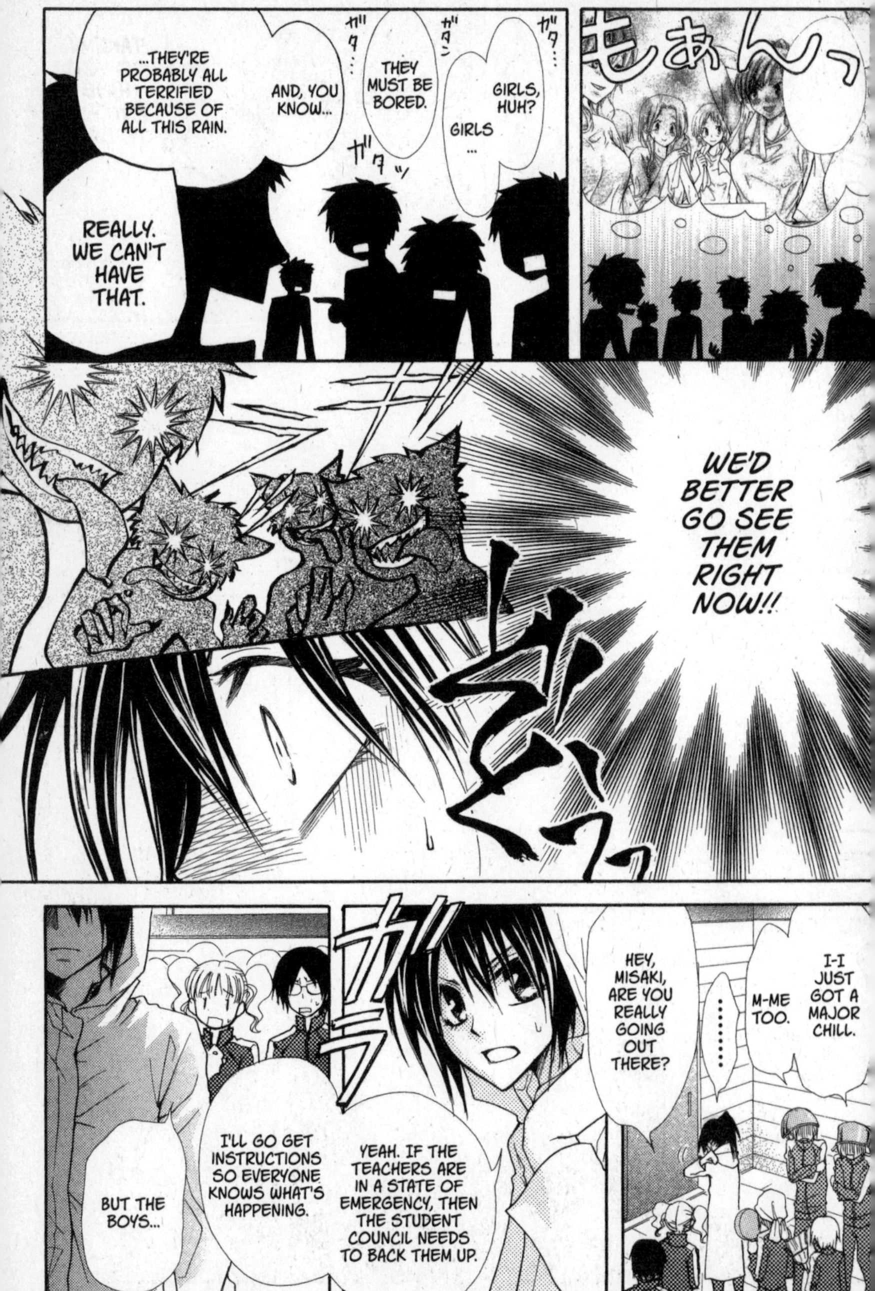
もぁんっ
ガタ…
GIRLS, HUH?
GIRLS ...
ガタン
THEY MUST BE BORED.
ガタ…
AND, YOU KNOW...
...THEY'RE PROBABLY ALL TERRIFIED BECAUSE OF ALL THIS RAIN.
ガタッ
REALLY. WE CAN'T HAVE THAT.
WE'D BETTER GO SEE THEM RIGHT NOW!!
I-I JUST GOT A MAJOR CHILL.
M-ME TOO.
......
HEY, MISAKI, ARE YOU REALLY GOING OUT THERE?
YEAH. IF THE TEACHERS ARE IN A STATE OF EMERGENCY, THEN THE STUDENT COUNCIL NEEDS TO BACK THEM UP.
I'LL GO GET INSTRUCTIONS SO EVERYONE KNOWS WHAT'S HAPPENING.
BUT THE BOYS...

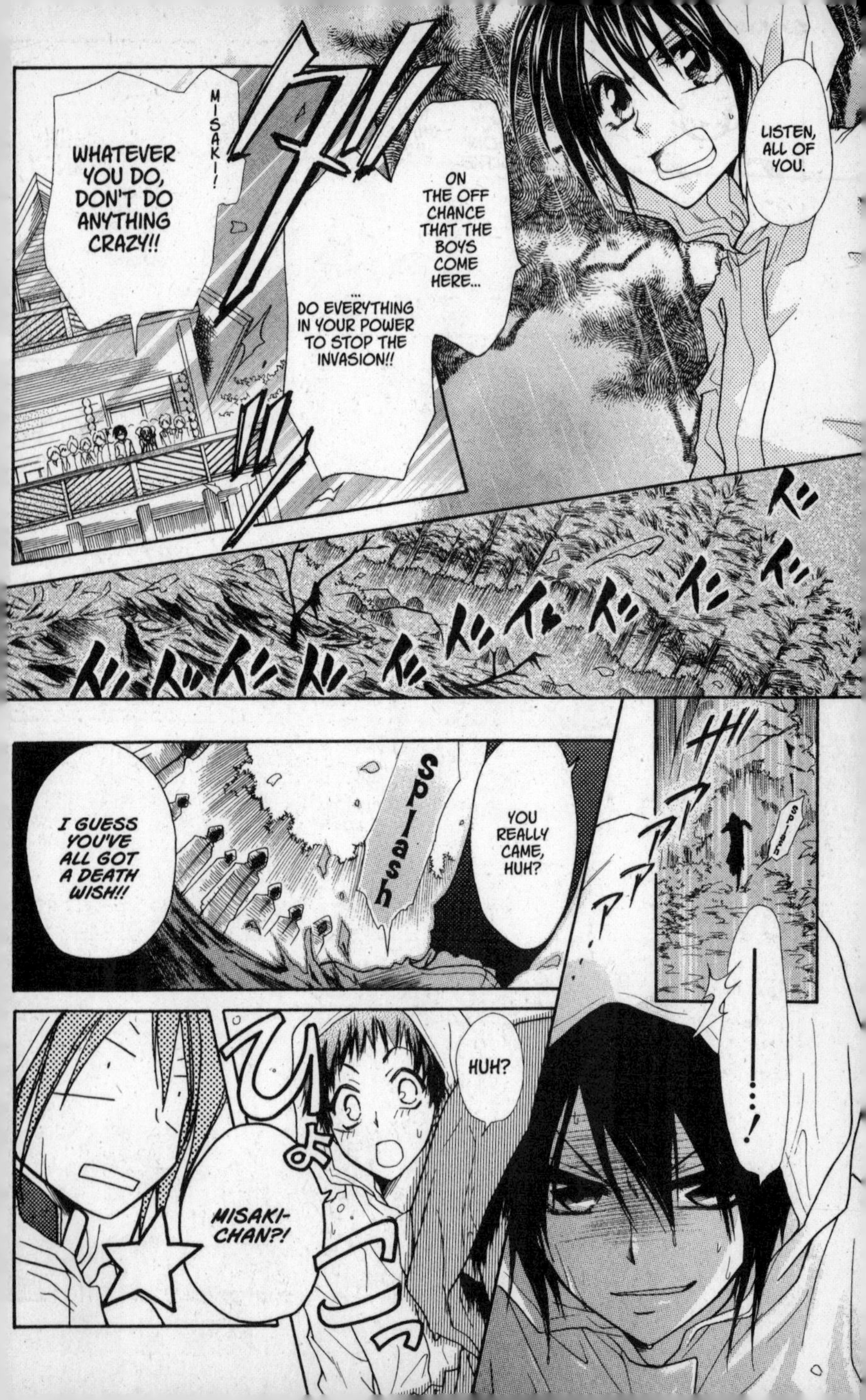
LISTEN, ALL OF YOU.
ON THE OFF CHANCE THAT THE BOYS COME HERE...
...DO EVERYTHING IN YOUR POWER TO STOP THE INVASION!!
MISAKI!
WHATEVER YOU DO, DON'T DO ANYTHING CRAZY!!
splash
...!
YOU REALLY CAME, HUH?
splash
I GUESS YOU'VE ALL GOT A DEATH WISH!!
HUH?
MISAKI-CHAN?!

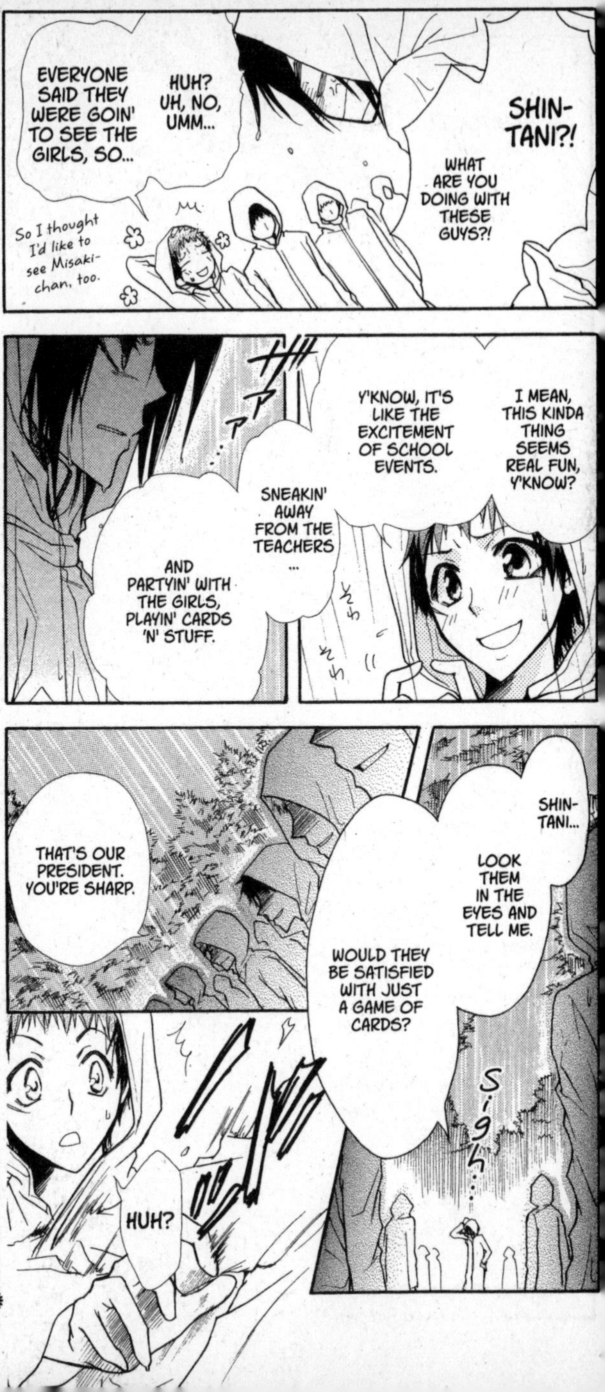
SHIN-TANI?!
WHAT ARE YOU DOING WITH THESE GUYS?!
HUH? UH, NO, UMM...
EVERYONE SAID THEY WERE GOIN' TO SEE THE GIRLS, SO...
So I thought I'd like to see Misaki-chan, too.
I MEAN, THIS KINDA THING SEEMS REAL FUN, Y'KNOW?
Y'KNOW, IT'S LIKE THE EXCITEMENT OF SCHOOL EVENTS.
SNEAKIN' AWAY FROM THE TEACHERS ...
AND PARTYIN' WITH THE GIRLS, PLAYIN' CARDS 'N' STUFF.
SHIN-TANI...
LOOK THEM IN THE EYES AND TELL ME.
WOULD THEY BE SATISFIED WITH JUST A GAME OF CARDS?
Sigh...
THAT'S OUR PRESIDENT. YOU'RE SHARP.
HUH?

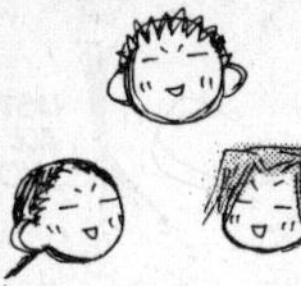

I got a request from my readers:

"Please rewrite the idiot trio's profile!"

Such ~~unusual~~ kind words.

And so, I think I will write the three idiots' individual profiles, starting with the next 1/4 column.

The subtle change in their weights comes from how they're always spending all their money at the maid cafe.

I went ahead and changed their special skills and favorite things too.

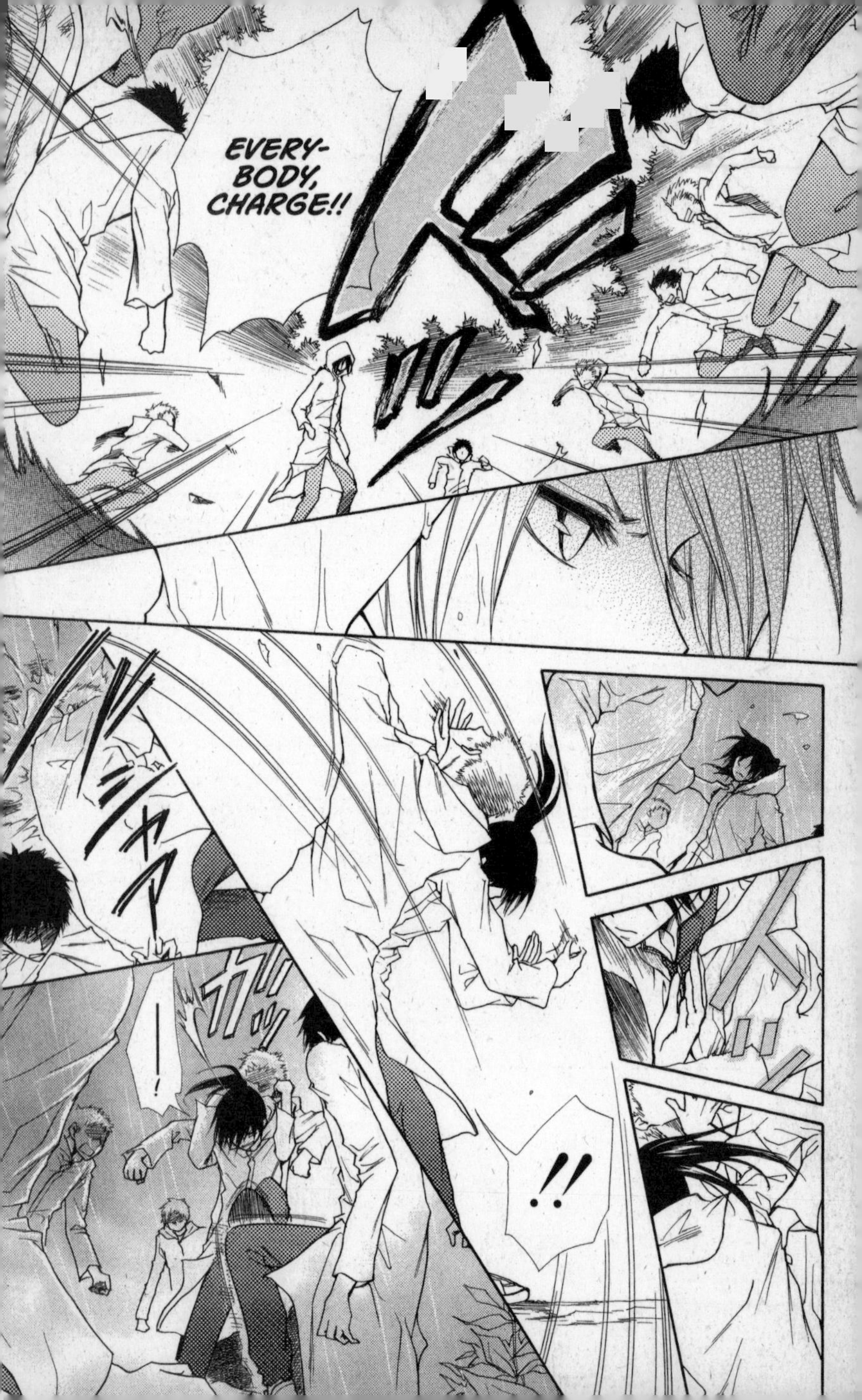
EVERY-BODY, CHARGE!!
ー!
!!

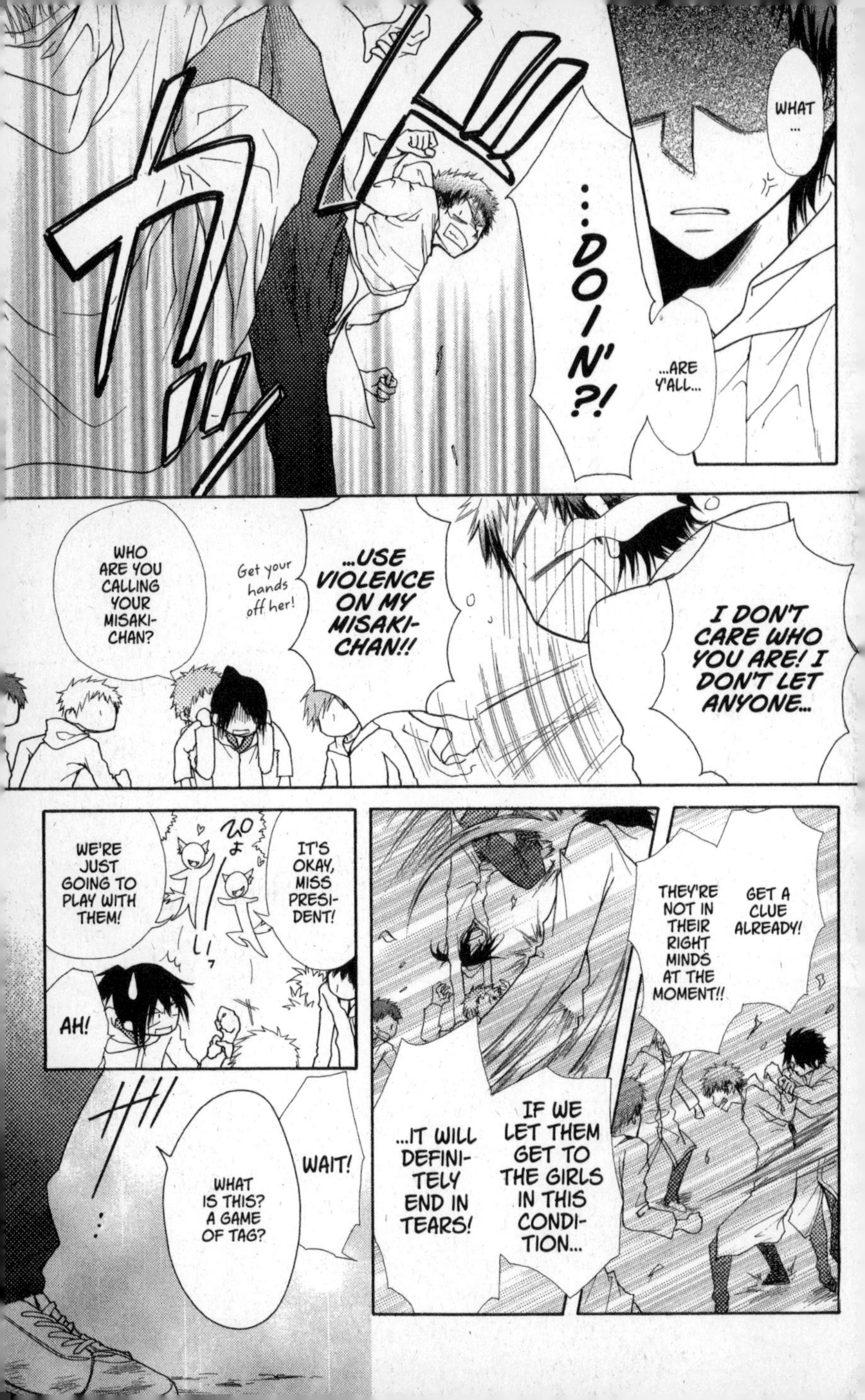
WHAT ...
...ARE Y'ALL...
...DOIN'?!
I DON'T CARE WHO YOU ARE! I DON'T LET ANYONE...
...USE VIOLENCE ON MY MISAKI-CHAN!!
Get your hands off her!
WHO ARE YOU CALLING YOUR MISAKI-CHAN?
GET A CLUE ALREADY!
THEY'RE NOT IN THEIR RIGHT MINDS AT THE MOMENT!!
IF WE LET THEM GET TO THE GIRLS IN THIS CONDITION...
...IT WILL DEFINITELY END IN TEARS!
IT'S OKAY, MISS PRESIDENT!
WE'RE JUST GOING TO PLAY WITH THEM!
AH!
WAIT!
WHAT IS THIS? A GAME OF TAG?

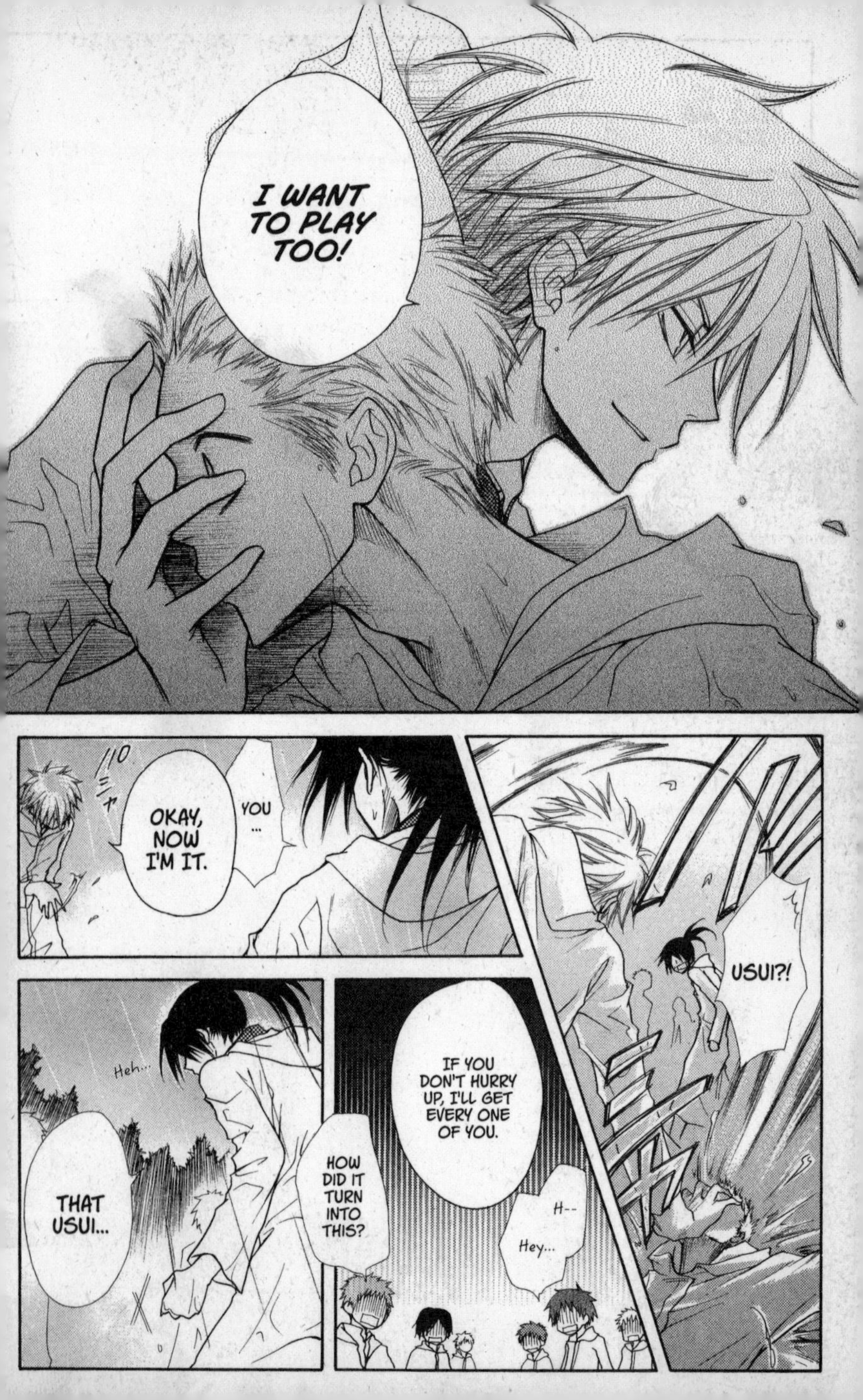
I WANT TO PLAY TOO!
USUI?!
YOU ...
OKAY, NOW I'M IT.
IF YOU DON'T HURRY UP, I'LL GET EVERY ONE OF YOU.
H--
Hey...
HOW DID IT TURN INTO THIS?
Heh...
THAT USUI...

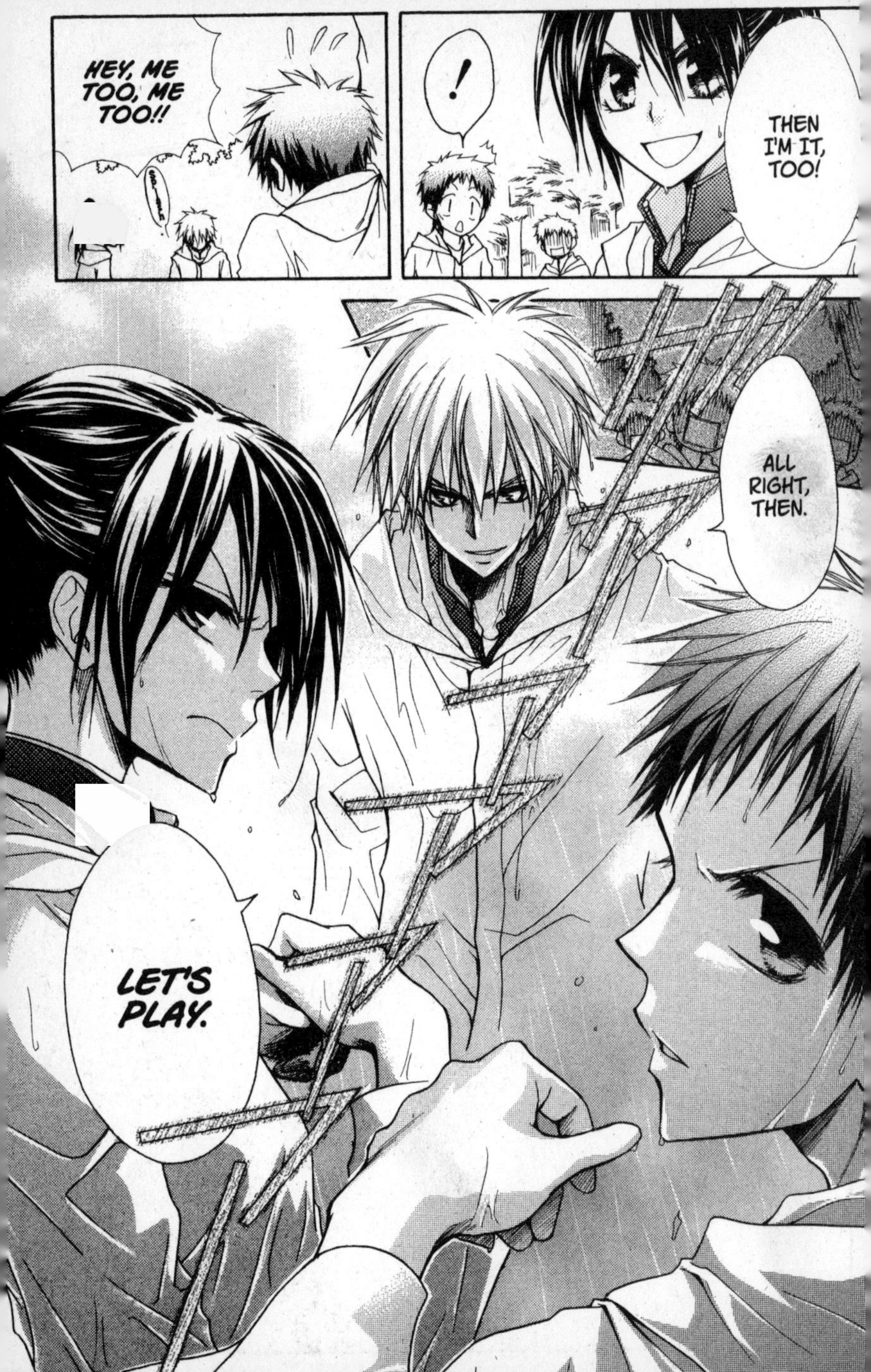
THEN I'M IT, TOO!
!
HEY, ME TOO, ME TOO!!
ALL RIGHT, THEN.
LET'S PLAY.

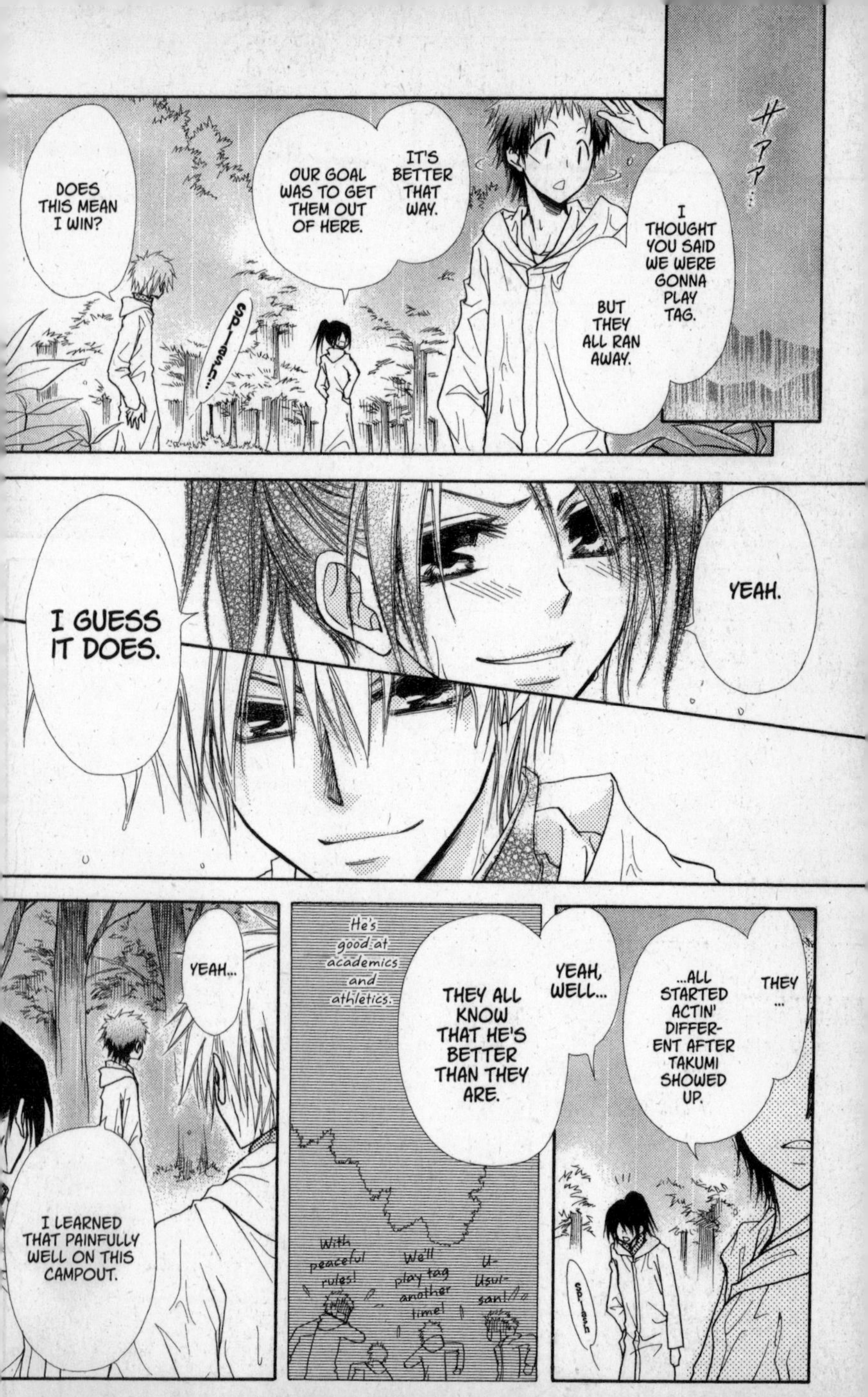
サァァ…
I THOUGHT YOU SAID WE WERE GONNA PLAY TAG.
BUT THEY ALL RAN AWAY.
IT'S BETTER THAT WAY.
OUR GOAL WAS TO GET THEM OUT OF HERE.
SPLASH...
DOES THIS MEAN I WIN?
YEAH.
I GUESS IT DOES.
THEY ...
...ALL STARTED ACTIN' DIFFER-ENT AFTER TAKUMI SHOWED UP.
splash
YEAH, WELL...
THEY ALL KNOW THAT HE'S BETTER THAN THEY ARE.
He's good at academics and athletics.
U-Usui-san!
We'll play tag another time!
With peaceful rules!
YEAH...
I LEARNED THAT PAINFULLY WELL ON THIS CAMPOUT.

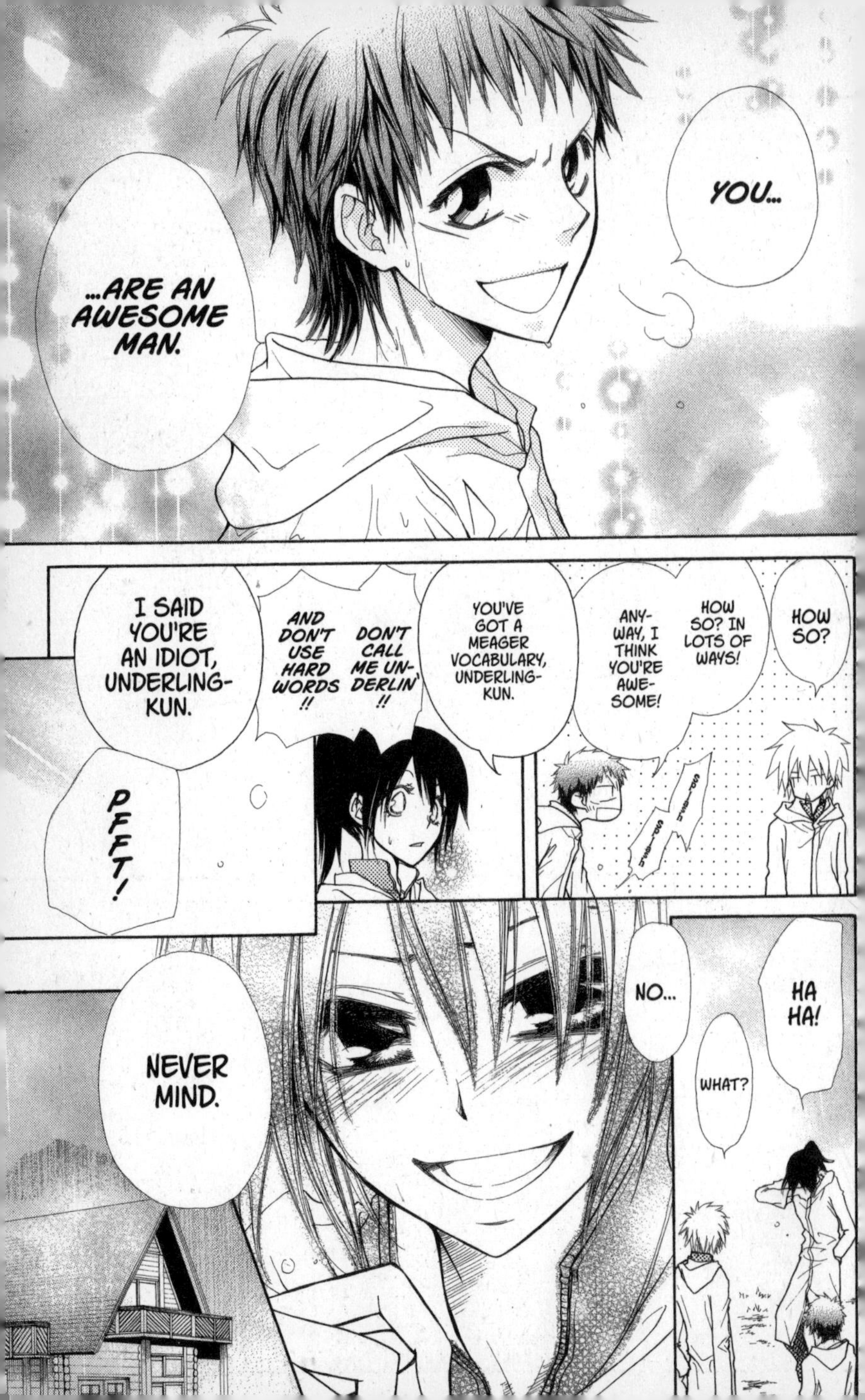
YOU...
...ARE AN AWESOME MAN.
HOW SO?
HOW SO? IN LOTS OF WAYS!
ANY-WAY, I THINK YOU'RE AWE-SOME!
YOU'VE GOT A MEAGER VOCABULARY, UNDERLING-KUN.
DON'T CALL ME UN-DERLIN'!!
AND DON'T USE HARD WORDS!!
I SAID YOU'RE AN IDIOT, UNDERLING-KUN.
PFFT!
HA HA!
WHAT?
NO...
NEVER MIND.

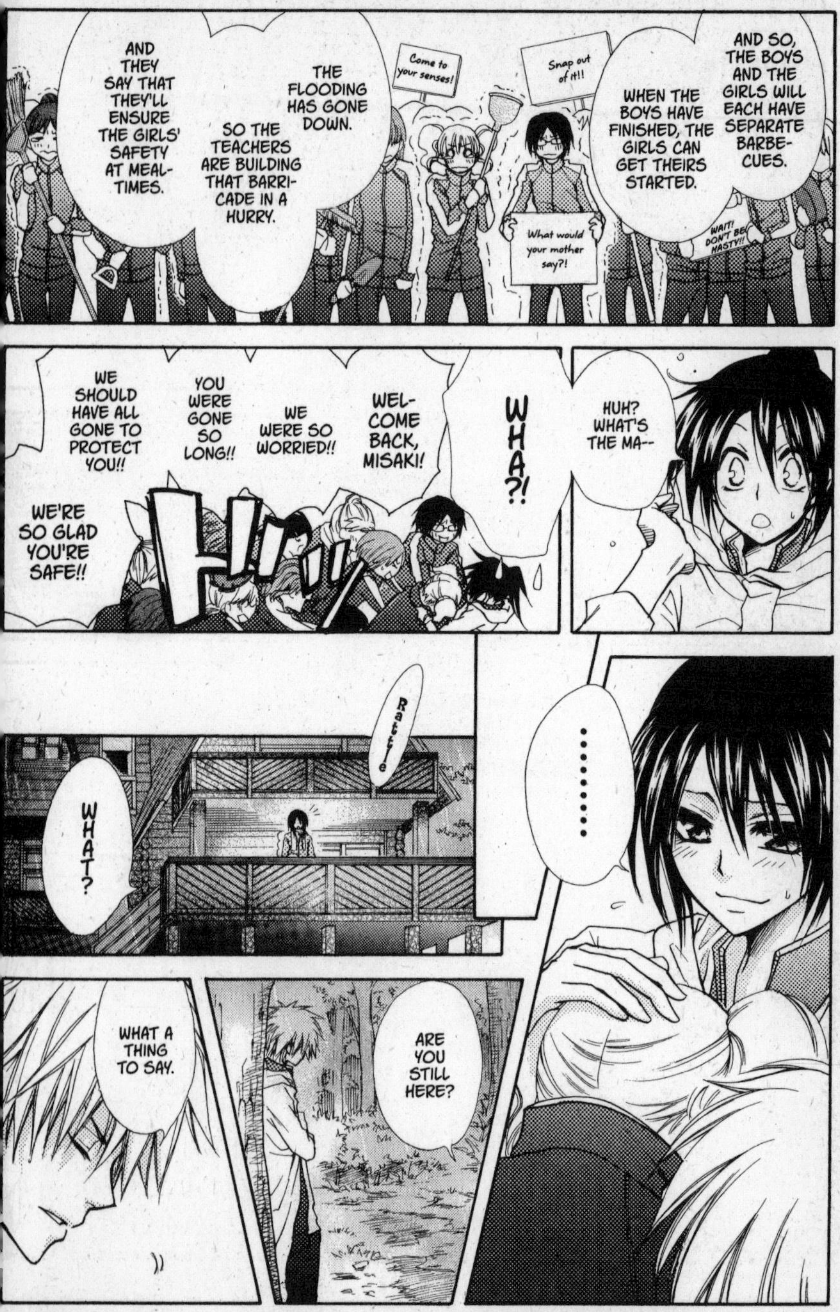
AND SO, THE BOYS AND THE GIRLS WILL EACH HAVE SEPARATE BARBECUES.
WHEN THE BOYS HAVE FINISHED, THE GIRLS CAN GET THEIRS STARTED.
WAIT! DON'T BE NASTY!!
What would your mother say?!
Snap out of it!!
Come to your senses!
THE FLOODING HAS GONE DOWN.
SO THE TEACHERS ARE BUILDING THAT BARRICADE IN A HURRY.
AND THEY SAY THAT THEY'LL ENSURE THE GIRLS' SAFETY AT MEALTIMES.
HUH? WHAT'S THE MA--
WHA?!
WELCOME BACK, MISAKI!
WE WERE SO WORRIED!!
YOU WERE GONE SO LONG!!
WE SHOULD HAVE ALL GONE TO PROTECT YOU!!
WE'RE SO GLAD YOU'RE SAFE!!
....
Rattle
WHAT?
ARE YOU STILL HERE?
WHAT A THING TO SAY.

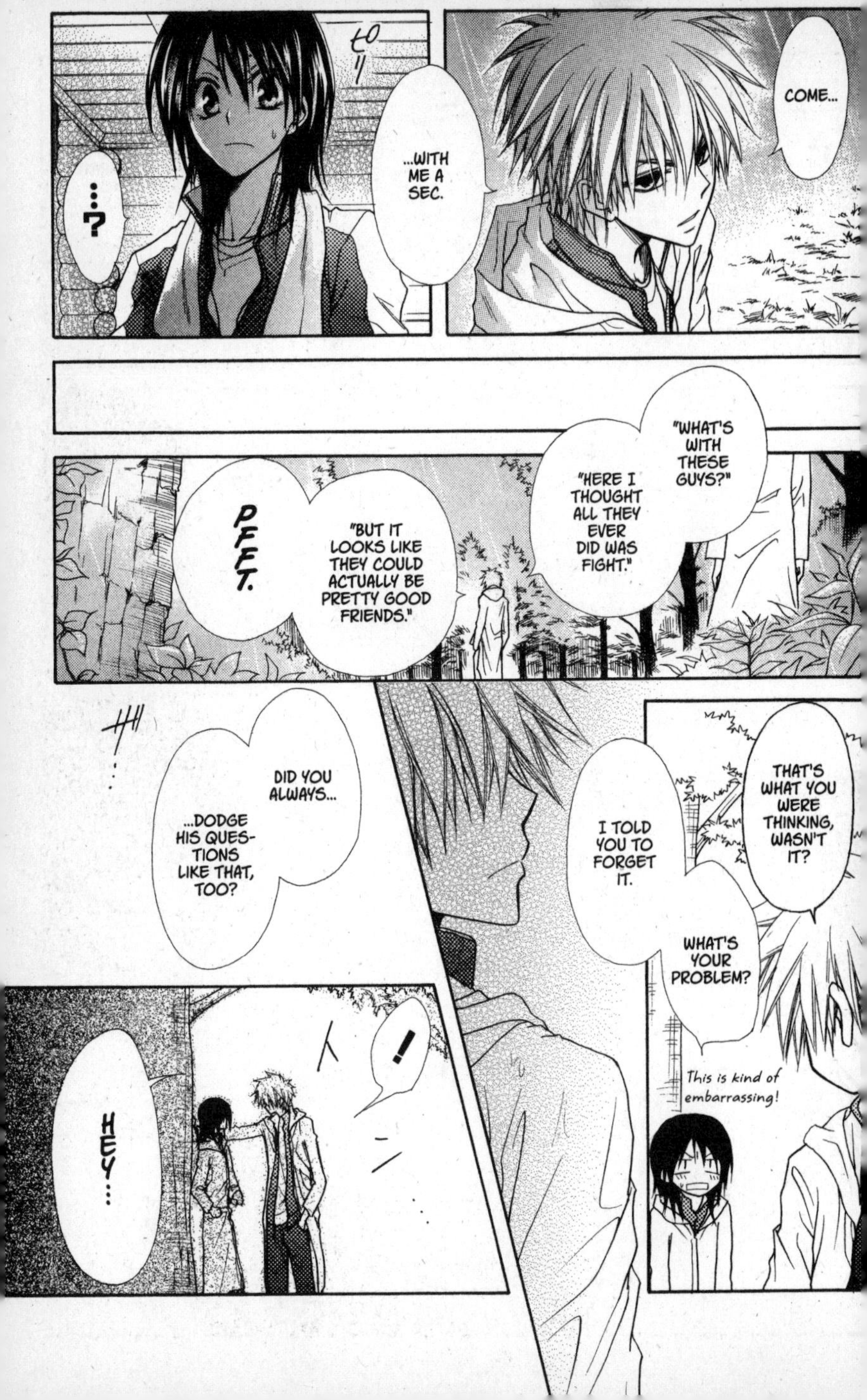
COME...
...WITH ME A SEC.
...?
"WHAT'S WITH THESE GUYS?"
"HERE I THOUGHT ALL THEY EVER DID WAS FIGHT."
"BUT IT LOOKS LIKE THEY COULD ACTUALLY BE PRETTY GOOD FRIENDS."
PFFT.
THAT'S WHAT YOU WERE THINKING, WASN'T IT?
I TOLD YOU TO FORGET IT.
WHAT'S YOUR PROBLEM?
This is kind of embarrassing!
DID YOU ALWAYS...
...DODGE HIS QUESTIONS LIKE THAT, TOO?
!
HEY...

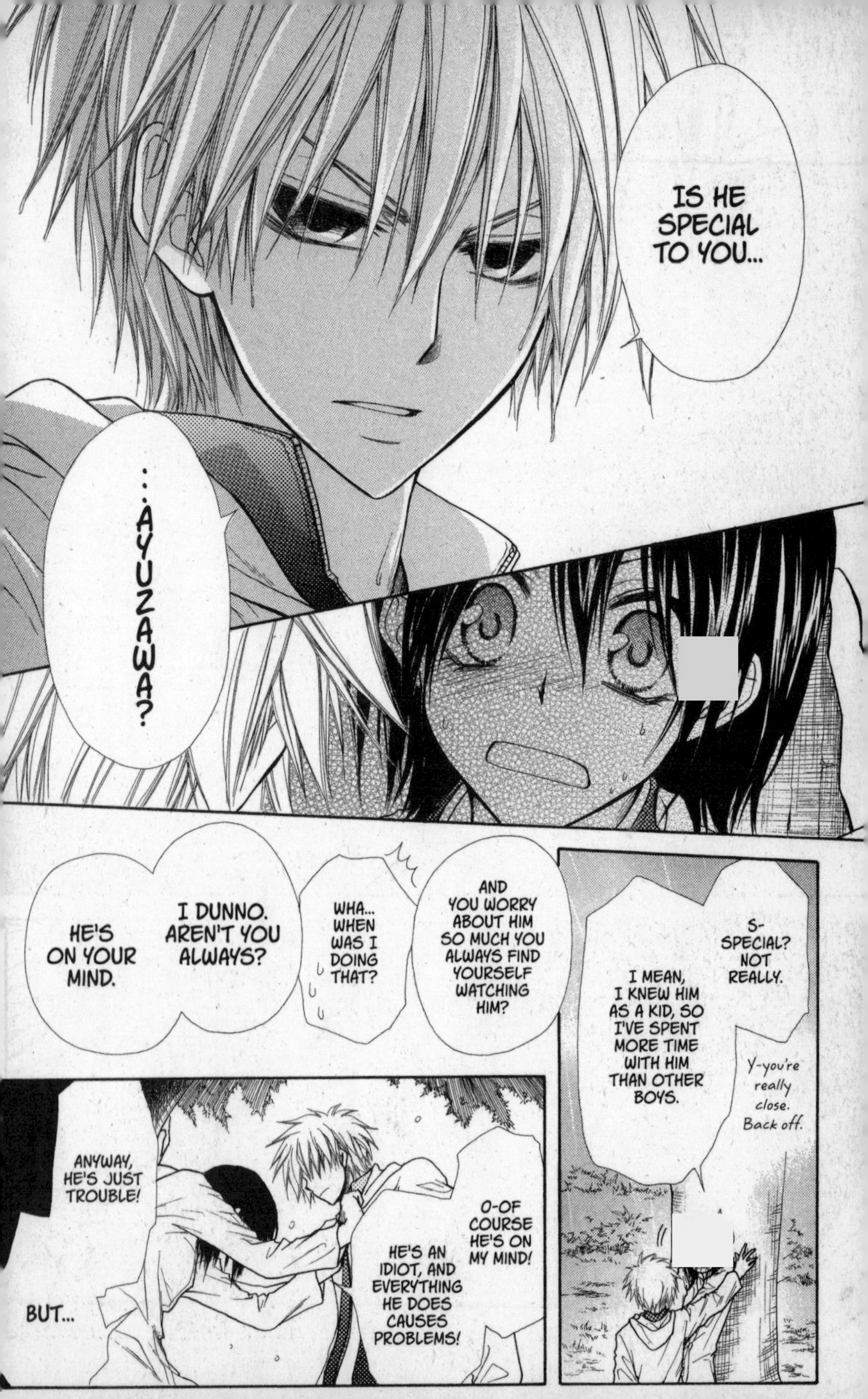

IS HE SPECIAL TO YOU...
...AYUZAWA?
S-SPECIAL? NOT REALLY.
I MEAN, I KNEW HIM AS A KID, SO I'VE SPENT MORE TIME WITH HIM THAN OTHER BOYS.
Y-you're really close. Back off.
AND YOU WORRY ABOUT HIM SO MUCH YOU ALWAYS FIND YOURSELF WATCHING HIM?
WHA... WHEN WAS I DOING THAT?
I DUNNO. AREN'T YOU ALWAYS?
HE'S ON YOUR MIND.
O-OF COURSE HE'S ON MY MIND!
HE'S AN IDIOT, AND EVERYTHING HE DOES CAUSES PROBLEMS!
ANYWAY, HE'S JUST TROUBLE!
BUT...

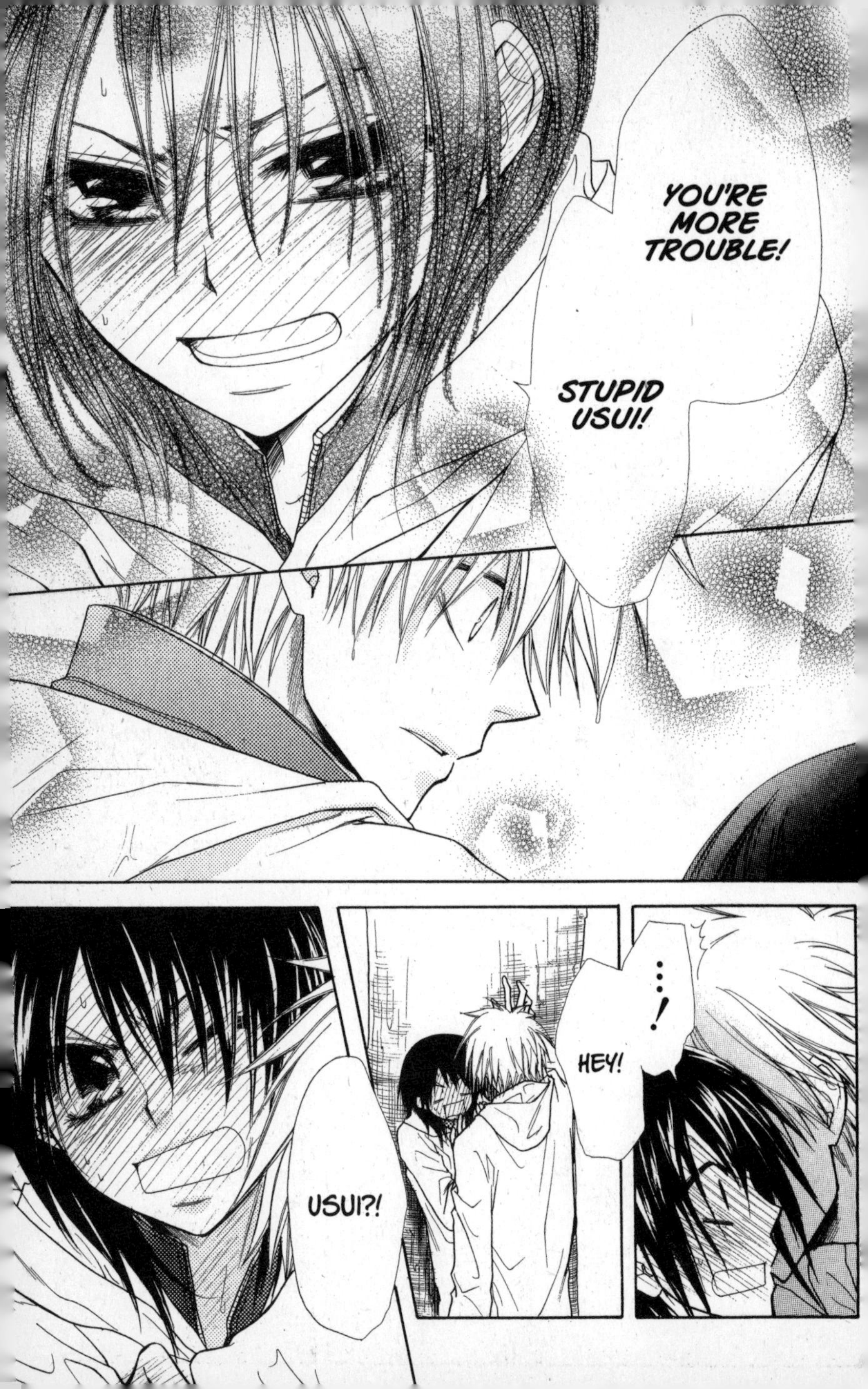
YOU'RE MORE TROUBLE!
STUPID USUI!
...!
HEY!
USUI?!

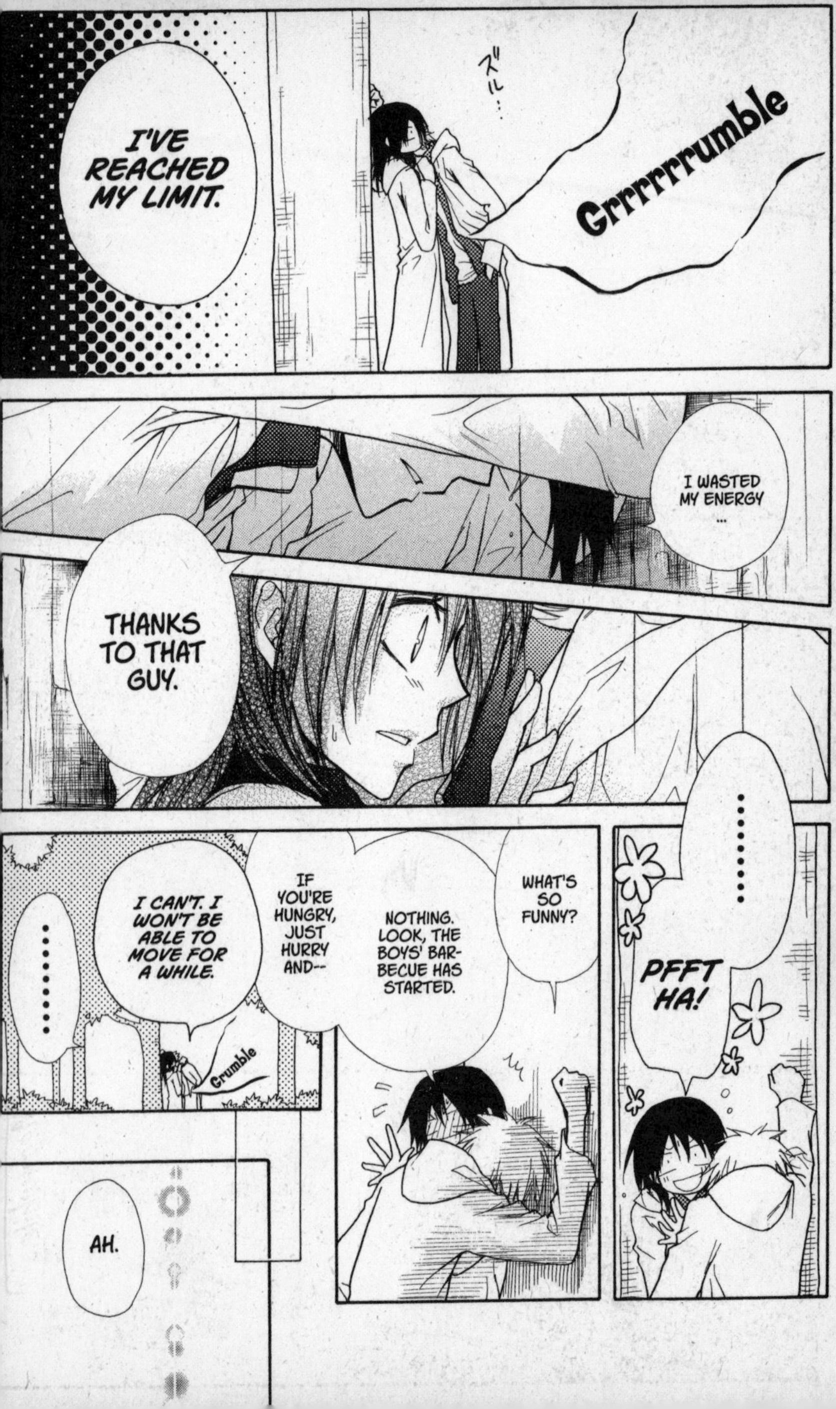
ズル…
Grrrrrrumble
I'VE REACHED MY LIMIT.
I WASTED MY ENERGY ...
THANKS TO THAT GUY.
......
PFFT HA!
WHAT'S SO FUNNY?
NOTHING. LOOK, THE BOYS' BAR-BECUE HAS STARTED.
IF YOU'RE HUNGRY, JUST HURRY AND--
I CAN'T. I WON'T BE ABLE TO MOVE FOR A WHILE.
......
Grumble
AH.

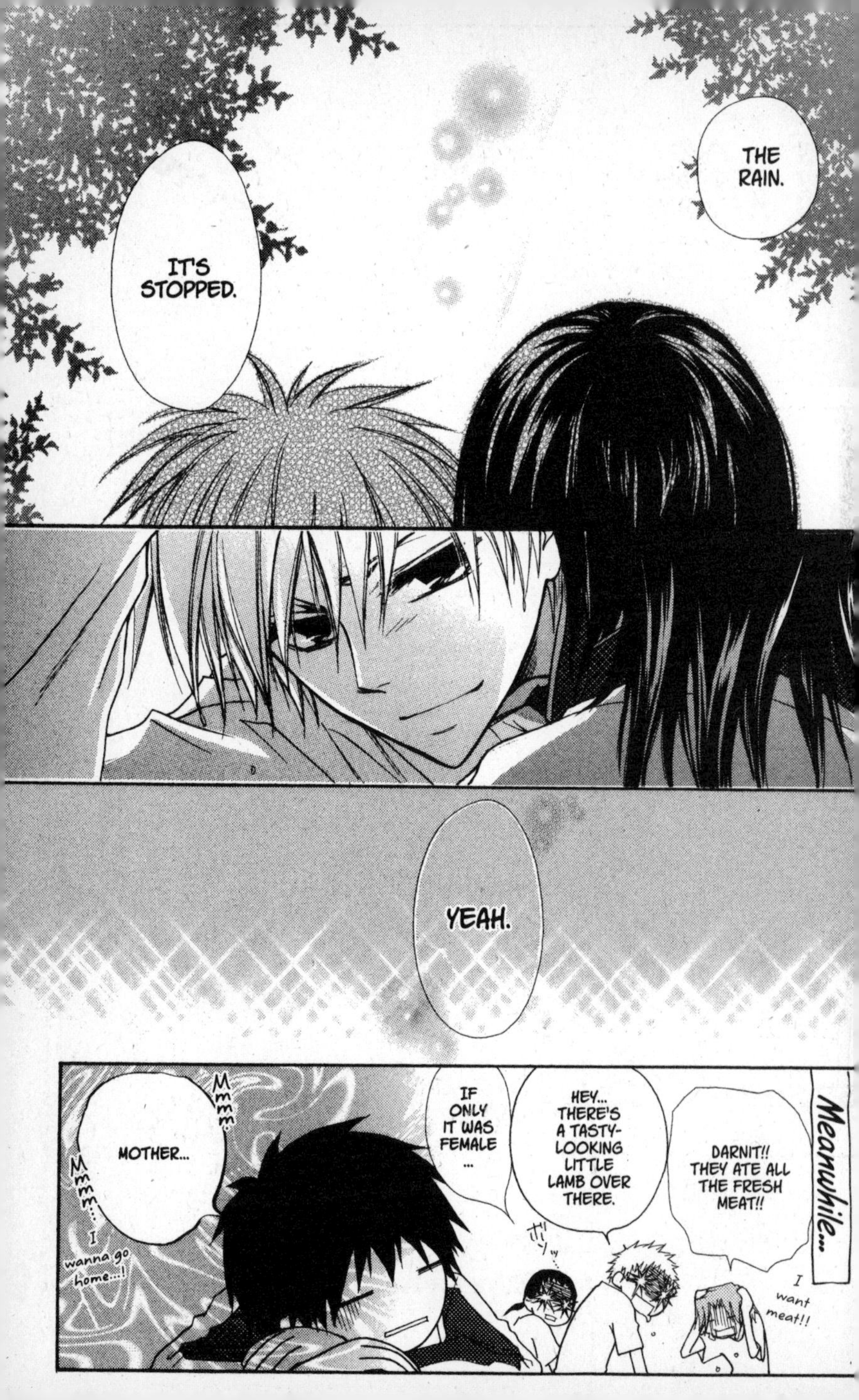
THE RAIN.
IT'S STOPPED.
YEAH.
Meanwhile...
DARNIT!! THEY ATE ALL THE FRESH MEAT!!
I want meat!!
HEY... THERE'S A TASTY-LOOKING LITTLE LAMB OVER THERE.
IF ONLY IT WAS FEMALE ...
Mmmm.
MOTHER...
Mmmm... I wanna go home...!

Q&A time...

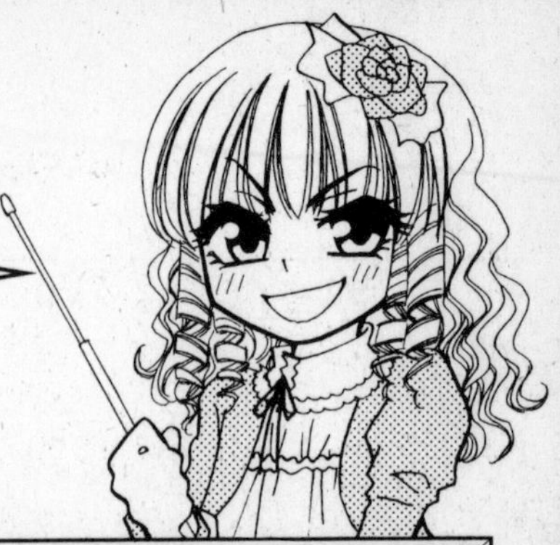

HMPH! YOU SAY YOU HAVE QUESTIONS FOR THE GREAT AOI-SAMA? I SUPPOSE I HAVE NO CHOICE. I'LL MAKE AN EXCEPTION AND ANSWER THEM FOR YOU! THERE'S NO WAY YOU'D BE ABLE TO RESIST SUCH AN ADORABLE INTERNET IDOL, AFTER ALL!

QUESTION11: WHAT DOES AOI-KUN THINK IS SO FUN ABOUT DRESSING LIKE A GIRL?

: ***JUST A--! WH-WHAT KIND OF A QUESTION IS THAT?! GIVE ME A BREAK! WHAT DO YOU KNOW ABOUT DRESSING LIKE A GIRL!?! HONESTLY, THIS IS UNBELIEVABLE!*** ARE YOU LISTENING?! I AM EXPRESSING MYSELF AS I AM BY WEARING ADORABLE CLOTHING! I LIKE LOOKING CUTE! AND IT LOOKS SO GOOD ON ME ♡***IT'S A MIRACLE!*** I CAN'T HAVE YOU TAKING SUCH MIRACLES SO LIGHTLY.♡

QUESTION 12: HAS AOI-CHAN'S VOICE CHANGED YET?

: M-MY VOICE...HASN'T CHANGED...YET...I THINK...AND HEY, STOP ASKING SUCH AWKWARD QUESTIONS! YOU MUST HAVE OTHER THINGS TO ASK!! LIKE, "ISN'T THERE AN ***AOI-SAMA'S BEST SHOTS COLLECTION OF POSTCARDS?*** " OR, "WILL THERE BE AN ***AOI-SAMA PHOTO COLLECTION?*** " OR SOMETHING!

QUESTION 13: DOES AOI-CHAN HAVE ANY FRIENDS AT SCHOOL?

: ***...!!! SHUT UP! LEAVE ME ALONE, STUPID!!!*** FORGET IT, I'M NEVER TAKING ANY MORE OF YOUR STUPID QUESTIONS EVER AGAIN!! AGAIN! AGAIN...AGAIN...(ECHO)

: HUH? DID AOI-CHAN RUN OFF SOMEWHERE? HE WAS SUPPOSED TO BE TAKING QUESTIONS HERE. THAT'S WEIRD. WELL, I GUESS WE'LL MOVE ON AND TAKE SOME QUESTIONS FOR YUKIMURA...WOW, ***THERE'S A LOT OF THEM!***

: ***REALLY, MISS PRESIDENT?!***

: OH, YOU'RE HERE, YUKIMURA?! YEAH, I HAVEN'T READ THEM YET, BUT I THINK YOU HAVE THE ***MOST OF ANYONE THIS TIME.***

: WOW, I'M SO HAPPY! I WONDER WHAT KIND OF QUESTIONS THEY ARE!

: ***WELL, LET'S GET STARTED, YUKIMURA!***

: ***YES, MA'AM!***

MY FAVORITE THINGS:

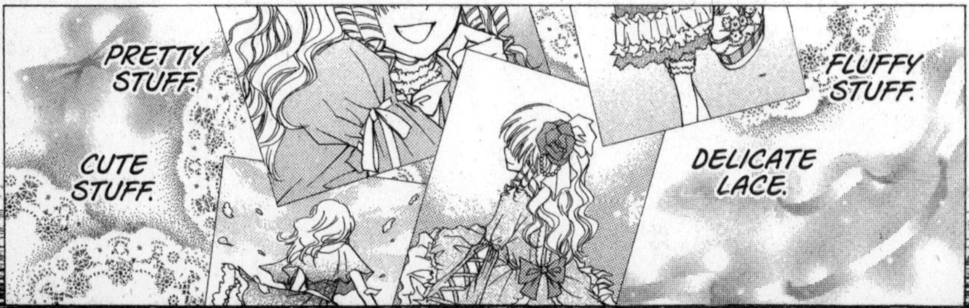
FLUFFY STUFF.
DELICATE LACE.
PRETTY STUFF.
CUTE STUFF.

MY LEAST FAVORITE THINGS:

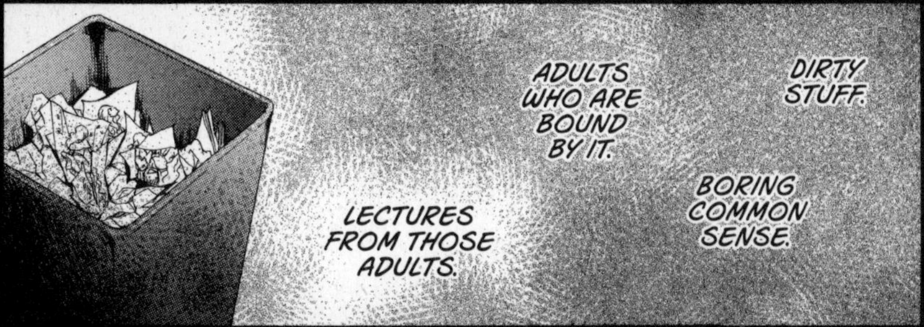
DIRTY STUFF.
BORING COMMON SENSE.
ADULTS WHO ARE BOUND BY IT.
LECTURES FROM THOSE ADULTS.

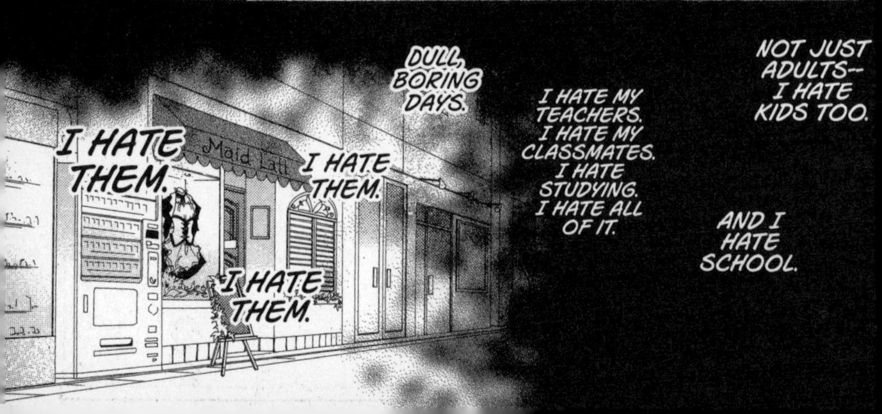
NOT JUST ADULTS-- I HATE KIDS TOO.
AND I HATE SCHOOL.
I HATE MY TEACHERS. I HATE MY CLASSMATES. I HATE STUDYING. I HATE ALL OF IT.
DULL, BORING DAYS.
I HATE THEM.
I HATE THEM.
I HATE THEM.
Maid Latte

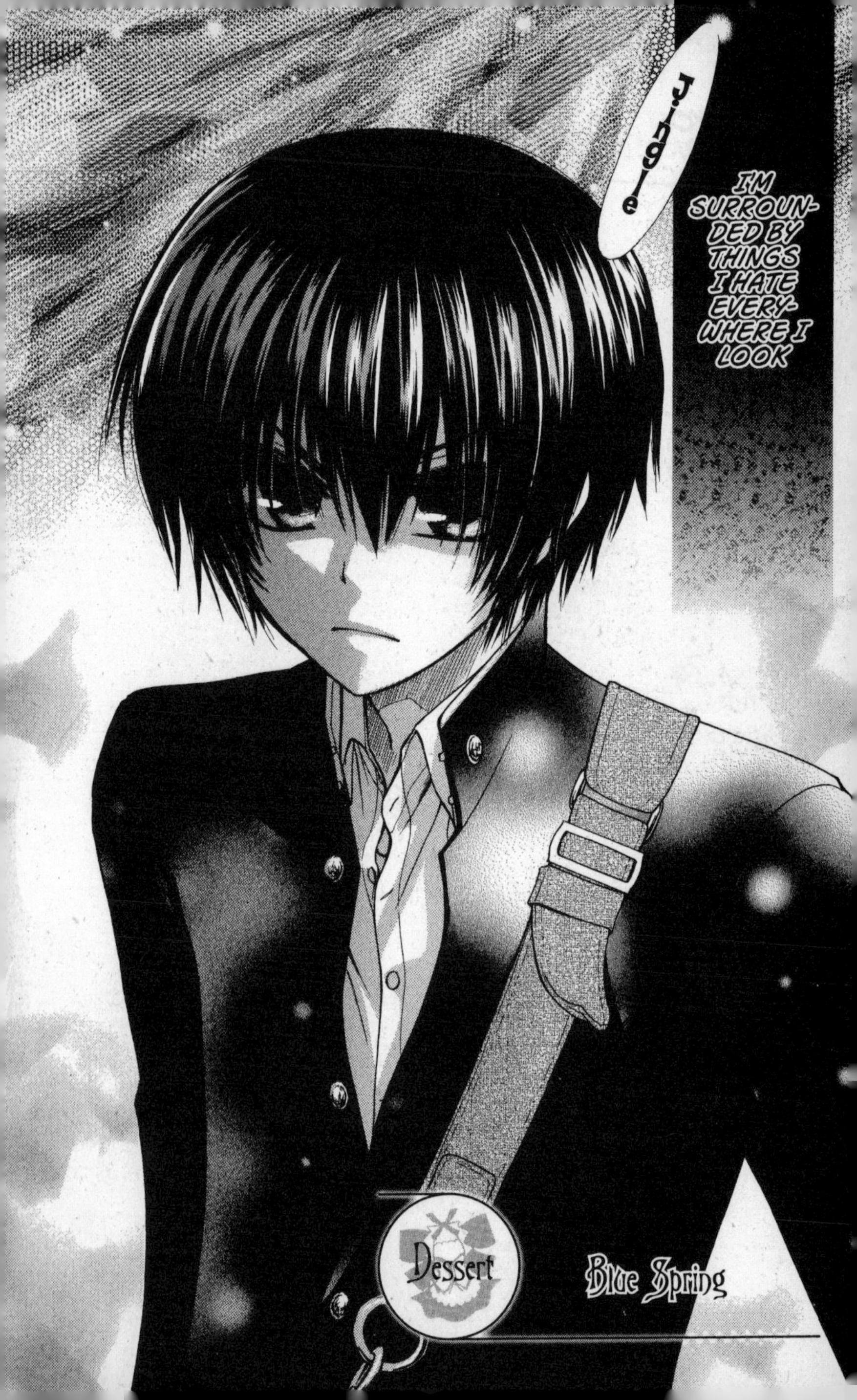
Jingle
I'M SURROUNDED BY THINGS I HATE EVERYWHERE I LOOK
Dessert
Blue Spring

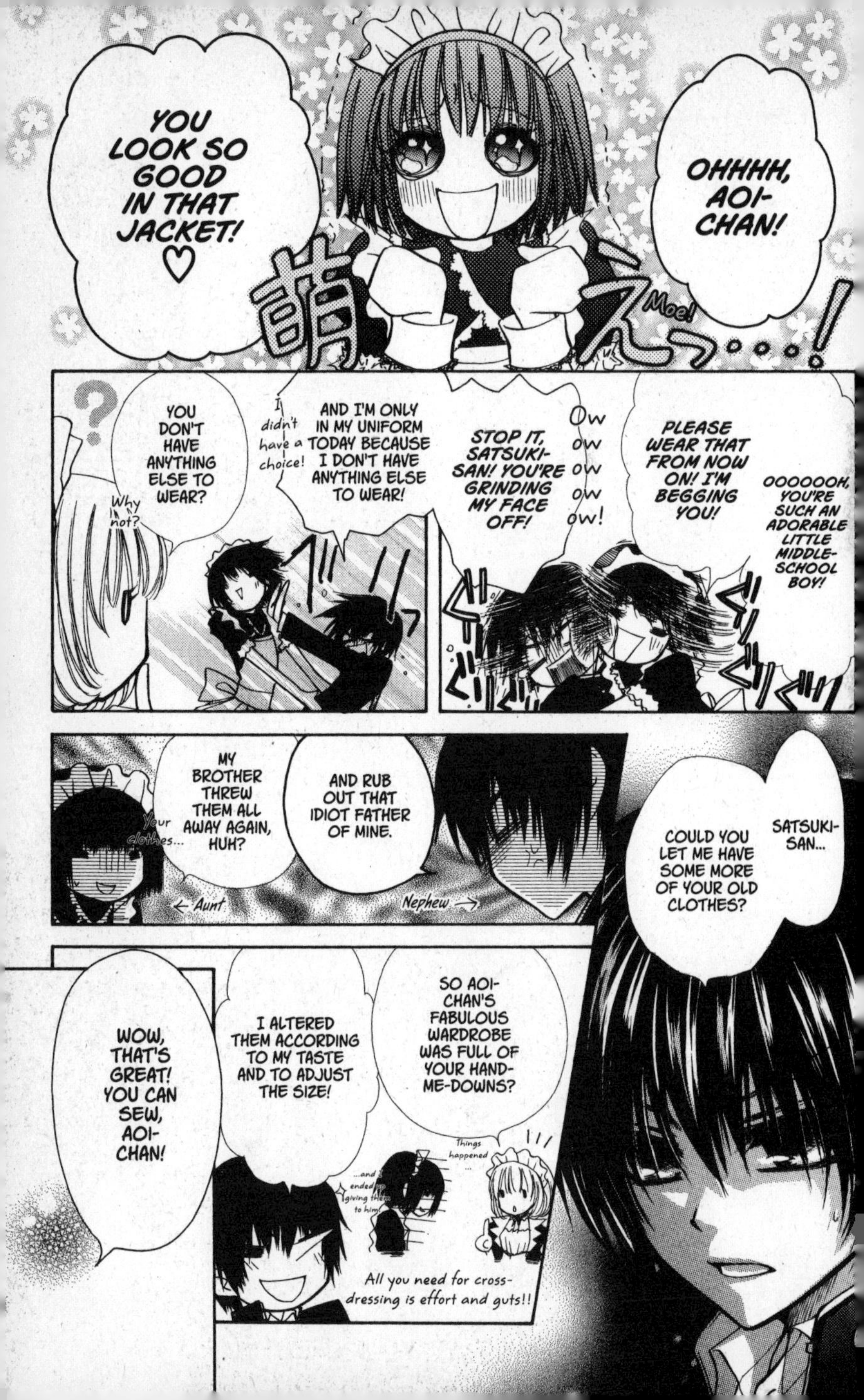
OHHHH, AOI-CHAN!
YOU LOOK SO GOOD IN THAT JACKET! ♡
萌えっ…!
Moe!
OOOOOOH, YOU'RE SUCH AN ADORABLE LITTLE MIDDLE-SCHOOL BOY!
PLEASE WEAR THAT FROM NOW ON! I'M BEGGING YOU!
STOP IT, SATSUKI-SAN! YOU'RE GRINDING MY FACE OFF!
Ow ow ow ow ow!
AND I'M ONLY IN MY UNIFORM TODAY BECAUSE I DON'T HAVE ANYTHING ELSE TO WEAR!
I didn't have a choice!
YOU DON'T HAVE ANYTHING ELSE TO WEAR?
Why not?
SATSUKI-SAN...
COULD YOU LET ME HAVE SOME MORE OF YOUR OLD CLOTHES?
AND RUB OUT THAT IDIOT FATHER OF MINE.
Nephew →
MY BROTHER THREW THEM ALL AWAY AGAIN, HUH?
Your clothes...
← Aunt
SO AOI-CHAN'S FABULOUS WARDROBE WAS FULL OF YOUR HAND-ME-DOWNS?
Things happened ...
I ALTERED THEM ACCORDING TO MY TASTE AND TO ADJUST THE SIZE!
...and I ended up giving them to him!
WOW, THAT'S GREAT! YOU CAN SEW, AOI-CHAN!
All you need for cross-dressing is effort and guts!!

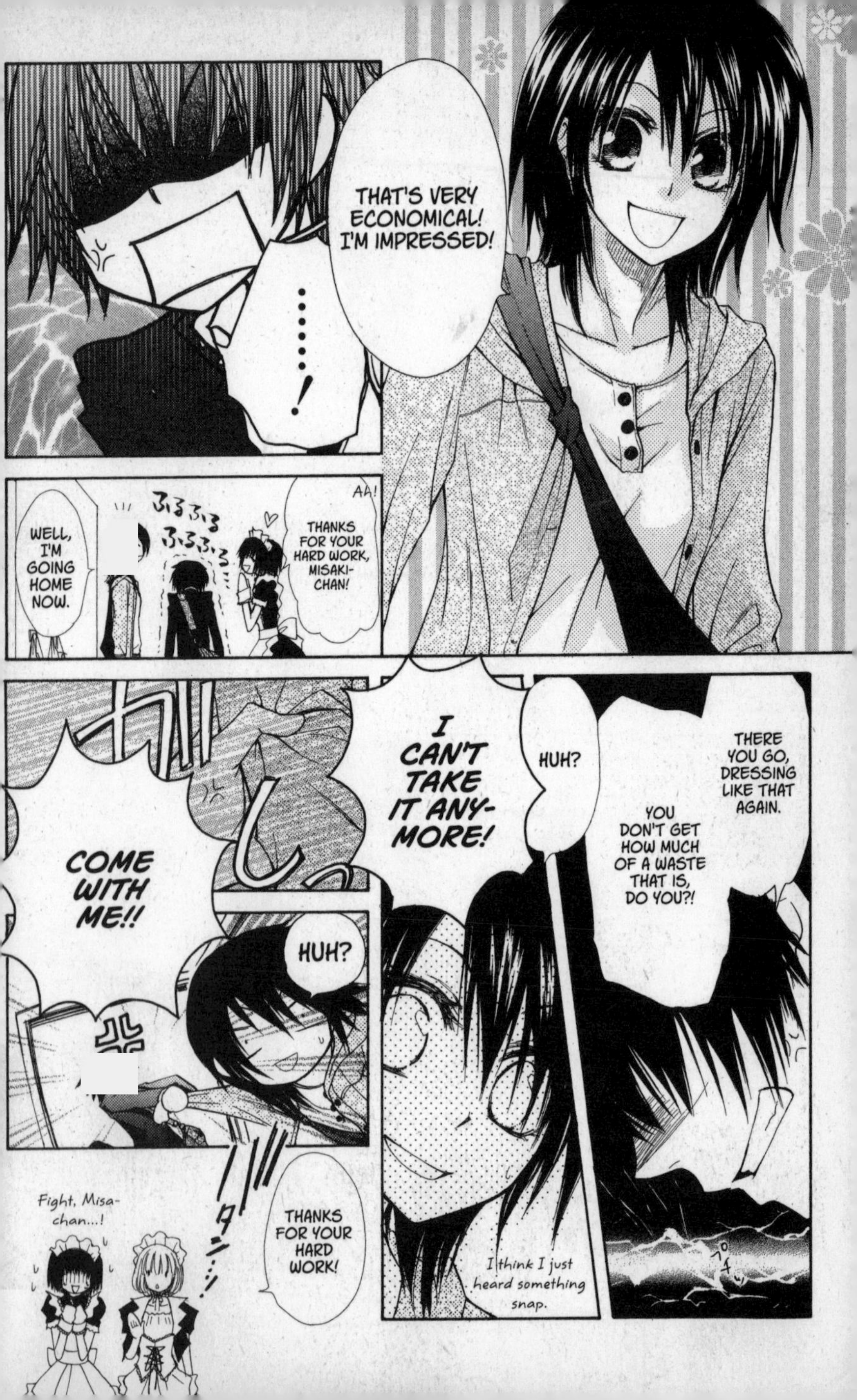
THAT'S VERY ECONOMICAL! I'M IMPRESSED!
......!
AH!
THANKS FOR YOUR HARD WORK, MISAKI-CHAN!
ふるふる ふるふる
WELL, I'M GOING HOME NOW.
THERE YOU GO, DRESSING LIKE THAT AGAIN.
YOU DON'T GET HOW MUCH OF A WASTE THAT IS, DO YOU?!
HUH?
I think I just heard something snap.
I CAN'T TAKE IT ANY-MORE!
COME WITH ME!!
HUH?
THANKS FOR YOUR HARD WORK!
Fight, Misa-chan...!

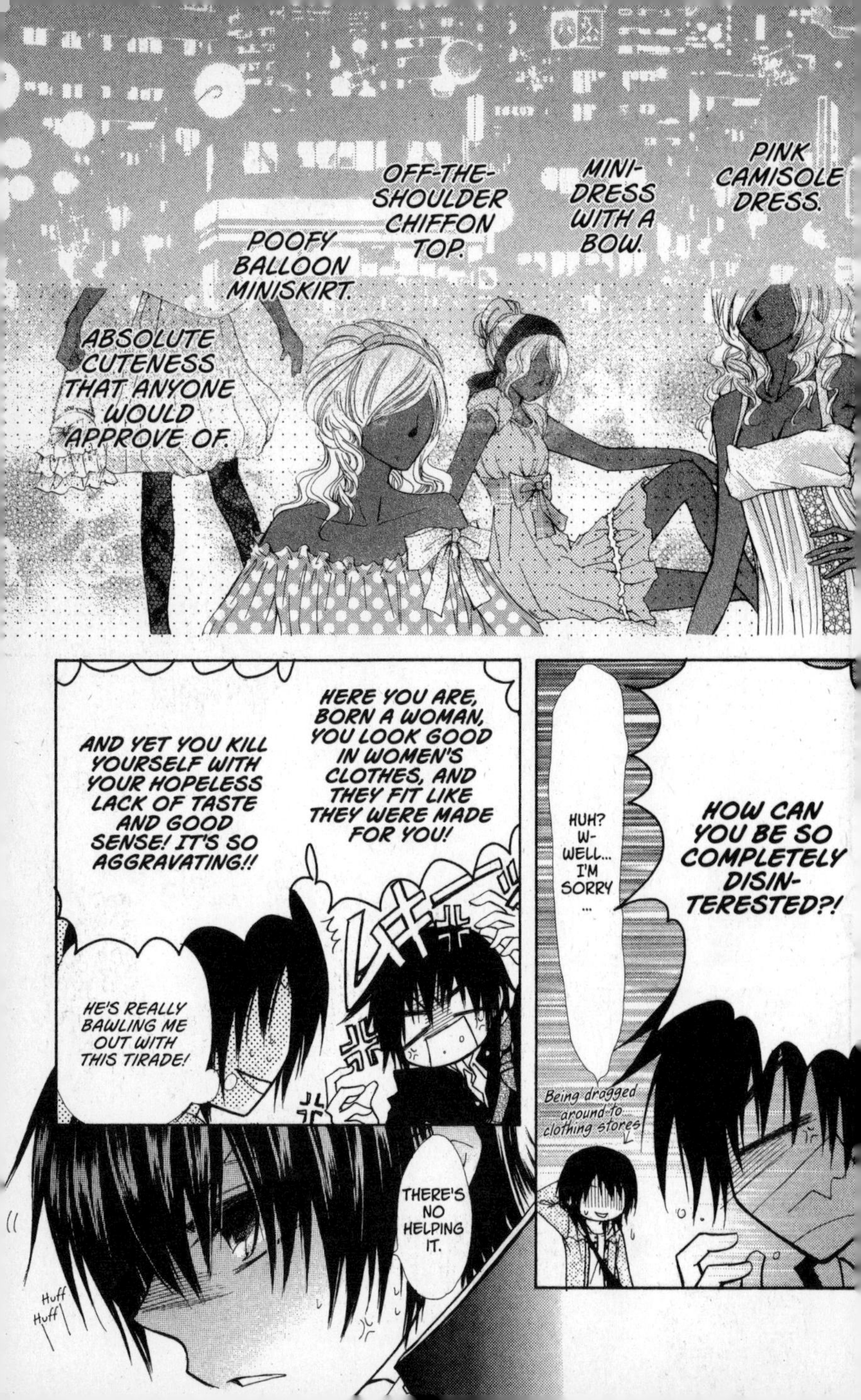
PINK CAMISOLE DRESS.
MINI-DRESS WITH A BOW.
OFF-THE-SHOULDER CHIFFON TOP.
POOFY BALLOON MINISKIRT.
ABSOLUTE CUTENESS THAT ANYONE WOULD APPROVE OF.
HOW CAN YOU BE SO COMPLETELY DISIN-TERESTED?!
HUH? W-WELL... I'M SORRY ...
Being dragged around to clothing stores
HERE YOU ARE, BORN A WOMAN, YOU LOOK GOOD IN WOMEN'S CLOTHES, AND THEY FIT LIKE THEY WERE MADE FOR YOU!
AND YET YOU KILL YOURSELF WITH YOUR HOPELESS LACK OF TASTE AND GOOD SENSE! IT'S SO AGGRAVATING!!
HE'S REALLY BAWLING ME OUT WITH THIS TIRADE!
THERE'S NO HELPING IT.
Huff Huff

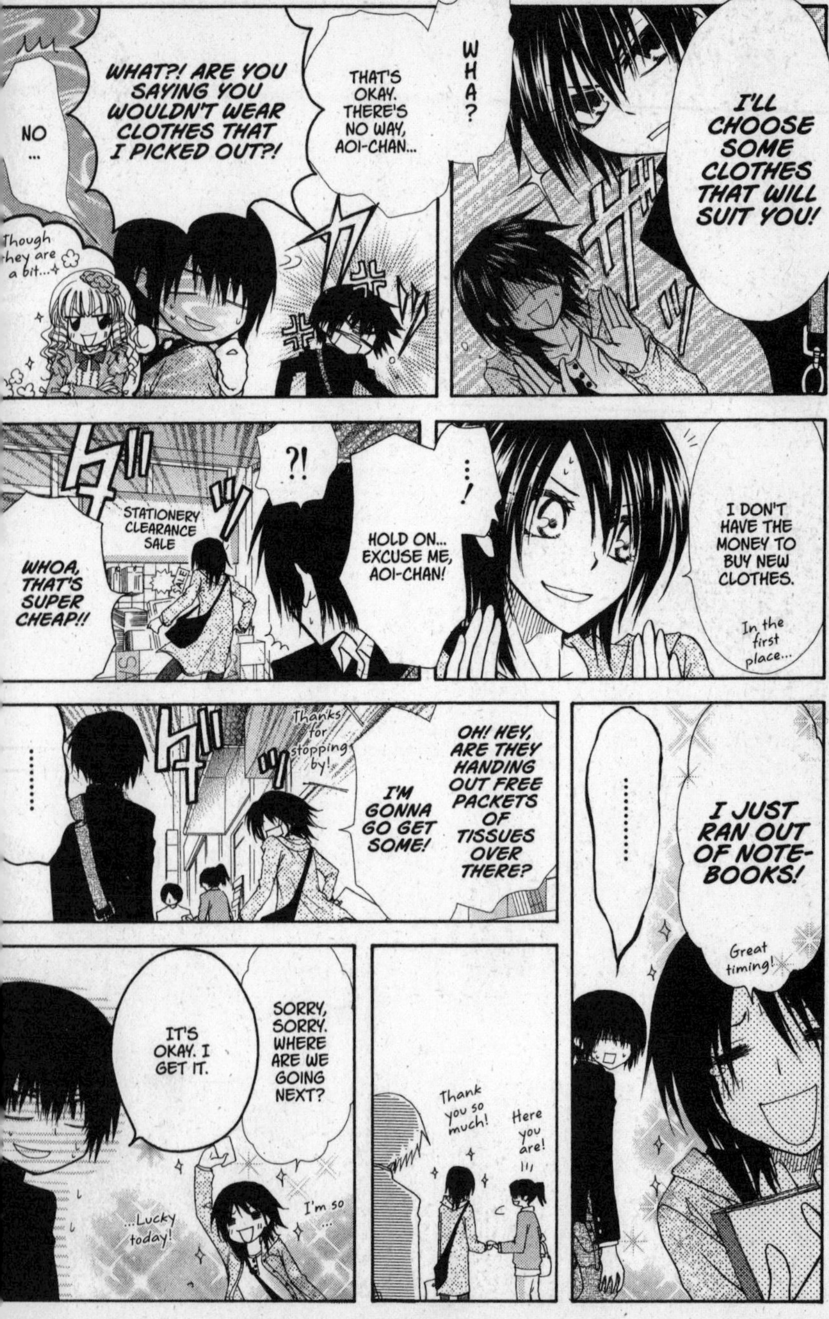
I'LL CHOOSE SOME CLOTHES THAT WILL SUIT YOU!
WHA?
THAT'S OKAY. THERE'S NO WAY, AOI-CHAN...
WHAT?! ARE YOU SAYING YOU WOULDN'T WEAR CLOTHES THAT I PICKED OUT?!
NO ...
Though they are a bit...
I DON'T HAVE THE MONEY TO BUY NEW CLOTHES.
In the first place...
...!
HOLD ON... EXCUSE ME, AOI-CHAN!
?!
STATIONERY CLEARANCE SALE
WHOA, THAT'S SUPER CHEAP!!
I JUST RAN OUT OF NOTE-BOOKS!
....
Great timing!
OH! HEY, ARE THEY HANDING OUT FREE PACKETS OF TISSUES OVER THERE?
I'M GONNA GO GET SOME!
Thanks for stopping by!
....
Here you are!
Thank you so much!
SORRY, SORRY. WHERE ARE WE GOING NEXT?
IT'S OKAY. I GET IT.
I'm so ...
...Lucky today!

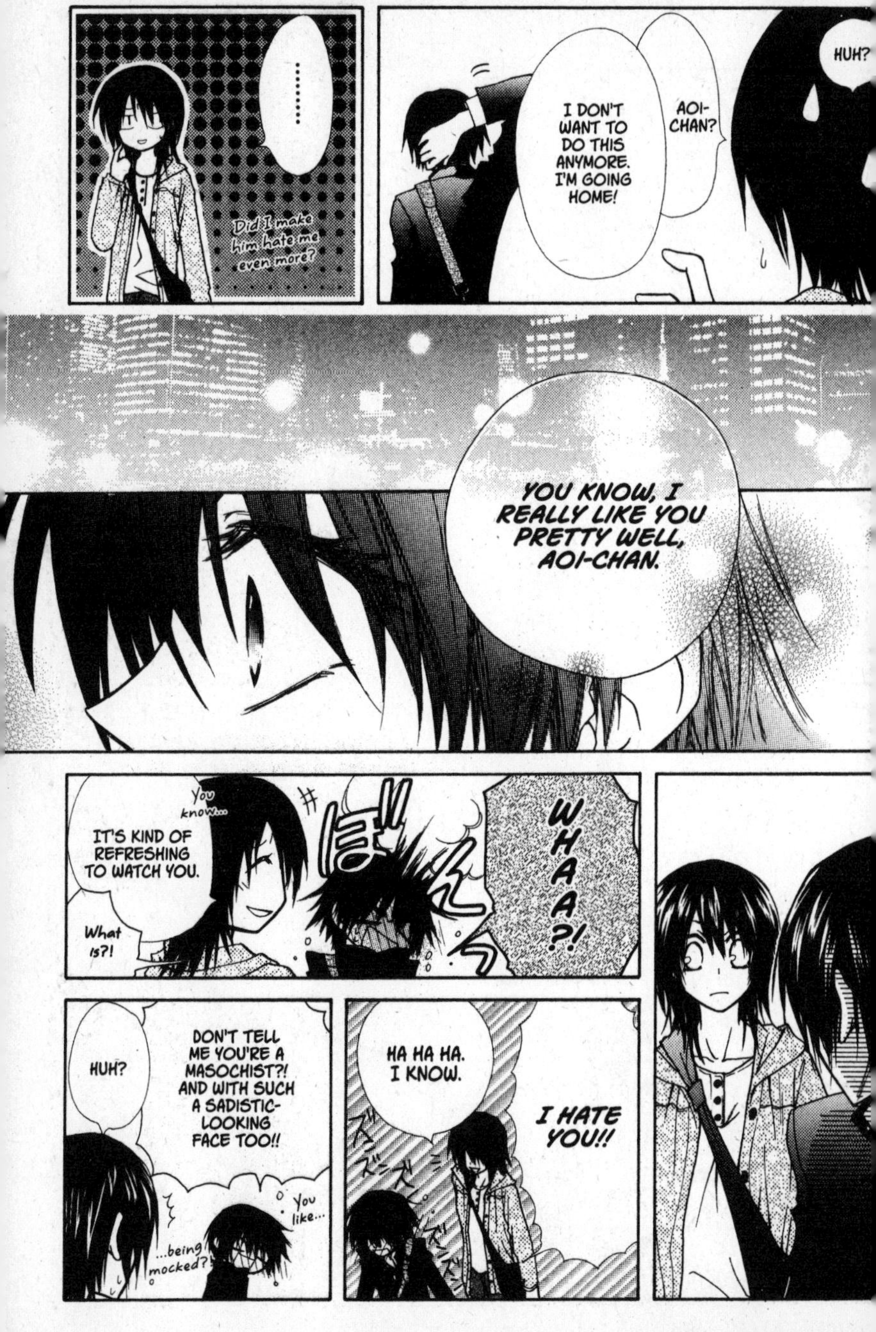
HUH?
AOI-CHAN?
I DON'T WANT TO DO THIS ANYMORE. I'M GOING HOME!
......
Did I make him hate me even more?
YOU KNOW, I REALLY LIKE YOU PRETTY WELL, AOI-CHAN.
WHAAA?!
You know...
IT'S KIND OF REFRESHING TO WATCH YOU.
What is?!
I HATE YOU!!
HA HA HA. I KNOW.
DON'T TELL ME YOU'RE A MASOCHIST?! AND WITH SUCH A SADISTIC-LOOKING FACE TOO!!
HUH?
You like...
...being mocked?

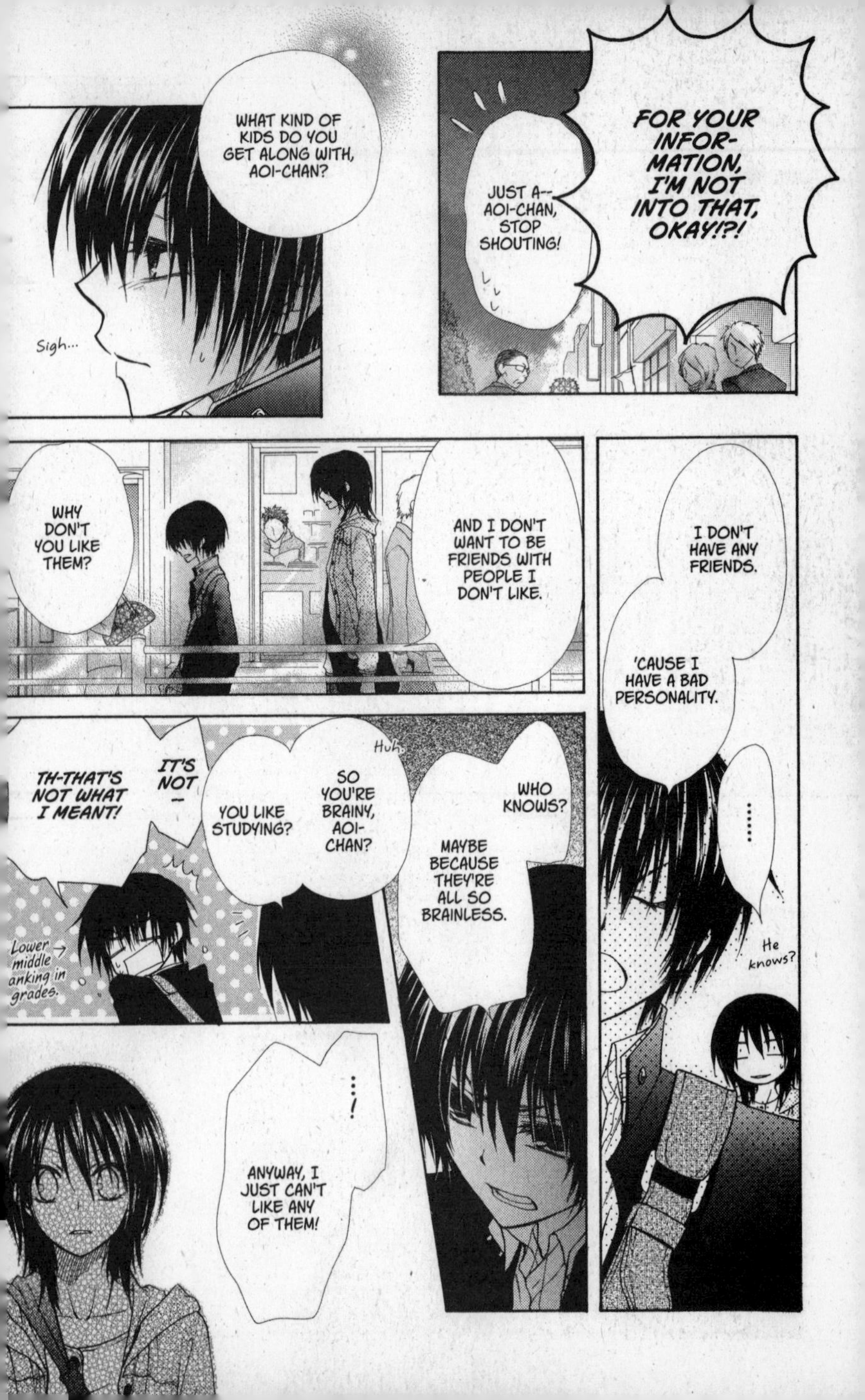
FOR YOUR INFORMATION, I'M NOT INTO THAT, OKAY!?!
JUST A-- AOI-CHAN, STOP SHOUTING!
WHAT KIND OF KIDS DO YOU GET ALONG WITH, AOI-CHAN?
Sigh...
I DON'T HAVE ANY FRIENDS.
'CAUSE I HAVE A BAD PERSONALITY.
......
He knows?
AND I DON'T WANT TO BE FRIENDS WITH PEOPLE I DON'T LIKE.
WHY DON'T YOU LIKE THEM?
WHO KNOWS?
MAYBE BECAUSE THEY'RE ALL SO BRAINLESS.
Huh.
SO YOU'RE BRAINY, AOI-CHAN?
YOU LIKE STUDYING?
IT'S NOT—
TH-THAT'S NOT WHAT I MEANT!
Lower middle anking in grades.
...!
ANYWAY, I JUST CAN'T LIKE ANY OF THEM!

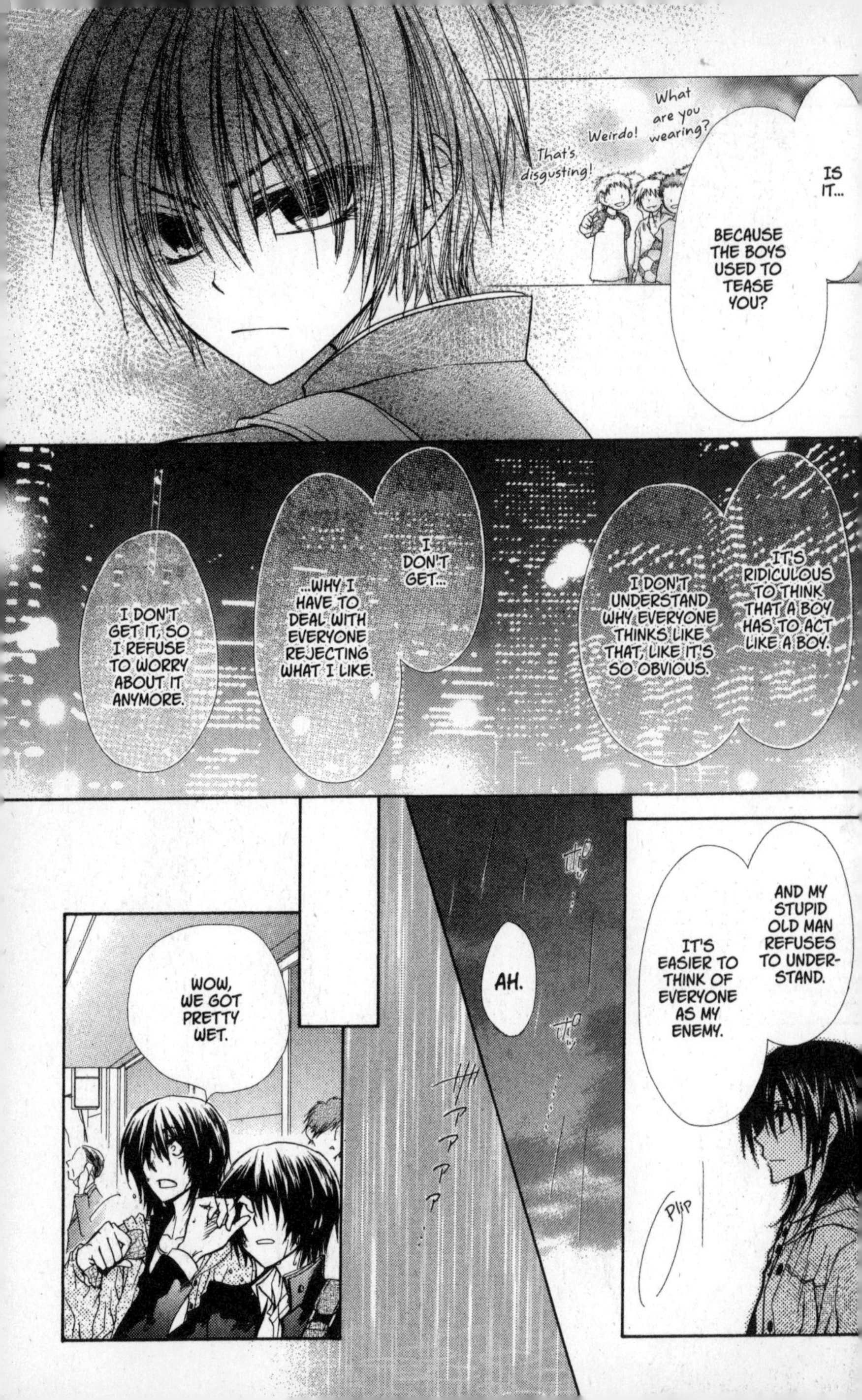
IS IT... BECAUSE THE BOYS USED TO TEASE YOU?
What are you wearing?
Weirdo!
That's disgusting!
IT'S RIDICULOUS TO THINK THAT A BOY HAS TO ACT LIKE A BOY.
I DON'T UNDERSTAND WHY EVERYONE THINKS LIKE THAT, LIKE IT'S SO OBVIOUS.
I DON'T GET...
...WHY I HAVE TO DEAL WITH EVERYONE REJECTING WHAT I LIKE.
I DON'T GET IT, SO I REFUSE TO WORRY ABOUT IT ANYMORE.
AND MY STUPID OLD MAN REFUSES TO UNDER-STAND.
IT'S EASIER TO THINK OF EVERYONE AS MY ENEMY.
Plip
AH.
WOW, WE GOT PRETTY WET.

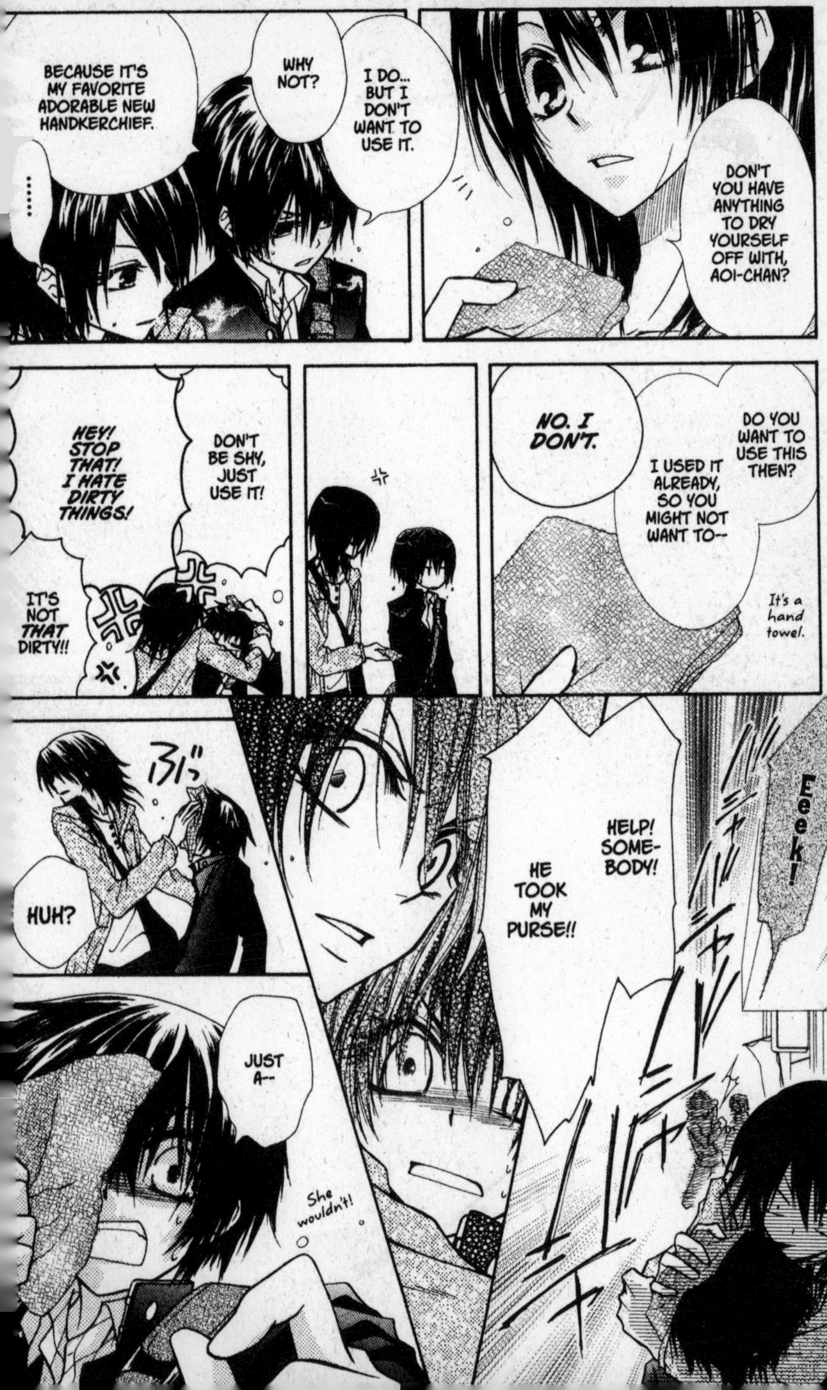
DON'T YOU HAVE ANYTHING TO DRY YOURSELF OFF WITH, AOI-CHAN?
I DO... BUT I DON'T WANT TO USE IT.
WHY NOT?
BECAUSE IT'S MY FAVORITE ADORABLE NEW HANDKERCHIEF.
......
DO YOU WANT TO USE THIS THEN?
I USED IT ALREADY, SO YOU MIGHT NOT WANT TO--
NO. I DON'T.
It's a hand towel.
DON'T BE SHY, JUST USE IT!
HEY! STOP THAT! I HATE DIRTY THINGS!
IT'S NOT THAT DIRTY!!
Eeek!
HELP! SOMEBODY!
HE TOOK MY PURSE!!
HUH?
JUST A--
She wouldn't!

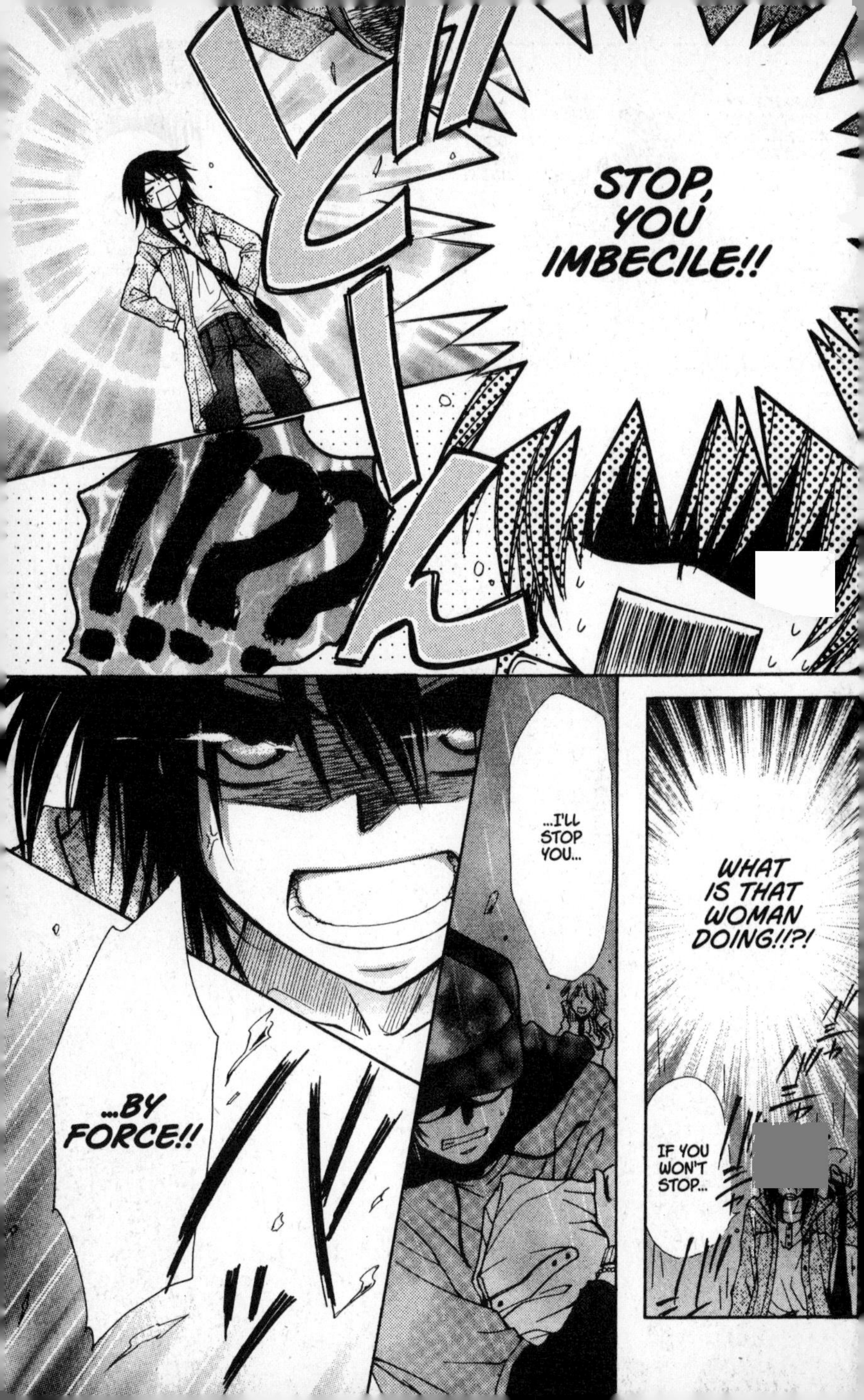
STOP, YOU IMBECILE!!
!!?...
WHAT IS THAT WOMAN DOING!!?!
IF YOU WON'T STOP...
...I'LL STOP YOU...
...BY FORCE!!

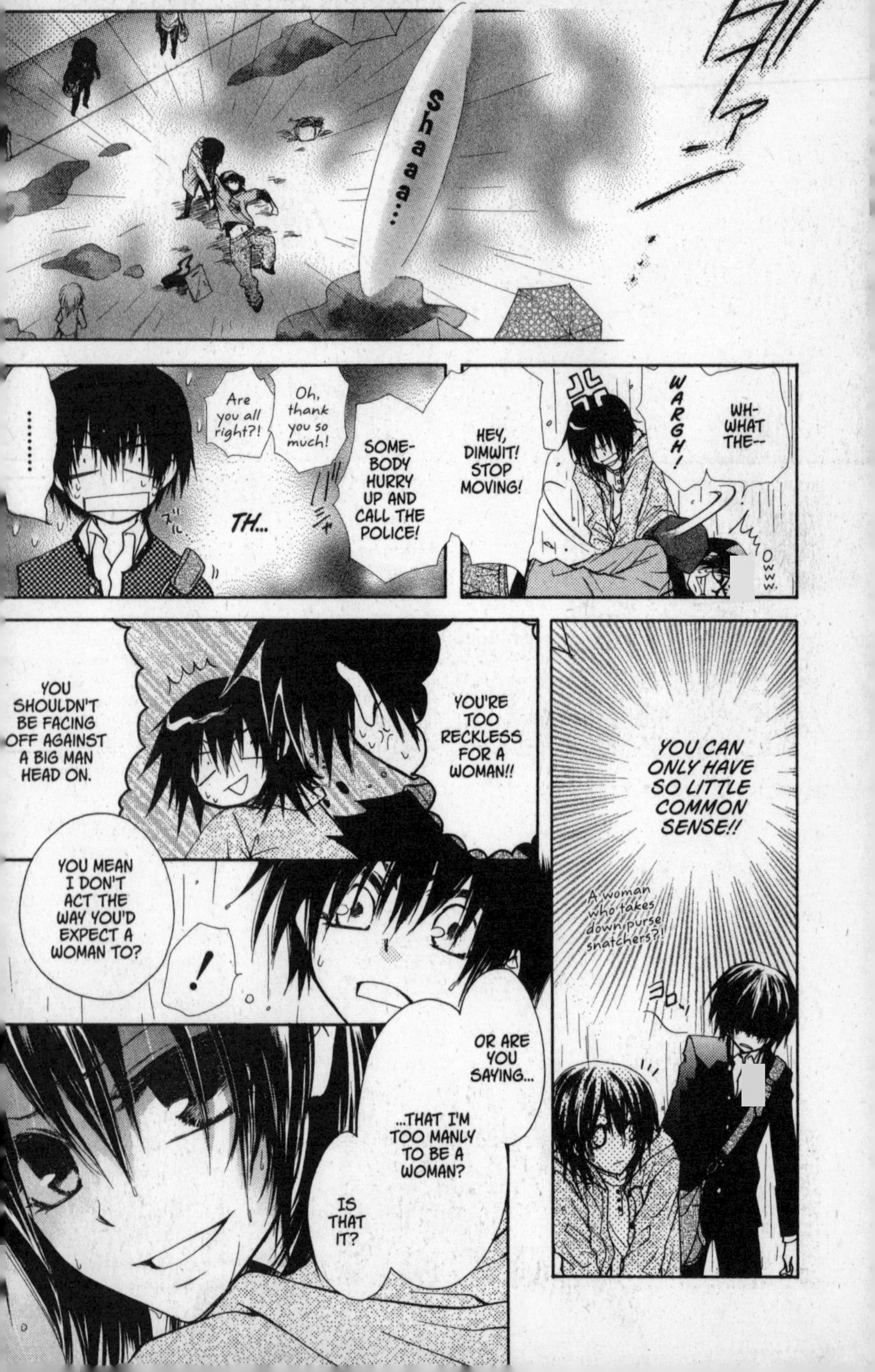
Shaaaa...
WH-WHAT THE--
WARGH!
Owww.
HEY, DIMWIT! STOP MOVING!
SOME-BODY HURRY UP AND CALL THE POLICE!
Oh, thank you so much!
Are you all right?!
TH...
......
YOU CAN ONLY HAVE SO LITTLE COMMON SENSE!!
A woman who takes down purse snatchers?!
YOU'RE TOO RECKLESS FOR A WOMAN!!
YOU SHOULDN'T BE FACING OFF AGAINST A BIG MAN HEAD ON.
!
YOU MEAN I DON'T ACT THE WAY YOU'D EXPECT A WOMAN TO?
OR ARE YOU SAYING...
...THAT I'M TOO MANLY TO BE A WOMAN?
IS THAT IT?

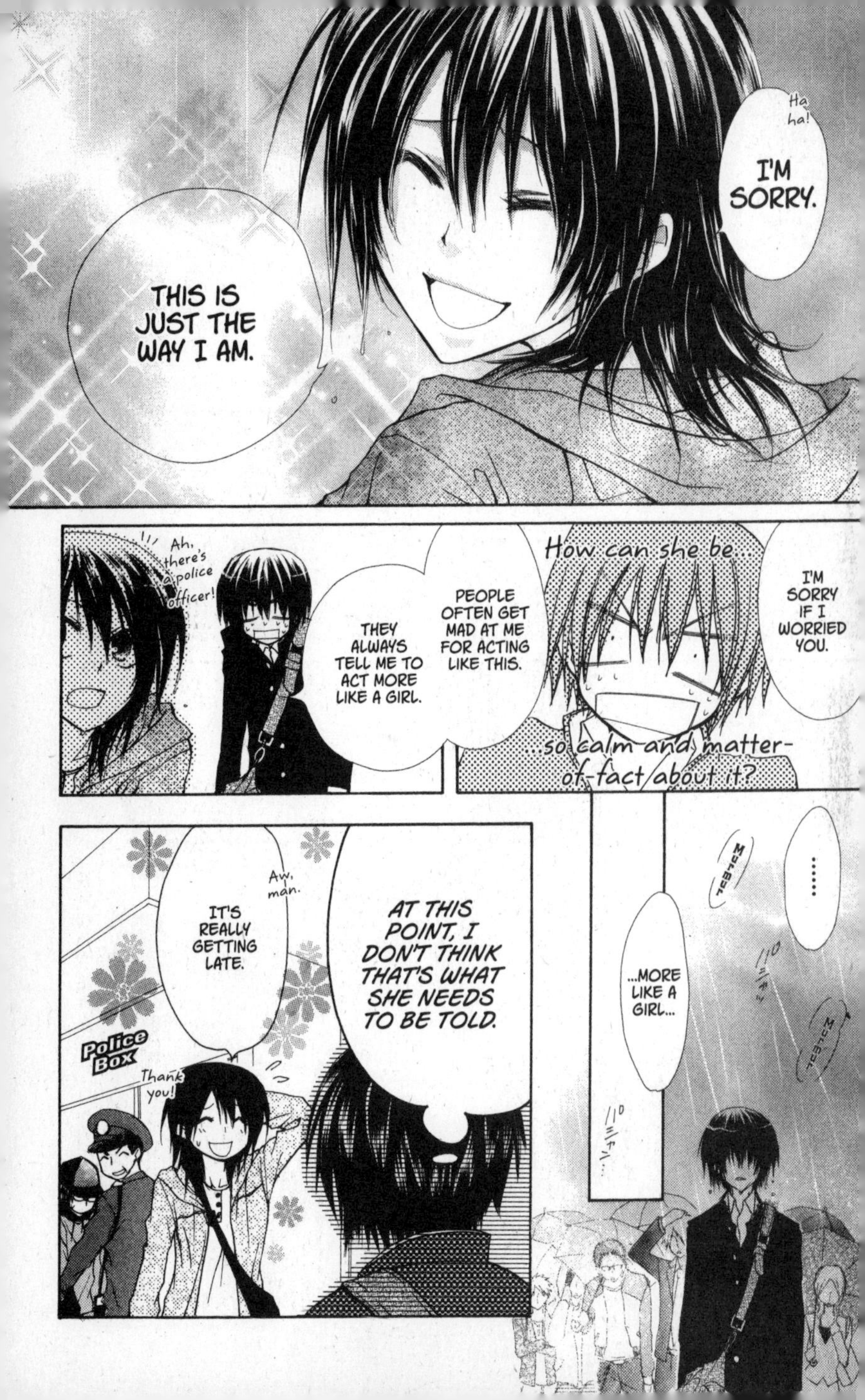
Ha ha!
I'M SORRY.
THIS IS JUST THE WAY I AM.
I'M SORRY IF I WORRIED YOU.
How can she be...
...so calm and matter-of-fact about it?
PEOPLE OFTEN GET MAD AT ME FOR ACTING LIKE THIS.
THEY ALWAYS TELL ME TO ACT MORE LIKE A GIRL.
Ah, there's a police officer!
......
MUMBLE
...MORE LIKE A GIRL...
AT THIS POINT, I DON'T THINK THAT'S WHAT SHE NEEDS TO BE TOLD.
Aw, man.
IT'S REALLY GETTING LATE.
Police Box
Thank you!

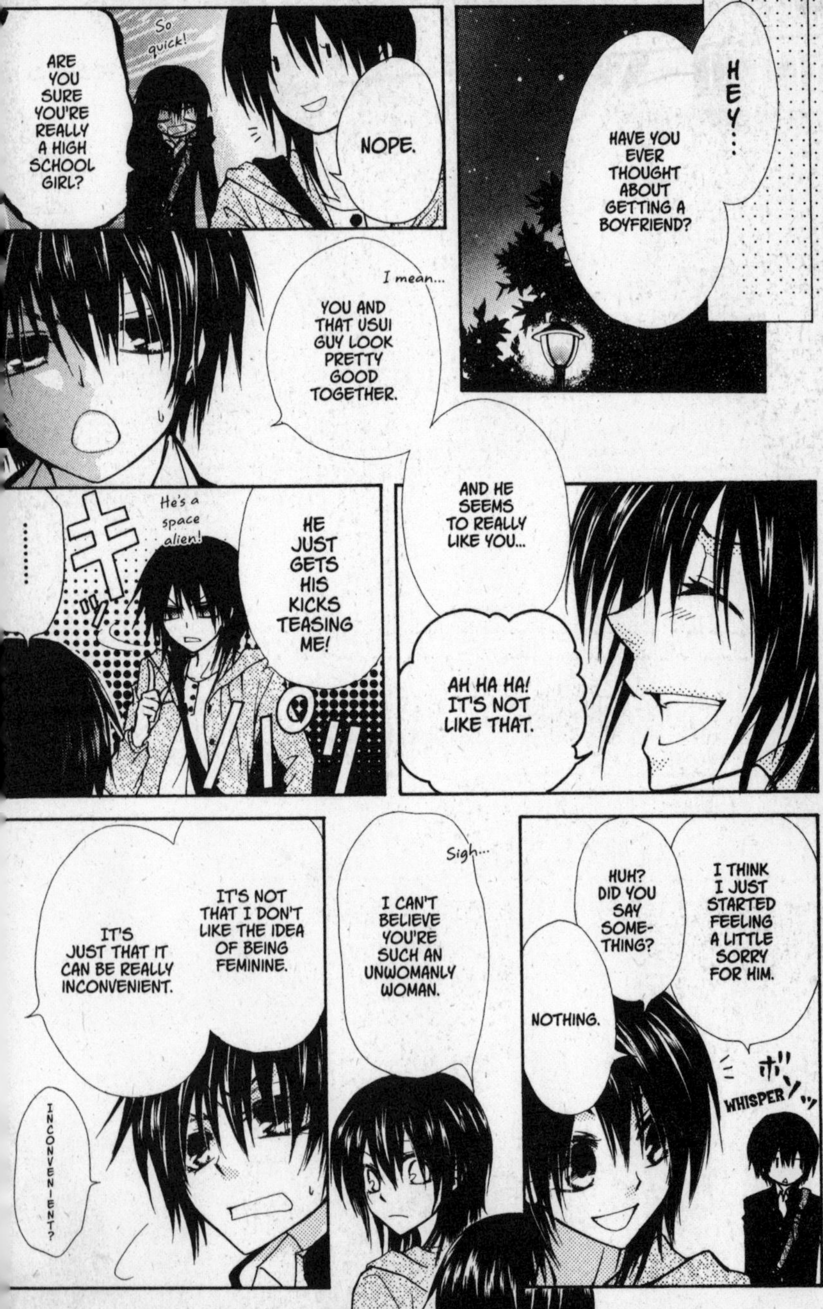
HEY...
HAVE YOU EVER THOUGHT ABOUT GETTING A BOYFRIEND?
NOPE.
So quick!
ARE YOU SURE YOU'RE REALLY A HIGH SCHOOL GIRL?
I mean...
YOU AND THAT USUI GUY LOOK PRETTY GOOD TOGETHER.
AND HE SEEMS TO REALLY LIKE YOU...
AH HA HA! IT'S NOT LIKE THAT.
HE JUST GETS HIS KICKS TEASING ME!
He's a space alien!
......
I THINK I JUST STARTED FEELING A LITTLE SORRY FOR HIM.
WHISPER
HUH? DID YOU SAY SOME-THING?
NOTHING.
Sigh...
I CAN'T BELIEVE YOU'RE SUCH AN UNWOMANLY WOMAN.
IT'S NOT THAT I DON'T LIKE THE IDEA OF BEING FEMININE.
IT'S JUST THAT IT CAN BE REALLY INCONVENIENT.
INCONVENIENT?

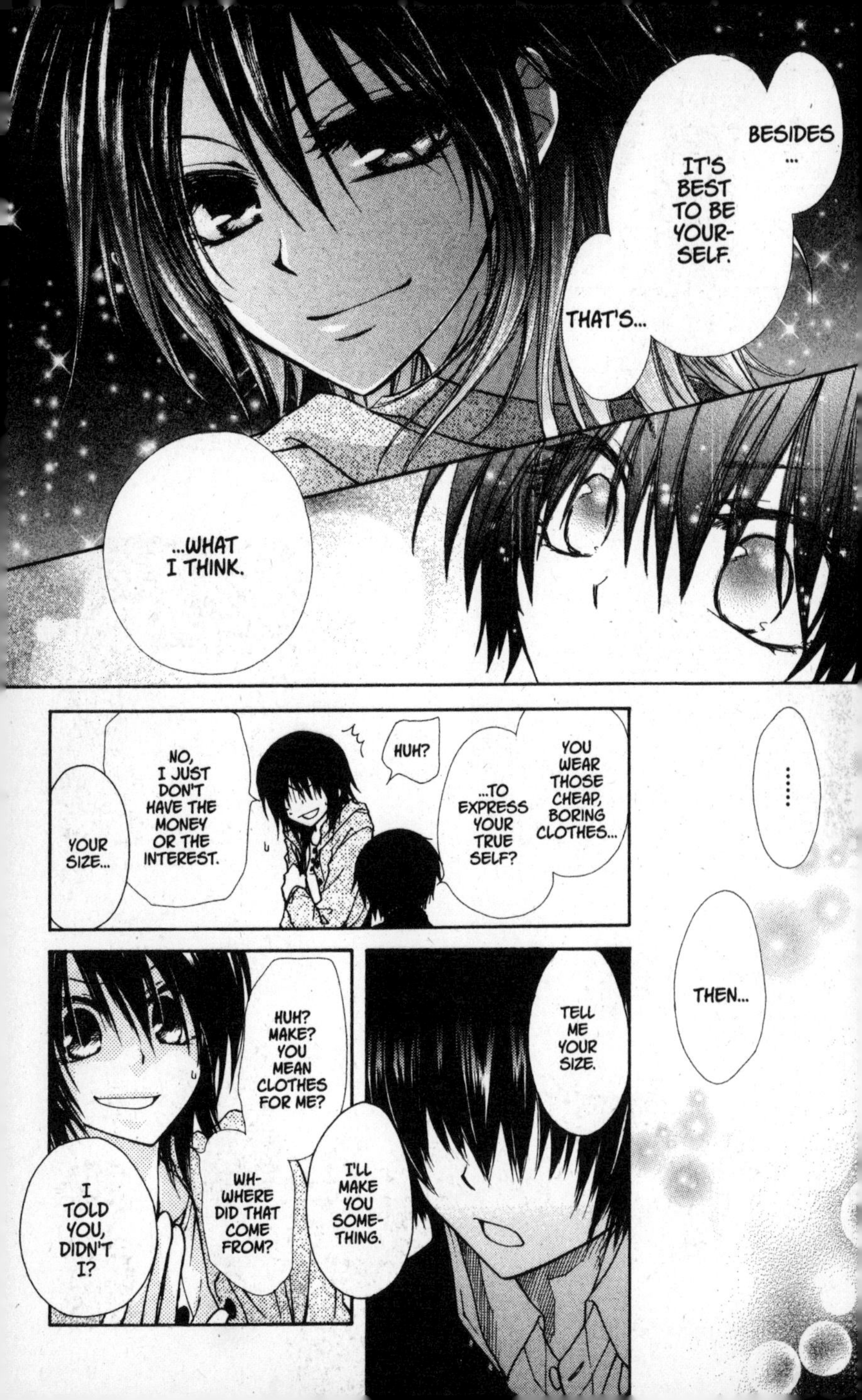
BESIDES...
IT'S BEST TO BE YOURSELF.
THAT'S...
...WHAT I THINK.
......
YOU WEAR THOSE CHEAP, BORING CLOTHES...
...TO EXPRESS YOUR TRUE SELF?
HUH?
NO, I JUST DON'T HAVE THE MONEY OR THE INTEREST.
YOUR SIZE...
THEN...
TELL ME YOUR SIZE.
I'LL MAKE YOU SOMETHING.
HUH? MAKE? YOU MEAN CLOTHES FOR ME?
WH-WHERE DID THAT COME FROM?
I TOLD YOU, DIDN'T I?

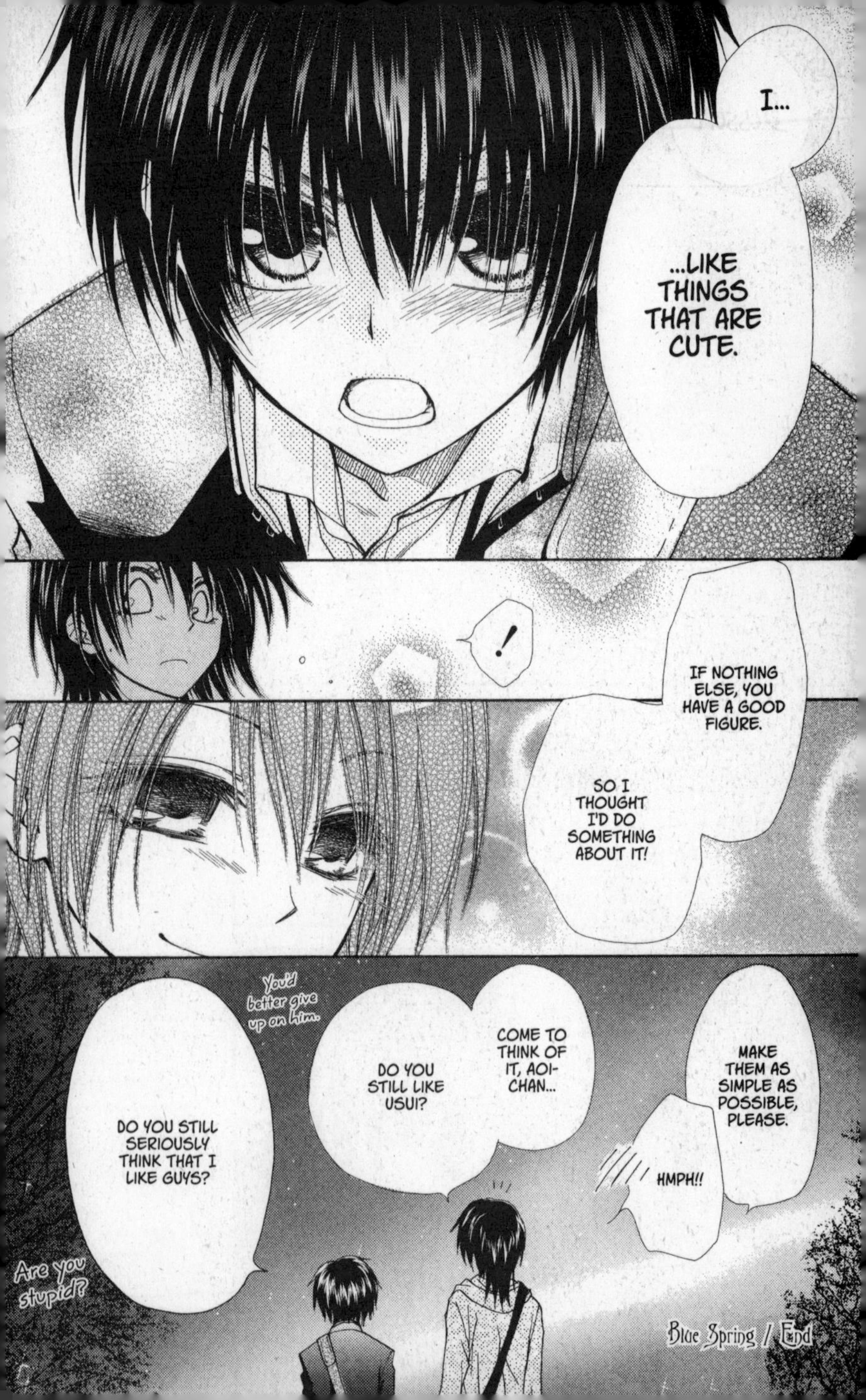
I...
...LIKE THINGS THAT ARE CUTE.
!
IF NOTHING ELSE, YOU HAVE A GOOD FIGURE.
SO I THOUGHT I'D DO SOMETHING ABOUT IT!
MAKE THEM AS SIMPLE AS POSSIBLE, PLEASE.
HMPH!!
COME TO THINK OF IT, AOI-CHAN...
DO YOU STILL LIKE USUI?
You'd better give up on him.
DO YOU STILL SERIOUSLY THINK THAT I LIKE GUYS?
Are you stupid?
Blue Spring / End

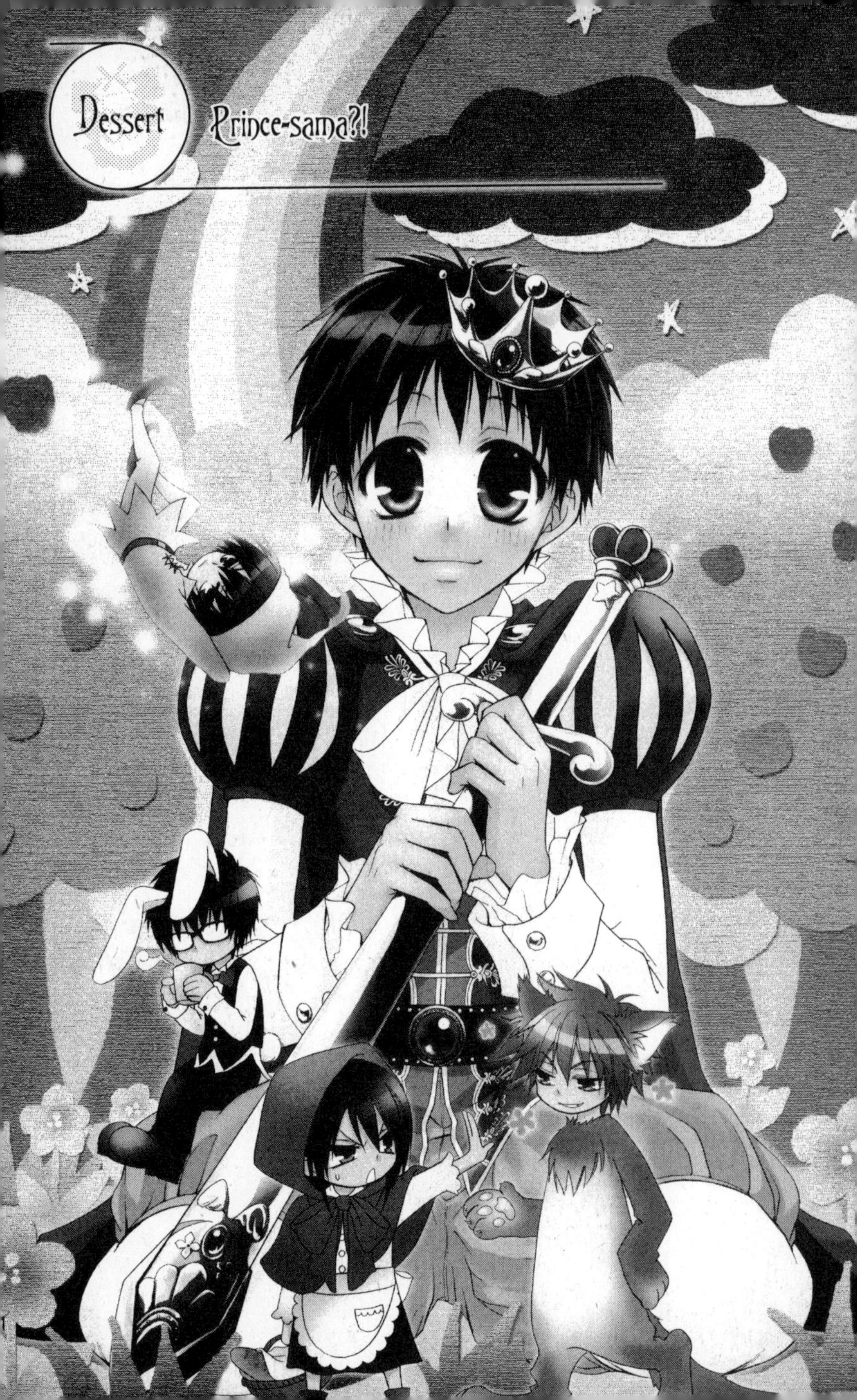
Dessert
Prince-sama?!

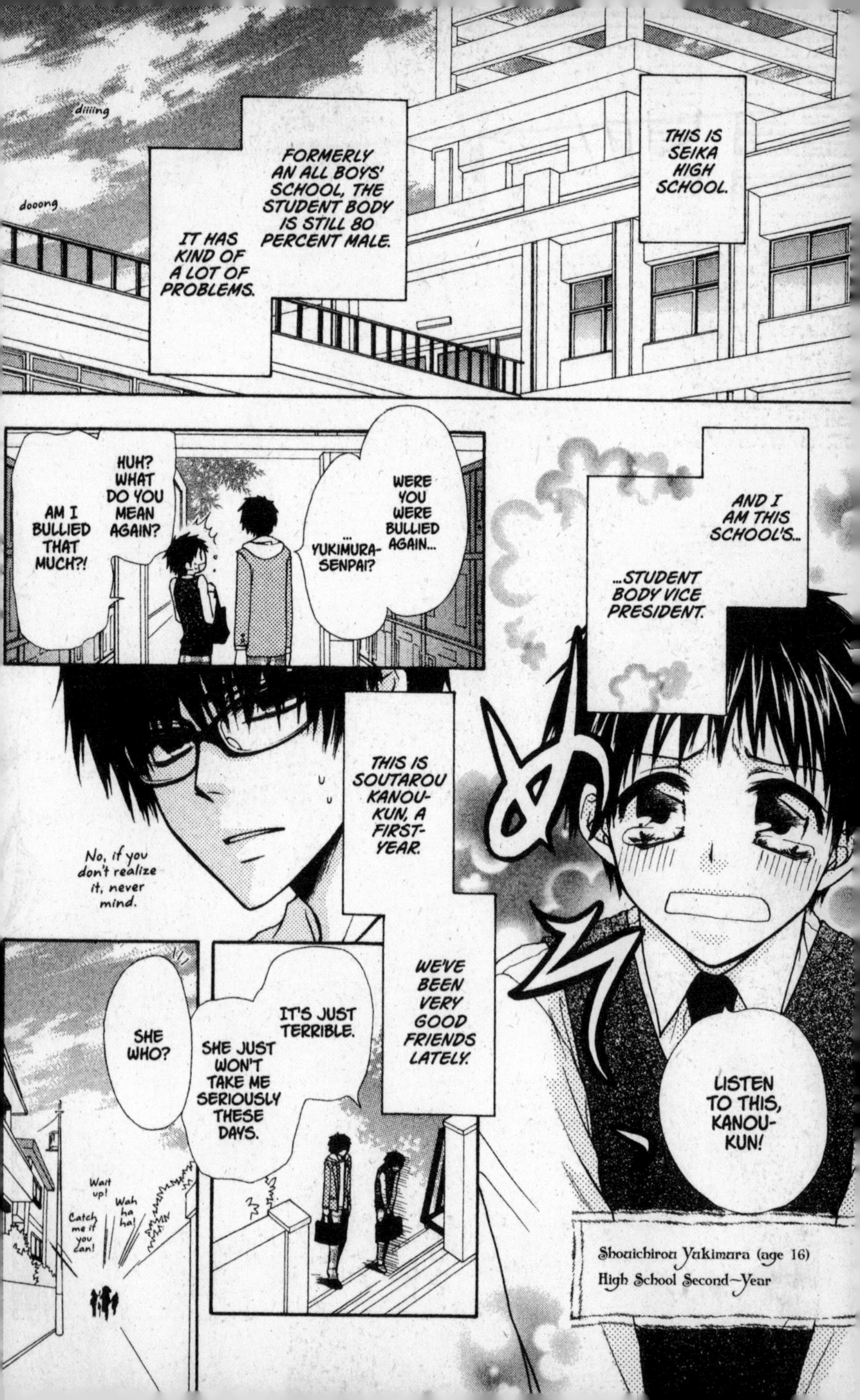
diiiing
dooong
THIS IS SEIKA HIGH SCHOOL.
FORMERLY AN ALL BOYS' SCHOOL, THE STUDENT BODY IS STILL 80 PERCENT MALE.
IT HAS KIND OF A LOT OF PROBLEMS.
AND I AM THIS SCHOOL'S...
...STUDENT BODY VICE PRESIDENT.
WERE YOU WERE BULLIED AGAIN...
... YUKIMURA-SENPAI?
HUH? WHAT DO YOU MEAN AGAIN?
AM I BULLIED THAT MUCH?!
LISTEN TO THIS, KANOU-KUN!
Shouichirou Yukimura (age 16)
High School Second-Year
THIS IS SOUTAROU KANOU-KUN, A FIRST-YEAR.
No, if you don't realize it, never mind.
WE'VE BEEN VERY GOOD FRIENDS LATELY.
IT'S JUST TERRIBLE.
SHE JUST WON'T TAKE ME SERIOUSLY THESE DAYS.
SHE WHO?
Wait up!
Wah ha ha!
Catch me if you can!

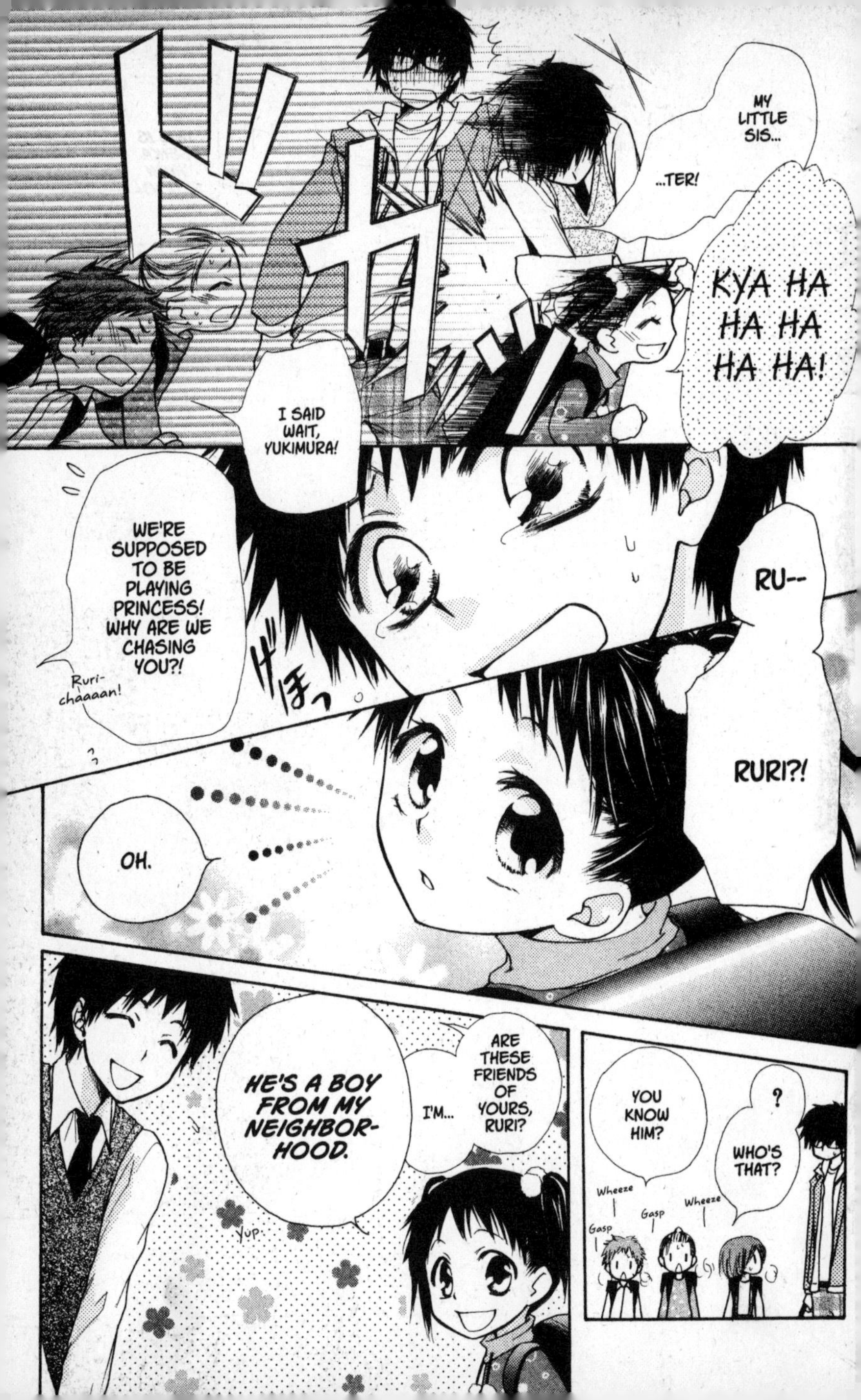
MY LITTLE SIS...
...TER!
KYA HA HA HA HA HA!
I SAID WAIT, YUKIMURA!
RU--
WE'RE SUPPOSED TO BE PLAYING PRINCESS! WHY ARE WE CHASING YOU?!
Ruri-chaaaan!
RURI?!
OH.
?
WHO'S THAT?
YOU KNOW HIM?
Wheeze
Gasp
Wheeze
Gasp
ARE THESE FRIENDS OF YOURS, RURI?
I'M...
HE'S A BOY FROM MY NEIGHBOR-HOOD.
Yup.

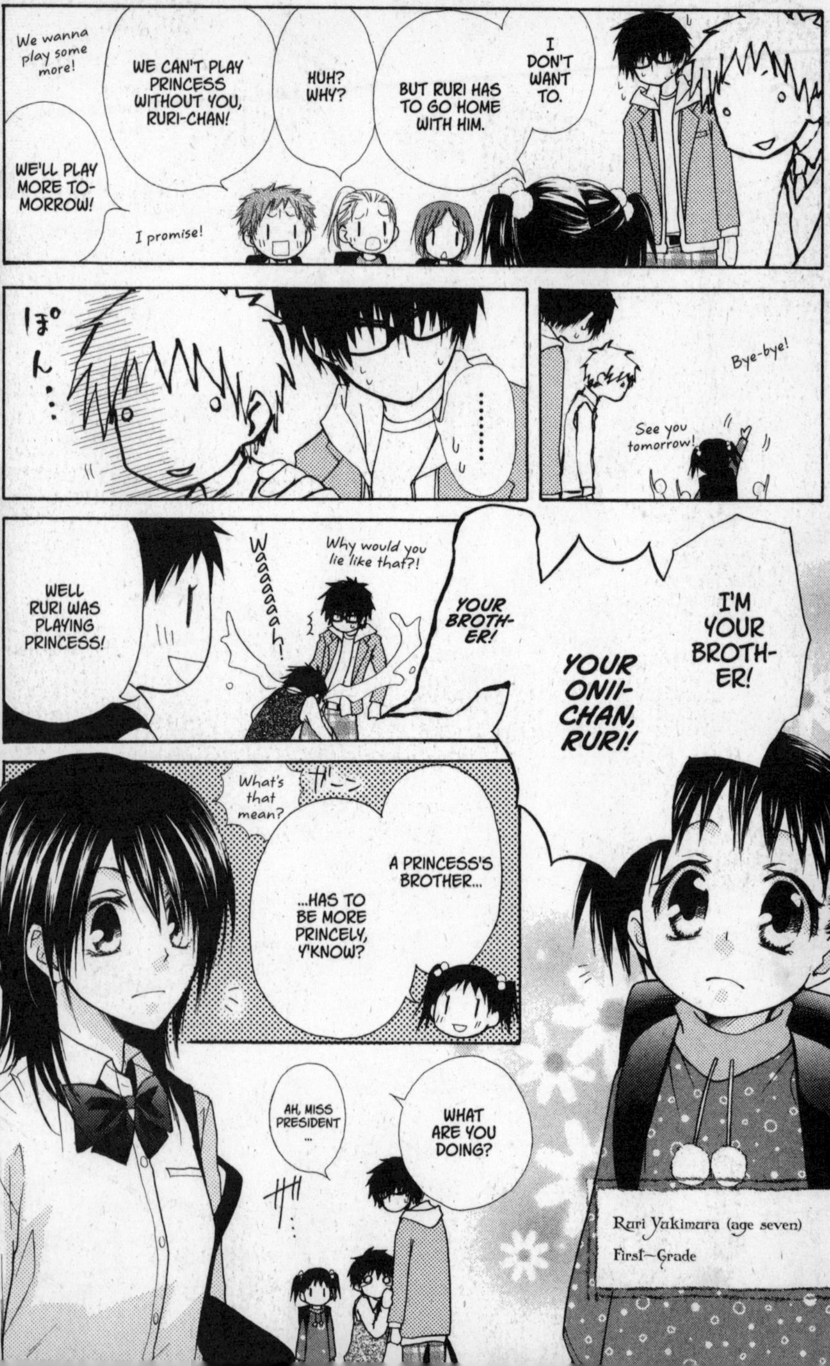
I DON'T WANT TO.
BUT RURI HAS TO GO HOME WITH HIM.
HUH? WHY?
WE CAN'T PLAY PRINCESS WITHOUT YOU, RURI-CHAN!
We wanna play some more!
WE'LL PLAY MORE TO-MORROW!
I promise!
Bye-bye!
See you tomorrow!
ぽん…
……
I'M YOUR BROTHER!
YOUR ONII-CHAN, RURI!
Ruri Yukimura (age seven)
First-Grade
YOUR BROTHER!
Why would you lie like that?!
Waaaaaaah!
WELL RURI WAS PLAYING PRINCESS!
What's that mean?
A PRINCESS'S BROTHER...
...HAS TO BE MORE PRINCELY, Y'KNOW?
WHAT ARE YOU DOING?
AH, MISS PRESIDENT ...

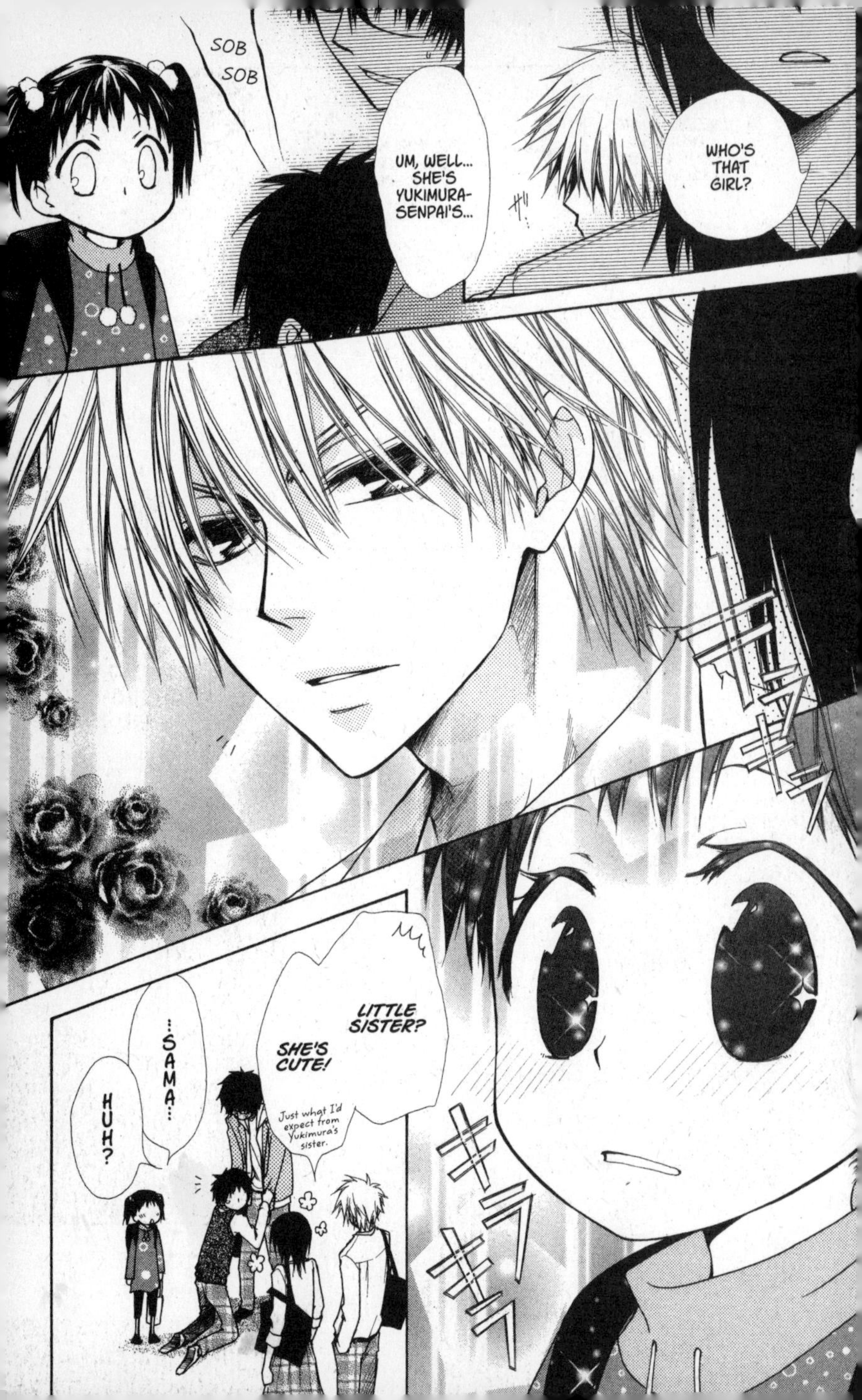

WHO'S THAT GIRL?
UM, WELL... SHE'S YUKIMURA-SENPAI'S...
SOB SOB
LITTLE SISTER?
SHE'S CUTE!
Just what I'd expect from Yukimura's sister.
...SAMA...
HUH?

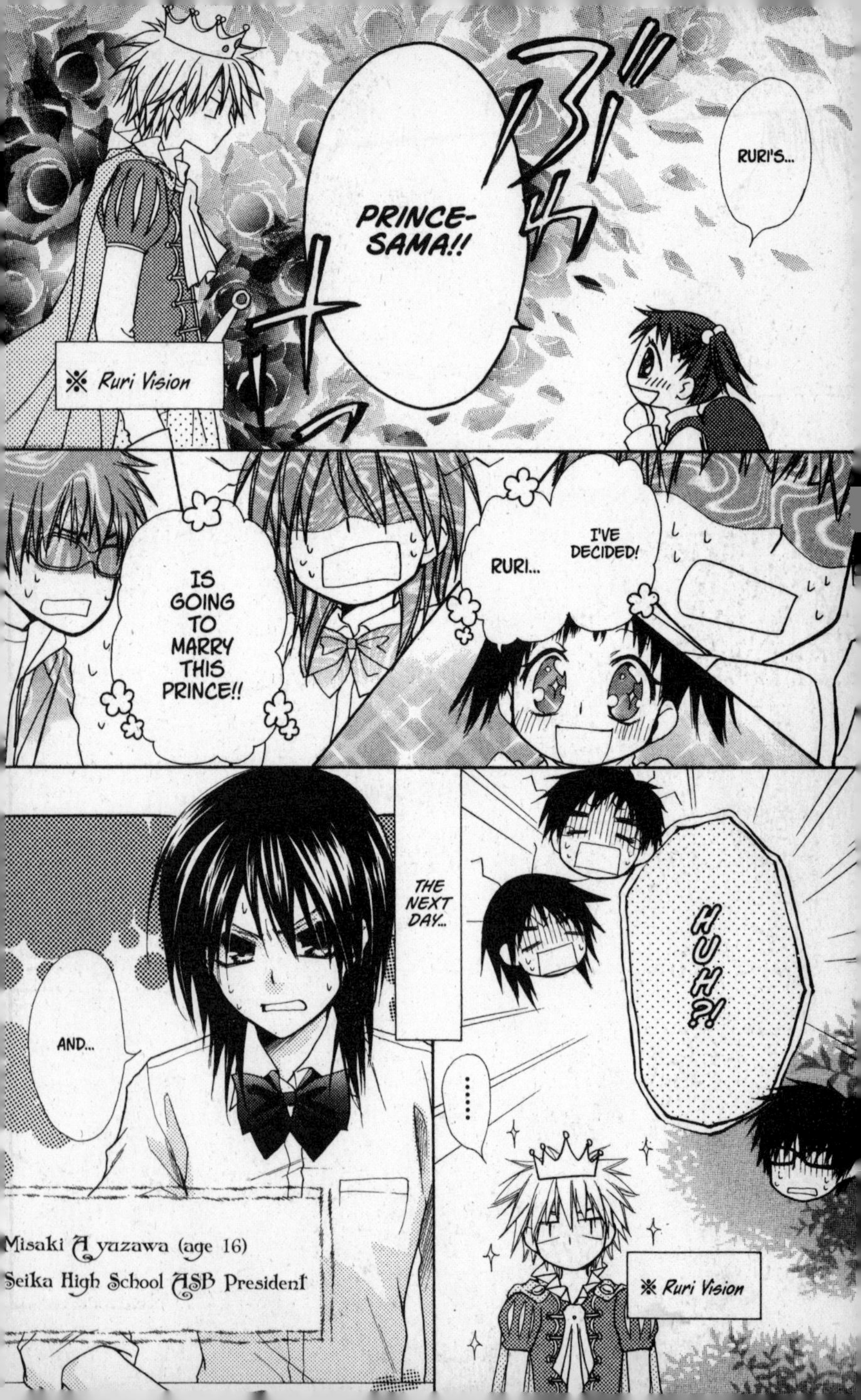
RURI'S...
PRINCE-SAMA!!
※ Ruri Vision
I'VE DECIDED!
RURI...
IS GOING TO MARRY THIS PRINCE!!
HUH?!
......
※ Ruri Vision
THE NEXT DAY...
AND...
Misaki Ayuzawa (age 16)
Seika High School ASB President

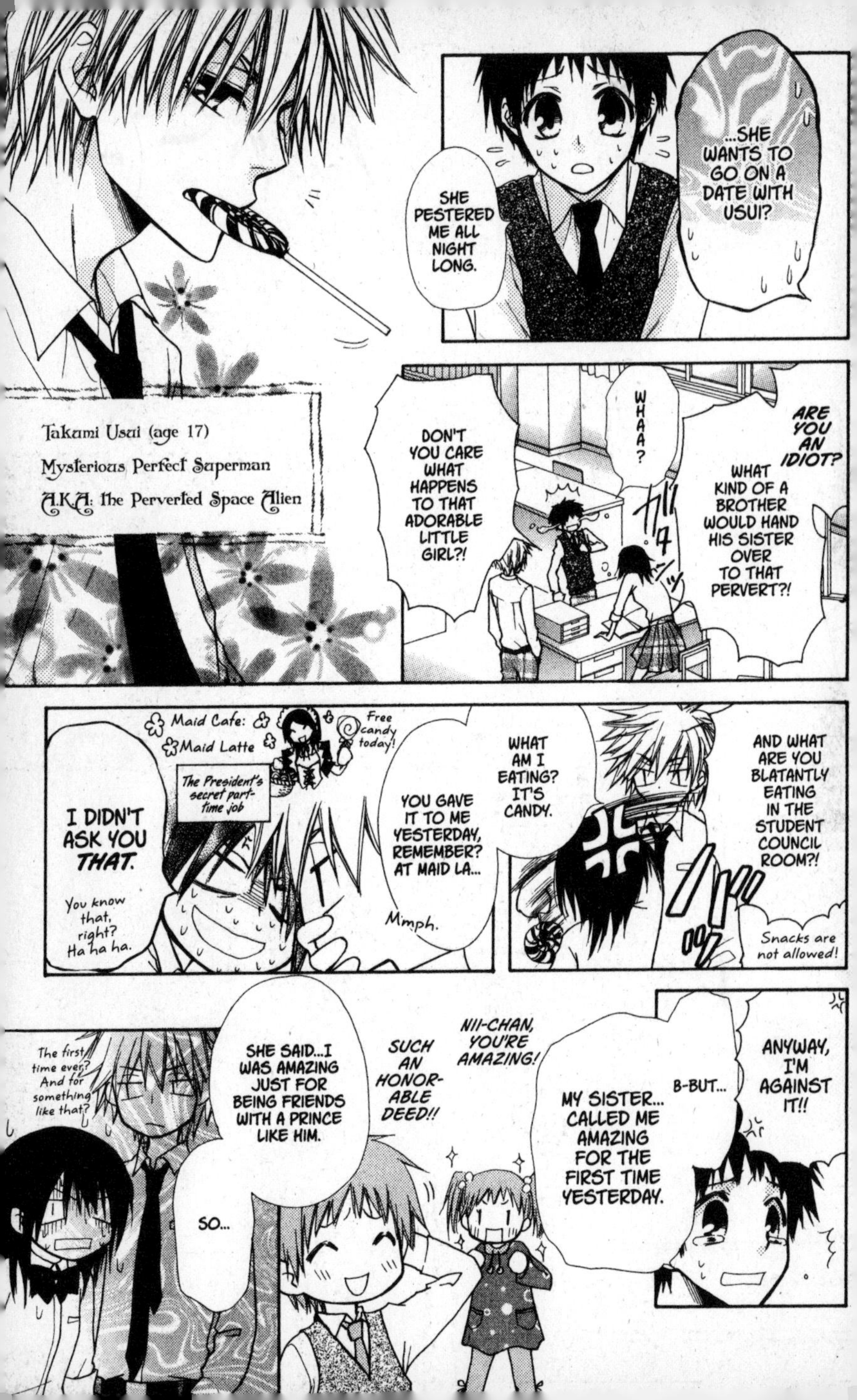
...SHE WANTS TO GO ON A DATE WITH USUI?
SHE PESTERED ME ALL NIGHT LONG.
ARE YOU AN IDIOT?
WHAT KIND OF A BROTHER WOULD HAND HIS SISTER OVER TO THAT PERVERT?!
WHAA?
DON'T YOU CARE WHAT HAPPENS TO THAT ADORABLE LITTLE GIRL?!
Takumi Usui (age 17)
Mysterious Perfect Superman
A.K.A: the Perverted Space Alien
AND WHAT ARE YOU BLATANTLY EATING IN THE STUDENT COUNCIL ROOM?!
Snacks are not allowed!
WHAT AM I EATING? IT'S CANDY.
YOU GAVE IT TO ME YESTERDAY, REMEMBER? AT MAID LA...
Mmph.
Maid Cafe:
Maid Latte
Free candy today!
The President's secret part-time job
I DIDN'T ASK YOU THAT.
You know that, right? Ha ha ha.
ANYWAY, I'M AGAINST IT!!
B-BUT...
MY SISTER... CALLED ME AMAZING FOR THE FIRST TIME YESTERDAY.
NII-CHAN, YOU'RE AMAZING!
SUCH AN HONORABLE DEED!!
SHE SAID...I WAS AMAZING JUST FOR BEING FRIENDS WITH A PRINCE LIKE HIM.
SO...
The first time ever? And for something like that?

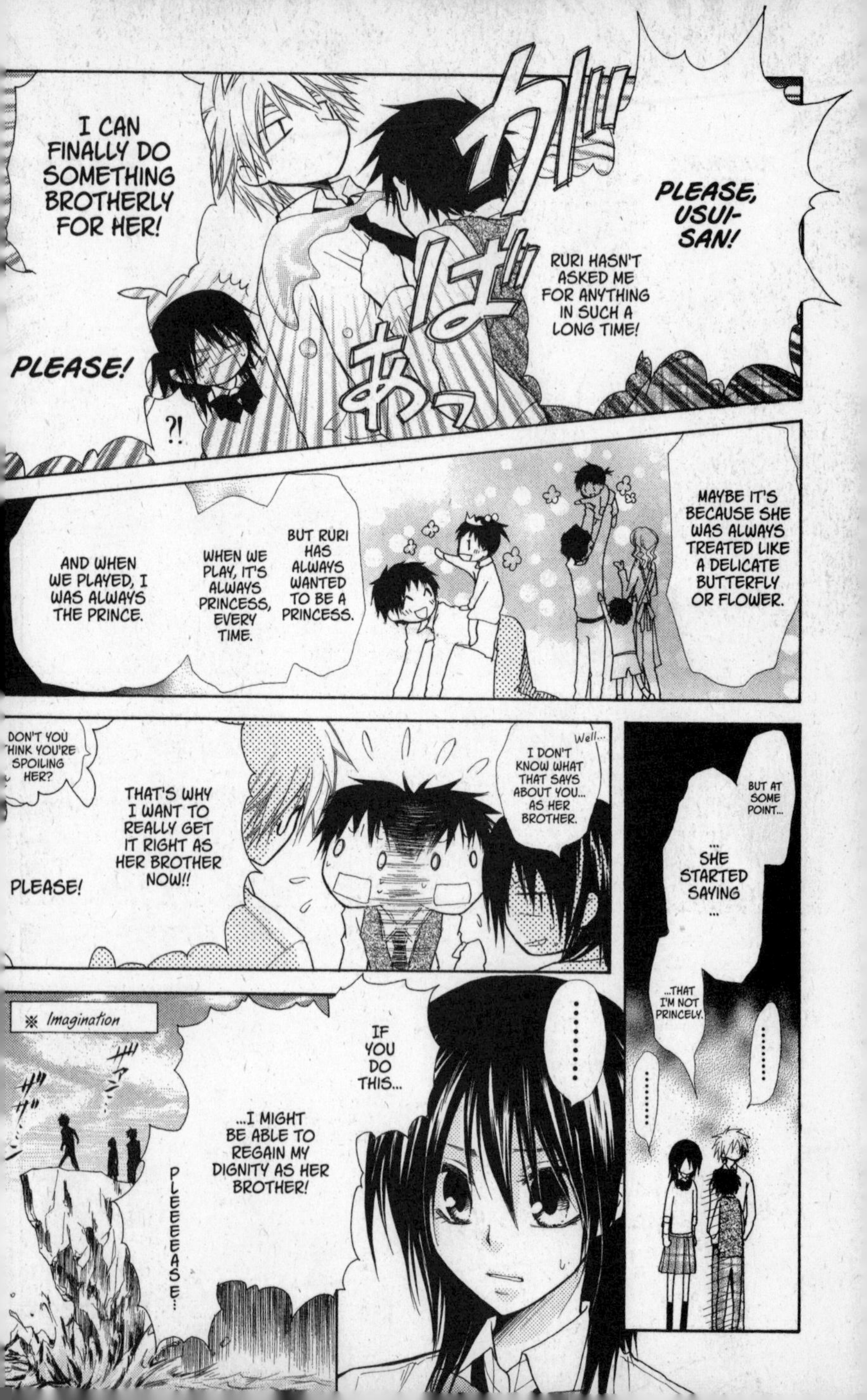
PLEASE, USUI-SAN!
RURI HASN'T ASKED ME FOR ANYTHING IN SUCH A LONG TIME!
I CAN FINALLY DO SOMETHING BROTHERLY FOR HER!
PLEASE!
?!
MAYBE IT'S BECAUSE SHE WAS ALWAYS TREATED LIKE A DELICATE BUTTERFLY OR FLOWER.
BUT RURI HAS ALWAYS WANTED TO BE A PRINCESS.
WHEN WE PLAY, IT'S ALWAYS PRINCESS, EVERY TIME.
AND WHEN WE PLAYED, I WAS ALWAYS THE PRINCE.
BUT AT SOME POINT...
...SHE STARTED SAYING...
...THAT I'M NOT PRINCELY.
......
......
Well...
I DON'T KNOW WHAT THAT SAYS ABOUT YOU... AS HER BROTHER.
THAT'S WHY I WANT TO REALLY GET IT RIGHT AS HER BROTHER NOW!!
DON'T YOU THINK YOU'RE SPOILING HER?
PLEASE!
......
IF YOU DO THIS...
...I MIGHT BE ABLE TO REGAIN MY DIGNITY AS HER BROTHER!
※ Imagination
PLEEEEASE...

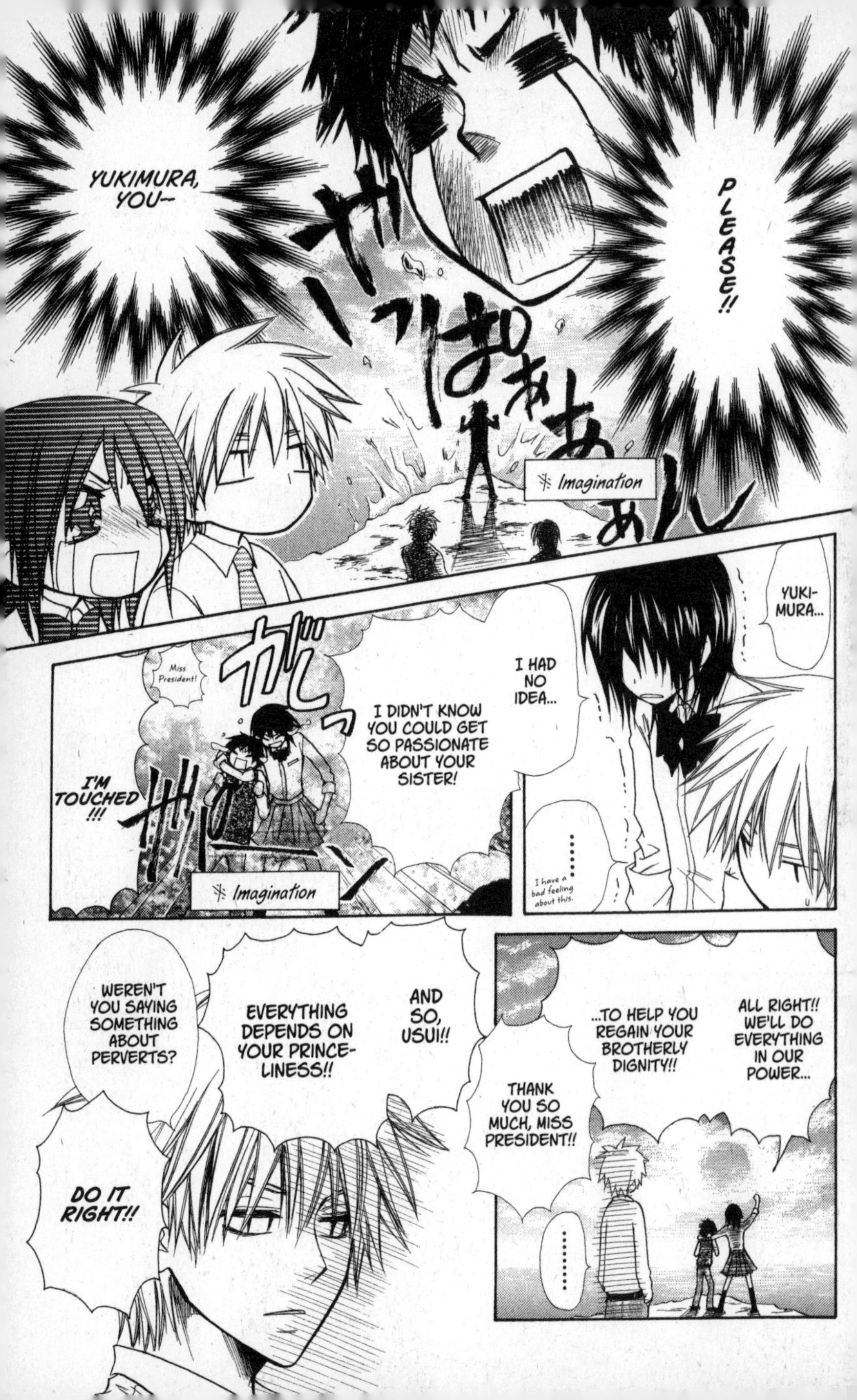
PLEASE!!
YUKIMURA, YOU--
※ Imagination
YUKI-MURA...
I HAD NO IDEA...
......
I have a bad feeling about this.
Miss President!
I DIDN'T KNOW YOU COULD GET SO PASSIONATE ABOUT YOUR SISTER!
I'M TOUCHED!!!
※ Imagination
ALL RIGHT!! WE'LL DO EVERYTHING IN OUR POWER...
...TO HELP YOU REGAIN YOUR BROTHERLY DIGNITY!!
THANK YOU SO MUCH, MISS PRESIDENT!!
......
AND SO, USUI!!
EVERYTHING DEPENDS ON YOUR PRINCE-LINESS!!
WEREN'T YOU SAYING SOMETHING ABOUT PERVERTS?
DO IT RIGHT!!

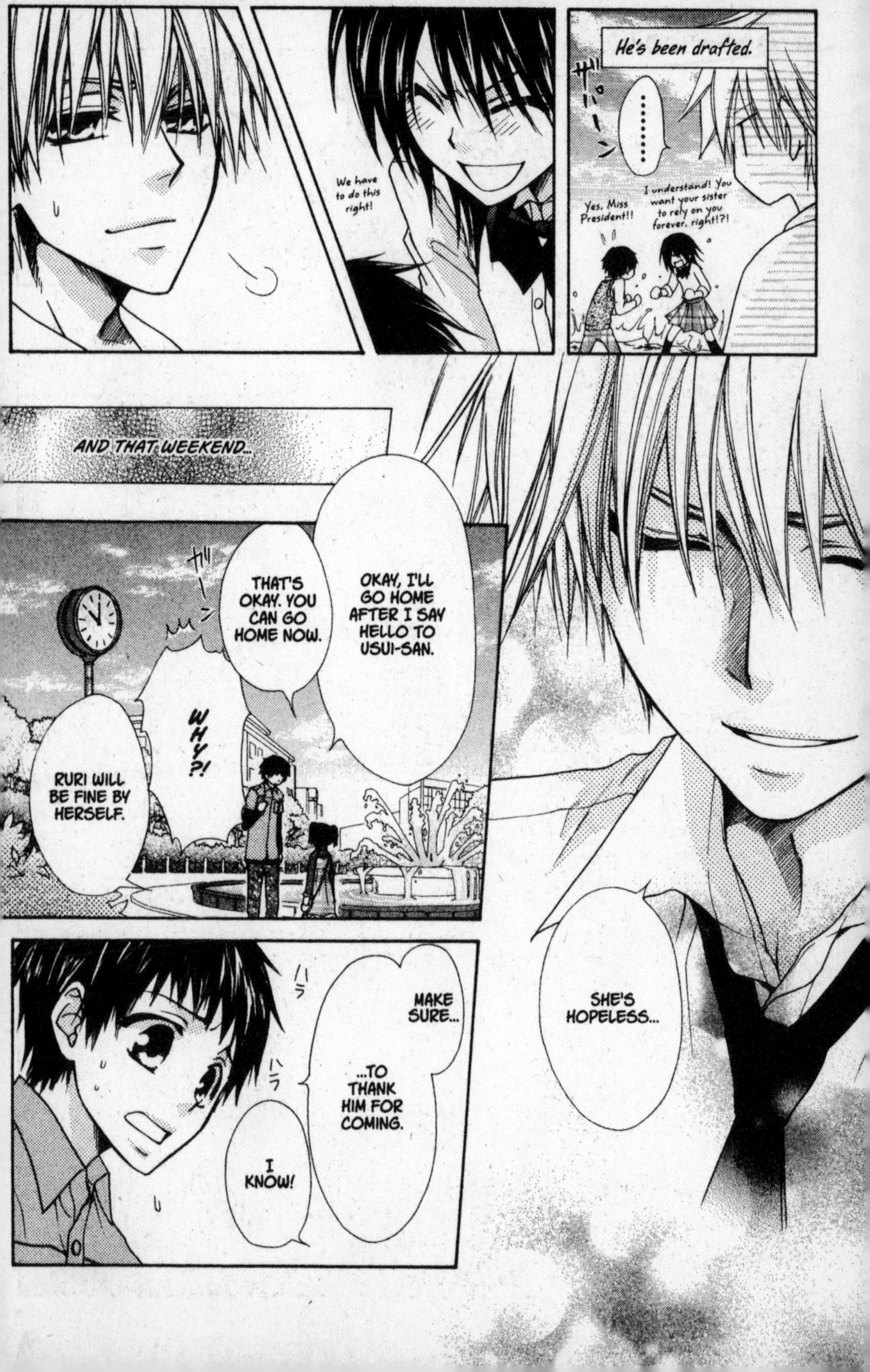
He's been drafted.
......
I understand! You want your sister to rely on you forever, right!?!
Yes, Miss President!!
We have to do this right!
SHE'S HOPELESS...
AND THAT WEEKEND...
OKAY, I'LL GO HOME AFTER I SAY HELLO TO USUI-SAN.
THAT'S OKAY. YOU CAN GO HOME NOW.
WHY?!
RURI WILL BE FINE BY HERSELF.
ハラ
ハラ
MAKE SURE...
...TO THANK HIM FOR COMING.
I KNOW!

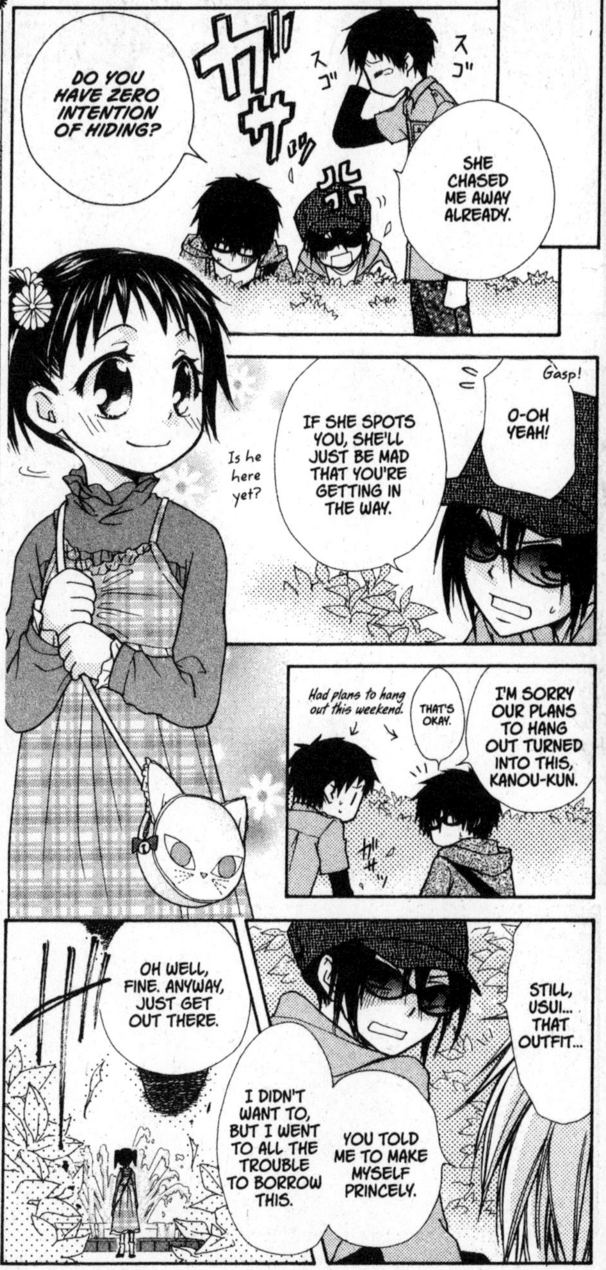
スゴ
スゴ
SHE CHASED ME AWAY ALREADY.
ガサッ
DO YOU HAVE ZERO INTENTION OF HIDING?
Gasp!
O-OH YEAH!
IF SHE SPOTS YOU, SHE'LL JUST BE MAD THAT YOU'RE GETTING IN THE WAY.
Is he here yet?
I'M SORRY OUR PLANS TO HANG OUT TURNED INTO THIS, KANOU-KUN.
THAT'S OKAY.
Had plans to hang out this weekend.
STILL, USUI... THAT OUTFIT...
YOU TOLD ME TO MAKE MYSELF PRINCELY.
I DIDN'T WANT TO, BUT I WENT TO ALL THE TROUBLE TO BORROW THIS.
OH WELL, FINE. ANYWAY, JUST GET OUT THERE.

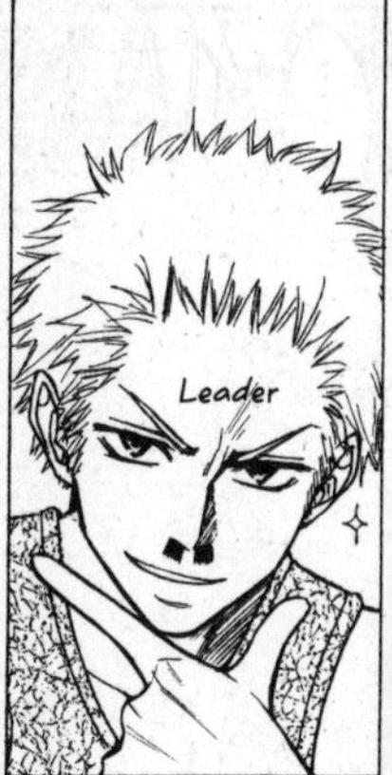
Leader

Name

Naoya Shirokawa

Age (Class)

17 (2-5)

Blood Type

B

Height

180 cm (5ft 11in)

Weight

73 kg (161 lbs)

Special Skills

Contests of strength!!

Likes

Fiery guys like sentai and superheroes!

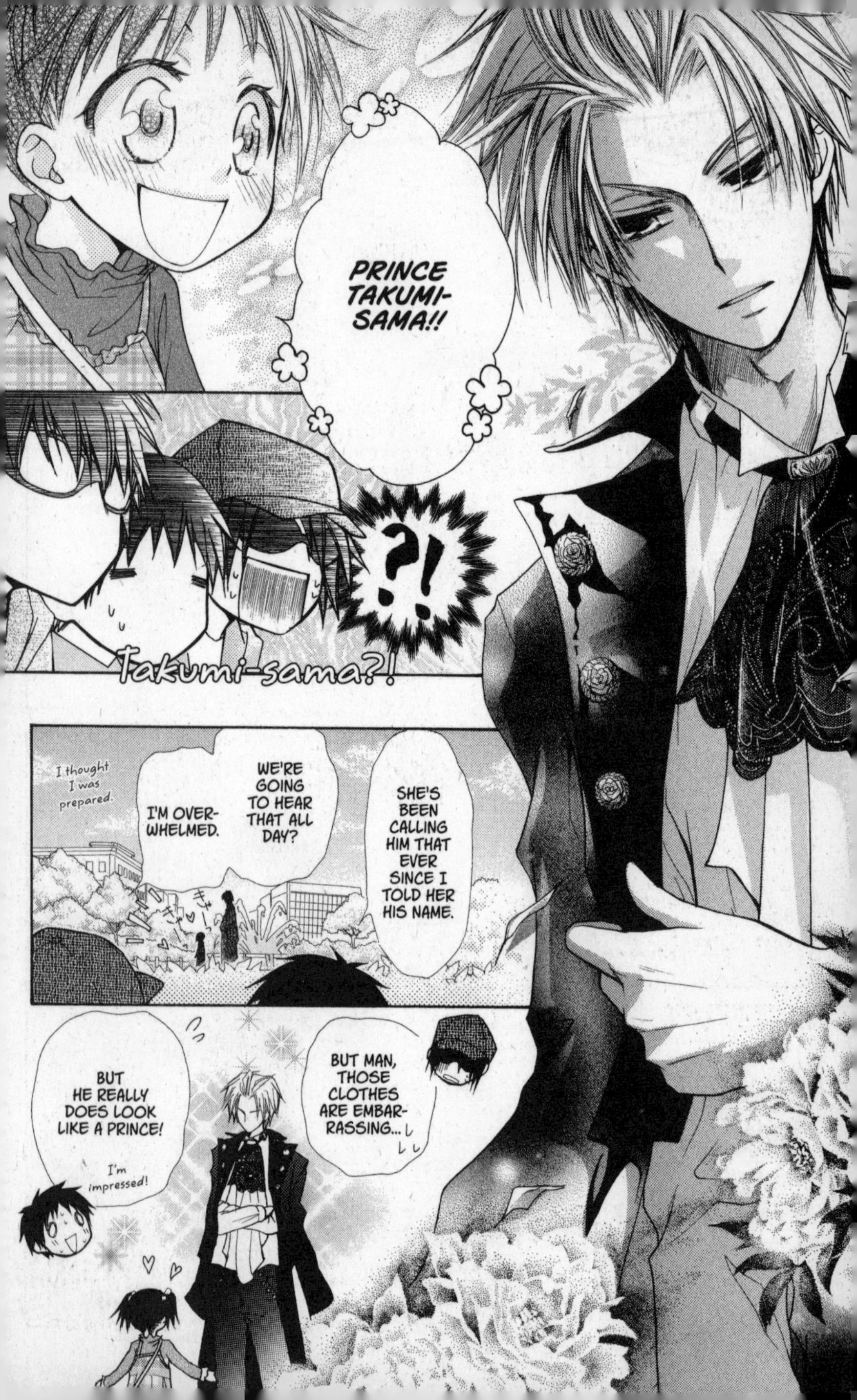
PRINCE TAKUMI-SAMA!!
?!
Takumi-sama?!
SHE'S BEEN CALLING HIM THAT EVER SINCE I TOLD HER HIS NAME.
WE'RE GOING TO HEAR THAT ALL DAY?
I'M OVER-WHELMED.
I thought I was prepared.
BUT MAN, THOSE CLOTHES ARE EMBAR-RASSING...
BUT HE REALLY DOES LOOK LIKE A PRINCE!
I'm impressed!

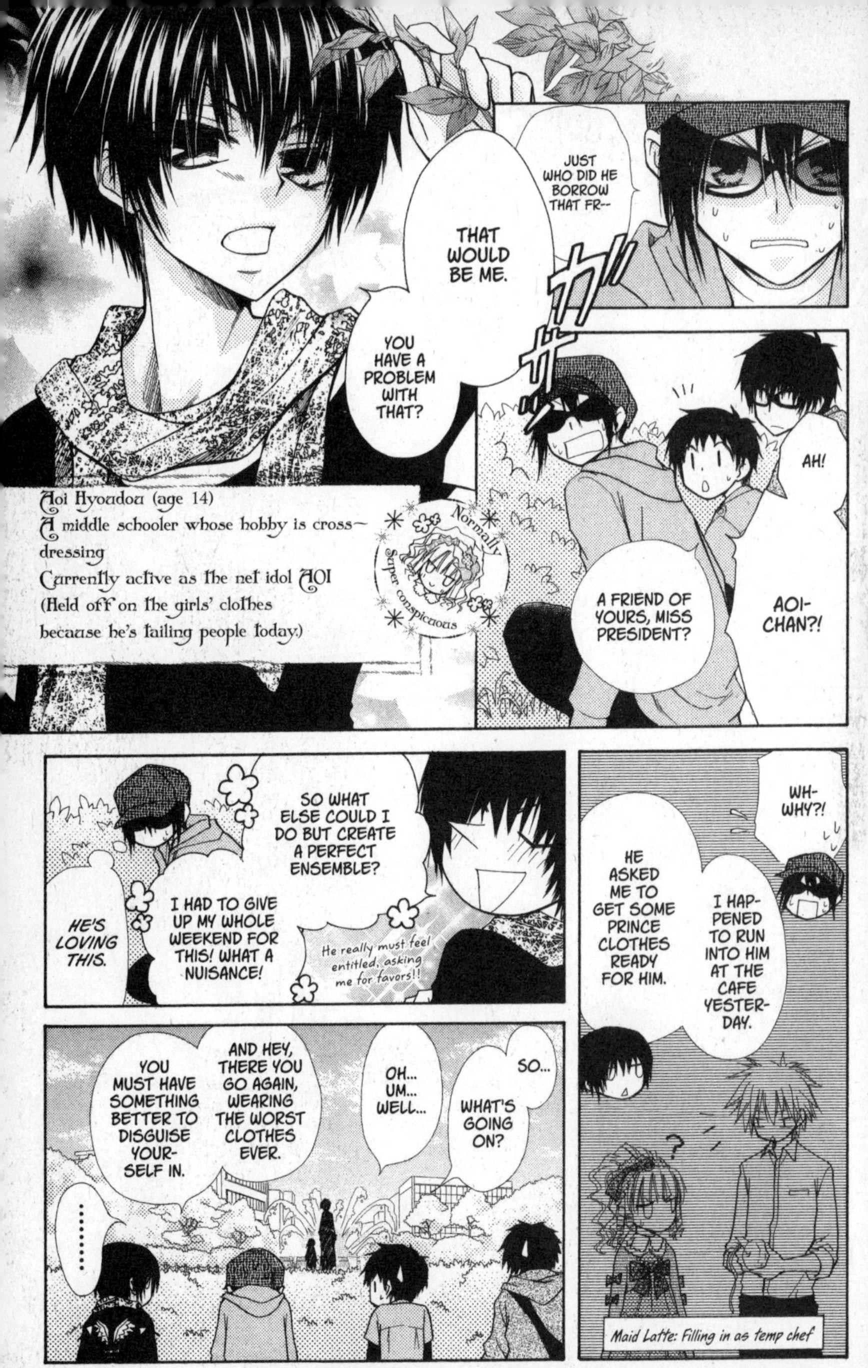
JUST WHO DID HE BORROW THAT FR--
ガッ
THAT WOULD BE ME.
YOU HAVE A PROBLEM WITH THAT?
Aoi Hyoudou (age 14)
A middle schooler whose hobby is cross-dressing
Currently active as the net idol AOI
(Held off on the girls' clothes because he's tailing people today.)
Normally Super conspicuous
AH!
AOI-CHAN?!
A FRIEND OF YOURS, MISS PRESIDENT?
WH-WHY?!
I HAPPENED TO RUN INTO HIM AT THE CAFE YESTERDAY.
HE ASKED ME TO GET SOME PRINCE CLOTHES READY FOR HIM.
Maid Latte: Filling in as temp chef
SO WHAT ELSE COULD I DO BUT CREATE A PERFECT ENSEMBLE?
I HAD TO GIVE UP MY WHOLE WEEKEND FOR THIS! WHAT A NUISANCE!
He really must feel entitled, asking me for favors!!
HE'S LOVING THIS.
SO...
WHAT'S GOING ON?
OH... UM... WELL...
AND HEY, THERE YOU GO AGAIN, WEARING THE WORST CLOTHES EVER.
YOU MUST HAVE SOMETHING BETTER TO DISGUISE YOURSELF IN.
......

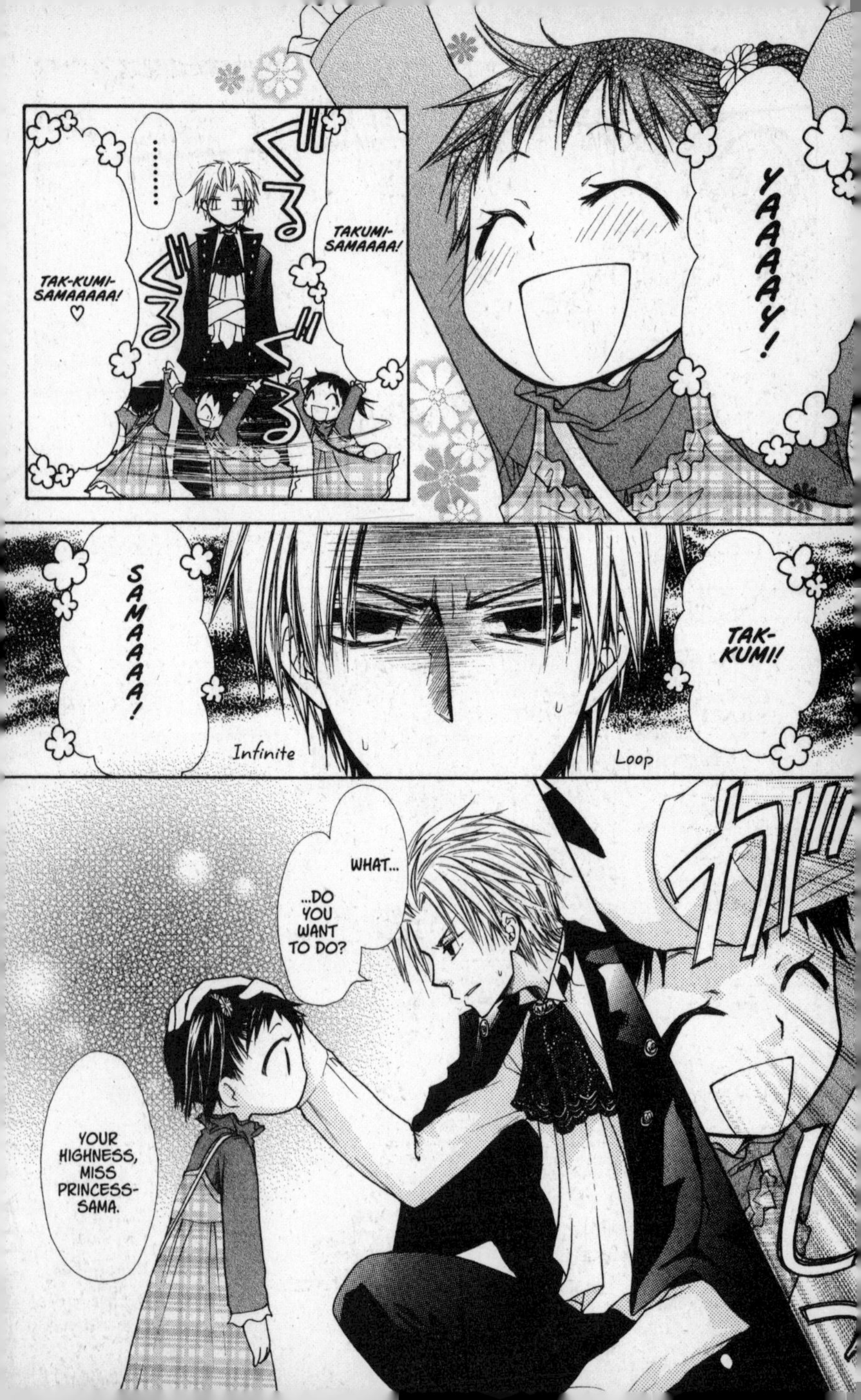
YAAAAAY!
TAKUMI-SAMAAAAA!
......
TAK-KUMI-SAMAAAAAA! ♡
TAK-KUMI!
SAMAAAAAA!
Infinite
Loop
WHAT...
...DO YOU WANT TO DO?
YOUR HIGHNESS, MISS PRINCESS-SAMA.

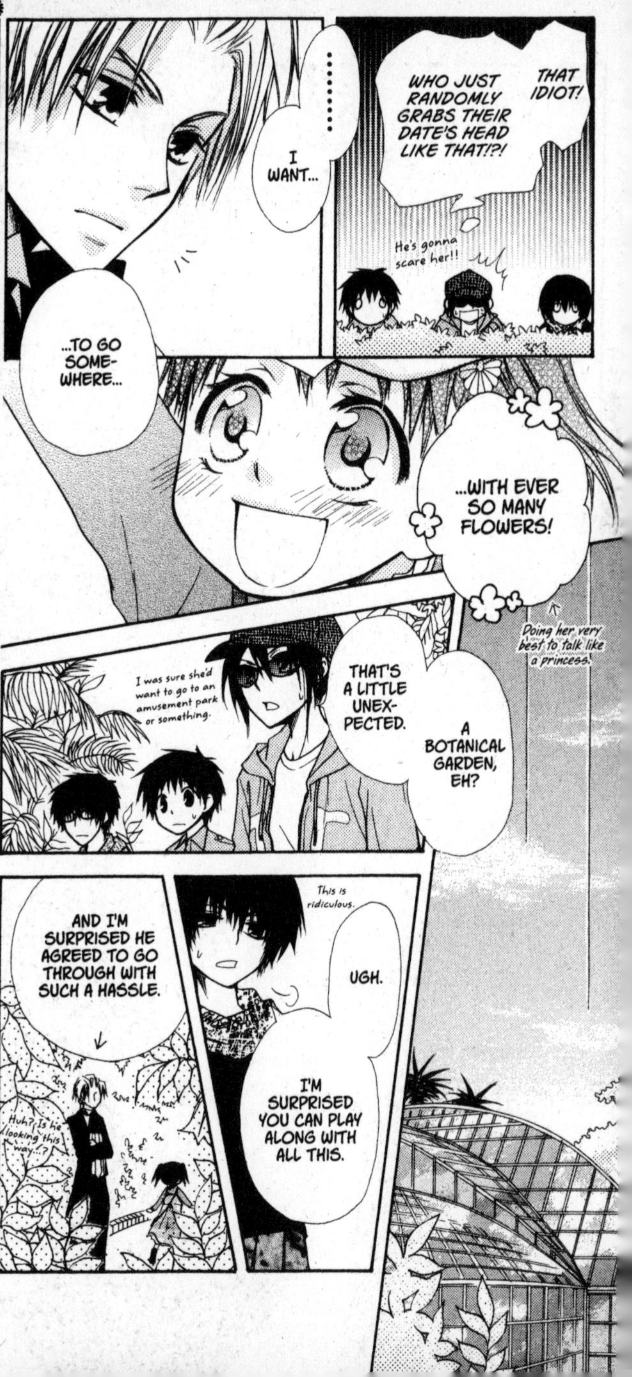
THAT IDIOT!
WHO JUST RANDOMLY GRABS THEIR DATE'S HEAD LIKE THAT!?!
He's gonna scare her!!
......
I WANT...
...TO GO SOME-WHERE...
...WITH EVER SO MANY FLOWERS!
Doing her very best to talk like a princess.
A BOTANICAL GARDEN, EH?
THAT'S A LITTLE UNEX-PECTED.
I was sure she'd want to go to an amusement park or something.
This is ridiculous.
UGH.
I'M SURPRISED YOU CAN PLAY ALONG WITH ALL THIS.
AND I'M SURPRISED HE AGREED TO GO THROUGH WITH SUCH A HASSLE.
Huh? Is he looking this way...?

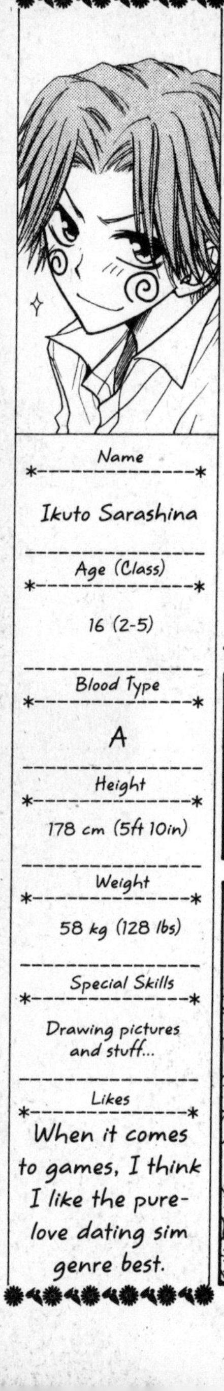

Name

Ikuto Sarashina

Age (Class)

16 (2-5)

Blood Type

A

Height

178 cm (5ft 10in)

Weight

58 kg (128 lbs)

Special Skills

Drawing pictures and stuff...

Likes

When it comes to games, I think I like the pure-love dating sim genre best.

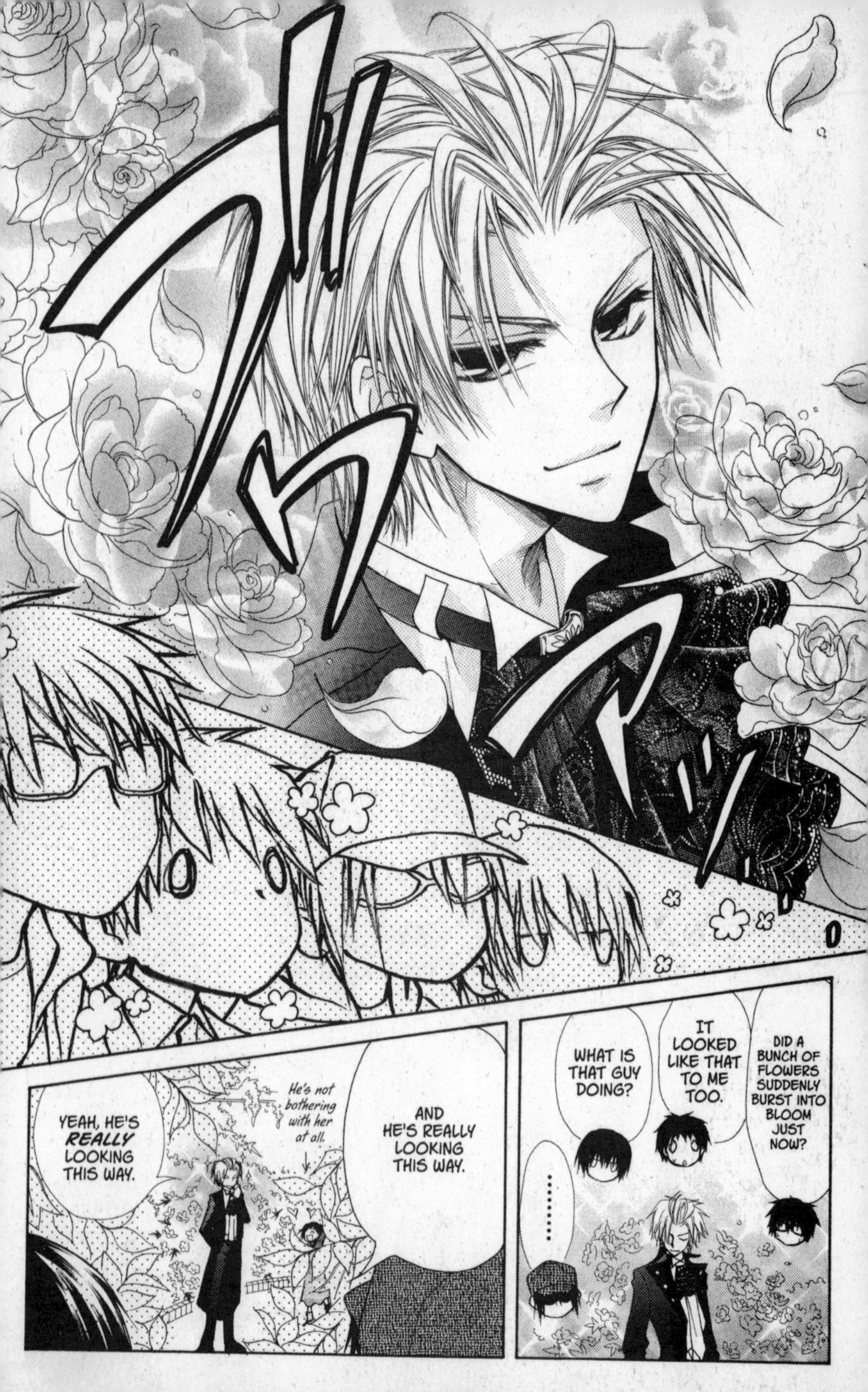
DID A BUNCH OF FLOWERS SUDDENLY BURST INTO BLOOM JUST NOW?
IT LOOKED LIKE THAT TO ME TOO.
WHAT IS THAT GUY DOING?
......
AND HE'S REALLY LOOKING THIS WAY.
He's not bothering with her at all.
YEAH, HE'S *REALLY* LOOKING THIS WAY.

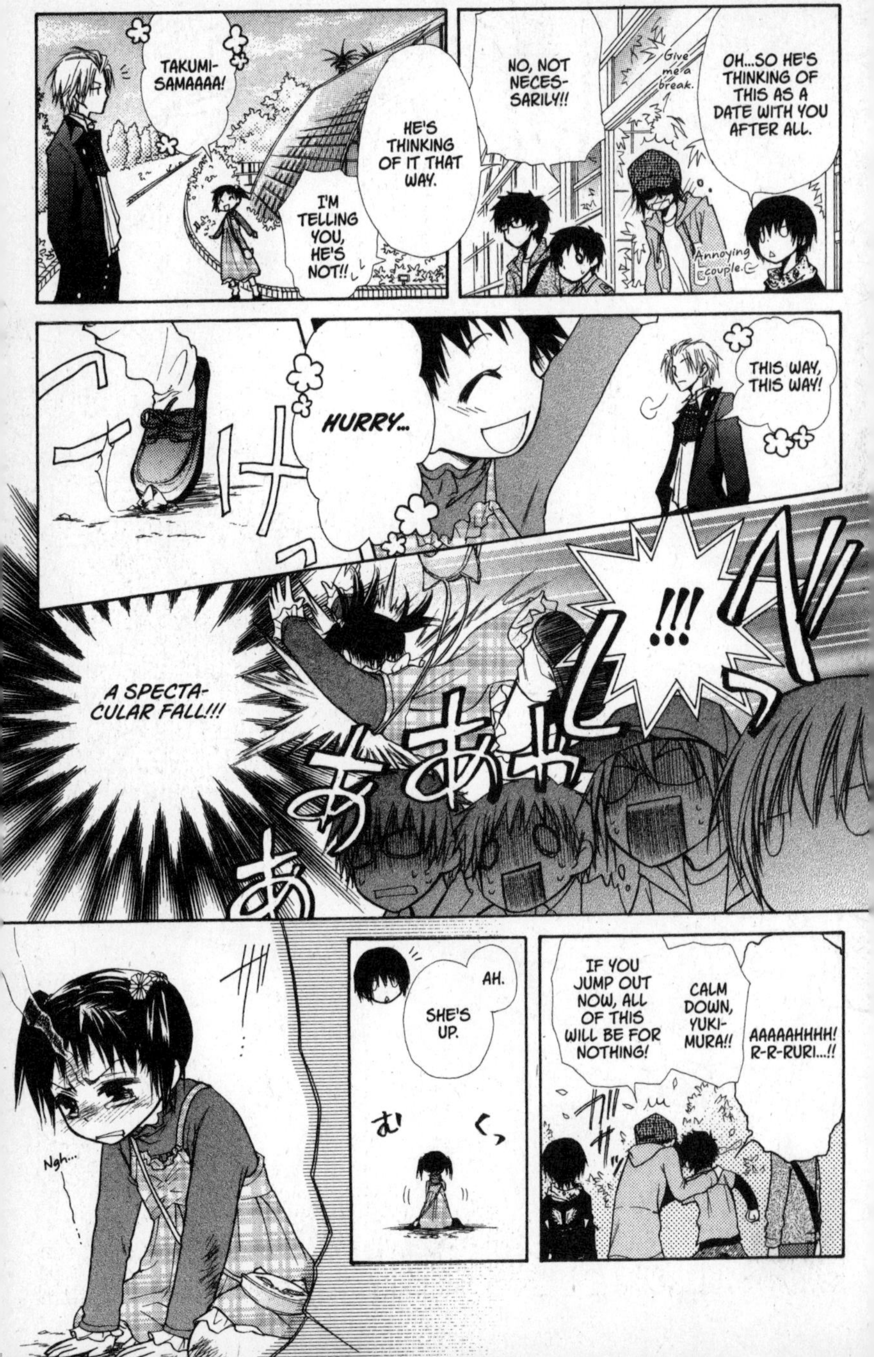
OH...SO HE'S THINKING OF THIS AS A DATE WITH YOU AFTER ALL.
Annoying couple.
Give me a break.
NO, NOT NECES-SARILY!!
HE'S THINKING OF IT THAT WAY.
I'M TELLING YOU, HE'S NOT!!
TAKUMI-SAMAAAA!
THIS WAY, THIS WAY!
HURRY...
!!!
A SPECTA-CULAR FALL!!!
AAAAAHHHH! R-R-RURI...!!
CALM DOWN, YUKI-MURA!!
IF YOU JUMP OUT NOW, ALL OF THIS WILL BE FOR NOTHING!
AH.
SHE'S UP.
むくっ
Ngh...

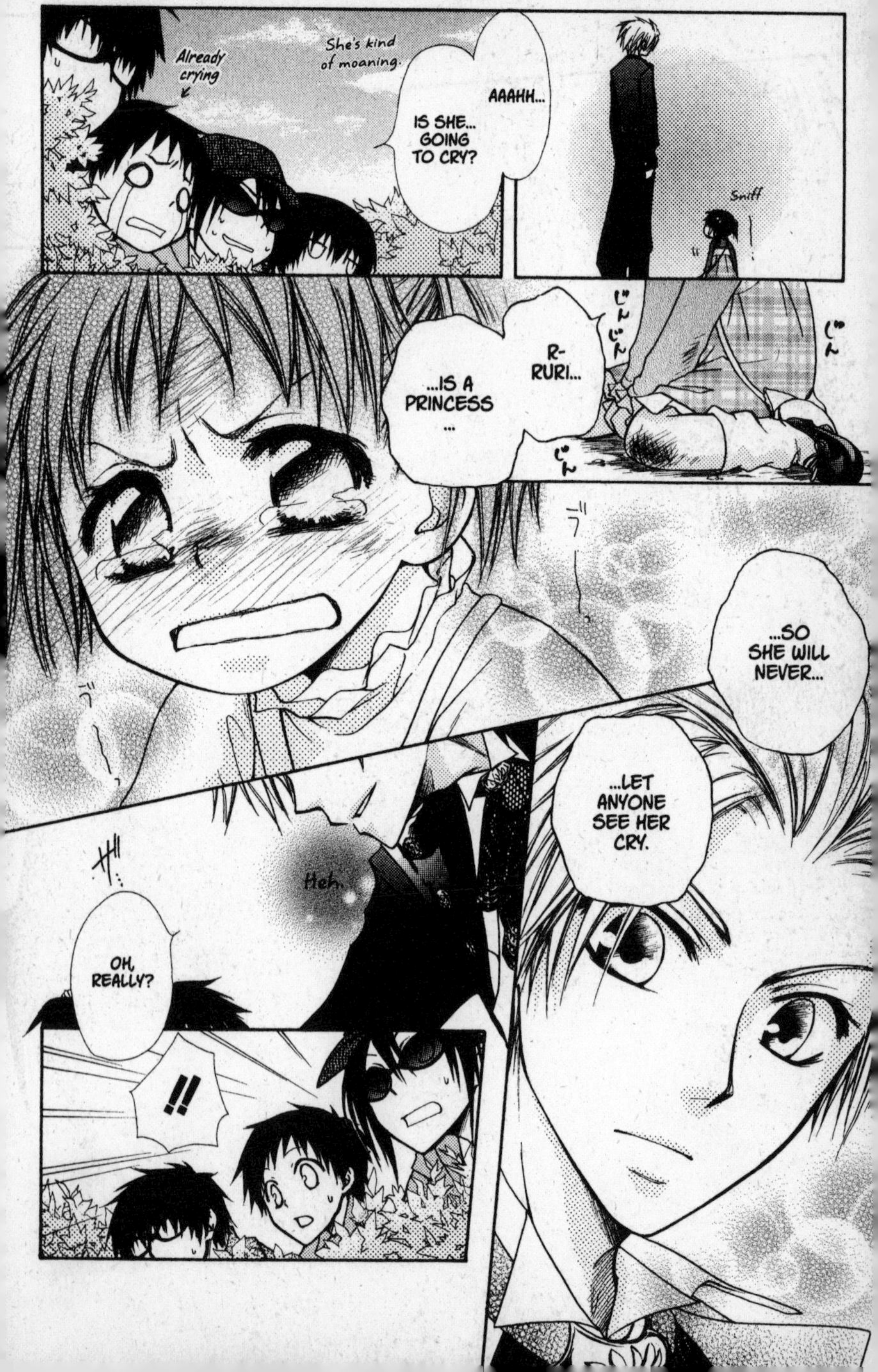
Sniff
AAAHH... IS SHE... GOING TO CRY?
She's kind of moaning.
Already crying
じんじん
じん
R-RURI... ...IS A PRINCESS ...
じん
...SO SHE WILL NEVER...
...LET ANYONE SEE HER CRY.
Heh.
OH, REALLY?
!!

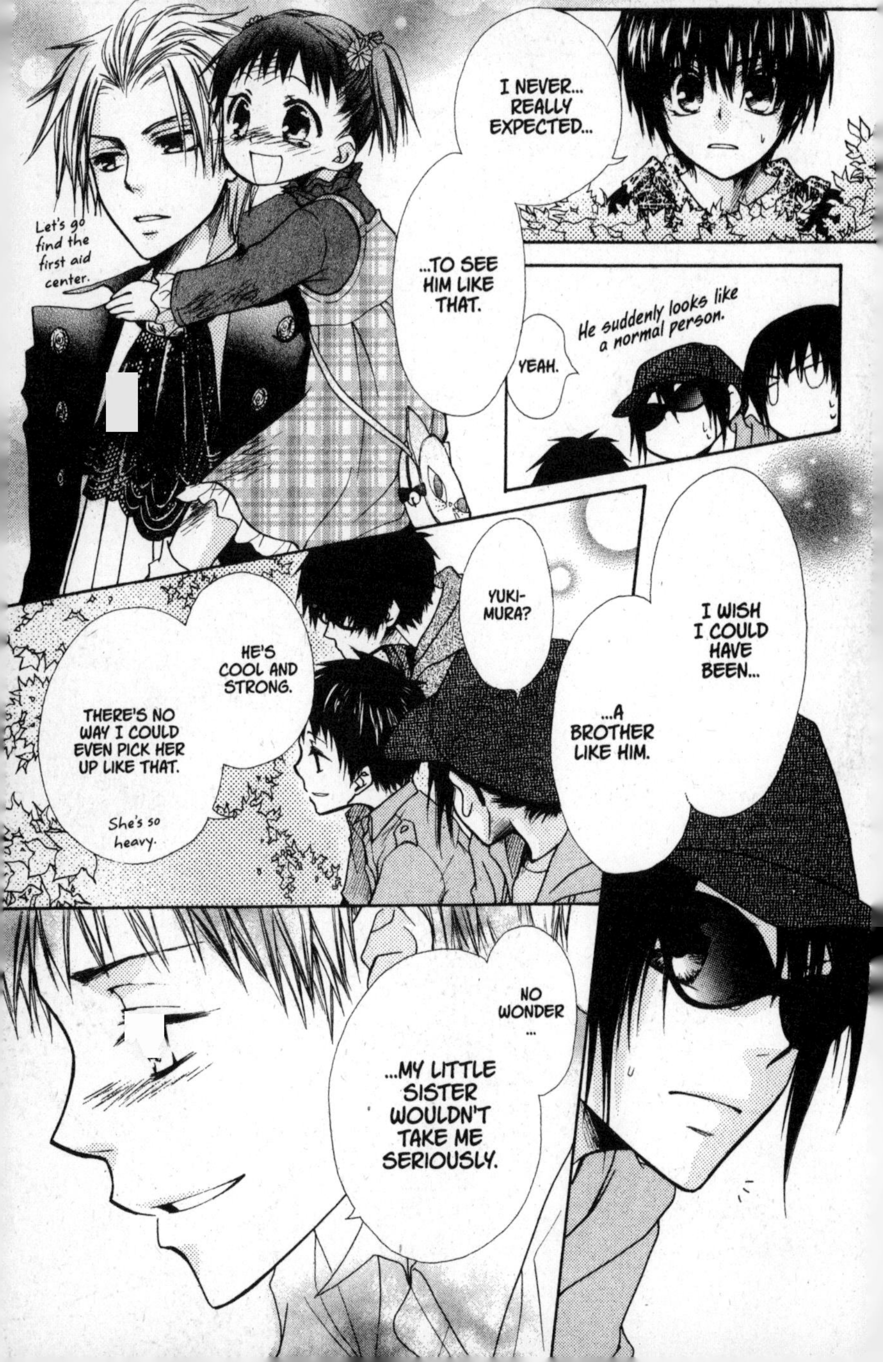
I NEVER... REALLY EXPECTED...
...TO SEE HIM LIKE THAT.
He suddenly looks like a normal person.
YEAH.
Let's go find the first aid center.
I WISH I COULD HAVE BEEN...
...A BROTHER LIKE HIM.
YUKI-MURA?
HE'S COOL AND STRONG.
THERE'S NO WAY I COULD EVEN PICK HER UP LIKE THAT.
She's so heavy.
NO WONDER...
...MY LITTLE SISTER WOULDN'T TAKE ME SERIOUSLY.

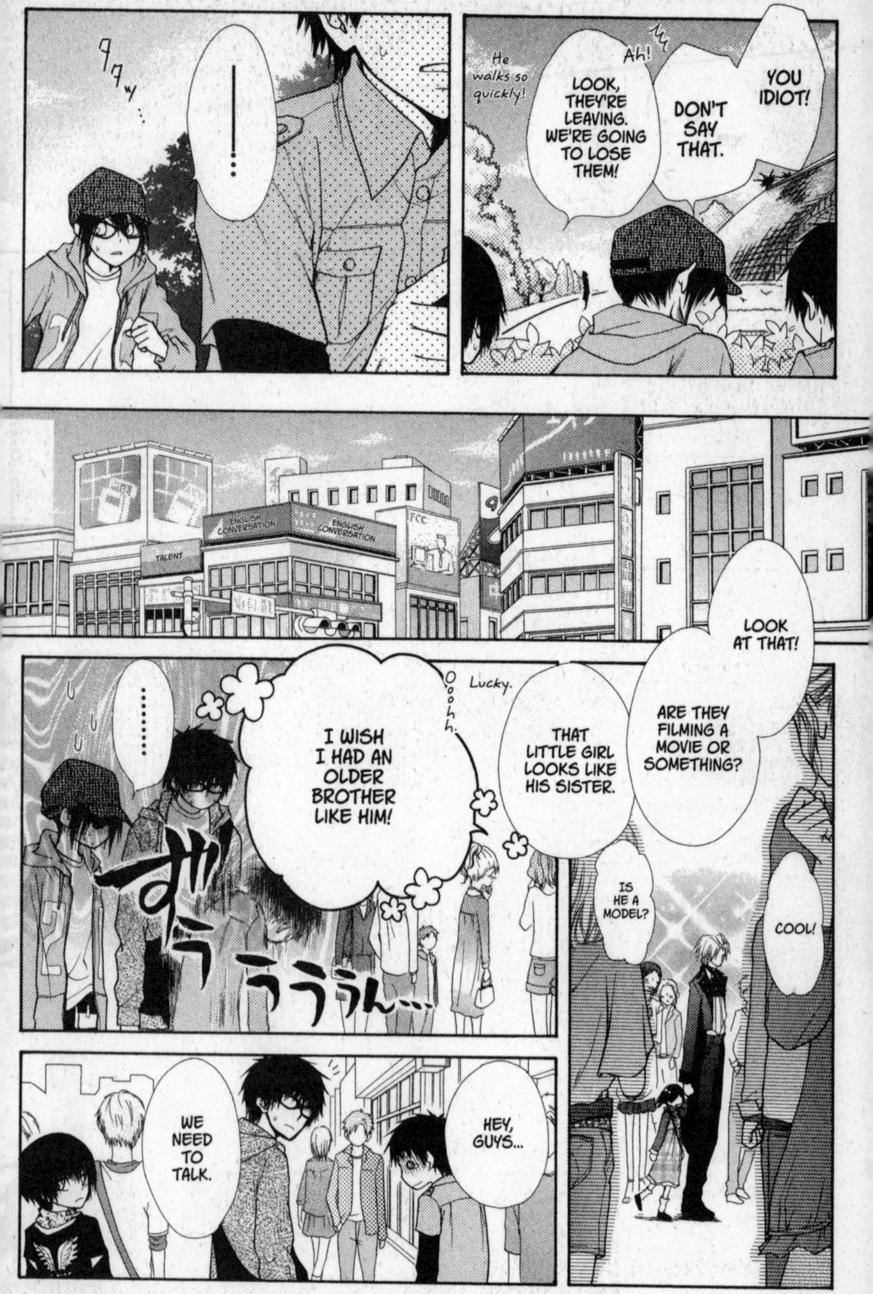
YOU IDIOT!
DON'T SAY THAT.
Ah!
LOOK, THEY'RE LEAVING. WE'RE GOING TO LOSE THEM!
He walks so quickly!
!......
タタッ...
ENGLISH CONVERSATION
ENGLISH CONVERSATION
TALENT
FCC
LOOK AT THAT!
COOL!
ARE THEY FILMING A MOVIE OR SOMETHING?
THAT LITTLE GIRL LOOKS LIKE HIS SISTER.
IS HE A MODEL?
Lucky.
Ooohh.
I WISH I HAD AN OLDER BROTHER LIKE HIM!
......
ずうううん...
HEY, GUYS...
WE NEED TO TALK.

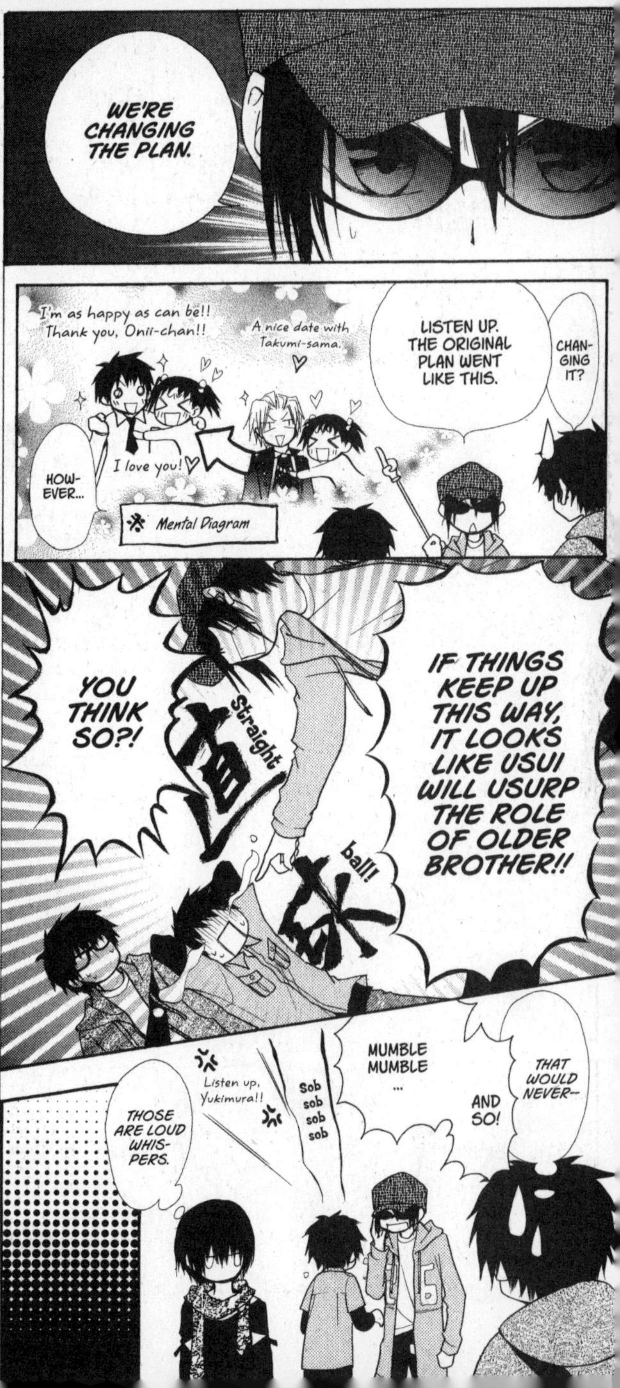
WE'RE CHANGING THE PLAN.
CHANGING IT?
LISTEN UP. THE ORIGINAL PLAN WENT LIKE THIS.
A nice date with Takumi-sama.
I'm as happy as can be!! Thank you, Onii-chan!!
I love you!
HOWEVER...
Mental Diagram
IF THINGS KEEP UP THIS WAY, IT LOOKS LIKE USUI WILL USURP THE ROLE OF OLDER BROTHER!!
Straight
ball!
YOU THINK SO?!
THAT WOULD NEVER--
AND SO!
MUMBLE MUMBLE ...
Sob sob sob sob
Listen up, Yukimura!!
THOSE ARE LOUD WHISPERS.

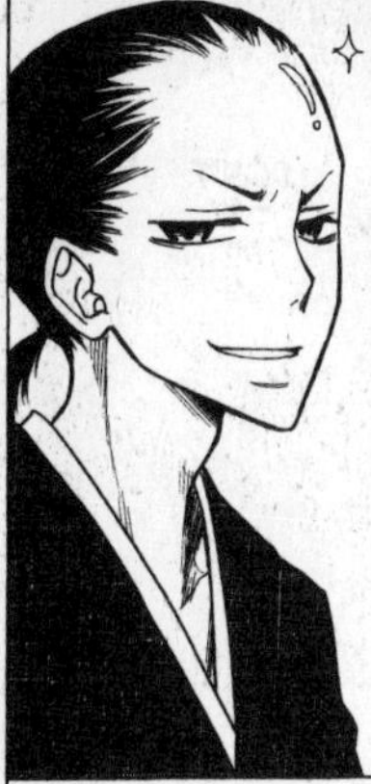

Name

Ryuunosuke Kurosaki

Age (Class)

17 (2-5)

Blood Type

O

Height

183 cm (6feet)

Weight

60 kg (132 lbs)

Special Skills

Sewing

Likes

Anything erotic

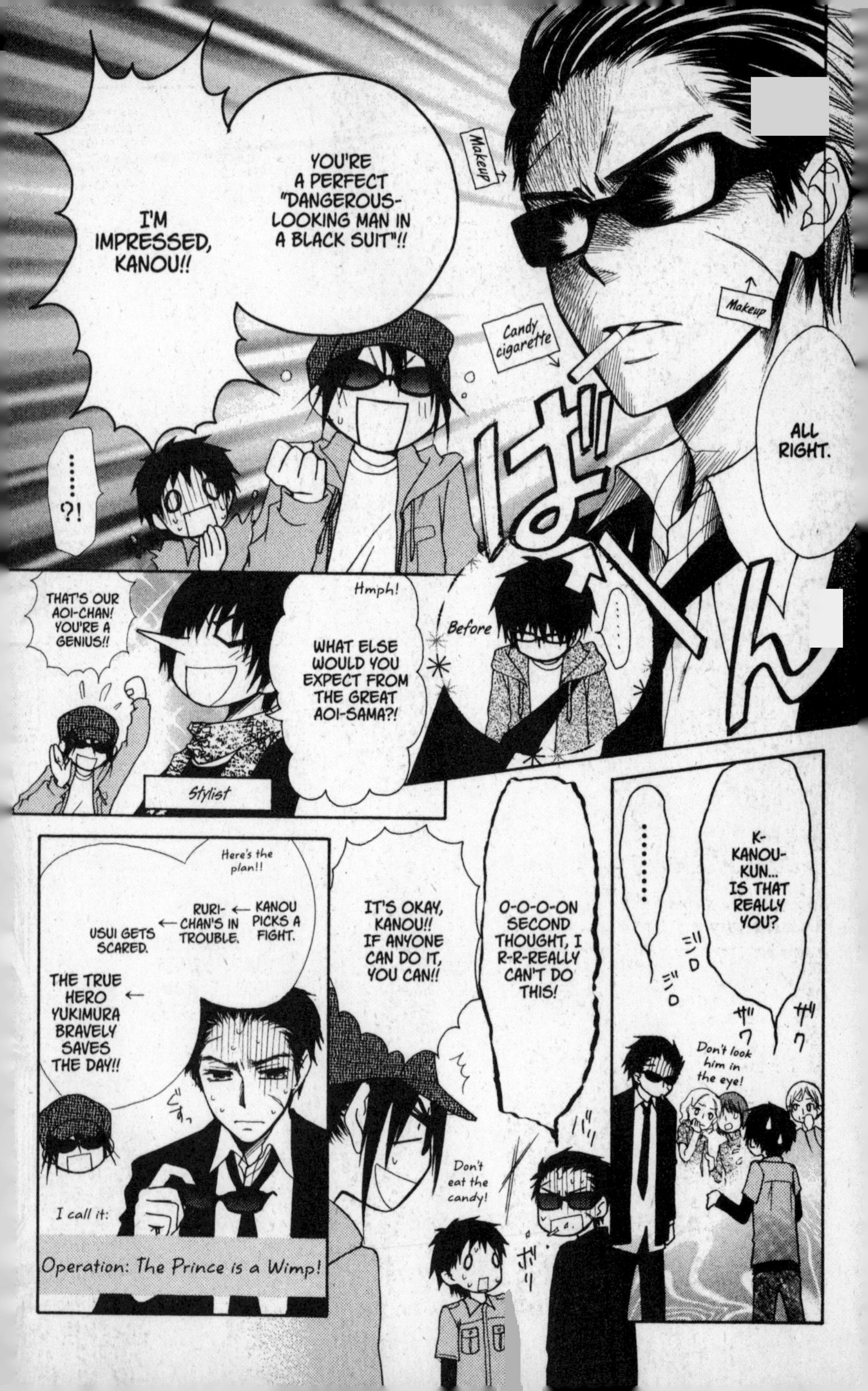
ALL RIGHT.
Makeup
Makeup
Candy cigarette
ばーん
YOU'RE A PERFECT "DANGEROUS-LOOKING MAN IN A BLACK SUIT"!!
I'M IMPRESSED, KANOU!!
......?!
Before
......
Hmph!
WHAT ELSE WOULD YOU EXPECT FROM THE GREAT AOI-SAMA?!
THAT'S OUR AOI-CHAN! YOU'RE A GENIUS!!
Stylist
K-KANOU-KUN... IS THAT REALLY YOU?
......
ジロ ジロ
ザワ ザワ
Don't look him in the eye!
O-O-O-ON SECOND THOUGHT, I R-R-REALLY CAN'T DO THIS!
IT'S OKAY, KANOU!! IF ANYONE CAN DO IT, YOU CAN!!
Don't eat the candy!
Here's the plan!!
KANOU PICKS A FIGHT. ← RURI-CHAN'S IN TROUBLE. ← USUI GETS SCARED.
← THE TRUE HERO YUKIMURA BRAVELY SAVES THE DAY!!
I call it:
Operation: The Prince is a Wimp!

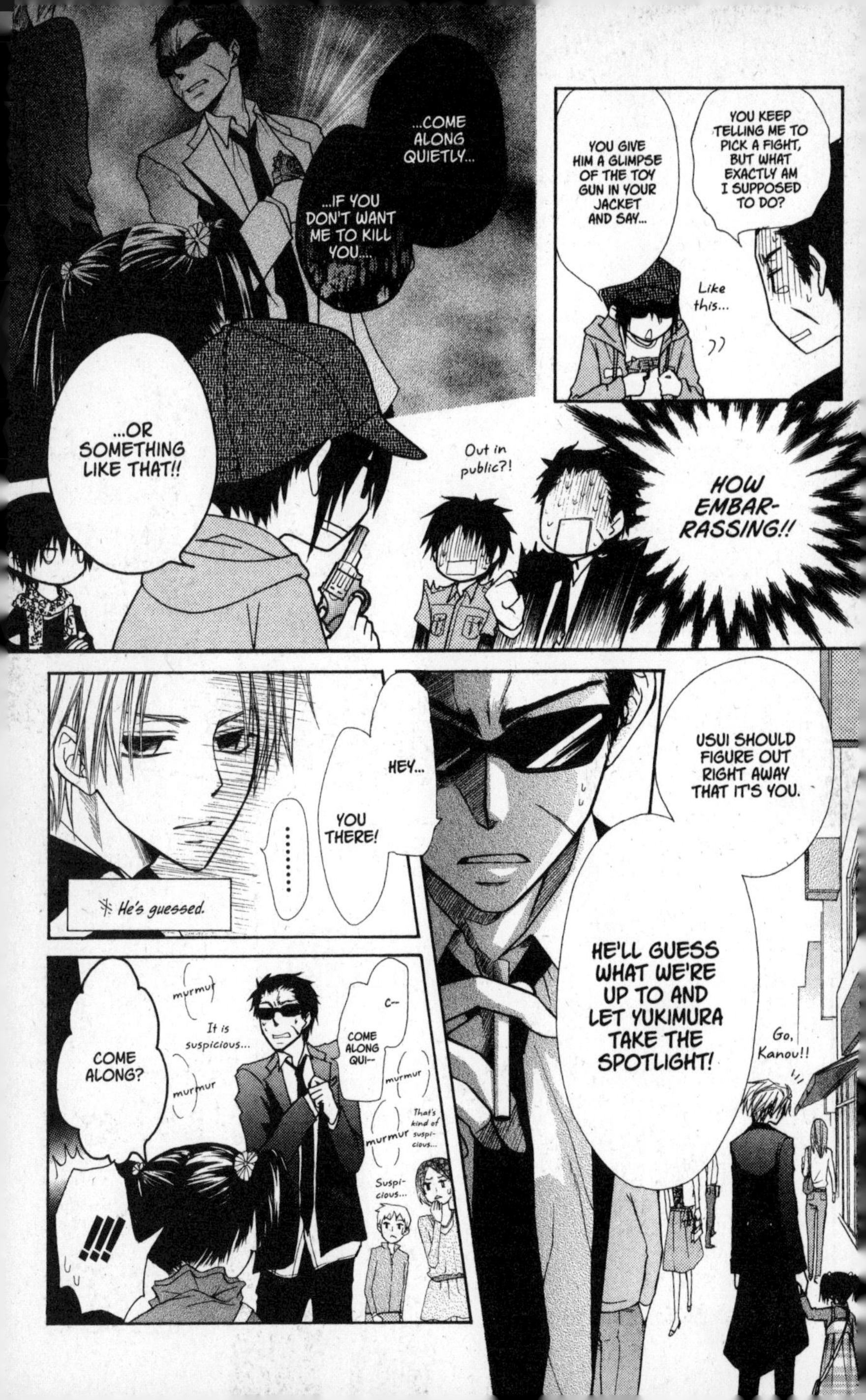
YOU KEEP TELLING ME TO PICK A FIGHT, BUT WHAT EXACTLY AM I SUPPOSED TO DO?
YOU GIVE HIM A GLIMPSE OF THE TOY GUN IN YOUR JACKET AND SAY...
Like this...
...COME ALONG QUIETLY...
...IF YOU DON'T WANT ME TO KILL YOU....
...OR SOMETHING LIKE THAT!!
HOW EMBAR-RASSING!!
Out in public?!
USUI SHOULD FIGURE OUT RIGHT AWAY THAT IT'S YOU.
HE'LL GUESS WHAT WE'RE UP TO AND LET YUKIMURA TAKE THE SPOTLIGHT!
Go, Kanou!!
HEY...
YOU THERE!
....
He's guessed.
C--
COME ALONG QUI--
murmur
murmur
That's kind of suspi-cious...
Suspi-cious...
It is suspicious...
murmur
murmur
COME ALONG?
!!!

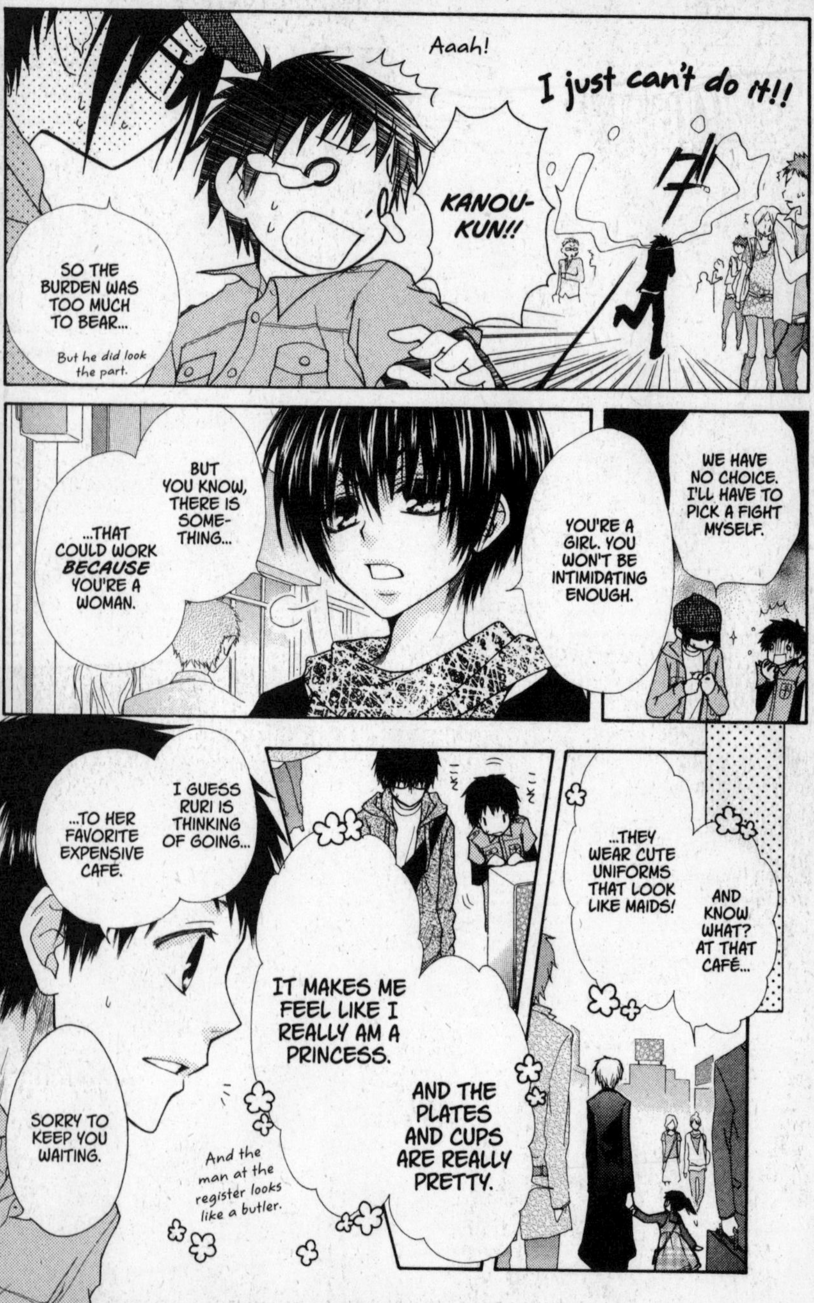
Aaah!
I just can't do it!!
KANOU-KUN!!
SO THE BURDEN WAS TOO MUCH TO BEAR...
But he did look the part.
WE HAVE NO CHOICE. I'LL HAVE TO PICK A FIGHT MYSELF.
YOU'RE A GIRL. YOU WON'T BE INTIMIDATING ENOUGH.
BUT YOU KNOW, THERE IS SOME-THING...
...THAT COULD WORK *BECAUSE* YOU'RE A WOMAN.
AND KNOW WHAT? AT THAT CAFÉ...
...THEY WEAR CUTE UNIFORMS THAT LOOK LIKE MAIDS!
IT MAKES ME FEEL LIKE I REALLY AM A PRINCESS.
AND THE PLATES AND CUPS ARE REALLY PRETTY.
And the man at the register looks like a butler.
I GUESS RURI IS THINKING OF GOING...
...TO HER FAVORITE EXPENSIVE CAFÉ.
SORRY TO KEEP YOU WAITING.

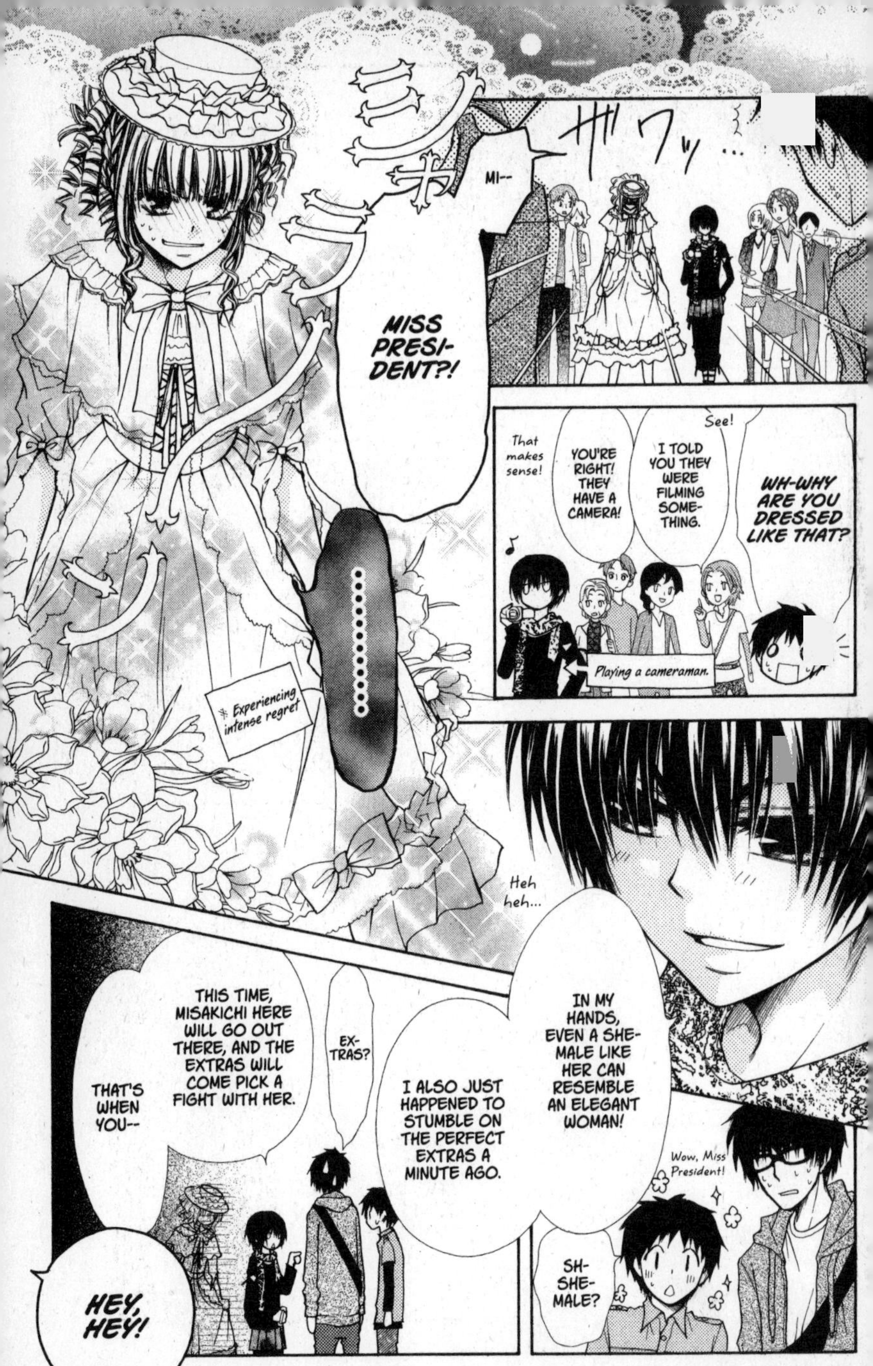
ザワッ…
MI--
MISS PRESIDENT?!
WH-WHY ARE YOU DRESSED LIKE THAT?
See!
I TOLD YOU THEY WERE FILMING SOMETHING.
YOU'RE RIGHT! THEY HAVE A CAMERA!
That makes sense!
Playing a cameraman.
Heh heh...
IN MY HANDS, EVEN A SHE-MALE LIKE HER CAN RESEMBLE AN ELEGANT WOMAN!
* Experiencing intense regret
Wow, Miss President!
SH-SHE-MALE?
I ALSO JUST HAPPENED TO STUMBLE ON THE PERFECT EXTRAS A MINUTE AGO.
EXTRAS?
THIS TIME, MISAKICHI HERE WILL GO OUT THERE, AND THE EXTRAS WILL COME PICK A FIGHT WITH HER.
THAT'S WHEN YOU--
HEY, HEY!

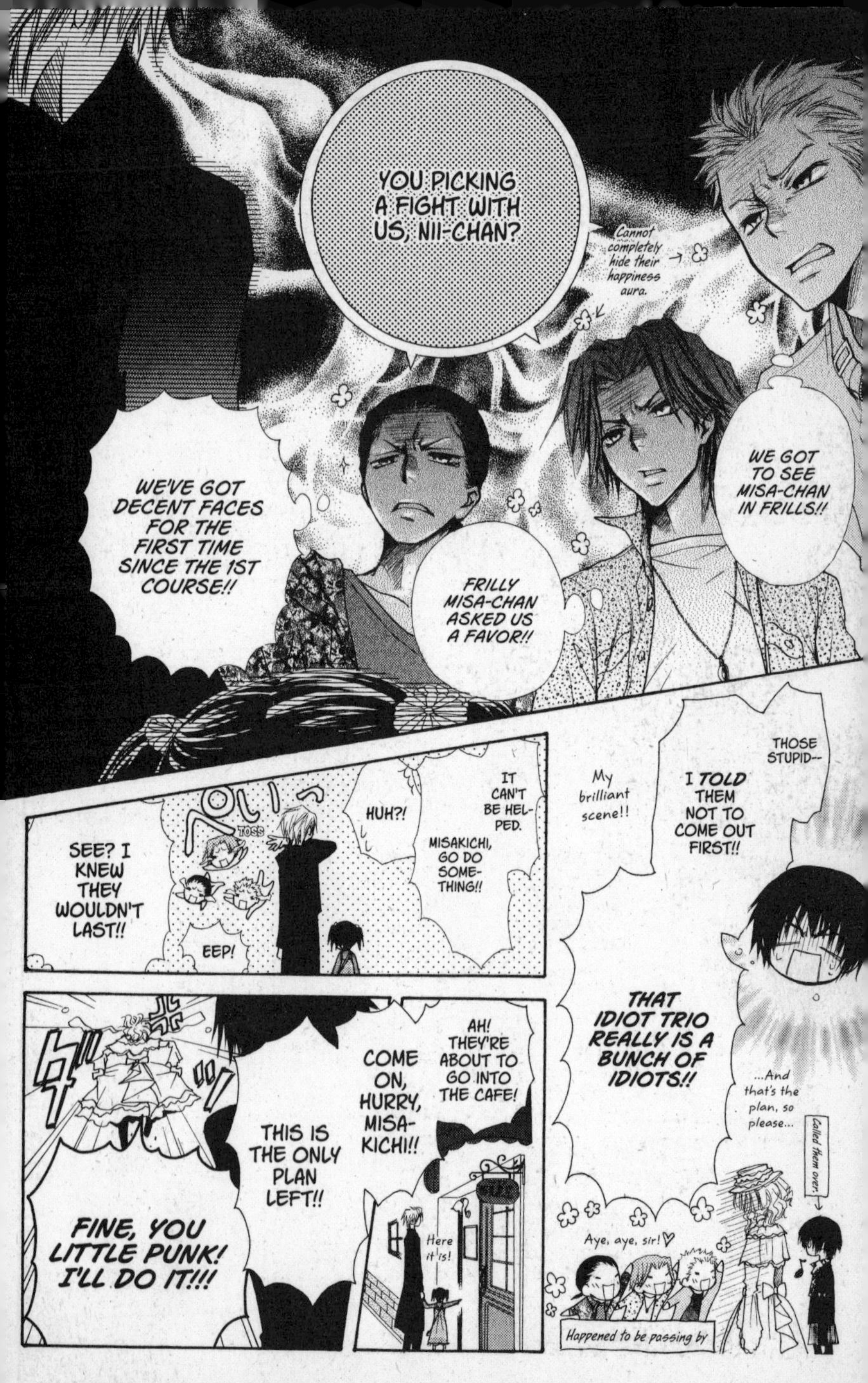
YOU PICKING A FIGHT WITH US, NII-CHAN?
Cannot completely hide their happiness aura.
WE GOT TO SEE MISA-CHAN IN FRILLS!!
FRILLY MISA-CHAN ASKED US A FAVOR!!
WE'VE GOT DECENT FACES FOR THE FIRST TIME SINCE THE 1ST COURSE!!
THOSE STUPID--
I TOLD THEM NOT TO COME OUT FIRST!!
My brilliant scene!!
THAT IDIOT TRIO REALLY IS A BUNCH OF IDIOTS!!
...And that's the plan, so please...
Called them over.
Aye, aye, sir!♡
Happened to be passing by
IT CAN'T BE HEL-PED.
MISAKICHI, GO DO SOME-THING!!
HUH?!
TOSS
SEE? I KNEW THEY WOULDN'T LAST!!
EEP!
AH! THEY'RE ABOUT TO GO INTO THE CAFE!
COME ON, HURRY, MISA-KICHI!!
Here it is!
THIS IS THE ONLY PLAN LEFT!!
FINE, YOU LITTLE PUNK! I'LL DO IT!!!

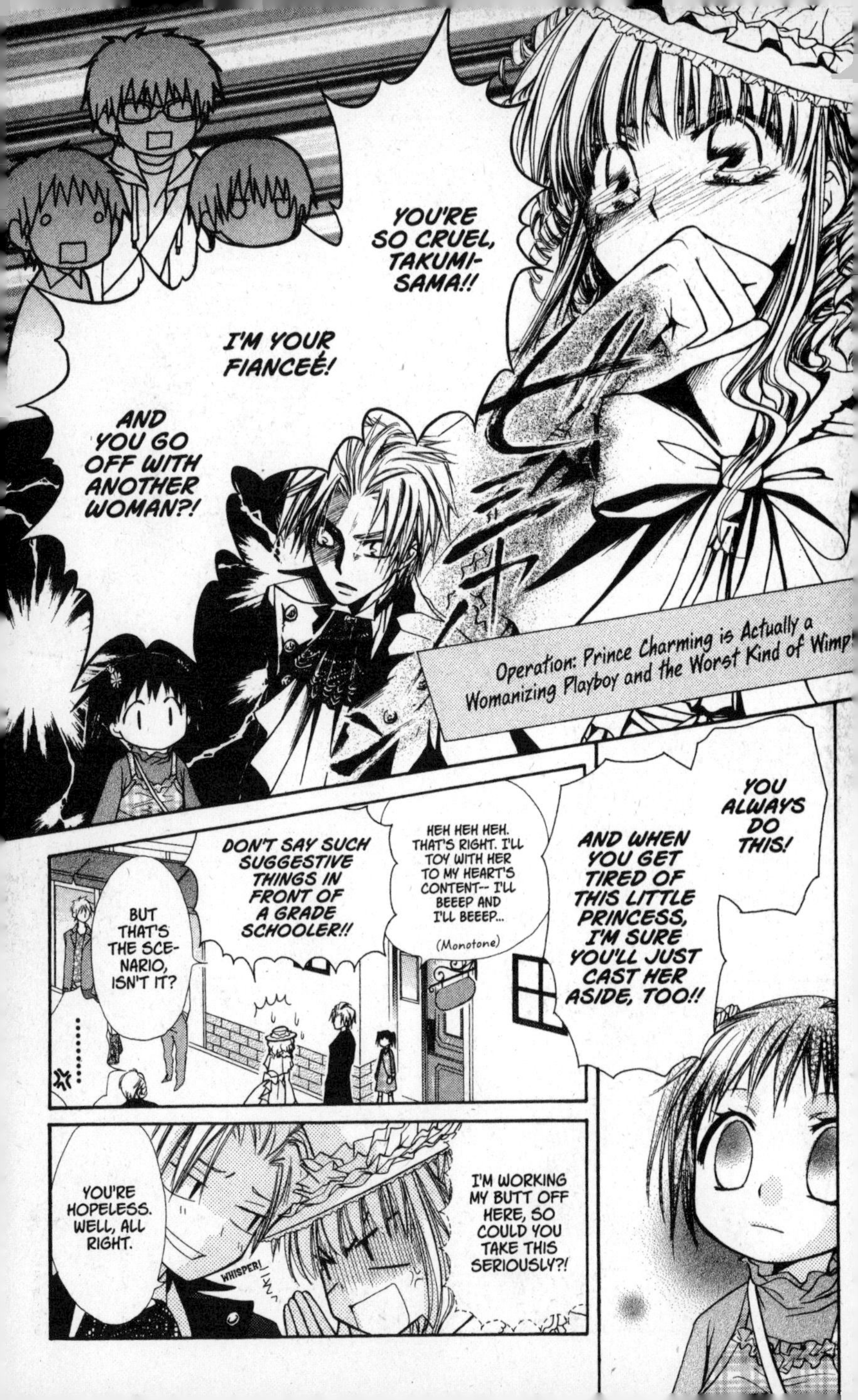
YOU'RE SO CRUEL, TAKUMI-SAMA!!
I'M YOUR FIANCEÉ!
AND YOU GO OFF WITH ANOTHER WOMAN?!
Operation: Prince Charming is Actually a Womanizing Playboy and the Worst Kind of Wimp
YOU ALWAYS DO THIS!
AND WHEN YOU GET TIRED OF THIS LITTLE PRINCESS, I'M SURE YOU'LL JUST CAST HER ASIDE, TOO!!
HEH HEH HEH. THAT'S RIGHT. I'LL TOY WITH HER TO MY HEART'S CONTENT-- I'LL BEEEP AND I'LL BEEEP...
(Monotone)
DON'T SAY SUCH SUGGESTIVE THINGS IN FRONT OF A GRADE SCHOOLER!!
BUT THAT'S THE SCE-NARIO, ISN'T IT?
I'M WORKING MY BUTT OFF HERE, SO COULD YOU TAKE THIS SERIOUSLY?!
WHISPER!
YOU'RE HOPELESS. WELL, ALL RIGHT.

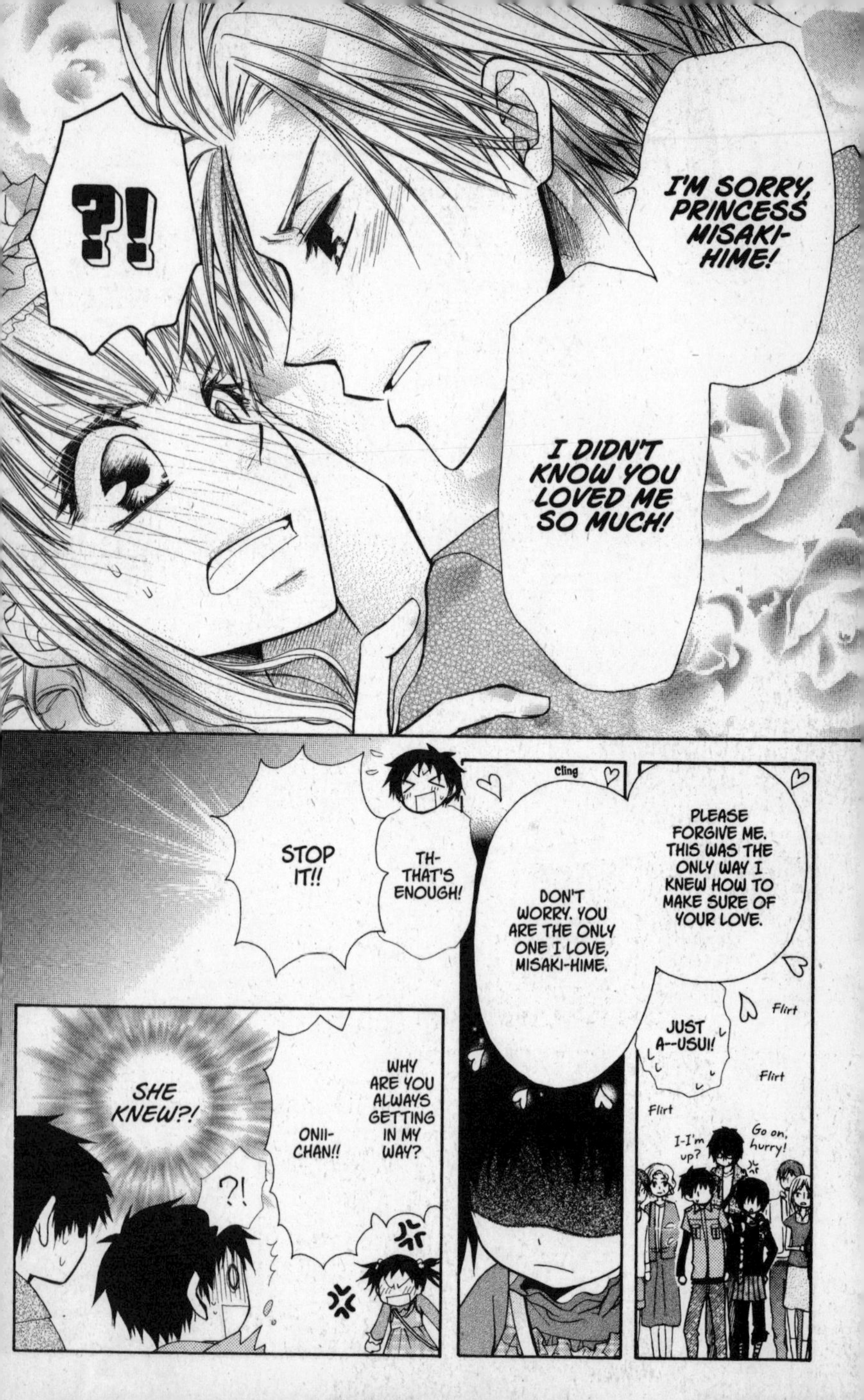
I'M SORRY, PRINCESS MISAKI-HIME!
I DIDN'T KNOW YOU LOVED ME SO MUCH!
?!
PLEASE FORGIVE ME. THIS WAS THE ONLY WAY I KNEW HOW TO MAKE SURE OF YOUR LOVE.
Flirt
JUST A--USUI!
Flirt
Flirt
Go on, hurry!
I-I'm up?
Cling
DON'T WORRY. YOU ARE THE ONLY ONE I LOVE, MISAKI-HIME.
TH-THAT'S ENOUGH!
STOP IT!!
WHY ARE YOU ALWAYS GETTING IN MY WAY?
ONII-CHAN!!
?!
SHE KNEW?!

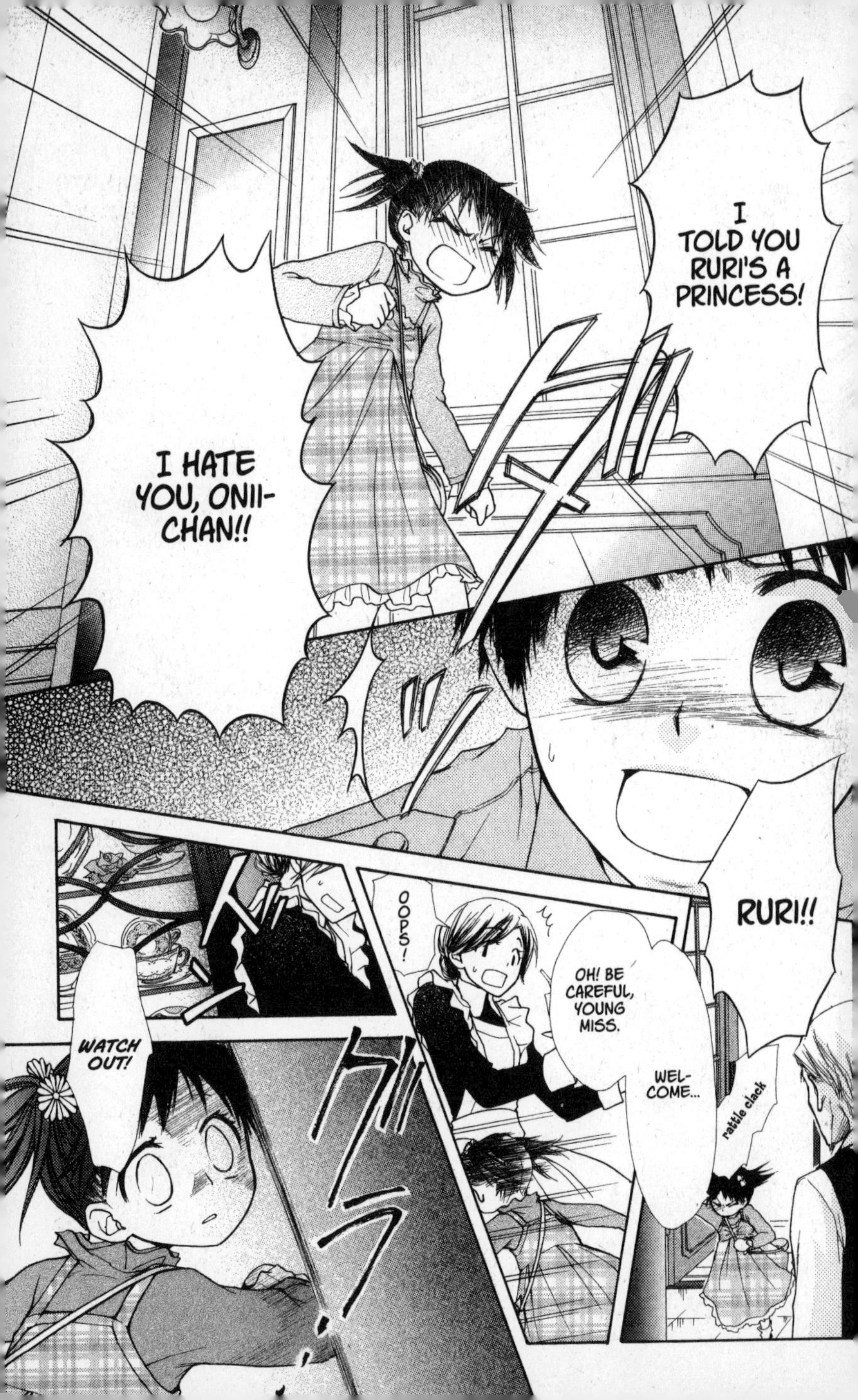
I TOLD YOU RURI'S A PRINCESS!
I HATE YOU, ONII-CHAN!!
RURI!!
rattle clack
WEL-COME...
OH! BE CAREFUL, YOUNG MISS.
OOPS!
WATCH OUT!

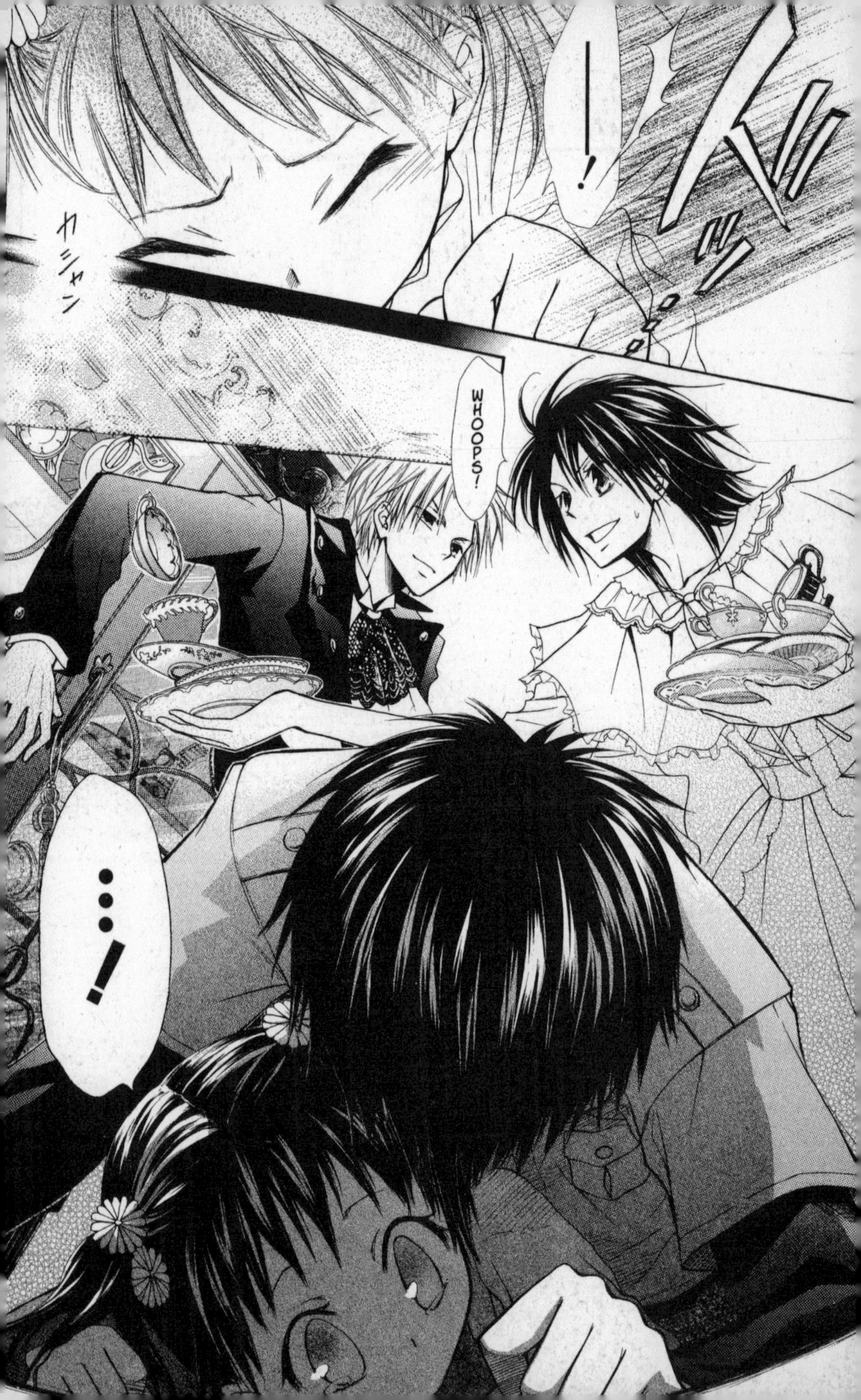
—!
カシャン
WHOOPS!
...!

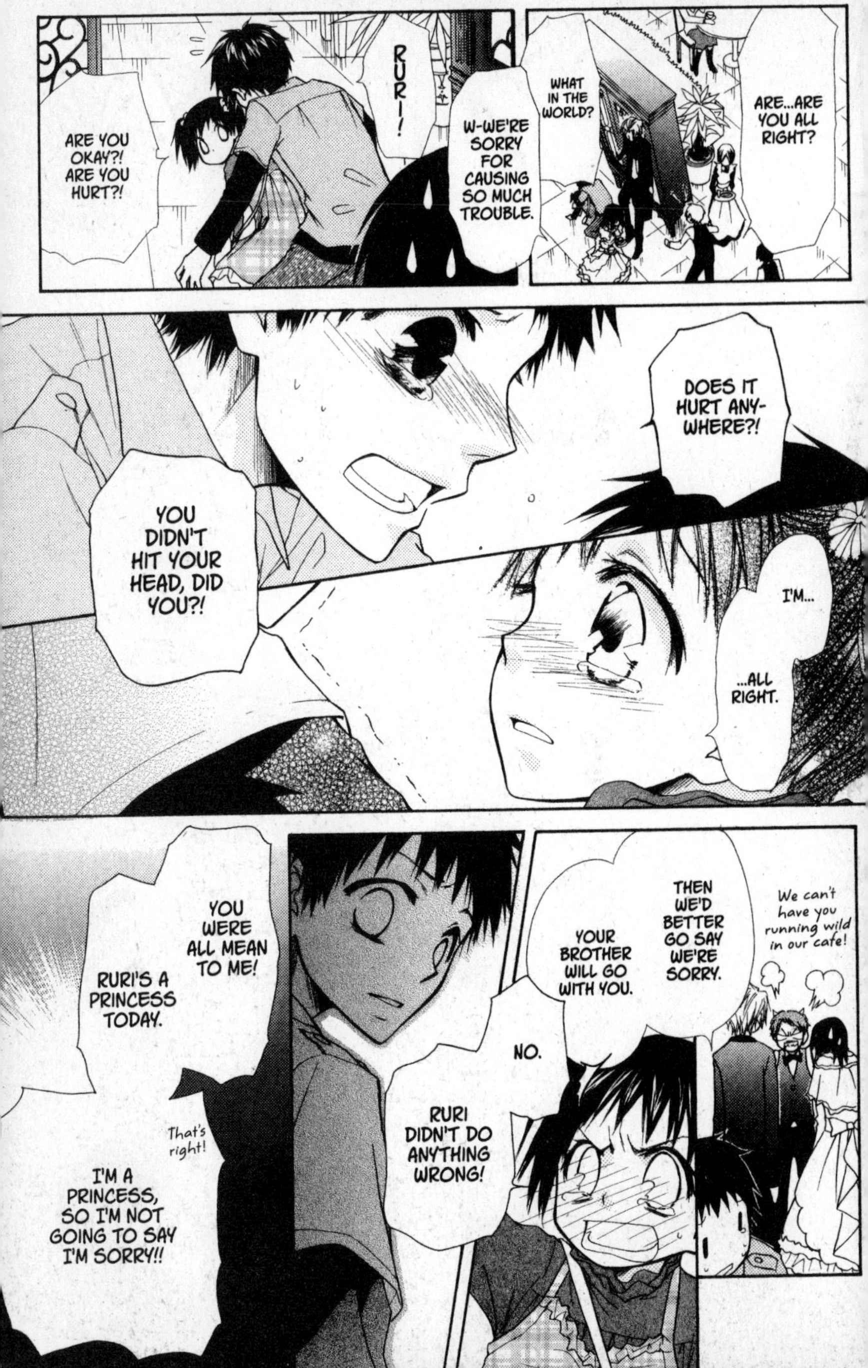
ARE...ARE YOU ALL RIGHT?
WHAT IN THE WORLD?
W-WE'RE SORRY FOR CAUSING SO MUCH TROUBLE.
RURI!
ARE YOU OKAY?! ARE YOU HURT?!
DOES IT HURT ANY-WHERE?!
YOU DIDN'T HIT YOUR HEAD, DID YOU?!
I'M...
...ALL RIGHT.
We can't have you running wild in our cafe!
THEN WE'D BETTER GO SAY WE'RE SORRY.
YOUR BROTHER WILL GO WITH YOU.
NO.
RURI DIDN'T DO ANYTHING WRONG!
YOU WERE ALL MEAN TO ME!
RURI'S A PRINCESS TODAY.
That's right!
I'M A PRINCESS, SO I'M NOT GOING TO SAY I'M SORRY!!

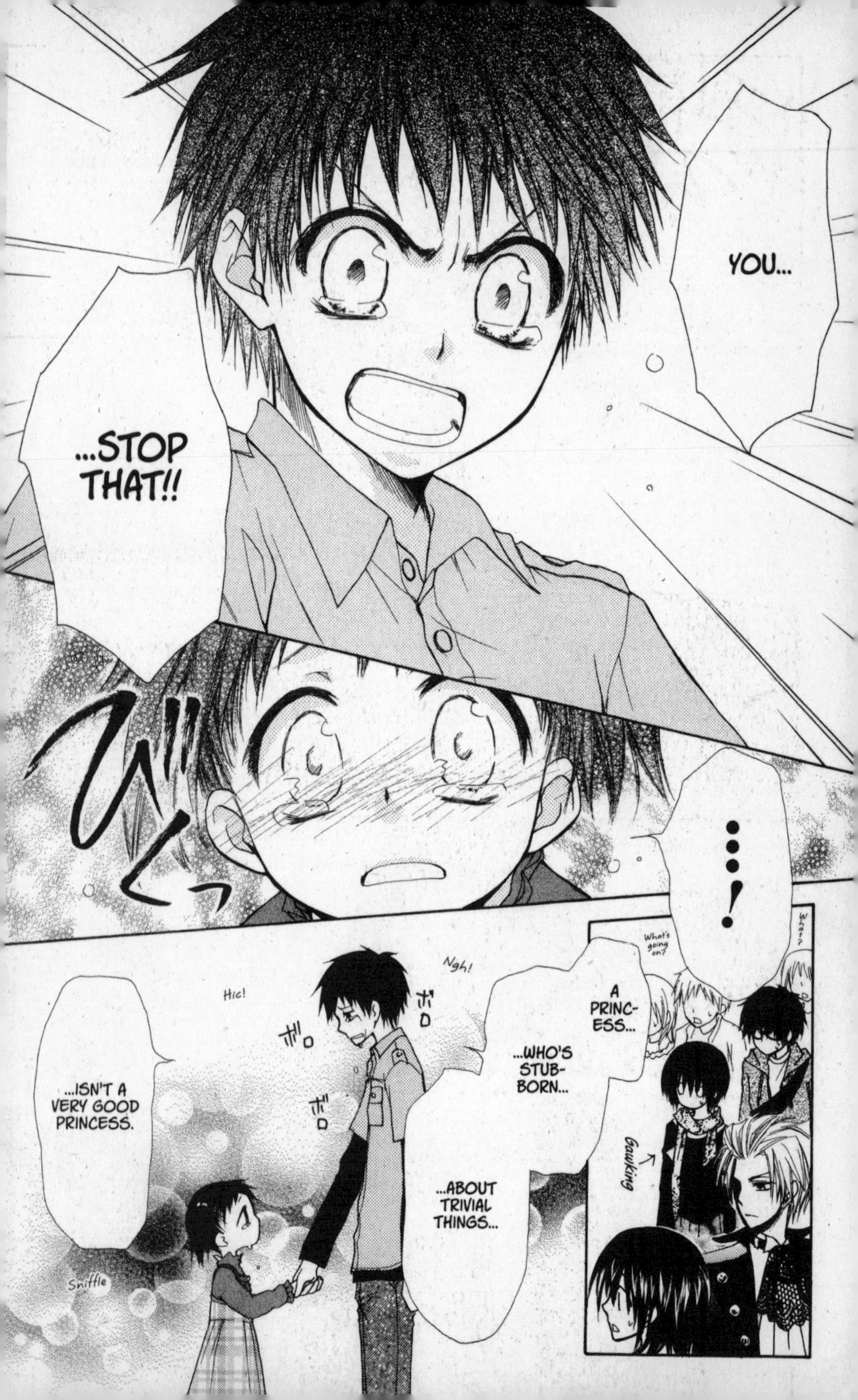
YOU...
...STOP THAT!!
ひっく
...!
What?
What's going on?
Gawking
A PRINC-ESS...
...WHO'S STUB-BORN...
...ABOUT TRIVIAL THINGS...
Ngh!
ボロ
Hic!
ボロ
ボロ
...ISN'T A VERY GOOD PRINCESS.
Sniffle

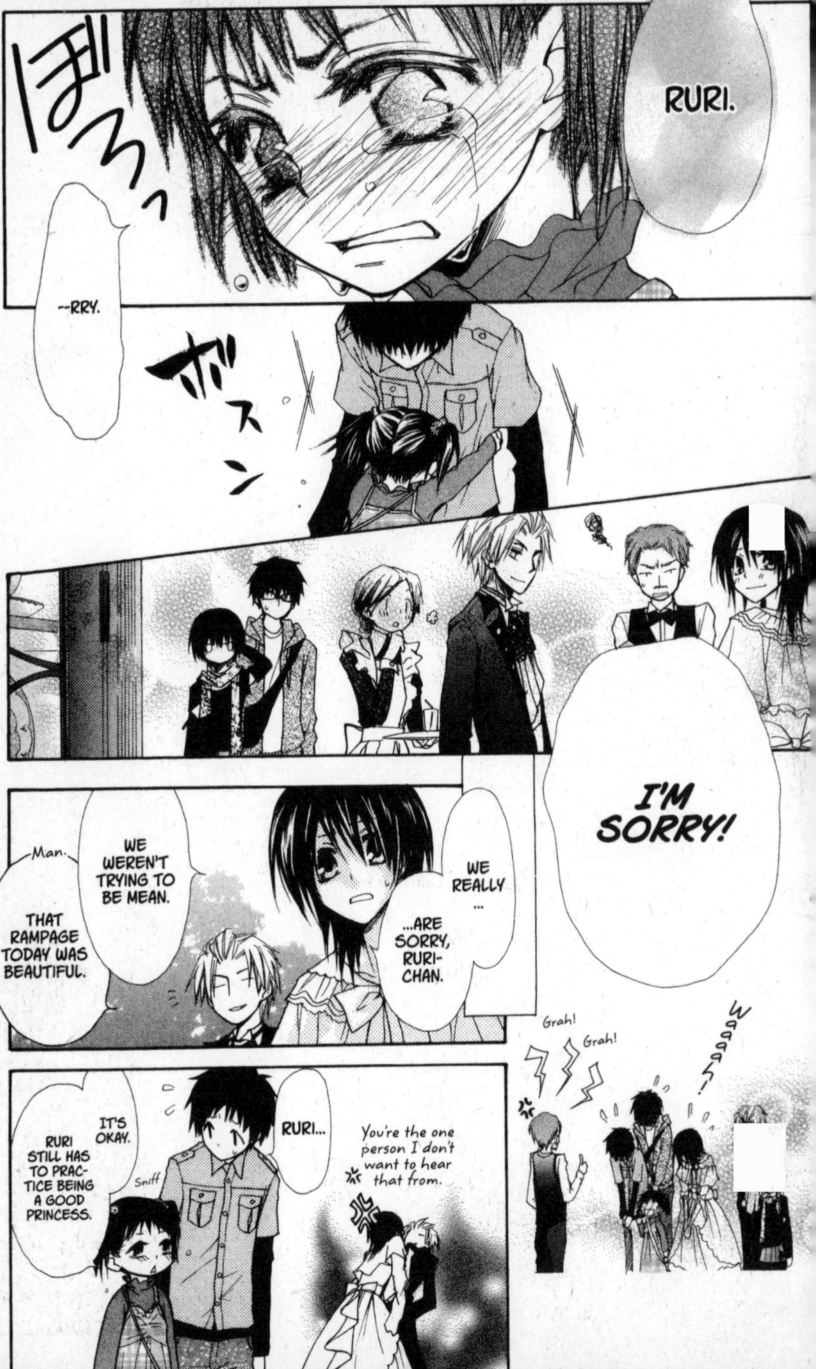

RURI.
ぽろっ
--RRY.
ボスン
I'M SORRY!
WE REALLY ...
...ARE SORRY, RURI-CHAN.
WE WEREN'T TRYING TO BE MEAN.
Man.
THAT RAMPAGE TODAY WAS BEAUTIFUL.
Waaaah!
Grah!
Grah!
RURI...
IT'S OKAY.
RURI STILL HAS TO PRAC-TICE BEING A GOOD PRINCESS.
Sniff
You're the one person I don't want to hear that from.

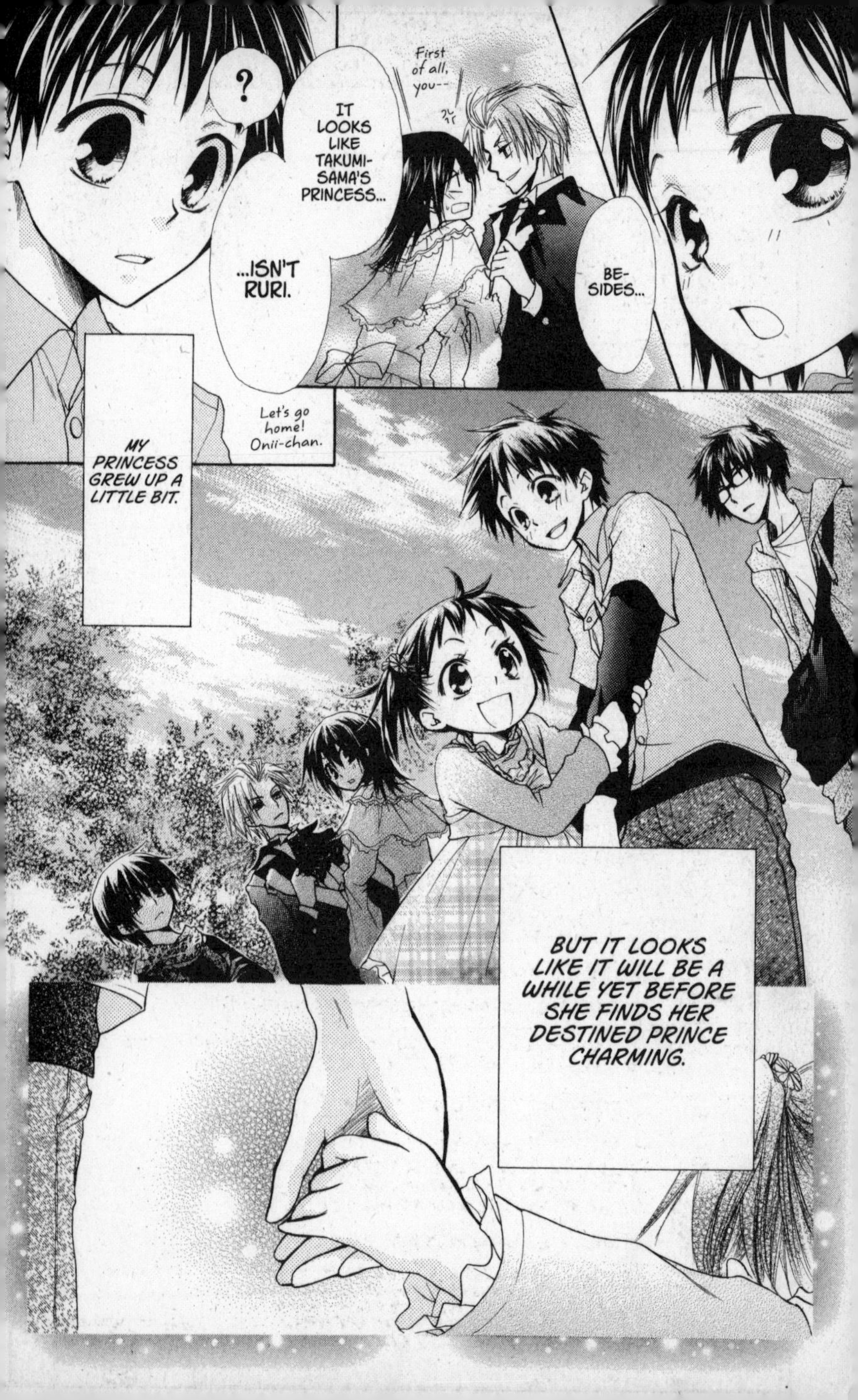
BE-SIDES...
IT LOOKS LIKE TAKUMI-SAMA'S PRINCESS...
...ISN'T RURI.
First of all, you--
?
MY PRINCESS GREW UP A LITTLE BIT.
Let's go home! Onii-chan.
BUT IT LOOKS LIKE IT WILL BE A WHILE YET BEFORE SHE FINDS HER DESTINED PRINCE CHARMING.

Q&A time...

IT LOOKS LIKE I'LL BE FINISHING UP THE Q+A CORNER THIS TIME! THEY TELL ME THAT THERE ARE LOTS OF QUESTIONS FOR ME--THAT MAKES ME KIND OF HAPPY! AND WE'RE STILL ACCEPTING QUESTIONS AND REQUESTS, SO KEEP THEM COMING!

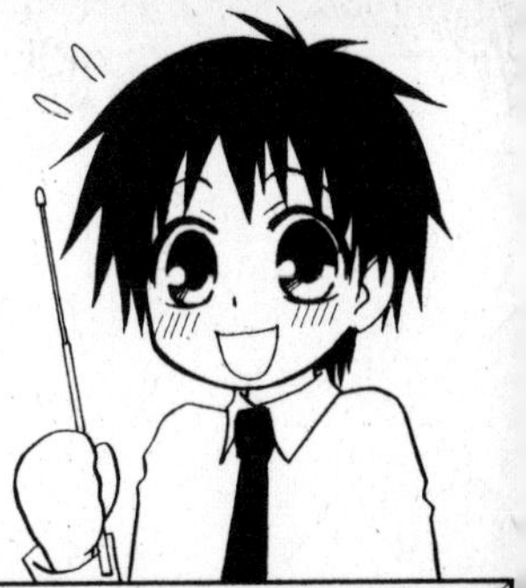

: ALL RIGHT THEN, HERE'S THE FIRST QUESTION.

QUESTION 14 : DOES YUKIMURA HAVE A BOY--I MEAN, GIRLFRIEND?

: I-I DON'T...AND HEY, HOW COULD YOU GET ***THAT*** PART OF THAT QUESTION WRONG?!

: I'M SURE ***IT WAS JUST A CARELESS MISTAKE!*** ALL RIGHT, LET'S KEEP UP THE PACE!

QUESTION 15 : YUKIMURA-KUN IS ALMOST CONSTANTLY IN GIRL'S CLOTHES. HAS HE EVER THOUGHT, "I WANT TO BE A GIRL!"?

: ***I-I HAVE NOT!!!*** AND HEY, WHAT DO YOU MEAN, ***ALMOST CONSTANTLY IN GIRL'S CLOTHES***?! I AM NOT! ***I'M ALWAYS A BOY!!!***

: R-RIGHT, YUKIMURA; YOU'RE ALWAYS A BOY. OKAY, NEXT!

QUESTION 16 : IS YUKIMURA REALLY A BOY?

: I ***AM*** A BOY!!!!! I'M TELLING YOU, I'M A GENUINE, BONA FIDE BOY!!!

: TH-THERE, THERE, YUKIMURA. DON'T CRY, DON'T CRY. YOU'RE A MAN, AREN'T YOU?

QUESTION 17 : WHAT DID IT FEEL LIKE WHEN USUI KISSED YOU, YUKIMURA?

: ---------!! WH-WHY WOULD THEY ASK THAT!?! NOOOOOO!

: S-SORRY, I'LL FIND ANOTHER QUESTION...H-HOW ABOUT THIS?!

QUESTION 18 : WOULD IT BE CORRECT TO FORM THE EQUATION YUKIMURA=MASOCHIST? OR SHOULD THAT "=MASOCHIST" GO WITH THE IDIOT TRIO?

: ***WHAT DO YOU KNOW, IT'S ACTUALLY FOR US!!!***

: I TOLD YOU-- THEY ***DO*** LOVE US A LITTLE!!

: FOR NOW, WE'LL SAY ***I JUST LOVE PUTTING PEOPLE IN BONDAGE AND BEING IN BONDAGE.***

: ***HA HA HA. YOU ERO-LOVING MORON!!***

: EH HEH HEH...I...JUST WANT...TO DISAPPEAR...

: TH-THERE, THERE, YUKIMURA. I'M SURE THAT SOMEDAY, A READER ***SHOULD*** APPEAR WHO WILL ACKNOWLEDGE YOUR MASCULINITY! R-RIGHT, EVERYONE?! C-COME ON, ***WE'RE WAITING FOR YOUR LETTERS SAYING, "YUKIMURA'S SO COOL!"***

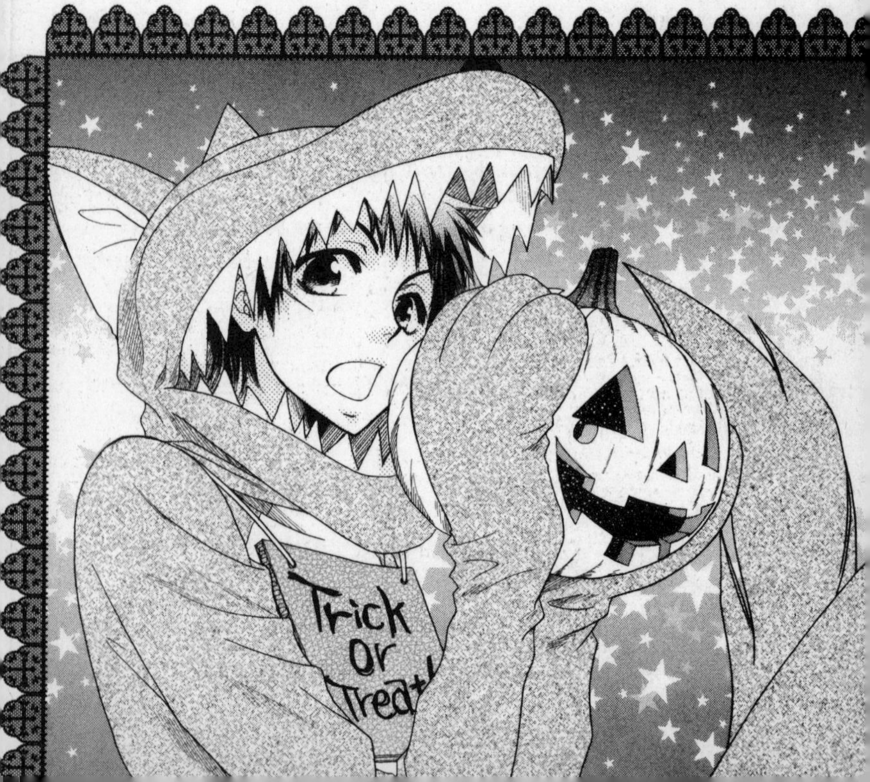
Trick Or Treat!

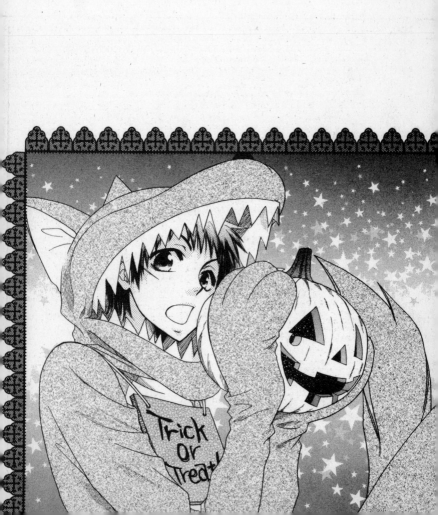

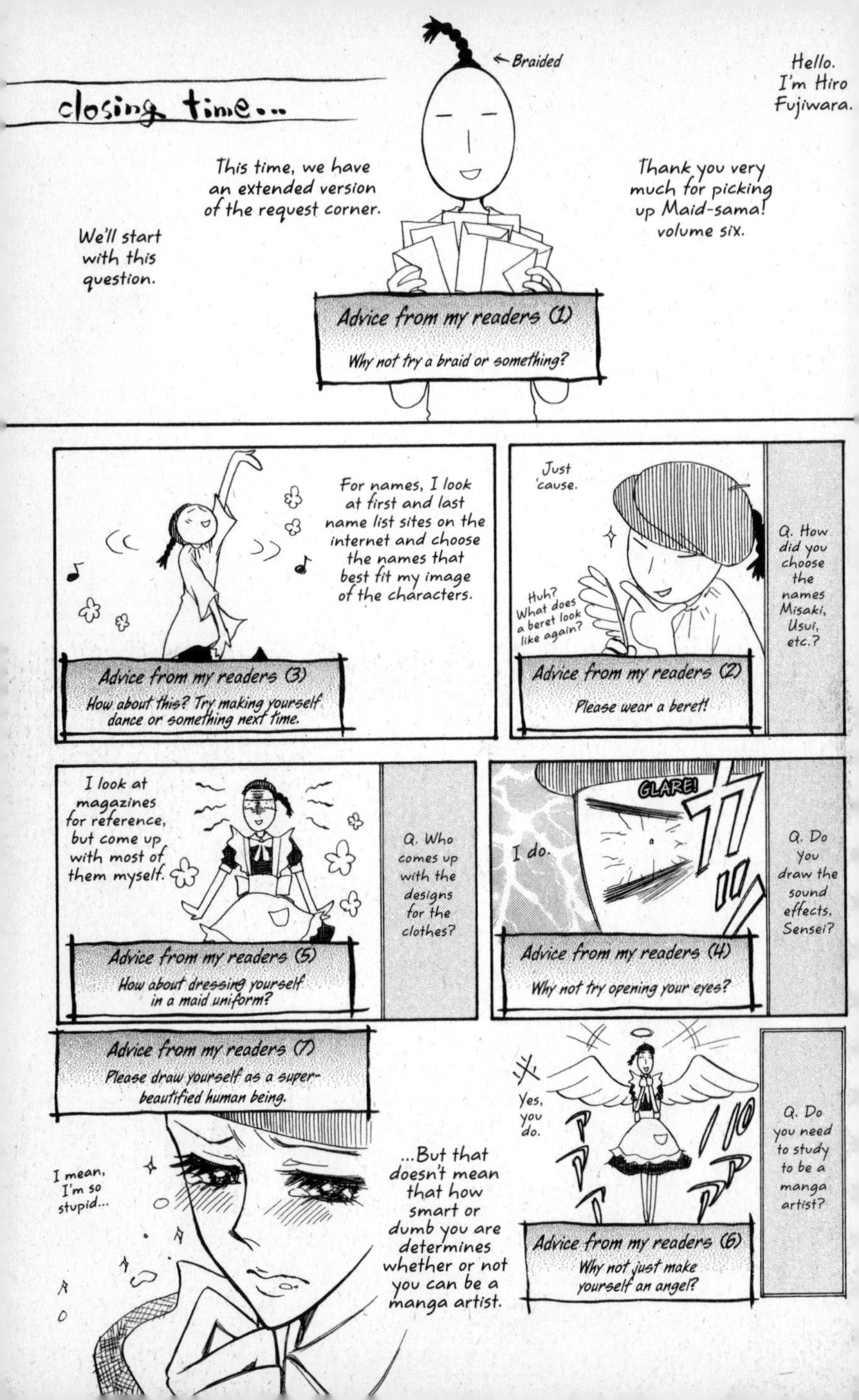
closing time...
Hello. I'm Hiro Fujiwara.
Thank you very much for picking up Maid-sama! volume six.
Braided
This time, we have an extended version of the request corner.
We'll start with this question.
Advice from my readers (1)
Why not try a braid or something?
Q. How did you choose the names Misaki, Usui, etc.?
Just 'cause.
Huh? What does a beret look like again?
Advice from my readers (2)
Please wear a beret!
For names, I look at first and last name list sites on the internet and choose the names that best fit my image of the characters.
Advice from my readers (3)
How about this? Try making yourself dance or something next time.
Q. Do you draw the sound effects, Sensei?
GLARE!
I do.
Advice from my readers (4)
Why not try opening your eyes?
Q. Who comes up with the designs for the clothes?
I look at magazines for reference, but come up with most of them myself.
Advice from my readers (5)
How about dressing yourself in a maid uniform?
Q. Do you need to study to be a manga artist?
Yes, you do.
Advice from my readers (6)
Why not just make yourself an angel?
Advice from my readers (7)
Please draw yourself as a super-beautified human being.
...But that doesn't mean that how smart or dumb you are determines whether or not you can be a manga artist.
I mean, I'm so stupid...

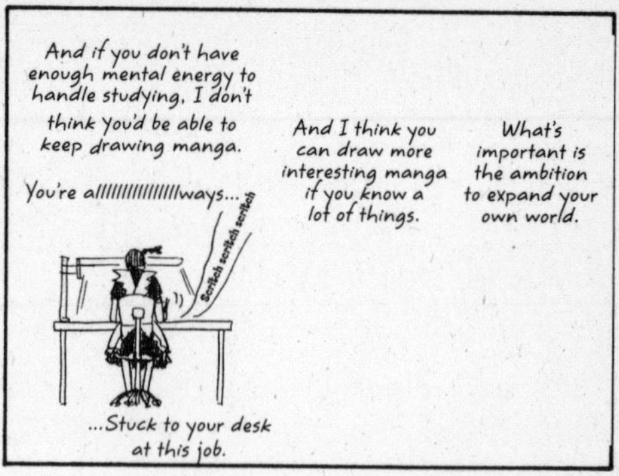
What's important is the ambition to expand your own world.
And I think you can draw more interesting manga if you know a lot of things.
And if you don't have enough mental energy to handle studying, I don't think you'd be able to keep drawing manga.
You're allllllllllllllways...
Scritch scritch scritch
...Stuck to your desk at this job.

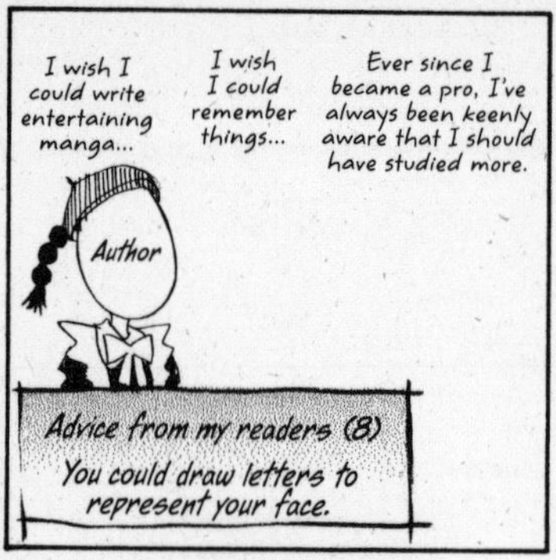
Ever since I became a pro, I've always been keenly aware that I should have studied more.
I wish I could remember things...
I wish I could write entertaining manga...
Author
Advice from my readers (8)
You could draw letters to represent your face.

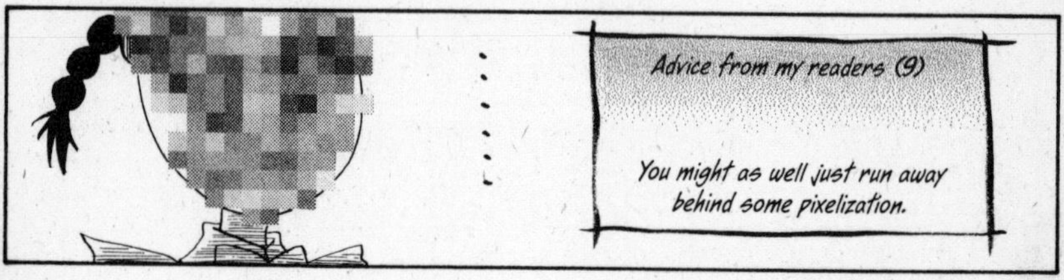
Advice from my readers (9)
You might as well just run away behind some pixelization.
......

Advice from my readers (10)

I think you're fine the way you are, Sensei. In a way, it brings out your charm.

Thank you... Thank you, everyone!

But why does this piece of advice...

...Emphasize that part?

They went to the trouble to use a colored pen in that one spot.

I wonder why... I really wonder why...

Special Thanks!

- Namino-san
- Eri Minakami-chan
- Miyabi Kawasaki-san
- Igusa Sasazuki-san
- Everyone who involved in the production of this book, everyone who helped me, and you, who are holding this book right now. Thank you!
- My editor, Junmi-sama
- My honorable mother

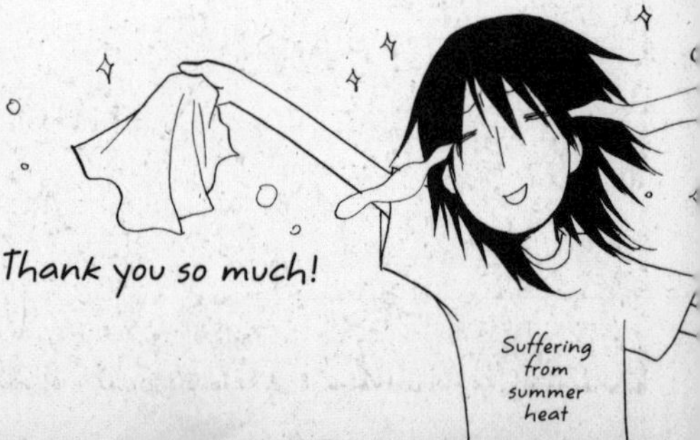
Thank you so much!
Suffering from summer heat

I welcome any questions, thoughts, or ideas!

Send:letters:here:

Hiro Fujiwara

TOKYOPOP Inc.

5900 Wilshire Blvd.
Suite 2000

Los Angeles CA 90036

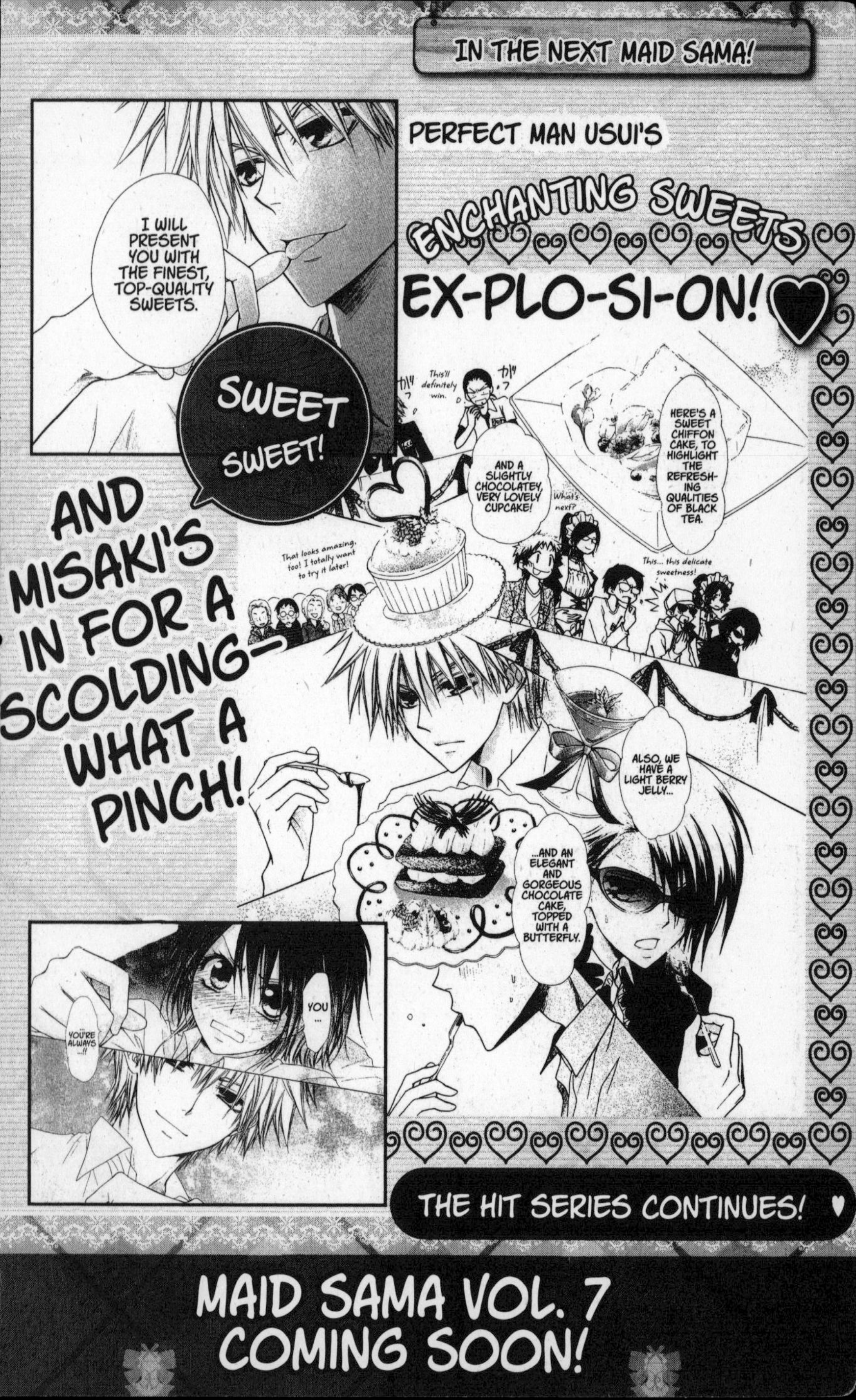

IN THE NEXT MAID SAMA!
PERFECT MAN USUI'S
ENCHANTING SWEETS
EX-PLO-SI-ON!
I WILL PRESENT YOU WITH THE FINEST, TOP-QUALITY SWEETS.
SWEET SWEET!
This'll definitely win.
HERE'S A SWEET CHIFFON CAKE, TO HIGHLIGHT THE REFRESHING QUALITIES OF BLACK TEA.
AND A SLIGHTLY CHOCOLATEY, VERY LOVELY CUPCAKE!
What's next?
This... this delicate sweetness!
That looks amazing, too! I totally want to try it later!
AND MISAKI'S IN FOR A SCOLDING— WHAT A PINCH!
ALSO, WE HAVE A LIGHT BERRY JELLY...
...AND AN ELEGANT AND GORGEOUS CHOCOLATE CAKE, TOPPED WITH A BUTTERFLY.
YOU...
YOU'RE ALWAYS ...!!
THE HIT SERIES CONTINUES!
MAID SAMA VOL. 7 COMING SOON!

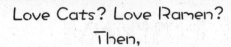

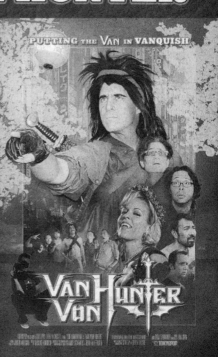

THE SMALLEST HERO!?
RATMAN

Not your typical good versus evil story

Even with a successful caper under his belt, Shuto Katsuragi is still not very comfortable with his role as the dark anti-hero "Ratman" for the evil secret organization "Jackal." Deciding to take advantage of Ratman's abilities, he tries his hand at some vigilante heroism on his off time from the organization. The first attempt goes well, and he even shows up in the papers as a "mysterious, unnamed hero." The second attempt does not go nearly as well, as he is mistaken for the criminal instead of the guy trying to stop the crime. The misunderstandings continue when he tries to break up a fight between members of a hero sentai team. He has to knock them out to do it, and a late-coming Ankaiser pounces on the excuse to pick a fight of his own!

the smallest hero?! | Story and Art by INUI Sekihiko | 2

OT
OLDER TEEN
AGE 16+

BE SURE TO VISIT WWW.TOKYOPOP.COM/SHOP FOR
EVERYTHING YOU COULD EVER WANT!

STOP!

This is the back of the book.
You wouldn't want to spoil a great ending!

This book is printed "manga-style," in the authentic Japanese right-to-left format. Since none of the artwork has been flipped or altered, readers get to experience the story just as the creator intended. You've been asking for it, so TOKYOPOP® delivered: authentic, hot-off-the-press, and far more fun!

1
2
3
4
5
6
7
8
9
10

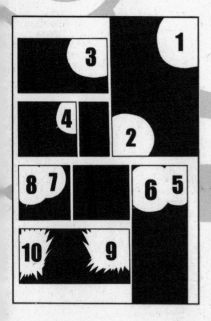

DIRECTIONS

If this is your first time reading manga-style, here's a quick guide to help you understand how it works.

It's easy... just start in the top right panel and follow the numbers. Have fun, and look for more 100% authentic manga from TOKYOPOP®!

THE MANGA REVOLUTION • LEADING THE MANGA REVOLUTION • LEADING
漫画革命